First World War
and Army of Occupation
War Diary
France, Belgium and Germany

24 DIVISION
73 Infantry Brigade
Northamptonshire Regiment
7th Battalion
21 August 1915 - 7 June 1919

WO95/2218/2

The Naval & Military Press Ltd
www.nmarchive.com
Published in association with The National Archives

Published by

The Naval & Military Press Ltd

Unit 10 Ridgewood Industrial Park,
Uckfield, East Sussex,
TN22 5QE England
Tel: +44 (0) 1825 749494

www.naval-military-press.com
www.nmarchive.com

This diary has been reprinted in facsimile from the original. Any imperfections are inevitably reproduced and the quality may fall short of modern type and cartographic standards.

© Crown Copyright
Images reproduced by permission of The National Archives, London, England, 2015.

Contents

Document type	Place/Title	Date From	Date To
Heading	WO95/2218/2		
Heading	7th Bn Northants Regt Aug 1915 June 1919		
Heading	7th Battn. The Northamptonshire Regiment. August And September (21.8.15 To 30.9.15) 1915 June 1919		
War Diary	Woking	21/08/1915	01/09/1915
War Diary	France	02/09/1915	30/09/1915
Heading	24th Division Oct 15		
War Diary	France	02/10/1915	07/10/1915
War Diary	Belgium	08/10/1915	31/10/1915
Heading	24th Division Nov 15		
War Diary	Belgium	01/11/1915	23/11/1915
War Diary	France	24/11/1915	30/11/1915
Map			
Heading	24th Div		
War Diary	France	01/12/1915	31/12/1915
Heading	7th Battalion Northampton Regiment January 1916		
Heading	7th Northern Vol 4		
War Diary	Eperleques	01/01/1916	07/01/1916
War Diary	Vlamertinghe	08/01/1916	14/01/1916
War Diary	Zillebeke Lake	15/01/1916	18/01/1916
War Diary	Hooge	19/01/1916	22/01/1916
War Diary	Zillebeke Lake	23/01/1916	26/01/1916
War Diary	Hooge	27/01/1916	31/01/1916
Heading	7th Battalion Northampton Regiment February 1916		
Heading	War Diary of 7th Service Battalion Northamptonshire Regt from 1st February 1916 To 29th Febry 1916		
War Diary	Ouderdom Vlamertinghe	01/02/1916	12/02/1916
War Diary	Ypres	13/02/1916	18/02/1916
War Diary	Vlamertinghe	19/02/1916	20/02/1916
War Diary	Ypres	21/02/1916	24/02/1916
War Diary	Vlamertinghe	26/02/1916	29/02/1916
Miscellaneous	7th B. Bn. Northamptonshire Regiment	11/02/1916	11/02/1916
Miscellaneous	C Form (Original). Messages And Signals.	22/02/1916	22/02/1916
Miscellaneous	Feb 11th 1916		
Heading	7th Battalion Northampton Regiment March 1916		
Heading	War Diary Of 7th Service Battalion Northamptonshire Regt In The Field March 1st To March 31st 1916		
War Diary	Nr Vlamertinghe	01/03/1916	04/03/1916
War Diary	Zillebeke Lake	05/03/1916	08/03/1916
War Diary	Hooge	09/03/1916	12/03/1916
War Diary	Zillebeke Lake	12/03/1916	16/03/1916
War Diary	Nr Vlamertinghe	17/03/1916	18/03/1916
War Diary	Meteren	19/03/1916	22/03/1916
War Diary	Kortepyp	23/03/1916	24/03/1916
War Diary	Nr Wulverghem	25/03/1916	31/03/1916
Miscellaneous	Operation Orders by Major E. R. Mobbs Commanding 7th. (S) Bn. Northamptonshire Regiment.	04/03/1916	04/03/1916
Miscellaneous	Working Parties to be found by 7. Northamptons	05/03/1916	05/03/1916
Miscellaneous	Working Parties to be found by 7. Northamptonshire Regt	06/03/1916	06/03/1916

Miscellaneous	Operation Orders By Major E R Mobbs Commanding 7th (S) Battalion Northamptonshire Regiment.	07/03/1916	07/03/1916
Miscellaneous	Working Parties to be Found	07/03/1916	07/03/1916
Miscellaneous	Working Parties to be Found	14/03/1916	14/03/1916
Operation(al) Order(s)	73rd. Infantry Brigade. Operation Order No. 31	13/03/1916	13/03/1916
Miscellaneous	Table Of Reliefs.		
Miscellaneous	Relief Of Lewis Guns.		
Miscellaneous	7th N H	15/03/1916	15/03/1916
Operation(al) Order(s)	73rd Infantry Brigade. Operation Order No. 32	17/03/1916	17/03/1916
Miscellaneous	March Table.		
Miscellaneous	Additions And Amendments To 73rd Infantry Brigade Operation Order No. 32	17/03/1916	17/03/1916
Miscellaneous	Battalion Orders by Major E.R. Mobbs, Commanding 7th (S) Bn. Northamptonshire Regiment.	17/03/1916	17/03/1916
Miscellaneous	Battalion Orders by Major E.R. Mobbs, Commanding 7th (S) Bn. Northamptonshire Regiment.	22/03/1916	22/03/1916
Heading	7th Battalion Northamptonshire Regiment April 1916		
Miscellaneous	Officer i/c A.G.s Office at the Base	07/05/1916	07/05/1916
Heading	War Diary Of 7th Services Battalion Northamptonshire Regiment For The North Of April 1916		
War Diary	Red Lodge	01/04/1916	07/04/1916
War Diary	Wulverghem	07/04/1916	13/04/1916
War Diary	Kortepyp	14/04/1916	18/04/1916
War Diary	Wulverghem	19/04/1916	24/04/1916
War Diary	Red Lodge	25/04/1916	30/04/1916
Operation(al) Order(s)	73rd Infantry Brigade Operation Order No. 35	10/04/1916	10/04/1916
Miscellaneous	Work Done In Trenches By 7th (S). Bn. Northamptonshire Regiment from April 6th to 12th	13/04/1916	13/04/1916
Miscellaneous	73rd. Infantry Brigade Order No. 36	16/04/1916	16/04/1916
Operation(al) Order(s)	73rd Infantry Brigade Operation Order No. 37	22/04/1916	22/04/1916
Heading	7th Battalion Northamptonshire Regiment. May 1916		
Heading	War Diary Of 7th Service Battalion Northamptonshire Regiment		
War Diary	Wulverghem	01/05/1916	06/05/1916
War Diary	Kortepyp	07/05/1916	12/05/1916
War Diary	Wulverghem	13/05/1916	18/05/1916
War Diary	Red Lodge	19/05/1916	31/05/1916
Heading	7th Battalion Northamptonshire Regiment June 1916		
Heading	7th Bn. Northamptonshire Regiment		
War Diary	Wulverghem	01/06/1916	03/06/1916
War Diary	Kortepyp	04/06/1916	11/06/1916
War Diary	Wulverghem	12/06/1916	17/06/1916
War Diary	Haegedoorne	18/06/1916	19/06/1916
War Diary	Locre	20/06/1916	20/06/1916
War Diary	Kemmel Shelters	21/06/1916	27/06/1916
War Diary	Kemmel	28/06/1916	30/06/1916
Miscellaneous	Offices i/c A.G. office at the Base	08/07/1916	08/07/1916
Miscellaneous	7th Service Battalion Northamptonshire Regiment	03/06/1916	03/06/1916
Miscellaneous	73rd Infantry Brigade. Preliminary Order	15/06/1916	15/06/1916
Operation(al) Order(s)	73rd Infantry Brigade. Operation Order No. 45	15/06/1916	15/06/1916
Miscellaneous	Relief Of The 73rd Infantry Brigade by The 7th Australian Brigade.		
Miscellaneous	Relief Of The 73rd Infantry Brigade By 7th Australian Brigade.		
Miscellaneous	Officer Commanding	15/06/1916	15/06/1916
Miscellaneous	Reference Operation Order No. 45	16/06/1916	16/06/1916

Operation(al) Order(s)	73rd. Infantry Brigade. Operation Order No. 46	16/06/1916	16/06/1916
Miscellaneous	Relief of The 150th Brigade by The 73rd Infantry Brigade.		
Operation(al) Order(s)	73rd Infantry Brigade. Operation Order No. 47	26/06/1916	26/06/1916
Operation(al) Order(s)	73rd Infantry Brigade Operation Order No. 48	01/07/1916	01/07/1916
Operation(al) Order(s)	73rd Infantry Brigade. Operation Order No. 48	30/06/1916	30/06/1916
Miscellaneous			
Heading	7th Battn. The Northamptonshire Regiment. July 1916		
Heading	War Diary of 7th (S) Battn. Northamptonshire Regiment For The Month Of July 1916		
War Diary	Kemmel	01/07/1916	04/07/1916
War Diary	Kemmel Shelters	05/07/1916	06/07/1916
War Diary	Locre	07/07/1916	11/07/1916
War Diary	Wulverghem	11/07/1916	20/07/1916
War Diary	Godewaersvelde	21/07/1916	24/07/1916
War Diary	Molliens-Vidame	24/07/1916	31/07/1916
Miscellaneous	Appendices 1 To 4		
Miscellaneous	Officer Commanding	28/06/1916	28/06/1916
Miscellaneous	7 Northamptonshire	29/06/1916	29/06/1916
Miscellaneous	Report On Enemy Word	30/06/1916	30/06/1916
Operation(al) Order(s)	73rd. Infantry Brigade. Operation Order No. 50	08/06/1916	08/06/1916
Miscellaneous	Relief Of The 73rd Infantry Brigade By The 150th Infantry Brigade.		
Operation(al) Order(s)	73rd. Infantry Brigade. Operation Order No. 51	11/07/1916	11/07/1916
Heading	7th Battalion Northamptonshire Regiment August 1916		
Heading	War Diary Of 7th (Service) Bn. Northamptonshire Regiment For The Month Of August 1916		
War Diary	Saillm-Le-Sec	01/08/1916	02/08/1916
War Diary	Happy Valley	03/08/1916	09/08/1916
War Diary	Nr. The Citadel	09/08/1916	13/08/1916
War Diary	Montauban	14/08/1916	17/08/1916
War Diary	Guillemont	18/08/1916	19/08/1916
War Diary	Montauban	20/08/1916	21/08/1916
War Diary	Nr. Meaulte	22/08/1916	25/08/1916
War Diary	Nr. Dernancourt	26/08/1916	31/08/1916
Diagram etc	Diagram Of Trenches		
Map			
Operation(al) Order(s)	73rd Infantry Brigade. Operation Order No. 57 Appendix No 1	01/08/1916	01/08/1916
Miscellaneous	Table "A"		
Miscellaneous	Table "B"		
Miscellaneous	Appendix No 2	18/08/1916	18/08/1916
Operation(al) Order(s)	73rd Infantry Brigade. Operation Order No. 59		
Miscellaneous	Continuation Of Operation Order No 59		
Miscellaneous		20/08/1916	20/08/1916
Miscellaneous	Operation Order No By Lieut Cole E.R. Mobbs		
Miscellaneous	7th (S) Bn Northamptonshire Regt.		
Miscellaneous	Appendice No 5		
Heading	7th Battalion. Northamptonshire Regiment. September 1916		
Heading	War Diary Of 7th Service Battalion Northamptonshire Regiment		
War Diary	Delville Wood	01/09/1916	04/09/1916
War Diary	Nr. Fricourt	05/09/1916	05/09/1916
War Diary	Dernancourt	06/09/1916	06/09/1916
War Diary	Villers-sous-Ailly	07/09/1916	19/09/1916

War Diary	Bruay	20/09/1916	21/09/1916
War Diary	Gauchie	22/09/1916	23/09/1916
War Diary	Carency	23/09/1916	30/09/1916
Operation(al) Order(s)	73rd. Infantry Brigade. Operation Order No. 70 Appendix 1	22/09/1916	22/09/1916
Miscellaneous	Table Issued With 73rd Infantry Brigade Operation Order No. 70		
Heading	7th Battalion Northamptonshire Regiment October 1916		
Heading	War Diary Of 7th (Service) Battn. Northamptonshire Regiment. From October 1st 1916 To October 31st 1916		
War Diary	Souchez	01/10/1916	10/10/1916
War Diary	Camblain L'Abbe	11/10/1916	18/10/1916
War Diary	Berthonval Wood	19/10/1916	25/10/1916
War Diary	Gouy Servin	27/10/1916	27/10/1916
War Diary	Mazingarbe	28/10/1916	28/10/1916
War Diary	Loos	29/10/1916	31/10/1916
Operation(al) Order(s)	73rd Infantry Brigade Operation Order No. 71	29/09/1916	29/09/1916
Miscellaneous	Defence Scheme		
Miscellaneous	Appendix No 3	04/10/1916	04/10/1916
Miscellaneous	Raid		
Operation(al) Order(s)	73rd Infantry Brigade. Operation Order No. 73	07/10/1916	07/10/1916
Miscellaneous	Table Issued With 73rd Infantry Brigade Operation Order No. 73		
Miscellaneous	Report On Minor Enterprise Carried Out By The 7th. Battalion Northamptonshire Regiment Appendix No 5	10/10/1916	10/10/1916
Diagram etc			
Miscellaneous	C Form (Original). Messages And Signals.	10/10/1916	10/10/1916
Miscellaneous	Work Parties to be Retailed For Work Under The 104th Field Coy. R.E.		
Heading	7th Battalion Northamptonshire Regiment December 1916		
Heading	War Diary Of 7th Service Battalion Northamptonshire Regiment. From December 1st 1916 To December 31st 1916		
War Diary	Maroc	01/12/1916	31/12/1916
Heading	7th Battalion Northamptonshire Regiment. November 1916		
Heading	War Diary Of 7th Service Battalion Northamptonshire Regiment. From November 1st 1916 To November 30th 1916		
War Diary	Maroc	01/11/1916	30/11/1916
Operation(al) Order(s)	73rd Infantry Brigade. Operation Order No. 80	16/11/1916	16/11/1916
Heading	War Diary Of 7th Service Battalion Northamptonshire Regiment. From January 1st 1917 To January 31st 1917		
War Diary	Maroc	01/01/1917	31/01/1917
Heading	War Diary Of 7th Service Battalion Northamptonshire Regiment From February 1st 1917 To February 28th 1917		
War Diary	Les Brebis	01/02/1917	03/02/1917
War Diary	Maroc	04/02/1917	10/02/1917
War Diary	Petit Sains	11/02/1917	11/02/1917
War Diary	Lapugnoy	12/02/1917	28/02/1917
Heading	War Diary Of 7th Service Battalion Of Northamptonshire Regiment. From March 1st 1917 To March 31st 1917		

War Diary	Lapugnoy	01/03/1917	02/03/1917
War Diary	Haillicourt	03/03/1917	03/03/1917
War Diary	Ablain St Nazaire	04/03/1917	10/03/1917
War Diary	Souchez	11/03/1917	16/03/1917
War Diary	Sains-En-Gohelle	17/03/1917	22/03/1917
War Diary	Souchez	23/03/1917	30/03/1917
War Diary	Ablain St Nazaire	31/03/1917	31/03/1917
Heading	7th Battn. Northamptonshire Regiment 73rd Infantry Brigade 24th Division April 1917		
Heading	War Diary Of 7th Service Battalion Northamptonshire Regiment. From April 1st 1917 To April 30th 1917		
War Diary	Ablain St Nazaire	01/04/1917	04/04/1917
War Diary	Souchez	05/04/1917	14/04/1917
War Diary	Roliencourt	15/04/1917	16/04/1917
War Diary	Cite Des Bureaux	17/04/1917	19/04/1917
War Diary	Petit Sains	20/04/1917	20/04/1917
War Diary	Marles Les Mines	21/04/1917	21/04/1917
War Diary	Febvin Paifart	22/04/1917	24/04/1917
War Diary	Camblain Chatlain	26/04/1917	26/04/1917
War Diary	Noeux Les Mines	27/04/1917	30/04/1917
Heading	War Diary Of 7th Service Battalion Northamptonshire Regiment From May 1st 1917 To May 31st 1917		
War Diary	Noeux Les Mines	01/05/1917	04/05/1917
War Diary	Lapugnoy	05/05/1917	08/05/1917
War Diary	L'Ecleme	09/05/1917	09/05/1917
War Diary	Thiennes	10/05/1917	11/05/1917
War Diary	Steenvoorde	12/05/1917	13/05/1917
War Diary	Vancouver	14/05/1917	28/05/1917
War Diary	Toronto	29/05/1917	31/05/1917
Heading	War Diary Of 7th Service Battalion Northamptonshire Regiment. From June 1st 1917 To June 30th 1917		
War Diary	Heksken	01/06/1917	27/06/1917
War Diary	Bayenghem	28/06/1917	30/06/1917
Heading	War Diary Of 7th Service Battalion Northamptonshire Regiment. From July 1st 1917 To July 31st 1917		
War Diary	Bayenghem	01/07/1917	17/07/1917
War Diary	Renescure	18/07/1917	18/07/1917
War Diary	La Kreule	19/07/1917	19/07/1917
War Diary	Eecke	20/07/1917	20/07/1917
War Diary	Reninghelst	21/07/1917	31/07/1917
Operation(al) Order(s)	Operation Orders No. 41	28/07/1917	28/07/1917
Miscellaneous	7th Service Battalion Northamptonshire Regiment. Appendix A	06/08/1917	06/08/1917
Miscellaneous	7th Service Battalion Northamptonshire Regiment.		
War Diary	Line	01/08/1917	01/08/1917
War Diary	Dickebusch	02/08/1917	10/08/1917
War Diary	Line	11/08/1917	15/08/1917
War Diary	Micmac	16/08/1917	20/08/1917
War Diary	Dickebusch	21/08/1917	23/08/1917
War Diary	Line	24/08/1917	27/08/1917
War Diary	Micmac	28/08/1917	30/08/1917
War Diary	Camp "J"	21/08/1917	31/08/1917
Miscellaneous	D.A.G. 3rd Echelon	21/08/1917	21/08/1917
Miscellaneous	Special Order Appendix B	06/08/1917	06/08/1917
Miscellaneous	Special Order Appendix "B"	06/08/1917	06/08/1917

Miscellaneous	7th Battn Northamptonshire Regiment War Diary For The Period 1st To 30th September 1917		
War Diary	Dickebusch	01/09/1917	03/09/1917
War Diary	Line	04/09/1917	07/09/1917
War Diary	Micmac	08/09/1917	10/09/1917
War Diary	Dickebusch	11/09/1917	13/09/1917
War Diary	Reninghelst	14/09/1917	15/09/1917
War Diary	Steenwerck	16/09/1917	19/09/1917
War Diary	Bapaume	20/09/1917	20/09/1917
War Diary	Barastre	21/09/1917	23/09/1917
War Diary	Haut Allaines	24/09/1917	25/09/1917
War Diary	Bernes	26/09/1917	26/09/1917
War Diary	Line	27/09/1917	30/09/1917
Heading	War Diary Of 7th Service Battalion Northamptonshire Regiment. From October 1st 1917 To October 31st 1917		
War Diary		01/10/1917	04/10/1917
War Diary	Hervilly	05/10/1917	07/10/1917
War Diary	Line	08/10/1917	27/10/1917
War Diary	Hervilly	28/10/1917	01/11/1917
Operation(al) Order(s)	Operation Order No 70	09/10/1917	09/10/1917
Heading	War Diary Of 7th (S) Bn Northamptonshire Regiment From Nov 1st 1917 To Nov 30th 1917		
War Diary	Hervilly	01/11/1917	03/11/1917
War Diary	Hargicourt	04/11/1917	21/11/1917
War Diary	Hervilly	22/11/1917	27/11/1917
War Diary	Hargicourt	28/11/1917	30/11/1917
Miscellaneous	Battn Northamptonshire Regiment		
Miscellaneous	Operation Order No. 5	03/11/1916	03/11/1916
Miscellaneous			
Miscellaneous		15/11/1917	15/11/1917
Miscellaneous	Operation Order No Lt By Lt Col		
Miscellaneous	7th (S) Bn Northamptonshire Regt Operation Order No. 63	14/11/1917	14/11/1917
Miscellaneous	7th Service Bn Northamptonshire Red Operation Order No 67	26/11/1917	26/11/1917
Heading	War Diary of 7th Service Battalion Northamptonshire Regiment From December 1st 1917 To December 31st 1917		
War Diary	Hargicourt	01/12/1917	20/12/1917
War Diary	Bernes	21/12/1917	31/12/1917
Operation(al) Order(s)	Operation Order No 69	03/12/1917	03/12/1917
Operation(al) Order(s)	Operation Order No 72	12/12/1917	12/12/1917
Miscellaneous	7th (S) Bn Northamptonshire Regt	17/12/1917	17/12/1917
Miscellaneous	Operation Orders No. 74 By Major S.S. Hayne, Commanding 7th Bn Northamptonshire Regt.	26/12/1917	26/12/1917
Heading	War Diary Of 7th Service Battalion Northamptonshire Regiment. From January 1st. 1918 To January 31st 1918		
War Diary	Templeux Quarries	01/01/1918	04/01/1918
War Diary	Bernes	05/01/1918	08/01/1918
War Diary	Vraignes	09/01/1918	20/01/1918
War Diary	Line	21/01/1918	24/01/1918
War Diary	Templeux Quarries	25/01/1918	29/01/1918
War Diary	Bernes	30/01/1918	31/01/1918

Miscellaneous	Operation Orders No. 1 By Major S.S. Hayne Commanding 7th Bn Northamptonshire Regiment	03/01/1918	03/01/1918
Miscellaneous	Operation Orders No.2 By Major S.S. Hayne Commanding 7th Bn Northamptonshire Regiment	07/01/1918	07/01/1918
Miscellaneous	7th S. Bn. Northamptonshire Regiment.	19/01/1918	19/01/1918
Miscellaneous		23/01/1918	23/01/1918
Miscellaneous			
Heading	7th (Service) Battalion Northamptonshire Regiment. War Diary Of The Month Of February 1918		
War Diary	Bernes	01/02/1918	11/02/1918
War Diary	Line	12/02/1918	19/02/1918
War Diary	Bernes	20/02/1918	20/02/1918
War Diary	Bervilly	21/02/1918	28/02/1918
Miscellaneous		11/02/1918	11/02/1918
Miscellaneous			
Heading	7th Battalion Northamptonshire Regiment March 1918		
Heading	7th (Service) Battalion Northamptonshire Regiment. War Diary For The Month Of March 1918		
War Diary	Hervilly	01/03/1918	01/03/1918
War Diary	Hancourt	02/03/1918	20/03/1918
War Diary	Jeancourt	21/03/1918	22/03/1918
War Diary	Flez	23/03/1918	23/03/1918
War Diary	Licourt	24/03/1918	24/03/1918
War Diary	Fonches	25/03/1918	26/03/1918
War Diary	Warvillers	26/03/1918	26/03/1918
War Diary	Meharicourt	27/03/1918	28/03/1918
War Diary	Castel	29/03/1918	29/03/1918
War Diary	Thezyglimont	30/03/1918	31/03/1918
Miscellaneous		27/03/1918	27/03/1918
Heading	7th Battn. The Northamptonshire Regiment. April 1918		
Heading	7th (Service) Battalion Northamptonshire Regiment. War Diary For The Month Of April 1918		
War Diary	Thezy Glimont	01/04/1918	03/04/1918
War Diary	Bois De Gentelles	04/04/1918	05/04/1918
War Diary	Longeau	06/04/1918	06/04/1918
War Diary	Escarbotin	07/04/1918	16/04/1918
War Diary	Houdain	17/04/1918	30/04/1918
Heading	7th Service Battalion Northamptonshire Regt. War Diary For The Month Of May 1918		
War Diary	Houdain	01/05/1918	01/05/1918
War Diary	Les Brebis	02/05/1918	02/05/1918
War Diary	Hill 70 Sector	03/05/1918	31/05/1918
Heading	7th Service Battalion Northamptonshire Regiment War Diary For June 1918		
War Diary	Hill 70	01/06/1918	11/06/1918
War Diary	Les Brebis	12/06/1918	17/06/1918
War Diary	Hill 70	18/06/1918	29/06/1918
War Diary	Les Brebis	30/06/1918	30/06/1918
Heading	7th (Service) Battalion Northamptonshire Regiment War Diary For The Month Of July 1918		
War Diary	Les Brebis	01/07/1918	05/07/1918
War Diary	Hill 70 Sector	06/07/1918	17/07/1918
War Diary	Les Brebis	18/07/1918	23/07/1918
War Diary	Hill 70 Sector	24/07/1918	31/07/1918
Heading	7th Service Battalion Northamptonshire Regiment. War Diary For Month Of August 1918		

War Diary	Hill 70 Sector	01/08/1918	04/08/1918
War Diary	Les Brebis	05/08/1918	11/08/1918
War Diary	Hill 70 Sector	12/08/1918	24/08/1918
War Diary	Les Brebis	25/08/1918	26/08/1918
War Diary	Lens Sector	27/08/1918	31/08/1918
War Diary	Les Brebis	10/08/1918	10/08/1918
War Diary	Hill 70 Sector	24/08/1918	24/08/1918
Heading	War Diary September 1918		
War Diary	Lens Sector	01/09/1918	07/09/1918
War Diary	Marqueffles Farm	08/09/1918	14/09/1918
War Diary	Lens Sector	15/09/1918	30/09/1918
Heading	War Diary For Month Of October 1918		
War Diary	Hersin Coupigny	01/10/1918	01/10/1918
War Diary	Grouches	02/10/1918	06/10/1918
War Diary	Moeuvres	07/10/1918	07/10/1918
War Diary	Caintaing	08/10/1918	08/10/1918
War Diary	Awoingt	09/10/1918	09/10/1918
War Diary	Cagnoncles	10/10/1918	10/10/1918
War Diary	Rieux	11/10/1918	14/10/1918
War Diary	Avesnes-Lez-Aubert	15/10/1918	15/10/1918
War Diary	St Aubert	16/10/1918	16/10/1918
War Diary	Haussy	17/10/1918	17/10/1918
War Diary	Avesnes Lez Aubert	18/10/1918	18/10/1918
War Diary	Caurior	19/10/1918	26/10/1918
War Diary	Haussy	27/10/1918	31/10/1918
Heading	War Diary Of 7th Service Battalion Northamptonshire Regiment From November 1st 1918 To November 30th 1918		
War Diary	Haussy	02/11/1918	02/11/1918
War Diary	Bermerain	03/11/1918	07/11/1918
War Diary	Bavay	08/11/1918	30/11/1918
Heading	7th Service Battalion Northamptonshire Regiment. War Diary December 1918		
War Diary	Mouchin	01/12/1918	05/12/1918
War Diary	Bachy	06/12/1918	20/12/1918
War Diary	Bachy And Tournai	21/12/1918	21/12/1918
War Diary	Tournai	22/12/1918	31/12/1918
Heading	7th Service Battalion Northamptonshire Regiment War Diary For The Month Of January 1918		
War Diary	Tournai	01/01/1919	31/01/1919
Heading	War Diary 7th (S) Bn Northamptonshire Regiment For The Month Of February 1919		
War Diary	Tournai	01/02/1919	28/02/1919
Miscellaneous	Headquarters 73rd Bde		
Miscellaneous			
Heading	War Diary Of The 7th (Service) Battalion Northamptonshire Regt. For The Month Of March 1919		
Miscellaneous			
War Diary	Tournai	01/03/1919	31/03/1919
Miscellaneous	To 25th Division	01/05/1919	01/05/1919
Heading	War Diary For The Month Of April 1919		
War Diary		01/04/1919	15/04/1919
War Diary	Tournai	16/04/1919	30/04/1919
Heading	War Diary For May 1919		
War Diary		01/05/1919	31/05/1919

Heading	7th Northamptonshire Regiment War Diary For The Month Of June 1919		
War Diary	?	01/06/1919	07/06/1919
Miscellaneous	Stray/WO/95/2		

3090 95
2218/2

24TH DIVISION
73RD INFY BDE

7TH BN NORTHANTS REGT
SEP 1915 — JUN 1919
AUG

73rd Inf.Bde.
24th Div.

Battn. disembarked
Boulogne from
England 2.9.15.

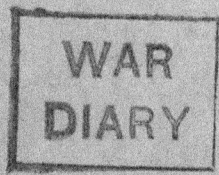

7th BATTN. THE NORTHAMPTONSHIRE REGIMENT.

AUGUST AND SEPTEMBER

(21.8.15 to 30.9.15)

1 9 1 5

June 1919

INTELLIGENCE SUMMARY.

(Erase heading not required.)

Instructions regarding War Diaries and Intelligence Summaries are contained in F. S. Regs., Part II. and the Staff Manual respectively. Title pages will be prepared in manuscript.

Place	Date	Hour	Summary of Events and Information	Remarks and references to Appendices
Woking	20/8/15		Orders were received that the Battalion would shortly be proceeding to France and had to get equipped and some fitting its mobilization establishment at once. Embarkation leave had commenced previous to this but there were already about five hundred who had no leave - the period was cut down to 48 hours. Practically all leave had finished by Saturday midnight. Major W.J. Ughy joined the Battn on the 13th of August & was posted to command "B" Coy. Captain W. Gordon took over command of "A" Coy.	
do	28/8/15 to 30/8/15		These days were spent mostly under Company arrangements the detail comprised of kit inspections, fitting each man with a new pair of service boots, completing each man's equipment, kit, ammunition etc. The Bn was one the strength of the service Bns but about 98 other ranks. It was ordered that on arrival Battalions in the division were under strength, viz Brigade transfers would take place. Those 98 men were transferred to the 9th Royal Fusiliers. Officers to men to the 9th Loyal Sussex Regt. A few were formed unfit for active service transferred to the 9th Battn Northants Regiment. The Bn left England at exactly war strength.	
do	31/8/15		The day was devoted to cleaning of barracks. The transport & machine gun section handed at 10 am proceeded to Southampton thence to Havre.	
	1/9/15		The Battn paraded for embarkation as follows: A.B. Coys at 5am under Major J.B. Fisher. Men proceeded to Brookwood Station. C&D Coys & Hdqrs paraded at 5.30pm and then proceeded to Brookwood Station. The Battn left Brookwood Stn in two trains first train at 7.8pm & 2nd train at 7.35pm. The weather was very hot during the whole time after leaving Barracks and each batch was ordered to be at the station two hours before the departure of the trains the men got very hot. Ref. The trains arrived at Folkestone at 9pm all men marched straight to the boat which left at 10.30pm for Boulogne. Disembarked at Boulogne at 1.30am, marched to a camp "Rest Camp" called Ostrohan just outside Boulogne. On arrival these (2.30pm) each man received a blanket. During the journey there were no casualties and no absentees from any of the parades.	
France	2/9/15		During the morning each man received two iron rations. The Bn paraded at 12.30pm (one man was reported absent.). The Bn's entrainment at Boulogne arrived at Marquet at 4.30pm. The Machine Gun transport had previously arrived at the station. The battn marched about a mile from the village to the cantons Nort Noit Lea.	

INTELLIGENCE SUMMARY.

(Erase heading not required.)

Instructions regarding War Diaries and Intelligence Summaries are contained in F. S. Regs., Part II. and the Staff Manual respectively. Title pages will be prepared in manuscript.

Place	Date	Hour	Summary of Events and Information	Remarks and references to Appendices
France	2/9/15 to 10/9/15		The Bn proceeded by route march via BEAURAMVILLE - OFFIN - ROYON - TORCY - CREQUY. A & B Coy went billets at CREQUY and C & D Coy at TORCY.	
	10/9/15		The Bn remained at TORCY - CREQUY, having was continued as usual. Officer classes etc were formed by the Division. Lectures etc. on the 8-15. Three Officers Lt King B Coy, Lt Fynn C Coy, Lt Clarke D Coy, went for a 24 hours tour of the trenches.	
	11/9/15		Brigade Exercise near EMERY, commenced 6-30 a.m., returned to billets 4 p.m. Grenade school	
	12/9/15 to 13/9/15		Exercise the Bn and 13th Middlesex Regt. This finished about 1 p.m. Capt. V.D. Short attended Brigade Intelligence Officers	
	14/9/15		Brigade operations, weather very wet. Bn returned 12 noon. Machine Gun Officers left for 24 hours trench tour	
	15/9/15		The Keeb. (reports about from Boulogne) we realised by the 4 coy to 3 mths ZPNO1 14 was for attending a battle of wine Bde Exercise 6 a.m. finished at 1-30 p.m.	
	17/9/15		Bn returned from Exercise 12 noon	
	19/9/15			
	21/9/15		B" paraded at 8 p.m. at TORCY and marched to LAIRES, arriving about 2 a.m. 22/9/15.	
	22/9/15		Paraded at LAIRES at 6 p.m. joined the Brigade about 1 mile west and marched to L'ECLEME, arriving about 3 a.m.	
	23/9/15		Stayed at L'ECLEME	

INTELLIGENCE SUMMARY.
(Erase heading not required.)

Place	Date	Hour	Summary of Events and Information	Remarks and references to Appendices
France	24/9/15		Proceeded at 7 p.m. [and] advanced guard of the 2nd I.S.W. and marched via GONNEHEN - CHOCQUES - BETHUNE to BEUVRY, arriving about 3 a.m. bivouacked for the remainder of the night (Except B Coy who were in a Barn) in the field.	
	25/9/15		Orders were received at 11-15 a.m. for the Bn to move. They marched to VERMELLES a halt in the village was made for 2 hours, the march was then continued until the Bn got up to the HOHENZOLLERN Redoubt met with the main German line trenches in front of this redoubt. (These had been captured earlier in the day by the Gordons, Seaforths, and Royal Scots), one of these Regts the Bn relieved.	VERMELLES
		8 p.m.	The German snipers were a constant attention, there was repulsed, but they shelled our trenches during the whole of the night.	
	26/9/15		During the whole of the day the enemy shelled heavily and made another counter attack at 7 p.m., these were repulsed, but the shelling continued on both sides all through the night.	
	27/9/15	6 a.m.	The enemy again made another attack and advanced on our front line trenches in mass, by 7-30 a.m. owing to the heavy casualties and no relief, we were driven from the front line trenches and with up a second line about 100 yds in rear, this was lost and re-taken several times during the day; highly exploding munitions	
		11 p.m.	the Batts were relieved when then both places we still held the second line of trenches.	

INTELLIGENCE SUMMARY.

(Erase heading not required.)

Instructions regarding War Diaries and Intelligence Summaries are contained in F.S. Regs., Part II. and the Staff Manual respectively. Title pages will be prepared in manuscript.

Place	Date	Hour	Summary of Events and Information	Remarks and references to Appendices
France	NOTE.		Owing to continued shelling no food or water reached the men, then they had no food except the iron ration, and during Saturday night rain fell heavily, with showers on Sunday; conditions were very much as those during a day machine made quick movements impossible. The casualties were very heavy. The 1/5th being N.C.2 – all ranks killed and wounded very heavy. The Commanding Officer (Lt. Col. A. Palmer), Capt. V. D. Scott & Lt. A. Phipps were killed. Major Tuke, Capt. S. E. Marshall, Capt. Boyd, Lt. Moorcroft, 2/Lt. Saunders were wounded, Capt. S. H. Fawssett wounded slightly but remained at duty. Lt. J. M. Hovey the Hospital, wounded and missing.	
	28/9/15		A Bivouac was formed in the village of SAILLY near VERMELLES where the enemy had a hot meal waiting for the troops as they retired. It was just impossible at 3 a.m. about, no men; every one without fighting and clock; it was difficult to get the men in.	
	28/9/15	2:30 p.m.	Another party, mostly A Coy arrived men fell during the march and about 11-30 p.m. The bivouac was in front of nights Reserve trenches.	
		8 p.m.	Bn paraded and marched for entrainment at NOEUX LES MINES, detraining at BERGETTE station, from there by route march to NORRENT-FONTES (about 6 miles) arriving there about 2 a.m.	
	29/9/15		Bn paraded at 4-30 p.m. and marched to LAMBRES (4 miles)	
	3/9/15		Carnellis Little returned from from information gathered from Corp, it was at first thought that gone but would be received from the trenches during steady but those did not arrive	

Army Form C. 2118.

WAR DIARY
or
INTELLIGENCE SUMMARY.
(Erase heading not required.)

Instructions regarding War Diaries and Intelligence Summaries are contained in F. S. Regs., Part II. and the Staff Manual respectively. Title pages will be prepared in manuscript.

Place	Date	Hour	Summary of Events and Information	Remarks and references to Appendices
France	30/9/15		The statement were as follows: Killed 21, wounded 182, missing 20w.	Passed 5
			This is in no way authentic	
		5/1 m	Major 14th Company arrived from the 12th Rl. Fusiliers and temporarily took over Command of the Battalion.	

23th
34th Division

7th Northamptons
Vol I
Aug Sept Oct 15

121/7608

WAR DIARY or INTELLIGENCE SUMMARY

Army Form C. 2118.

7/Northants.

October 1915

Place	Date	Hour	Summary of Events and Information	Remarks and references to Appendices
[FRANCE]	2/10/15		Bn paraded at 11.30 a.m. and proceeded by route march to BERGUETTE. Bn entrained at 12.45 p.m. and proceeded to BOESWAERSVELDE. From thence by route march to HERZEELE via STEENVOORDE arriving at 6.30 p.m. The transport went by road.	
	3/10/15		Col. P.C.B. Skinner, North Hamptonshire Regt. arrived and took over command from Major Coughlan from the 4th. Inspection by Major-General J.E. Capper C.B. the new commander of the 24th Division.	
	4/10/15	10 a.m		
	6/10/15	10.30 a.m	A party of 40 or so all ranks left for a 48 hours tour of the trenches.	
		12 noon	The remainder of the Bn paraded and proceeded to the various billeting areas in the Bde. and the Bn. had the following officers with them — 9/ H. Raynd Surrees. 2/Lt J.C Gurney, 2/Lt Mahin, 2/Lt Shadbolt, 2/Lt. Mackway.	
	7/10/15		Draft of 50 N.C.O.'s men arrived at 10.15 p.m. These included 19 of the old Batln men who have been slightly wounded etc and had been attached at the Divisional Base. Five new officers also joined from the 3rd Battalion as follows 2/Lt. G.T. Shebbeard — 2/Lt. P.B. Borzeger, 2/Lt. A.F.S.B. Wenham 2/Lt. E.F.D. Vreusthorne — 2/Lt. H.H. Williamson.	

Army Form C. 2118.

WAR DIARY
or
INTELLIGENCE SUMMARY.
(Erase heading not required.)

Instructions regarding War Diaries and Intelligence Summaries are contained in F. S. Regs., Part II. and the Staff Manual respectively. Title pages will be prepared in manuscript.

Place	Date	Hour	Summary of Events and Information	Remarks and references to Appendices
Belgium	8/9/15		The parts of 400 returned from the trenches.	
	10/9/15		The 10 officers rejoined from the 9th Bn. Sussex Regt.	
	11/9/15	8.45 am	Bn paraded and marched to RENINGHELST via PROVEN and POPERINGHE arriving at 2 p.m.	
	12/9/15		A party of 1 officer & 4 N.C.O. + men per platoon went up to the sector of trenches the Baln was watching over tonight in much in parties inspecting them. Companies re-organised and promotions made up as far as an establishment. The Coys assigned as under. Capt: Brennan to Command A Coy, H: Hts King B Coy, H: Hts Tyson C Coy, Capt. Cooper D Coy. Various junior subaltern Changes also left for the trenches.	
	13/9/15	9 p.m	The Bn in follows joined the 84th&82nd North amptonshire Regt. 27th. W.W. Taylor, 27th A&B Coys, 27th S.G. Parsons 27th S.C. Percival 27th M.C.S Vaile. The Bn paraded at 3.15 p.m and marched to the sector of trenches, which they completed by 9 oclock.	
	14/9/15		The village of ST ELOI, the relief from the Durham Light Infantry was completed by 9 oclock.	
	15/9/15		Klein Zillebeke quiet, a little trench mortar fighting, our artillery 3 guns were our responding 5 others, this was retaliation by the enemy.	
	16/9/15		Work in trenches continued.	

Army Form C. 2118.

WAR DIARY
or
INTELLIGENCE SUMMARY.
(Erase heading not required.)

Place	Date	Hour	Summary of Events and Information	Remarks and references to Appendices
Belgium	16/9/15		Some artillery firing, and trench mortar fighting, an enemy trench mortar has caused rather a lot of trouble, but at 4-45 p.m. we replied with shrapnel at 5-30 p.m. and after every trench mortar sent in was well and slightly damaged and pumped. Both sides - enemy trenches generally. Roof of 7 elven men arrived from Blatzley a few shells exchanged. Ammunition normal.	
	17/9/15			
	18/9/15		Enemy sent over 9 trench mortar rounds wounding one man - enemy to live but if we were sniping Ethelbert both sides hard at it, in about half an hour however we replied, no work could be carried on outside trenches owing wounded Normal	
	19/9/15			
	20/9/15		no	
	21/9/15		27th S.C. Personnel left the Bn. in transition with Royal Engineers. Everything very quiet. Enemy sent one shell over, this killed his own and wounded one	
	22/9/15	1-30 p.m.		
		3-15 a.m.	our artillery shelled German Trench his Trenches returned every reply but this soon ceased	
		8 p.m.	Baths relieved by the 13th Middlesex Regt. the relief was completed by about 9-30 p.m. and the Bn. returned to the rest camp at RENINGHELST.	
	23/9/15		ROSENHILL camp 'C' was reached late P.M. then the attached with the 13th Middlesex Regt N.C.O.'s were turned out - 11 a.m. Mil uniforms, cleaning etc during the day. A short - of me have crossed	

2353 Wt. W2544/1454 700,000 5/15 D. D. & L. A.D.S.S./Forms/C. 2118.

Army Form C. 2118.

WAR DIARY
or
INTELLIGENCE SUMMARY.
(Erase heading not required.)

Instructions regarding War Diaries and Intelligence Summaries are contained in F. S. Regs., Part II. and the Staff Manual respectively. Title pages will be prepared in manuscript.

Place	Date	Hour	Summary of Events and Information	Remarks and references to Appendices
Belgium	24/10/15		Drafts allotted as follows A.1. B.2. C.19. D.39.	
		3 p.m	300 men provided for R.E. fatigue in the trenches. Have returned about midnight	
	25/10/15		Individuals drilled	
	26/10/15	3 p.m	300 men provided for R.E. fatigue as on the 24th. Have returned about 4 a.m. the 27th.	
	27/10/15		Twenty men picked from the Battalion have proceeded to a camp at Renninghelst for one inspection by his majesty the King, who also made up from the Division, the men selected by his majesty	
RENINGHELST.		10 a.m	Battn. found the use of the Divisional baths, everyone with the exception of 3 had a good bath, this being the first allotment of baths of the Bn. since arrival in France.	
	28/10/15	2–4.5 p.m	Building of Individual continued. Bn. proceeded and marched to the trenches to relieve the 13th Middlesex Regt, now jet trams heavily all the way	
		9 p.m	Relief completed.	
	29/10/15		Trenches dangerous and all is very bad condition many within the mud.	
	30/10/15		Situation unchanged	
	31/10/15		Enemy fired heavy bombardment of with trench mortar place in our left, doing the 6 a.m. and evening also bombarded trenches with rents into 8r.E101 no damage done a few casing things	

2353) Wt.W2544/M54 700,000 5/15 D.D.&L. A.D.S.S./Forms/C.2118.

Army Form C. 2118.

WAR DIARY
or
INTELLIGENCE SUMMARY.
(Erase heading not required.)

Place	Date	Hour	Summary of Events and Information	Remarks and references to Appendices
Belgium	31/10/15		2nd transferred that the (1st Bn Staffords) Bn in our left had taken during the night a rather point in front of their lines.	
		6.30 p.m	one man of ration fatigue wounded in the leg. this was probably our own from the [illegible] lines.	

Per Shirra R Oland
Com Off. 7" Northamptonshire R.

14/11/15.

24th Division 7th Rothbank's vol: 2

12/7635

Nov 15

WAR DIARY
or
INTELLIGENCE SUMMARY

Army Form C. 2118.

(Erase heading not required.)

Place	Date	Hour	Summary of Events and Information	Remarks and references to Appendices
BELGIUM	1/11/15		The 1st Staffords (Bn in our left) still held the trenches as it is thought the Germans were in for sniping. The Battalion Bomb. to Staffords and machine Gun section, have went up into the trenches and told it will returned to same afternoon by a section from the 9th Royal Sussex Regt. Situation quiet, some artillery fire served by R.E. working parties repairing trenches, two artillery retaliated and eventually silenced them. Normal, one casualty accidentally.	
	2/11/15		Some artillery firing during the night. Enemy shelled some working parties casualties. The relief by the 13th Middlesex Regt. commenced during afternoon & was completed by 10 p.m. (Bomber-machine gunner taking over during afternoon) Lt. Flynn R.E. Co commander wounded (not seriously) by a piece of shrapnel. In Rest. Camp at RENINGHELST. Day spent in cleaning kit.	
	3/11/15			
	4/11/15		Training of specialists, further members of Clothing were issued - number of RE.	
	5/11/15	2 p.m	Camp very muddy - difficulty experienced in getting clothes dry. Fatigue party of 30-0 men - 8 officers provided for work on the Trenches under the R.E.	
	6/11/15		Bootless & "Holdsworth" continued Bn had some of Division at Bailles during the afternoon. Fatigue party made from bully beef tin ashes etc.	
	7/11/15	2.15	Bathing Veronica morning Camp cleaned up from 15 Bays for Transport. Bn marched off - halted for tea about 4-30 p.m. Relief of 13th Middlesex Regt completed by 9 p.m.	

Army Form C. 2118.

WAR DIARY
or
INTELLIGENCE SUMMARY
(Erase heading not required.)

Instructions regarding War Diaries and Intelligence Summaries are contained in F. S. Regs., Part II. and the Staff Manual respectively. Title pages will be prepared in manuscript.

Place	Date	Hour	Summary of Events and Information	Remarks and references to Appendices
BELGIUM	8/11/15		Lunch done at 8th Hdqrs. Artillery fairly active	
	9/11/15		Head artillery duels. BUS HOUSE ROAD shelled intermittently. Difficult to catch working parties etc. Trenches in bad state. Work continued. German snipers seen taking water from their trenches.	
	10/11/15		Normal	
	11/11/15	4·30 am	Patrol went round the craters reporting enemy activity. One man killed between 1st & 2nd Bavarian(?)	
	12/11/15	7·45 am 9·15 am	German shelled R1 & R4 with shot & shrapnel when a light French Mortar on artillery retaliated. Artillery both light & big guns active. Enemy's own comn. of French continued.	
	13/11/15		Heavy rain during the night. Communication trenches practically impassable. Some of Hdqr. dugouts flooded. Civilian guides.	
		6·20 pm	First Company of 131st Hohenz. Rgt arrived, relief completed by 9 pm	
	14/11/15		C Camp RENINGHELST, very dismal owing to the mud.	
	15/11/15		Company ordered to Canfield's Farm and defence work undertaken. Lent for 7th march in G.R.O. Helmet plan framed by 7 specialists.	

2333 Wt. W2544/1454 700,000 5/15 D.D.&L. A.D.S.S./Forms/C.2118.

WAR DIARY or INTELLIGENCE SUMMARY.

(Erase heading not required.)

Army Form C. 2118.

Place	Date	Hour	Summary of Events and Information	Remarks and references to Appendices
BELGIUM	16/11/15		Building of flicknacks continued. Bn. Route march. Training of specialists in afternoon.	
	17/11/15		Bathing at Divisional baths. in morning. Bn. paraded (Bn and Coy HQrs) formed at 1.30 p.m. - 1.45 p.m to march to brickfields, who day. The Bn. was to spend in billets at DICKEBUSCH. During the time Bn. was marching up, three men were killed, one other wounded; the rest were killed by the enemy.	
	18/11/15		Stay in DICKEBUSCH to act as Brigade Reserve for the right Section. Fatigue parties furnished for work under the R.E.	
	19/11/15		Fatigue parties furnished during morning. The rest of J., 16, 13 & 14 Middlesex completed about 8 p.m.	
	20/11/15		Drainage of trenches continued. Normal situation.	
	21/11/15	5.30 am	Artillery action. Enemy fairly dispersed. Enemy working party dispersed.	
		10	Our Artillery shelled strongly enemy Batterie	
		9.30 am	Place empty in morning. 2/Lt Mackay wounded slightly, also 4 other men. 2 by own gun. strafed railway level.	
	22/11/15		Bn. relieved by the 2nd & 13th Royal Fusiliers machine gunners between 5 & 7 pm. Bn. arrived in RENINGHELST at 21.45. Bn. retired to RENINGHELST.	
	23/11/15	4.10 pm	Bn. left RENINGHELST marched via POPERINGHE to the village of ECKE near STEENWOORDE distance about 8 miles completed about 7 p.m.	

Army Form C. 2118.

WAR DIARY
or
INTELLIGENCE SUMMARY.
(Erase heading not required.)

Instructions regarding War Diaries and Intelligence Summaries are contained in F. S. Regs., Part II. and the Staff Manual respectively. Title pages will be prepared in manuscript.

Place	Date	Hour	Summary of Events and Information	Remarks and references to Appendices
FRANCE	24/11/15		Bn. remained for the day at ECKE.	
	25/11/15	10-15	B.n left ECKE and marched via CASSEL to ARNEKE distance about 12 miles	
	26/11/15	9 a.m	Left ARNEKE marched to EPERLECQUES a village about 6 miles N.W. of ST. OMER arriving about 4 p.m.	
	27/11/15		Day spent in cleaning equipment etc.	
	28/11/15		Divine Service morning. 2/Lt. G.H.NUTT "B" Coy; 2/Lt. D.W Norris "D" Coy, joined the Battalion men posted on schemes.	
	29/11/15		Training of Specialists. C.O. inspection of B & C Coys. men extra blankets for men chosen.	
	30/11/15		C.O. inspection A & B Coys. Training of Specialists. S/6 C. miles Billets for Bn —	
	30/11/15		[illegible]	

Map attached showing position of German & English trenches round STEL01, shows the Bn's both of [illegible] with an [illegible]

Army Form C. 2118.

WAR DIARY
or
INTELLIGENCE SUMMARY.
(Erase heading not required.)

Instructions regarding War Diaries and Intelligence Summaries are contained in F.S. Regs., Part II. and the Staff Manual respectively. Title pages will be prepared in manuscript.

Place	Date	Hour	Summary of Events and Information	Remarks and references to Appendices

SHEET 28.
SCALE
GERMAN TRENCHES
ST ELOI
WHITE HORSE CELLARS
BUS HOUSE
VORMEZEELE

7th Northamptons
Vol: 3 December 1915

121/7931

24th

Army Form C. 2118.

WAR DIARY
or
INTELLIGENCE SUMMARY.
(Erase heading not required.)

Instructions regarding War Diaries and Intelligence Summaries are contained in F. S. Regs., Part II. and the Staff Manual respectively. Title pages will be prepared in manuscript.

Place	Date	Hour	Summary of Events and Information	Remarks and references to Appendices
1/12/15 FRANCE	2/12/15		Brigade route march during morning. Training of specialists continued.	
	3/12/15 to 6		Training continued — have commenced 6 successive abettors with Battalions, period 8 days.	
	7/12/15		Training continued.	
	8/12/15		Brigade Route march (raining heavy)	
	9/12/15		do	
	10/12/15		Draft of 30 other ranks arrived	
	11/12/15		Provisions made up as far as possible. Brigade now 6 under, inspection during march by Army Commander. Party from Battalion attended a course of instruction in engineering lately three days.	
	12/12/15		2/Lt I.H Stevenson, 2/Lt F.R. Beveridge, 2/Lt J.E. Goode joined and were posted to A.B.+A. Coy respectively	
	13/12/15		Brigade Route march	
	14/12/15 15/12/15		Training continued. Spieshoh, Tomboun, machine Gunners, etc.	

Army Form C. 2118.

WAR DIARY

~~INTELLIGENCE SUMMARY.~~
(Erase heading not required.)

Instructions regarding War Diaries and Intelligence Summaries are contained in F.S. Regs., Part II. and the Staff Manual respectively. Title pages will be prepared in manuscript.

Place	Date	Hour	Summary of Events and Information	Remarks and references to Appendices
FRANCE.	16/12/15		Battalion Route march — Party of 300 all ranks attended a gas demonstration at HOUVILLE.	
	17/12/15		Battalion paraded for practice in the attack, on zenie model trenches built near the Rifle Range.	
	18/12/15		Musketry and manual training	
	19/12/15		Divine Service	
	20/12/15		Battalion route march — Draft of 17 other ranks arrived	
	21/12/15		Manual training — 27/- P.J. Smail joined reported to B Coy.	
	22/12/15		Battalion again practised in the attack on model trenches	
	23/12/15		Manual training — Party (40 all ranks) detailed for engineering course at ADDLE. Two men found test for machine making left the Battn for HAVRE.	
	24/12/15		All clothing arms bike helmets etc completed and inspections made. Inter company football competition. Draft of 23 other ranks joined from 8/K.R.R.	
	25/12/15		Church parade. Additional purchases (cigars, oranges, beer etc) made from the canteen fund for Xmas dinner. Pudding (gigantic size) by people of N'ampton.	
	26/12/15		Battalion undertook ………… to ………… new area —	

Army Form C. 2118.

WAR DIARY
or
INTELLIGENCE SUMMARY.
(Erase heading not required.)

Instructions regarding War Diaries and Intelligence Summaries are contained in F. S. Regs., Part II. and the Staff Manual respectively. Title pages will be prepared in manuscript.

Place	Date	Hour	Summary of Events and Information	Remarks and references to Appendices
France	27/12/15		Orders for move cancelled. Training continued in full swing.	
	28/12/15		Hand Training. Permission obtained for Lt. H.J.B. King (O.C. B Coy) & H.R. Surrey (O.C. C Coy) to assume the rank of Captain as Company Commanders. 9 other ranks promoted.	
	29/12/15		Hand Training.	
	30/12/15		Inspection of 73rd Inf. Bde. by General E.S. Coffin C.B. Comdg. 24th Division, at Moulle.	
	31/12/15		The attack practised through the FORÊT D'EPERLECQUES.	

Bryant R. Hobbs Major,
Comdg. 7 K.O. Yorkshire Regiment.

72rd Brigade,
24th Division.

7th BATTALION

NORTHAMPTON REGIMENT.

January 1916.

7th Northants
Vol: 4

Army Form C. 2118.

WAR DIARY
or
INTELLIGENCE SUMMARY.
(Erase heading not required.)

Instructions regarding War Diaries and Intelligence Summaries are contained in F.S. Regs., Part II. and the Staff Manual respectively. Title pages will be prepared in manuscript.

Place	Date	Hour	Summary of Events and Information	Remarks and references to Appendices
EPERLEQUES.	1-1-16.		EPERLEQUES. Passes to locate the Billeting area were disallowed to N.C.Os and men by Division Order	
	2-1-16.		Divine Service .... 4 Other ranks proceeded on leave	
	3-1-16.		Usual training or geopisitats etc.	
	4-1-16.		Preliminary movement orders issued for the movement of the Battalion back to the trenches	
	5-1-16.		Command of 73rd Infantry Brigade assumed by Lieut.Col. P.C.B. Skinner during absence on leave of Brigadier General Jelf R.E. Further ord rs fir move to new Divisional Area issued.	
	6-1-16.		Advance party proce ded to POPERINGHE at 6-45 a.m. llst. Clarke in charge of party. Cleaning up of Billets. Blankets tied up in bundles of 10 and conveyed in Motor lorries to new Divisional Area. Officers Kit. Company Stores etc. packed in 2 G.S. Wagons. Capt. R. Gurney proceeded to England on leave with 3 other ranks.	
	7-1-16.		Transport moved to St.Omer at 12H15 am with Machine Gun Section with an extra 20 men to assist loading and unloading limbers etc. Battalion paraded at 2 am and moved off at 2-10am to St.Omer arriving at 5am. The men were given tea. Battalion entrained at 6-45am for QUINTIN one mile from POPERINGHE. Destination of Transport. The Battalion arrived at QUINTIN at 10-30am. The Camp which the Battalion was to take over was situated about 2 miles S.E. of POPERINGHE Station. The 3rd. Bn. Rifle Brigade were still in occupation but they left during the afternoon and we took over. No casualties during the move	

Army Form C. 2118.

WAR DIARY
or
INTELLIGENCE SUMMARY.

(Erase heading not required.)

Instructions regarding War Diaries and Intelligence Summaries are contained in F. S. Regs., Part II. and the Staff Manual respectively. Title pages will be prepared in manuscript.

Place	Date	Hour	Summary of Events and Information	Remarks and references to Appendices
VLAMERTINGHE.	8-1-16.		Day spent in cleaning up. Inspection of Helmets etc.	
	9-1-16.		Training of Specialists. Major General Capper visited Camp Notification received that Capt. E. R. Mobbs appointed 2nd. in Command of the Battalion, to hold the rank of Major while in the appointment.	
	10-1-16.		Training, Inspections, etc. The Commanding Officer inspected all Huts and gave a prize of 40 francs for the best one. This was won by 'A' Coy.	
	11-1-16.		2nd. Lieut. Heaton appointed Brigade Machine Gun Officer during the temporary absence of Capt. Godwin. Usual Training.	
	12-1-16.		Notification received that 2nd. Lieut. Motion, 2nd.Lieut.Martyn promoted to the rank of Lieutenant to date from 28-8-15. Parades under Company arrangements. At 11-1 pm orders were received from Brigade Headquarters for Battalion to 'stand to' and to be ready to proceed to BELGIAN CHATEAU – the Brigade rendezvous – in an hour. The Battalion was paraded and ready to move off with Transport loaded and in-spanned in 56 minutes. At 12-0pm the Brigade Major dismissed the parade. A message expressing the satisfaction of the G.O.C. Division was received by the Regiment.	
	13-1-16.		Lieut. Col. Skinner rejoined the Battalion. Draining of Camp etc. Training of Specialists. 2nd. Lieut. F.S.Hadley promoted Lieutenant to date from 28-8-15. Taube flew over the Area and dropped Bombs near POPERINGHE-VLAMERTINGHE Railway. 2 men of R.F. killed	

Instructions regarding War Diaries and Intelligence Summaries are contained in F. S. Regs., Part II. and the Staff Manual respectively. Title pages will be prepared in manuscript.

WAR DIARY

or

INTELLIGENCE SUMMARY.

(Erase heading not required.)

Place	Date	Hour	Summary of Events and Information	Remarks and references to Appendices
VLAMERTINGHE.	13-1-16.		Working Party of 4 Officers and 235 other ranks proceeded to KRUISSTRAAT DICKEBUSCH area to bury Cables under the supervision of R.E.	
	14-1-16.		Oders were issued to Battalion to proceed to BELGIAN CHATEAU and ZILLEBEKE LAKE dug-outs the following day. Roy-1 Artillery Band from England played in the Camp of the 5th. Royal Sussex. (C Camp). Machine Gun Section proceeded to occupy fortified points in front of ZILLEBEKE LAKE.	
ZILLEBEKE LAKE.	15-1-16.		Battalion moved off by Companies at 3 p.m. and proceeded Via VLAMERTINGHE, YPRES RLY, KRUISSTRAAT, YSER CANAL, arriving 7-30 pm. Outgoing Regiment, 9th East Surreys.	
	16-1-16.		Day opened very quietly. Our Aeroplanes reconnoitring were fired at with no success. Enemy Artillery quiet. Our Artillery fairly active all round the Salient. Wind in our favour, no fear of Gas attack. Large Working Party of 350 proceeded at 5 pm to GORDON HOUSE for entrenching and rebuilding under supervision of R.E. Cpl. Agaiit of Working Party was killed by a Sniper. One of our detached men wounded by shell fire in YPRES Ramparts.	
	17-1-16.		Day opened quietly. Great Aeroplane activity in early morning. A British AEROPLANE came down in our lines in front of YPRES apparently undamaged. Our artillery became very active during the early part of the day. The Germans were fairly quiet. Wind more in favour of the enemy.	
	18-1-16.		Draft of 40 other ranks arrived at Battalion Base from 5th. Battalion Colchester 12-8-26. Fairly quiet day. Little Artillery activity. Working party of 300 men for R.E. Reconnoitring of Trenches at HOOGE.	
HOOGE.	19-1-16.		Morning opened quietly.	

Instructions regarding War Diaries and Intelligence Summaries are contained in F. S. Regs., Part II. and the Staff Manual respectively. Title pages will be prepared in manuscript.

INTELLIGENCE SUMMARY.

or

(Erase heading not required.)

Place	Date	Hour	Summary of Events and Information	Remarks and references to Appendices
HOOGE.	19-1-16.		At 11-15am. our Artillery opened on enemy lines, probable objectives HILL 60 and BILLEWAARDE LAKE. No enemy reply. Battalion moved up into left sector of trenches at HOOGE from ZILLEBEKE LAKE. Headquarters, HALF WAY HOUSE. Outcoming Battalion, 2nd.Liensters commanded by Lieut.Col.Bullen-Smith. The relief was carried out without casualties to either Battalions.	
	20-1-16.		Wind safe. S.W. Artillery activity on both sides. Our Grenadiers were busy during night of 29th-21st in front of STABLES at HOOGE. Enemy Snipers shewed activity. Trenches are bad. Close proximity of enemy does not permit of movement in daylight. R.E. and parties attached doing excellent work.	
	21-1-16.		Wind S.W. Still unfavourable for enemy Gas. Our Grenadiers under Lieut. Hadley obtained superiority over enemy bombs. Enemy shelled our front line dropping 12 shells, 8 of which failed to explode. Work on night of 21st-22nd. continued by R.E. and our own men. Wire in front of trenches strengthened and traverses built up. This work is necessarily gradual, otherwise enemy observes too much progress and shells more frequently.	
	22-1-16.		Wind safe. Minor shelling by enemy on our section proceeded throughout the day. Attitude of enemy, alert. Snipers active. Night of 22nd-23rd our Grenadiers patroled and caused enemy Snipers to become less active.	
ZILLEBEKE LAKE.	23-1-16.		Wind very light and in our favour. Situation, normal.	

Instructions regarding War Diaries and Intelligence Summaries are contained in F.S. Regs., Part II. and the Staff Manual respectively. Title pages will be prepared in manuscript.

INTELLIGENCE SUMMARY.
or
(Erase heading not required.)

Place	Date	Hour	Summary of Events and Information	Remarks and references to Appendices
ZILLEBEKE LAKE.	23-1-16.		Night of 23rd-24th Battalion relieved by 2nd.Liensters. and proceeded to ZILLEBEKE dugouts. Casualties for first 4 days tour of HOOGE TRENCHES amounted to 6 O.R.	
	24-1-16.		Day spent in cleaning up. Working party of 300 provided under supervision of R.E.	
	25-1-16.		Men rested all day. Nothing of importance to report. Usual working party provided	
	26-1-16.		Aeroplane activity on either side and increased shelling from our Guns. Enemy replied without effect. Working party provided for R.E.	
HOOGE.	27-1-16.		Wind favourable. Battalion relieved 2nd.Liensters in HOOGE Trenches on night of 27th-28th. Machine Gun caused a few casualties on the MENIN ROAD.	
	28-1-16.		All quiet during day. Wind still in our favour. Attitude of enemy fairly quiet. Enemy threw Bombs in front of our trenches at STABLES at HOOGE. all fell short. General activity along the line. Trenches shewed improvement, less water and good progress of retrenchments. The Commanding Officer personally inspected the wire in front of our trenches on the night of 28th-29th. Many dead bodies of the enemy revealed by digging parties.	
	29-1-16.		Wind favourable. Morning opened quietly. Mid-day our light Artillery bombarded enemy front line with good effect. He retaliated by shelling our sector of trenches for 15 minutes,	

INTELLIGENCE SUMMARY.

(Erase heading not required.)

Instructions regarding War Diaries and Intelligence Summaries are contained in F. S. Regs., Part II and the Staff Manual respectively. Title pages will be prepared in manuscript.

Place	Date	Hour	Summary of Events and Information	Remarks and references to Appendices
HOOGE.	29-1-16.		putting over a great quantity of shells, without, however, doing much damage, and causing no casualties. The Officers and men behaved splendidly throughout this intensive bombardment.	
	30-1-16.		Wind in favour of the enemy. 'Gas alert' issued by Division and all men prepared for Gas attack. Night of 30th-31st sniping and Grenade throwers very active on both sides. Work continued. Trenches shewed improvement.	
	31-1-16.		Wind still in favour of the enemy. 'Gas alert' continued. Pumping and revetting of trenches continued. Night of 31stJan-1st Feb, the Battalion was relieved by 3rd. Rifle Brigade, and proceeded to Camp E, via YPRES and VLAMERTINGHE. Men were supplied with Cocoa and Soup under Divisional arrangements at YPRES ASYLUM, and Gum Boots were handed in on the way to Camp. Total Casualties for four days tour of HOOGE TRENCHES, 5 other ranks. Last Company of Battalion arrived in Camp E at 4pm. on the morning of Feb. 1st.	

73rd Brigade.
24th Division.

7th BATTALION

NORTHAMPTON REGIMENT.

February 1916.

Army Form C. 2118.

WAR DIARY
or
INTELLIGENCE SUMMARY.
(Erase heading not required.)

Instructions regarding War Diaries and Intelligence Summaries are contained in F.S. Regs., Part II. and the Staff Manual respectively. Title pages will be prepared in manuscript.

Place	Date	Hour	Summary of Events and Information	Remarks and references to Appendices
			CONFIDENTIAL	
			WAR DIARY	
			of	
			7th Service BATTALION NORTHAMPTONSHIRE REGT	
			from 1st February 1916 to 29th Febry 1916	

2353 Wt. W2544/1454 700,000 5/15 D.D.&L. A.D.S.S./Forms/C. 2118.

Army Form C. 2118.

WAR DIARY
or
INTELLIGENCE SUMMARY.
(Erase heading not required.)

Instructions regarding War Diaries and Intelligence Summaries are contained in F.S. Regs., Part II. and the Staff Manual respectively. Title pages will be prepared in manuscript.

Place	Date	Hour	Summary of Events and Information	Remarks and references to Appendices
OUDERDOM = VLAMERTINGHE.	1-2-16.		Nothing doing during the day with the exception of cleaning up Equipment etc.	
	2-2-16.		Baths at POPERINGHE allotted to the Battalion and C Company are detailed to bathe. The remainder of the Battalion, Platoon Drill and Short run. The new draft of 40 are inspected by the Commanding Officer and reported on. TrenchStores are inspected by the Commanding Officer. Afternoon devoted to washing clothes etc. The Battalion is held in readiness to move at one hours' notice.	
	3-2-16.		D and B Companies bathe this morning at Divisional Baths, POPERINGHE and A Company at the Labour Battalion Baths OUDERDOM. Training of Specialists etc. Brigadier General, 73rd. Infantry Brigade inspected the new draft.	
	4-2-16.		Usual training. Swedish drill, Bayonet fighting, Musketry exercises etc. Duck-boards are being relaid and new ones placed.	
	5-2-16.		Usual training of Sepcialists etc and cleaning up Camp.	
	6-2-16.		ChurchParade at 10-30 am at the Canteen of Labour Battalion. Rest of day left free. Two Food Containers issued by Brigade and report on their efficacy rendered.	
	7-2-16.		Mats having been drawn for the purpose of crossing barbed wire, experiments made by Lieut Goode and party. A report rendered thereon. Mats then forwarded to 9th. Royal Sussex Regt. Training - Infantry in Attack and ShortRun. Feet massage in the afternoon. Battalion received order to "Stand to" at 2-40 pm and were ready to move off with Transport Inspanned by 3-5 pm. G.O.C. expressed great satisfaction at manner and promptness of turnout.	

2353 Wt W2544/1454 700,000 5/15 D.D.&L. A.D.S.S./Forms/C.2118.

Army Form C. 2118

WAR DIARY
or
INTELLIGENCE SUMMARY.
(Erase heading not required.)

Instructions regarding War Diaries and Intelligence Summaries are contained in F.S. Regs., Part II. and the Staff Manual respectively. Title pages will be prepared in manuscript.

Place	Date	Hour	Summary of Events and Information	Remarks and references to Appendices
	8-2-16.		Today the Brigade returns to the line but the Battalion remains at Camp E.. Brigade Operation Orders were issued on the 6th. Working party for R.E. of 150 proceeded to the trenches. Covering for ablution stands erected and more duck-boards leading hereto will be put down tomorrow. Infantry in Attack (with Gas Helmets).	
	9-2-16.		Training. Training of Cutting out parties etc. Gas Helmet Inspection.	
	10-2-16.		Training. Wire cutting - Company drill - Inspection of Ammunition - Training of Cutting out parties - Iron Rations Inspected by the Commanding Officer.	
	11-2-16.		Operation orders for the move of the Battalion into the trenches tomorrow evening were issued.* (see appendix No. 1.)	* See Appendix No. 1.
BELGIAN CHATEAU DUGOUTS.	12-2-16.		The Battalion left Camp E, First Company starting at 4.30 pm. Heavy bombardment of VLAMERTINGHE ROAD is taking place. First Company of Battalion had arrived at the R.E.Dump when orders were received not to proceed further owing to shelling of Roads and approach to YPRES. The Commanding Officer distributed the Battalion as follows :- C Company at BELGIAN CHATEAU, D Company ½ mile N.". of BELGIAN CHATEAU DUG-OUTS in line of trenches, A & B Companies in trenches extending North and South of R.E. Dump. Battalion remained in this disposition for two and a half hours, when orders were received to return to Camp E. This was accomplished by 1 am with no casualties.	
YPRES.	13-2-16.		The Battalion relieved the 2nd. Battn Leinster Regiment in the trenches tonight, shelling having subsided very considerably. Advanced Headquarters are at Dug-outs close to F.13. Relief carried out in good order and completed by 12-5 am. Intense bombardment of HELL FIRE CORNER in which we lost men of Ration party, killed and wounded.	

Army Form C. 2118.

WAR DIARY
or
INTELLIGENCE SUMMARY.
(Erase heading not required.)

Instructions regarding War Diaries and Intelligence Summaries are contained in F.S. Regs., Part II. and the Staff Manual respectively. Title pages will be prepared in manuscript.

Place	Date	Hour	Summary of Events and Information	Remarks and references to Appendices
	14-2-16.		Wind safe. Enemy Artillery shelled HELL FIRE CORNER, WEST LANE, and Battery in rear of F.13 since 8-30 am. Otherwise situation normal. At 6-45 pm orders to "Stand to" were issued. Three squads of Grenadiers and six Machine Gunners under 2nd. Lt. Passmore sent up to 5.23 at 6 pm.	
	15-2-16.		At 4-45 am and again at 5-15 am an enemy Field Gun firing from our direct front landed 20 shells just right of Railway on the right of F.13. On both occasions all these shells failed to explode. All relief and working parties were suspended and extra precautions taken. The Crater has been reconnoitred and found untenable owing to the depth of mud therein. Heavy shelling heard some distance away.	
	16-2-16.		Artillery on this sector, quiet. Reconnoitring patrol reported that enemy listening post off left of Crater in front of H.30 appeared to be strongly held by Bombers and Riflemen. Enemy fired a few Trench Mortars at H.49-30 but did no damage, and enemy Snipers opposite this section of trench were very active. Otherwise situation quiet during the night.	
	17-2-16.		Enemy exceptionally quiet in this section. At 2-35 pm the enemy put over 3 Trench Mortars into 9th. Royal Sussex trenches and we retaliated with effect at 3-45 pm. Wind, S.W. Battalion relieved by 2nd. Leinsters this evening. Hot Soup etc., provided at the ASYLUM - YPRES. During this tour of the trenches we had the misfortune to lose our Intelligence Officer. He went out to reconnoitre the wire one night the Bosch evidently saw him, opened fire with Rifles, Bombs and Trench Mortars. He did not return, and shortly afterwards a patrol was sent out but was unable to find any trace of this Officer.	
	18-2-16.		Most of day devoted to cleaning up, washing clothes etc and resting for the troops.	

2353 Wt. W2544/1454 700,000 5/15 D. D. & L. A.D.S.S.Forms/C.2118.

Army Form C. 2118.

WAR DIARY
or
INTELLIGENCE SUMMARY.
(Erase heading not required.)

Instructions regarding War Diaries and Intelligence Summaries are contained in F. S. Regs., Part II. and the Staff Manual respectively. Title pages will be prepared in manuscript.

Place	Date	Hour	Summary of Events and Information	Remarks and references to Appendices
VLAMERTINGHE.	19-2-16.		Feet. Clothing and Gas Helmet Inspection held today and further issue of Shrapnel proof helmets. Gas Alert ordered by 24th. Division and instructions issued accordingly.	
	20-2-16.		Morning and afternoon devoted to cleaning up Camp and preparing for the trenches tonight. Battalion move off at 4-45 pm and relieve 2nd.Leinsters without Casualties.	
YPRES.	21-2-16		Today the enemy's attitude is more or less quiet but the wind is still East and favourable for enemy Gas. Artillery is also quiet. IDENTIFICATION. Two Germans were seen going out from their Crater this morning, one dressed in dark blue and blue cap with black peak, the other in ordinary grey with usual cap and red band. Our Artillery fired about 20 rounds during the early hours of the morning to which the enemy did not reply. WORK. It is proposed to build parapet and parados at S. end of H.49 and N. end of H.30. The wiring of S.21 continued during the night. Three Aeroplanes passed over during the night at 11 pm and dropped coloured lights. (Report attached. Appendix No. 2.)	
	22-2-16.		Wind still dangerously East and temperature low. Night very quiet. Enemy Snipers very active in the early morning. During the morning the Artillery becomes more active, enemy shelling SUNKEN ROAD at 1 pm and communication trench leading therefrom between 2 pm and 2-30 pm with H.E. without causing material damage. A German entering the CRATER was accounted for by one of our Snipers early in the morning. Enemy Whizzbanged RAILWAY WOOD at 12 noon. As a Platoon of B.Company was leaving their trench this morning to go into their Sap the enemy sent over eight H.E's but none of them fell into the trench. On our left, Artillery seems very active. A wiring party of ours early this morning was sniped rather heavily but no casualties occurred.	

Army Form C. 2118.

WAR DIARY
or
INTELLIGENCE SUMMARY.
(*Erase heading not required.*)

Instructions regarding War Diaries and Intelligence Summaries are contained in F. S. Regs., Part II. and the Staff Manual respectively. Title pages will be prepared in manuscript.

Place	Date	Hour	Summary of Events and Information	Remarks and references to Appendices
	23-2-16.		WORK DONE. 50 yards of wire put up in front of S.21. Traverse built in H.20 and Fire steps in H.19. Towards evening wind changes to N.E. Trench repaired where shelled and drained in three places. NOTE. Enemy seems to be still working in the CRATER judging by the sounds of hammering and sawing, although nothing can be seen of them. About 8-40 pm a train was heard - it soon opened fire with H.E. knocking in one trench in two places which was repaired the same evening. An enemy Machine Gun was also very active enfilading a trench after working parties. Wind still N.E. but slightly dangerous for Gas. Morning passed quietly. Our Artillery bombarded CRATER at 2-15 pm with H.E. to which the enemy retaliated weakly and ineffectually. Early this morning the parapet and parados in H.19 and H.20 were built up. At 4-30 am an enemy patrol on right of A.1. was fired at and immediately dispersed. At 4 pm enemy dropped a few H.E's behind S.23. A working party heard in German crater was dislodged by our Artillery fire. Snipers fairly active during the night. WORK DONE. Trenches repaired where shelled and several new fire-bays constructed. Owing to the cold and hardness of the ground progress tonight has been slow. Wing now changed East again. Between 10-30 pm and 12-50 am enemy shelled behind H.19 with Howitzers doing very little damage. Nothing heard tonight of enemy in CRATER.	
	24-2-16.		Two enemy Machine Guns firing from a point opposite end of H.19 were engaged by the 9th. Royal Sussex and our own Machine Guns. Wind N.E. Weather cold. Attitude during today quiet. During the evening several coloured lights were sent up No working parties heard but relief train was heard loaded about 11-45pm but did not appear to go away and no gun fired from it and by the puffing it seemed to be heavily laden.	

Army Form C. 2118.

WAR DIARY
or
INTELLIGENCE SUMMARY.
(Erase heading not required.)

Instructions regarding War Diaries and Intelligence Summaries are contained in F. S. Regs., Part II. and the Staff Manual respectively. Title pages will be prepared in manuscript.

Place	Date	Hour	Summary of Events and Information	Remarks and references to Appendices
VLAMERTINGHE.	26-2-16.		WORK DONE. Wiring at H.20 completed. S.21 repaired and duck-boards in C.1 behind H.20 with replaced.	
	27-2-16.		Wind N. to S.E. There has been some shelling of C.1 behind H.20 with H.E. during the morning. Enemy Snipers very alert at 5 am this morning. The Battalion was relieved tonight by the 1st.Bn. The Buffs. The Companies after resting at the ASYLUM for hot cocoa and soup proceeded to a point selected where a train awaited them and were detrained just outside Camp. A, near POPERINGHE arriving in the Camp at 2-45 pm. This tour of the trenches particularly significant in many ways, principally in the extreme restlessness of the Hun, his Artillery in particular more especially of the small Field Gun type which apparently he has close up and not so far behind his Support line. His activity in front of HOOGE was apparently due to the fact of a premeditated attack on the BLUFF, and an endeavour to occupy the attention of the whole front with a view to not disclosing exactly as to where his attack should take place.	
	28-2-16.		Bathing started at 8-30 am this morning and continued all day. Cleaning up equipment etc during the day. DIVINE SERVICE in the Y.M.C.A.Hut, Camp A at 11 am. Remainder of the day free to the troops.	
	29-2-16.		TRAINING. Platoon drill - Company drill etc. Inspection of Gas Helmets etc. Promotions in the Battalion made up to Establishment. Today taken up by the selection of Grenadiers, Signallers, Machine Gunners, etc. Machine Gun Sections are being re-organized on the basis of two Guns per Company as soon as the additional guns are delivered. Clothing and equipment issued in the afternoon. Lieut.Col.P.C.B.Skinner takes over command of 73rd. I.B. during absence of Brigadier General Jelf and Major E.R.Mobbs takes over command of the Battn.	

2353 Wt.W2544/1454 700,000 5/15 D.D.&L. A.D.S.S./Forms/C.2118.

7th S. Bn NORTHAMPTONSHIRE REGIMENT

No. 9

OPERATION ORDERS   No. 17.   FEBRUARY 11th 1916

1. The Machine Gunners under Sergeant Ruston will start from Camp E. at 4 pm. today, and will march via R.E. Dump, BELGIAN CHATEAU - KRUISTRAAT and YPRES, and will draw Gum Boots from Brigade Headquarters in YPRES and march to HELL FIRE CORNER. 2nd Leinsters Guides will meet them there at 7.30 p.m.

2. GRENADIERS. Lt. Hedley, 12 N.C.O.'s and 6 men will leave Camp E. at 4.15 pm today, and march as above. They will draw gum boots from Brigade Headquarters and march to HELL FIRE CORNER. Leinster's Guides will meet them there at 7.30 p.m.

3. 1 N.C.O. per Platoon will leave Camp E. at 4.30 p.m. today, and march as above, drawing Gum Boots from Brigade Headquarters at YPRES and march on to HELL FIRE CORNER. The Leinster Guides will meet them there.   A Company's N.C.O.'s will remain in the Ramparts.

4. SIGNALLERS. Leave Camp E. at 4.30 pm today, and will march as above, and report to 2nd Leinsters in the RAMPARTS for instructions.

5. All men to carry tomorrow's rations.

6. Dress - Marching orders

                                              nd Lt. A/Adjt
7th Service Bn Northamptonshire Regiment.

Copy. 1. File.
      2. A. Coy
      3. B. Coy
      4. C. Coy
      5. D. Coy
      6. M.G.O.
      7. Signg O.

"C" Form (Original).
MESSAGES AND SIGNALS.

Army Form C. 2123

No. of Message...........

Prefix CM Code Words 61	Received From AN By King B	Sent, or sent out At.......m. To By	Office Stamp. NR6 2/2/16

Charges to collect

Service Instructions AN

Handed in at .... Office ....m. Received ....m.

TO ADJT **No 2**

*Sender's Number	Day of Month	In reply to Number.	AAA	
PSH1	22			
Enemy	very	quiet	aaa	three
aeroplanes		passed	over	our
lines	last	night	at	11PM
they	returned at	11.50	and	
dropped	lights	the	one	on
the	right	dropped	a	white
light	the	one	in	the
centre	a	white	followed	
by	a	red	and	green
and	then	another	white	
one	on	the	left	dropped
two	white	a	green	and
a	red	one	aaa	
(war diary)				

FROM: P S HADLEY LT

PLACE & TIME:

* This line should be erased if not required.

W 12550/4103 75,000 Pads. A.J.W. & Co. 11/15 Forms/C.2123.

FEB 11th 1916

NO1

73rd Brigade.
24th Division.

7th BATTALION

NORTHAMPTON REGIMENT.

March 1916.

Army Form C. 2118.

WAR DIARY
or
INTELLIGENCE SUMMARY.
(Erase heading not required.)

7/Northants
Vol 6

CONFIDENTIAL

WAR DIARY

of

7th SERVICE BATTALION NORTHAMPTONSHIRE REGT.

IN THE FIELD

MARCH 1st TO MARCH 31st
1916

9.4.1916.

Army Form C. 2118.

WAR DIARY
or
INTELLIGENCE SUMMARY.
(Erase heading not required.)

Instructions regarding War Diaries and Intelligence Summaries are contained in F.S. Regs., Part II and the Staff Manual respectively. Title pages will be prepared in manuscript.

Place	Date	Hour	Summary of Events and Information	Remarks and references to Appendices
Nr. VLAMERTINGHE.	1/3/16.		TRAINING. Physical Exercises. Wiring with the Whitnall Portable Knife Rests. Training of Specialists. No.1 Baths POPERINGHE allotted to the Battalion from 8 am to 12 noon. Specialists and employed men excused. The Battalion is held in readiness to move off at an hours' notice in the event of being required as reserves of the BUFF. They are eventually not required.	
	2/3/16.		TRAINING. as usual. The Battalion is still held in readiness to move at an hours' notice and nobody is to leave camp till further orders.	
	3/3/16.		Training of Specialists. Inspection of Arms and Ammunition. Making of High wire entanglements with Pickets. New Pioneers have been appointed in consequence of the casualties occurring amongst them lately. A working party for the R.E. is found. Concert for the men in Y.M.C.A is arranged for this evening is posponed till tomorrow evening.	
	4/3/16.		TRAINING - NIL. PARADES.- Inspection of Gas Helmets, Trench Stores etc. Cleaning up Huts, Rolling Blankets etc. Operation Orders No.18 for the move of the Battalion to ZILLEBEKE LAKE DUG-OUTS in relief of the 8th Bn.East Surreys under Col. de la Fontaine issued in the morning. The Battalion moved off at 7-45 pm. and entrained at a point G.5.c.10.0 not far from A.Camp and detrained close to the ASYLUM - YPRES marching from there to the dug-outs ZILLEBEKE. The relief was completed by about 11-30 pm. Since our last tour the dug-outs have been shelled and several smashed in. 73rd. Brigade Headquarters have been shifted to the RAMPARTS YPRES. Draft of 20 O.R. arrived this afternoon including several old members of the Battalion.	See Appendices No.1

Army Form C. 2118.

WAR DIARY
or
INTELLIGENCE SUMMARY.

(Erase heading not required.)

Instructions regarding War Diaries and Intelligence Summaries are contained in F. S. Regs., Part II. and the Staff Manual respectively. Title pages will be prepared in manuscript.

Place	Date	Hour	Summary of Events and Information	Remarks and references to Appendices
ZILLEBEKE LAKE.	5/3/16.		Everything quiet here. Enemy shell YPRES and Batteries around us heavily. Working parties found tonight.	See Appendices No. 2.
	6/3/16.		Nothing of an exciting nature happens today. Weather is cold with snow, otherwise not bad. Not very much enemy artillery activity today - our own Artillery seem to be doing most. Further supply of 5 Trench Mgs of HOOGE Section received from 73rd.Brigade. Working party of 335 for R.E. required. No casualties among them.	
	7/3/16.		Snow falling again today. Wind - NIL. Enemy Artillery fairly quiet excepting towards the evening when they sent a few over. Operation Orders No..5 for relief of 2nd.Leinsters in HOOGE SECTOR on night of 8/9th issued. A party of 12 F.E. are attached to us for the purpose of erecting Gas Curtains to the dug-outs here and with the aid of our own men this work is commenced. - Working party found for RE.	See Appendix No 4 See Appendix No 5
	8/3/16.		Gas Curtains erected to several dug-outs. Battalion left ZILLEBEKE LAKE about 6 pm and relieved 2nd.Leinsters in HOOGE SECTOR - left section trenches - completing about 11 pm without casualties. "Gas Alert" still continues. Night passes quietly. Enemy inactive and sends up very few lights. Enemy transport is heard about 350 yards down the MENIN ROAD and again in early morning.	
HOOGE.	9/3/16.		Enemy quiet during the early hours. Our Lewis Gun quietened an enemy gun firing from their second line opposite C.4.	

Army Form C. 2118.

WAR DIARY
or
INTELLIGENCE SUMMARY.
(Erase heading not required.)

Instructions regarding War Diaries and Intelligence Summaries are contained in F.S. Regs., Part II. and the Staff Manual respectively. Title pages will be prepared in manuscript.

Place	Date	Hour	Summary of Events and Information	Remarks and references to Appendices
HOOGE.	9/3/16.		Wind N.N.E. Temperature Low. Enemy snipers inactive during the early hours but become active later on and remain so all day. About 5-30 am enemy transport again heard on MENIN ROAD - also mens' voices. (see report bombing attack). Until 3-15 pm the German Artillery has been very quiet, when they dropped about 25 in the direction of a dug-out in our lines known as "German Dug-outs". Casualties for today are fair - ill caused by Snipers. In C.4. at about 6-15 pm whilst B.Company were "Standing to", the enemy threw a few bombs at the left bombing post a few of which fell into the trench and it is belived these were thrown from slings or a machine. To prevent reinforcements the enemy wizzbanged the MENIN ROAD and several parts of our trench especially TRENCH STREET. The whole action lasted one hour and we threw over 350 bombs. The enemy certainly suffered casualties as he was seen carrying men down his trench. A few smoke bombs were thrown by him to hid. several of the casualties. Our Casualties were seven wounded. The trench was considerably damaged. WORK DONE. C.3. repairs to parapet - two traverses built up. Wiring in front of STABLE RETRENCHMENT continued. No.4 and 2 posts in C.5. sandbagged and C.7. drained.	
	10/3/16.		Wind. N.E. Cold with sleet and snow. Enemy Machine Gun has several times played on our new listening post in C.2. during the night. General situation - quiet. Machine Guns and Sniping activity during early hours but between 4-30 am and 6-0 am, quiet. Artillery on both sides fairly quiet. At 6-45 am a whistle was heard coming from the German lines, this being after our bombardment with Trench Mortars. At 10-45 am one of our Snipers fired at a periscope missing it with his first shot, this being duly signalled with a spade in the German lines after this, it was hit twice, but replaced both times.	

Army Form C. 2118.

WAR DIARY
or
INTELLIGENCE SUMMARY.
(Erase heading not required.)

Instructions regarding War Diaries and Intelligence Summaries are contained in F. S. Regs., Part II. and the Staff Manual respectively. Title pages will be prepared in manuscript.

Place	Date	Hour	Summary of Events and Information	Remarks and references to Appendices
HOOGE.	10/3/16.		Smoke was observed coming from German trench I.12.C.41, and in I.12.B.67 two Germans were seen wearing soft grey caps with red bands. Enemy dropped 4 H.E. on MENIN ROAD and a few near GERMAN dug-out. WORK DONE. Drainage of C.7 continued. 2 traverses in C.3. MMK built and bays therein drained. In front of the trench 6 coils of barbed wire were used in wiring. It is proposed to rebuild bombing posts in front of retrenchments which are knocked about badly. A & B Companies relieved in front line trenche s by C & D Companies, A.Company staying at HALF-WAY HOUSE AND B.Company proceeding back to BELGIAN CHATEAU.	
	11/3/16.		Flammenwerfer demonstration held near "A"Camp at which 35 were detailed to attend. Early morning very quiet. Wind in the East. At 5-50 am the enemy commenced throwing bombs on the STABLES, most of them however, falling short. A few fell in trench behind STABLES and in trench occupied by D.Company. Our bombers replied, throwing about 100 bombs. At 6-15 am our Artillery sent five shells into their front line trench and later some on our right, upon which the enemy quietened down. At 8-15 am enemy Transport heard on MENIN ROAD. Enemy Artillery shelled HOOGE and bend of GRAFTON STREET with H.E. and Whizzbangs between 2 pm and 2-45 pm. Sanctuary Wood also heavily shelled. Our Artillery retaliated. No casualties caused by the enemy's fire. WORK DONE. Strong traverse built at left end of C.4. C.3.cleared. Enemy shelled SANCTUARY WOOD and MENIN ROAD actively during night and early morning.. Working party of 100 for R.E. found by B.Company.	
	12/3/16.		Artillery active during night. Otherwise everything quiet. Wind - N.E. But very quiet.	

Army Form C. 2118.

WAR DIARY
or
INTELLIGENCE SUMMARY.
(Erase heading not required.)

Instructions regarding War Diaries and Intelligence Summaries are contained in F. S. Regs., Part II. and the Staff Manual respectively. Title pages will be prepared in manuscript.

Place	Date	Hour	Summary of Events and Information	Remarks and references to Appendices
ZILLEBEKE LAKE.	12/3/16.		Enemy Artillery on our left very active bombarding front line trenches. Battalion was relieved by the 2nd.Leinsters and returned to the ZILLEBEKE LAKE DUG-OUTS. No casualties during relief. Total casualties during four days tour - 22 other ranks.	
	13/3/16.		Working parties as usual found in the evening. Nothing of note occurred during the day. Draft on One O.R. arrived. Brigade O.O.No.31 for the relief of the Battalion on the night of 16/17th were issued today.	See Appendix No 6.
	14/3/16.		Morning quiet. Weather fine. Enemy shelled ZILLEBEKE LAKE DUG-OUTS in the afternoon, most of the shells dropping in the fields in front. No damage or casualties. CHATEAU BELGE also shelled causing one casualty. Working parties found. Casualties - Nil.	See Appendix No 6.
	15/3/16.		Morning quiet. Weather damp. Enemy shelled ZILLEBEKE BUND in the afternoon at 2-30 p.m. doing no damage and again at 5 p.m.heavily. Casualties - Nil. Working parties found.	See Appendix No Y.
	16/3/16.		Enemy Artillery quiet. Did not shell our section today. Battalion relieved by the 5th East Surrey Regt. and entrained near the ASYLUM - YPRES arriving in Camp "B" about 3 a.m. Artillery during this tour extraordinarily intensive. Both sides have shewn marked increase. The men are wonderfully cheerful in view of the fact that the time spent in the SALIENT has been a particularly trying one. Brigade Operation Orders No.32 for the move to new area received today.	See Appendix No /A
Nr.VLAMERTINGHE	17/3/16.			

Army Form C. 2118.

WAR DIARY
OF
INTELLIGENCE SUMMARY.
(Erase heading not required.)

Instructions regarding War Diaries and Intelligence Summaries are contained in F. S. Regs., Part II. and the Staff Manual respectively. Title pages will be prepared in manuscript.

Place	Date	Hour	Summary of Events and Information	Remarks and references to Appendices
VLAMERTINGHE.	17/3/16.		A draft of 50 O.R. arrived today and were inspected by the Commanding Officer.	See Appendix No 8
	18/3/16.		The Battalion moved to the KEMMEL area via Route march via WESTOUTRE and BERTHEN. This march was accomplished in good order and more than satisfactory after a spell in wet trenches. Battalion Headquarters are at LINDENHOEK. (X.8.a.2.0.) Sheet 27. The Battalion was here able to get thoroughly cleaned up and rested.	
KEMMEL.	19/3/16.		The Baths at X.8.C.2.7. are allotted to Battalion from 10-30 am to 12-15 am today and 275 are thus accommodated.	
	20/3/16.		TRAINING. Usual training of Bombers, Signallers, Machine Gunners etc.	
	21/3/16.		Training as usual. The Commanding Officer and Company Commanders, Machine Gun Officer, and Battalion Grenade Officer proceeded to reconnoitre the new line today.	See Appendix No 9
	22/3/16.		Brigade Operation Orders for the forward move to take over the new line received tonight. Operation Orders issued by Commanding Officer.	
KORTEPYP.	23/3/16.		The Battalion moved from KEMMEL D FENCES AREA to KORTEPYP a distance of 10 miles and there relieved the 16th. Battalion Canadian Highlanders, 3rd.-Brigade. Relief completed by 1 p.m. Transport lines situated about a mile from Battalion. Orders for move into trenches following night issued. 1 party of One Officer per Company, 1 N.C.O. per Platoon and M.G. Sgt. proceeded to trenches to take over.	
	24/3/16.		Heavy Snow. Mens' feet treated with Anti-Frost oils. Day spent in storing surplus kit in transport field.	

Army Form C. 2118.

WAR DIARY
or
INTELLIGENCE SUMMARY.

(Erase heading not required.)

Instructions regarding War Diaries and Intelligence Summaries are contained in F. S. Regs., Part II. and the Staff Manual respectively. Title pages will be prepared in manuscript.

Place	Date	Hour	Summary of Events and Information	Remarks and references to Appendices
KORTEPYP.	24/5/16.		At 5-45 p.m. first Company moved off followed by remaining 3 Coys. at 5 minutes interval. Relief of 15th.Bn.Canadian Highlanders complete by 8-30 p.m. Trenches Good. Enemy attitude quiet. Interesting Front. Enemy some distance away. Good opportunities for Patrols. Acting Brigadier P.C.B.Skinner admitted to Hospital. Lt.Col.Bullen-Smith, 2nd. Leinsters took over the Brigade. Weather good overhead. All safe.	
Nr. WULVERGHEM.	25/5/16.		Trenches on examination proved good. Wire excellent. Day opened fine. Wind safe. Draft of 40 O.R. arrived. Nothing of note occurred during morning, artillery etc being very quiet. The enemy is generally alert. At 9 p.m. two green lights were sent up from the trenches on our right and were immediately followed by 6 shells. At 11-30 p.m. some rifle grenades were fired by the enemy but with no effect as they landed behind trench 149. Parapets and traverses built and repaired during night. When relieving listening post on right of 141 our bombers were bombed but no damage was done. Working party of 260 under R.E. were required to dig trenches but owing to shelling etc of front line only 50 were available. At 2-30 p.m. enemy shelled WULVERGHEM--MESSINES ROAD T.6.D. with H.E. Shrapnel, Whizzbangs and Howitzers. At 5-0 p.m. he began to shell FORT OSBORNE, IRISH FARM, and front line trenches 144, 145, C.1., and C.2. Firing ceased at 5 p.m. Several direct hits were obtained on FORT OSBORNE and 141 was knocked in in several places. Our Artillery retaliated with Whizzbangs on trenches left on ONTARIO FARM at 3-30 p.m. and again at 5-15 p.m. on front line trenches.	

Army Form C. 2118.

WAR DIARY
or
INTELLIGENCE SUMMARY.
(Erase heading not required.)

Instructions regarding War Diaries and Intelligence Summaries are contained in F.S. Regs., Part II. and the Staff Manual respectively. Title pages will be prepared in manuscript.

Place	Date	Hour	Summary of Events and Information	Remarks and references to Appendices
Nr. WULVERGHEM.	25/3/16.		Approximate number of enemy shells:- 2000.	
	26/3/16.		At 1-45 a.m. today enemy bombarded trenches on our right with Whizzbangs and Crumps. until 2-45 a.m.	
			At 3-0 a.m. 6 Whizzbangs landed behind trench 140. W While bombardment was proceeding on our right enemy sent up 12 Red single lights from his trenches.	
			Sniping very quiet.	
			We sent out two patrols to examine our wire in front of 141. They report wire not broken by bombardment.	
			Enemy had no working parties or patrols in front.	
			Aeroplane dropped two bombs at U.4.c.. These were apparently intended for parties which were moving in vicinity.	
			At 12 noon our Artillery fired on enemy's front line to the left of ONTARIO FARM U.1.a.5.7.	
			About 1 p.m. enemy retaliated with Whizzbangs on C.2., 142, and WULVERGHEM - MESSINES ROAD getting only one hit in 143 near Company Headquarters.	
			About 6-30 a.m. our observers noticed a working party of about 30 men. in front of enemy's front line T.6.b.7.0.. They were immediately fired on with Whizzbangs by our Artillery and dispersed.	
			At 7-0 p.m. enemy Machine Gun fired on C.2. and Road. It is situated somewhere-rear N.36.d.5.2. but bearing was not taken.	
			During the night enemy fired very lights from his listening posts, some of them almost reached 141.	
			Work done:- Traverse repaired and large island traverse nearly completed in 141.	
			2nd. Lieut. Warton joined the Battalion from the Cadet School.	
	27/3/16.		At 4 a.m. our artillery opened fire on XXX enemy's front line and set up a very accurate barrage. Enemy replied with Whizzbangs almost immediately but only one gun continued to fire.	

Army Form C. 2118.

WAR DIARY
or
INTELLIGENCE SUMMARY.
(Erase heading not required.)

Instructions regarding War Diaries and Intelligence Summaries are contained in F. S. Regs., Part II. and the Staff Manual respectively. Title pages will be prepared in manuscript.

Place	Date	Hour	Summary of Events and Information	Remarks and references to Appendices
Nr. WULVERGHEM	27/3/16		Enemy shelled neighbourhood of FORT OSBORNE, BOYLES FARM, and C.1. at intervals during the day. 142 was knocked about by Whizzbangs and a Trench Mortar which hit the parados. Sniping very inactive. Smoke was rising from enemy's trench at 4-30 p.m. at T.6.b.9.2.. Enemy moves about in his lines freely, about 30 have been seen during the last three days. None of these had equipment on or rifles. Patrol went out at 8-30 p.m. in front of 142 and found wire in good condition, but night was too wet to do any patrolling. At 7-30 a.m. searchlight was worked from left of MESSINES. Several of the enemy seen walking in his trench at U.1.a.6.6½. They were wearing grey overcoats and soft hats and were fired on. D Company relieved C.Company in the trenches. This was carried out satisfactorily. The night passed quietly with scarcely any sniping.	
	28/3/16		Situation Normal. Wind - S.W. Two fires occurred in the enemy's lines, N.E. of ONTARIO FARM at 10 p.m. and N.W. of ONTARIO FARM at 7-30 pm. No bearings were taken.	
	29/3/16		Artillery activity at 2 p.m.. 2 rounds of H.E. Shrapnel on road and behind C.2. At 1 p.m. 3 Whizz Bangs were fired at C.2. No sniping during the day. Machine Gun firing on Road from U.1.a.3.1. to T.6.d.3.8. at 7-5 p.m. Enemy attitude very quiet. About 12 light H.E. were fired at the DIAGONAL between 8-45 p.m. and 9-15 p.m. Wind. N.W. Machine Guns active during night- on road and on our parapet at C.2. 142, 142. Very little sniping during the night. Parapets and fire bays improved and drainage of trench commenced.	

Army Form C. 2118.

WAR DIARY
or
INTELLIGENCE SUMMARY.

(Erase heading not required.)

Place	Date	Hour	Summary of Events and Information	Remarks and references to Appendices
Nr. WULVERGHEM.	30/3/16.		Wind. S.W. At 3-30 a.m. red light was sent up from enemy trench about 100 yards West of ONTARIO FARM. Nothing unusual followed. At 1-40 a.m. two bombs were thrown from the enemy's Listening post at U.1.a.8.5., accompanied by rifle fire. We had no patrol out there. We sent patrol out in front of DIAGONAL. Enemy not moving. Regiment on our left heavily shelled with H.E. and Shrapnel between 2-0 p.m. and 3-30 p.m. Our Artillery retaliated. At 2 p.m. Hostile Aeroplane flew low over144. It was fired on and returned. Work done :- Traverse built and repairs to trench. Battalion relieved by 2nd. Leinsters tonight and returned to RED LODGE.	
	31/3/16.		Day devoted to cleaning up Huts, equipment etc. No other work done.	

Edgar Knott Major
Comm. 7 North'n'ptonshire Regt.

OPERATION ORDERS by MAJOR E.R.MOBBS commanding 7th. (S).Bn.
NORTHAMPTONSHIRE REGIMENT.

In the Field.   No.18.   March 4th.1916.

1. The Battalion will move into ZILLEBEKE LAKE DUG-OUTS today.
   Parade at 7-45 pm.
   Train will convey Battalion leaving junction G.5.C.10.0. at 8-30 pm.

2. "A")
   "B") Companies - ZILLEBEKE DUG-OUTS.
   "C")

   "D" Company to BELGIAN CHATEAU. (100).
   Forts 1K and 1H occupied by "B" Company.

3. One Blanket and Waterproof Sheet per man will be taken by Transport.
   One Blanket taken to Transport Stores.
   One day's rations will be carried on the men.
   Trench Stores will be carried by Transport.
   Four men (1 per Company) to report to Brigade Corporal at ASYLUM for charge of Gum Boots.
   2nd.Lt.A.B.Cox, 4 N.C.O's, and 4 O.R. will proceed to ZILLEBEKE to take over.
   One man per Company will report to Brigade Headquarters to act as Runners.

In the Field.   .... 2nd.Lt.A/Adjt.
March 4th. 1916.   7th.(S).Bn. Northamptonshire Regiment.

HEADQUARTERS 73RD
No. .... **№ 70**
Date **5/3/16**

No. 2

WORKING PARTIES to be found by .J. McKampton...... on ....5. 3. 16......

TIME	PLACE.	TO REPORT TO.	STRENGTH OF PARTY.	TOOLS AND WIRE DRAWN.	GUM BOOTS THIGH REQUIRED.	REMARKS.
① 6.30 p.m.	GORDON HOUSE	13 Middlesex	1 Officer 40 ♂ k ♂ k ♂ (consolidation)	from unit (shovels)	Yes	
② 7 p.m.	Head of New Pits Comm. (branch of 177 C Rly)	177 Tunnelling Co R.E.	20	—	"	
③ 9 p.m.	Repairing tram and (Rat/Rent Jn (new named) Must be notified in man party to us send for further instruction to Tuffs	Officers to reconnoitre beforehand and discuss any material required from R.E. dump Gordon House	2 Officers 50 men	unit	No	

H.Q. 73rd.I.B.

P Hoste
Major,
Brigade Major, 73rd.Infantry Brigade.

No 3

HEADQUARTERS, 73rd B
No. Bm/S.9
Date. 6/3/16

WORKING PARTIES to be found by 7 th Northamptonshire Regt. Bn. 6/3/16.

TIME	PLACE	TO REPORT TO	STRENGTH OF PARTY	TOOLS AND APPLIANCE DRAWN	GUM BOOTS THIGH REQUIRED	REMARKS
1. 8.30pm	Menin Gate	Sherwood Foresters	50 /p.m	Sherwoods	50	
2. 9 pm	Gordon Farm	do.	50	do.	50	
3. 7 pm	Culvert	2/ Leinster Regt.	100 p.m.		100	To draw 1000 Sandbags at Gordon Ho on the way, & take with them
4. 7 pm	Dump W. of Hell Fire Corner	177 Tunnelling Co.	35 p.m.	Nil.	Nil	Carrying party
5. 7.30 pm	Zillebeke dugouts	104 Co. R.E.	50	50 shovels	Nil	" "
6. 7.30 pm	dump 250x W. Hell Fire Corner	25th T.M. Battery	50	Nil	Nil	Carrying party

H.Q. 73rd. I.B.
6/3/16

Maugerid Capt.
Major,
Brigade Major, 73rd Infantry Brigade.

OPERATION ORDERS by MAJOR E.R.MOBBS commanding 7th. (S). Battalion
NORTHAMPTONSHIRE REGIMENT.

SECRET.

No 4

In the Field.   No.19.   March 7th.1916.

---

1. The Battalion will move into the trenches in the front line on the night of 8th/9th March where it will be disposed as follows:-

   Battalion Headquarters & Reserve Machine Gunners. HALFWAY HOUSE.
   "A" Company (3 Platoons). Culvert R.S.4., R.S.3., C5, C6, C7, (left sector
   "B" Company (4 Platoons and one Platoon of "A" Company. C2, C3, C4,.
                                                           (right sector).

   "C" Company. (3 Platoons).   HALFWAY HOUSE.
   " "   "   (1 Platoon).   ZILLEBEKE DUG-OUTS.
   "D" Company.   ZILLEBEKE DUG-OUTS.

   Machine Gunners and Grenadiers will relieve the same night.

2. The undermentioned will proceed to the trenches tomorrow at 2 pm.
   Signalling Sergeant and 4 Signallers.
   1 N.C.O. from "A", "B", and "C" Companies to take over.

3. All Blankets will be stored at the ASYLUM with the exception of the "D" Company and one Platoon of "C" Company at ZILLEBEKE DUG-OUTS. Blankets for the ASYLUM will be ready rolled in the usual manner by 5 pm on the day of departure.

4. Ankle Boots and Trench Stores will be carried by the men.

5. Troops from ZILLEBEKE DUG-OUTS WILL MARCH VIA GORDON HOUSE, HALFWAY HOUSE, and REGENT STREET.

6. Ration Dump will be 300 yards W. of HELL FIRE CORNER on the MENIN ROAD.

7. Officers' Kit, Headquarters and Company Stores will be brought by the Transport from ZILLEBEKE DUG-OUTS to the Dump and GORDON HOUSE.

8. All Companies will draw their own rations from the Dump and GORDON HOUSE
   "C" Company will carry for Headquarters.

9. "B" Company will move off at 5-45 pm.
   "A"   "   "   "   "   " 6-15 pm.
   "C"   "   (3 Platoons) will move off at 6-30 pm.
   "D"   "   will move up from BELGIAN CHATEAU at 5-30 pm. They will leave a Guard and loading party over their Blankets and those men without Gum Boots will march via the ASYLUM, draw Gum Boots and carry them to ZILLEBEKE DUG-OUTS.

In the Field.   ....2nd.Lt.A/Adjt.
March 7th. 1916.   7th. (S). Bn. Northamptonshire Regiment.

No 5

HEADQUARTERS 73RD BDE.
Pmn 111
Date 7/3/16

WORKING PARTIES to be found by 7. Northamptonshire Regt. on 7.3.16

TIME	PLACE.	TO REPORT TO.	STRENGTH OF PARTY.	TOOLS AND VIHNCE DRAWN.	GUM BOOTS THIGH REQUIRED.	REMARKS.
① 7 pm	Illiers depot	Reg Co RE	100 ✓	RE	Yes	① Shod on Rd line
② 7.30 pm	"	"	50 ✓	"	"	② "
③ 7.45 pm	"	"	70	"	"	③ "
④ 5 pm	Mesnin Gatte	"	42 ✓	" ✗	No	④ Work on Gordon House road
⑤ 6.30 pm	Rd dump Gordon House	"	10 ✓	"	"	⑤ Unloading etc
⑥ 7 pm	CULVERT	2 dismounted	Ssunday anit	"	Yes	⑥ Has two an Officer with pack Chevala
⑦ 7.30 pm	200 yds W. of R.E. corner	TN Railway	40 ✓	NiLL	"	⑦ Carrying part to "
⑧ 6 pm	Gordon House	M.G. Coy	20 ✓	"	No	⑧ " Dummy Post
⑨ 7.30 pm	TRANSPORT PARK	Rev. Transport bugs?	6 ✓	"	"	⑨ To unload bags & carry material for R.E. Battalion

1.416

R. Rosslett Major.
Bg. Battalion

H.C. 73rd. I.B. Guides for parties ①, ②, ③ will come to Northampton HQ. at times stated.

R.T.

Brigade Major, 73rd. Infantry Brigade.

No 6

WORKING PARTIES to be found by 7/N.H. ZILLEBECKE on 14th Feb. 1916

TIME	PLACE.	TO REPORT TO.	STRENGTH OF PARTY.	TOOLS AND WIRE NCE DRAWN.	GUM BOOTS THIGH REQUIRED.	REMARKS.
1) 6 pm.	ZILLEBEKE LAKE.	104th Co. R.E. B Coy	60	30 Shovels (Large)	Yes. for 30	To unload stores.
2) 6.30 pm.	GORDON HOUSE.	103 Co. R.E. B Coy	10	Nil	No	
3) 7 pm.	GORDON HOUSE.	73rd Bde. M.G. Coy. B Coy	10	Nil.	Yes.	Carrying Party.
4) 7.15 pm.	200 × W of HELLFIRE C.	177th Coy R.E. D Coy	40.	Nil.	No	
5) 8.30 pm	DORMY LANE N.W. CORNER MAPLE COPSE	I.O. 13th MIDDLESEX. D. Coy.	20	16 Shovels. 4 Picks	Yes.	Erection Rifle Battens

N.B. Parties from BELGIAN CHATEAU issued dried.

H.Q. 73rd. I.B.

L.B. Daly Capt. & m. Major,
Brigade Major, 73rd. Infantry Brigade.

SECRET.   COPY NO. 13

N° 6ᴬ

Ref.Sheet 28   73rd. INFANTRY BRIGADE.
1/40,000.   OPERATION   ORDER   NO. 31.

                                              H.Q. 73 I.B. March 13th. 1916.

1.   The 72nd. Infantry Brigade will relieve the 73rd. Infantry Brigade in the trenches on the nights of 15/16th. inst., and 16/17th. inst. as per relief table attached.(A).

2.   Lewis guns and Grenadiers of the 72nd. Infantry Brigade will relieve those of 73rd. Infantry Brigade night previous to that on which their battalion goes into the trenches. Table of Lewis Gun reliefs is attached (B).

3.   All other details will be arranged between O's.C. direct.

4.   Trench Store cards duly receipted will be forwarded to Brigade Headquarters within 24 hours of relief.

5.   The command of the HOOGE Sector will pass to B.G.C. 72nd. Infantry Brigade at 3.30 p.m. on March 16th., 1916.

6.   ACKNOWLEDGE.

                                       R Howlett
ISSUED AT 8 p.m.   Major,
                     Brigade Major, 73rd. Infantry Brigade.

          Copy No.1. War Diary.
               2. File.
               3. "G" 24 Div.
               4. "Q" 24 Div.
               5. 72 I.B.
               6. 17 I.B.
               7. 16 I.B.
               8. Left Group Artillery.
               9. 103rd. Fd.Coy.R.E.
              10. O.C. T.M. Batteries, 24 Div.
              11. 2nd. Leinsters.
              12. 9th. Royal Sussex.
              13. 7th. Northamptons.
              14. 13th. Middlesex.
              15. B.T.O., 73rd. I.B.
              16. B.M.G.O., 73 I.B.
              17. Bde.Sigs.Officer.

"A"

TABLE OF RELIEFS.

DATE.	UNIT.	FROM.	TO.
Night 15th/16th. March.	1st. North Staffords.	Camp "F".	Left Section trenches.
"	2nd. Leinsters.	Left Section trenches.	Camp "F".
Night 15th/16th. March.	8th. Queens.	Camp "E".	BELGIAN CHATEAU.
"	9th. Royal Sussex.	BELGIAN CHATEAU.	CAMP "E".
Night 16/17th. March.	8th. Queens.	BELGIAN CHATEAU.	Right Section trenches.
"	13th. Middlesex.	Right Section trenches.	CAMP "A" @
"	8th. Royal West Kents.	Camp "A".	BELGIAN CHATEAU.
Night 16/17th. March.	9th. East Surreys.	Camp "F".	ZILLEBEKE.
"	7th. Northamptons.	ZILLEBEKE & BELGIAN CHATEAU.	CAMP "B" @.
16. 3. 16.	H.Q. 73rd. Infantry Brigade.	RAMPARTS.	H.14.a.3.4.

@. It is hoped to arrange trains for these reliefs.

RELIEF OF LEWIS GUNS.

Night of 14/15th. March.

1st. North Staffords relieve 2nd. Leinsters: guides to be at CULVERT, MENIN ROAD at 7.30 p.m.
On relief 2nd. Leinsters to Camp "F".

8th. Royal West Kents relieve 9th. Royal Sussex guides to be at HALF WAY HOUSE at 7.45 p.m.
On relief 9th. Royal Sussex to BELGIAN CHATEAU.

Night 15th./16th. March.

8th. Queens relieve 4 guns of 13th. Middlesex and 1 gun 7th. Northamptons: guides to be at GORDON FARM at 7.30 p.m.
On relief 13th. Middlesex to Camp "A".
7th. Northamptons join battalion.

9th. East Surreys relieve 3 guns of 7th. Northamptons: guides at TRANSPORT FARM at 7.45 p.m.
On relief 7th. Northamptons join battalion.

VICKERS GUNS.

The Vickers teams of the 13th. Middlesex and 7th Northamptons at YEOMANRY POST will be relieved on 14th./15th. inst.: guides to be at GORDON FARM at 7.30 p.m.
These teams will join their battalions when relieved.

---oOo---

HEADQUARTERS 73RD BDE.
No. Bm 786
Date. 15/3/16

7th N.H.

Will you please arrange the following working parties for tonight.

1) 6.30 pm. GORDON HOUSE Dump - 10 men
unloading Stores for 103rd RE. B
No tools. No gum boots.

2) 6 pm. ZILLEBEKE LAKE. ... 50 men
for 104th Co R.E. B 1 Officer.
½ Shovels & Gumboots.

3) 9.30 pm. GORDON HOUSE. ... 80 men
for 13th MIDDLESEX. D
Shovels if possible & gum boots. 1 Officer.

N.B. Det't at BELGIAN CHATEAU has been detailed separately.

L. ☐ Bah Capt.
for Bde. Major
73rd I.B.

15. 3. 16.

SECRET.

Ref. Sheets 27 & 28. 1/40,000.

No 7ᴬ
COPY NO:- 13

73rd. INFANTRY BRIGADE.

OPERATION ORDER NO.32.

H.Q. 73 I.B., March 17th. 1916.

1. The 73rd. Infantry Brigade (less 2nd. Leinster Regt. and 9th. Royal Sussex) 129th. Field Coy. R.E., 197th. Coy. A.S.C., and 72nd. Field Ambulance, will move on 18th. March, to Canadian Rest Area (2), as per attached table.

2. 2nd. Leinster Regt. and 9th. Royal Sussex Regt. under the command of Lt. Colonel G.M.Bullen-Smith, D.S.O., 2nd. Leinster Regt., will move to same destination on 19th., March.

3. The Officer Commanding, 13th. Middlesex Regt. will detail two sections under an Officer and accompanied by the Medical Officer to march 50 yards in rear of the Infantry to collect stragglers.

4. All transport will march in rear of respective units.

5. Billetting Officers will proceed to new area to-day under arrangements already made.
Billetting parties, mounted or provided with bicycles, will report to the Staff Captain, 73rd. Infantry Brigade, at RENINGHELST CHURCH at 10 a.m. on the 18th. inst. Attention is drawn to para 1 of 24th. Divisional letter G.960 dated 8. 12. 15.

6. Further instructions will be issued re transport of blankets, surplus stores, refilling points, etc.

7. ACKNOWLEDGE.

R.Howlett.
Major,
Brigade Major, 73rd. Infantry Brigade.

ISSUED AT 8 a.m.

Copy No. 1. File.
2. War Diary.
3. 24 Div. "G".
4. 24 Div. "Q".
5. 8th. Canadian I.B.
6. 72nd. Field Ambulance.
7. 129th. Field Coy. R.E.
8. 197th. Coy. A.S.C.
9. 73/1 T.M.Battery.
10. 73rd. Coy. Machine Gun Corps.
11. 2nd. Leinsters.
12. 9th. Royal Sussex.
13. 7th. Northamptons.
14. 13th. Middlesex.
15. B.M.G.O.
16. B.T.O., 73 I.B.
17. Bde. Sigs.

MARCH TABLE.

DATE.	UNIT.	STARTING POINT.	TIME.	ROUTE.	DESTINATION.	REMARKS.
18th. March.	Brigade H.Q. Signal Section.	Road junction G.34.d.3.8.	2 p.m. 2 p.m.	RENINGHELST-HESKIN-WESTOUTRE-MT.VIDAIGNE-LA.MANCHE-SCHAEXKEN.	Canadian Rest Area (2). LE ROUKLOSHILLE-HAEGEDOORNE	
	7th. Northamptons.	do.	2.1 p.m.	do.	LETTREN. H.Q. at RETAKEN).	
	13th. Middlesex Regt.	do.	2.6 p.m.	do.		
	72rd. Coy. Machine Gun Corps.	do.	2.12 p.m.	do.	do.	
	72/1 T.M. Battery.	do.	2.15 p.m.	do.	do.	
	72nd. Field Ambulance (less motor ambulance)	do.	2.17 p.m.	do.	do.	
	Ambulances 72nd.Fd.Amb. (less 2 ambulances).	do.	3.15 p.m.	do.	do.	
	129th.Field Coy.R.E.	Will be on KEMMEL-WESTOUTRE road with head at road junction M.9.c.5.3 at 3 p.m.ready to take its place in the column.				
	197th. Coy. A.S.C.			do.	do.	Will not leave camp before 1 p.m.
19th. March.	2nd. Leinster Regt. 9th. Royal Sussex Regt. 2 Ambulances 72nd.F.A.			do.	do.	

H.Q. 73 I.B., March 18th., 1916.

SECRET.

No 7A

HEADQUARTERS 73RD BDE.
No. B.M.320.
Date 17. 3. 16.

ADDITIONS AND AMENDMENTS TO 73rd. INFANTRY
BRIGADE OPERATION ORDER NO.32.

Reference 73rd. Infantry Brigade Operation Order No.32, the following additions and amendments are notified:-

March Table.

129th. Field Coy. R.E. will join the column at starting point at 2.20 p.m.

Para 3.

The Rear Guard to be detailed by Officer Commanding, 13th. Middlesex Regt. will march 50 yards in rear of the 129th. Field Coy. R.E.

Refilling Point.

18th. March.   At WIPPENHOEK as usual.
19th. March.   Probably near FLETRE. Exact position will be notified later.

ACKNOWLEDGE.

ISSUED AT 6 p.m.

R Howlett
Major,
Brigade Major, 73rd. Infantry Brigade.

Copy No. 1. File.
2. War Diary.
3. 24 Div. "G".
4. 24 Div. "Q".
5. 8th. Canadian I.B.
6. 72nd. Field Ambulance.
7. 129th. Field Coy. R.E.
8. 197th. Coy. A.S.C.
9. 73/1 T.M.Battery.
10. 73rd. Coy. Machine Gun Corps.
11. 2nd. Leinsters.
12. 9th. Royal Sussex Regt.
13. 7th. Northamptons.
14. 13th. Middlesex.
15. B.M.G.O.
16. B.T.O., 73 I.B.
17. Bde. Sigs.

No 8

BATTALION ORDERS by MAJOR E.R.MOBBS, commanding 7th. (S). Bn.
NORTHAMPTONSHIRE REGIMENT.

In the Field.   March 17th. 1916.

----

1. MOVE.   The Battalion will move to new area tomorrow the 18th. inst.
           Parade 12-15 pm. on Battalion Parade Ground.
           Dress. Full Marching Order.
           Battalion will move off at 12-30 pm in the following order:-
           Headquarters - A.B.C.D. - Machine Gunners - Stretcher
Bearers.
           All Company spare kit, Sniperscopes, Company Trench Stores,
etc. etc., will be ready to be loaded by 6-30 am.
           All Officers' Kit etc., ready by 9-30 am.
           Officers' Kit necessary for journey will be conveyed in the
small handcarts. these will move in rear of the Battalion.

WATER.   The water cart will be in camp filled by 8.30.a.m. O.C.Coys
will arrange that all mens water bottles are filled.   The unconsumed
portion of the days rations will be carried on the man.

CAMP STORES. Bowls hurricane lamps etc will be stored in No.1. hut
Quartermasters Stores in Camp B, by 10.A.M.

Sick parade 9.30.a.m.

                                        ....2/Lt A.ADJT.
17.3.16   7th Northamptonshire Regiment.

OPERATION ORDERS by Major E.R.Mobbs commanding

7TH BN NORTHAMPTONSHIRE REGIMENT.

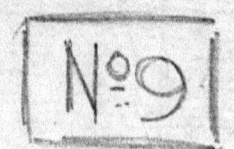

In the Field.   23.3.1916.

1. The Battalion will move to KORTEPYP tomorrow in the following order:-
D. C. B. A. Coys, transport, the head of the column will rest on point
K.19.A.9.9. and will start at 9.a.m.

2. Dress marching order - men will carry tomorrows ration less meat, tea
and sugar which will be carried by the cookers.

3. Officers kit will be marked and ready by 7.a.m. and called for by the
transport.
Mess kit will be ready by 8.a.m. and also called for by the transport.
Blankets will be ready rolled by 8.a.m. and called for by Motor transport.

4. Breakfast 7.30.a.m., dinner will be served on arrival at the new camp.

                                                    ....2/Lt A.Adjt.
                                                    7th Northamptonshire Regiment.

73rd Brigade.
24th Division.

7th BATTALION

NORTHAMPTONSHIRE REGIMENT.

April 1916

7 Northants

Officer i/c A.G.s Office at the

Base

Herewith Appendices for attachment to

my War Diary for April 1916

———————————— 2/Lt Actg
Adjutant 7th Northamptonshire Regt

In the Field

7/5/16

Army Form C. 2118.

T Nattcan(s
Vol 7

XXIV

WAR DIARY
or
INTELLIGENCE SUMMARY.
(Erase heading not required.)

CONFIDENTIAL.

WAR DIARY

of 7th. (SERVICE) BATTALION NORTHAMPTONSHIRE REGIMENT.

FOR THE MONTH OF APRIL 1916.

IN THE FIELD.

Army Form C. 2118.

WAR DIARY
or
INTELLIGENCE SUMMARY.
(*Erase heading not required.*)

Instructions regarding War Diaries and Intelligence Summaries are contained in F. S. Regs., Part II. and the Staff Manual respectively. Title pages will be prepared in manuscript.

Place	Date	Hour	Summary of Events and Information	Remarks and references to Appendices
RED LODGE.	1/4/16.		No training. Working parties for R.E. at night. Draining of Camp and collection of water for purpose of forming washing places.	
	2/4/16.		Weather fine. Aerial activity during day. Usual woking parties at night for R.E.	
	3/4/16.		Nothing done in day-time. Working parties during evening.	
	4/4/16.		R.E. Working party at night.	
	5/4/16.		During morning enemy shelled RED LODGE without causing any damage. Working parties found as usual	
	6/4/16		Huts and dug-outs cleaned up in view of the Battalion relieving 2nd.Bn. Leinster Regt tonight. At 5-30 p.m. the enemy commenced shelling RED LODGE with H.E. Shrapnel, and Whiz-bangs lasting for 3/4 hour and causing some damage. Our casualties were 3 Killed and 23 Wounded. At 7 p.m. the Battalion moved off and completed the relief without casualties. 150 men working party found for R.E. Night very quiet. Very little rifle fire and flares. 73rd.Brigade Headquarters move to ENGLISH FARM.	
	7/4/16.		At 2-40 a.m. an enemy working party were heard working on the front line trench and wire at ONTARIO FARM. The Barrier behind DIAGONAL in our lines was shelled with a few crumps during the afternoon. Working party of 80 for WULVERGHEM DUMP and 20 for RATION FARM were found for R.E. 129th Coy at 7-30 p.m.	

Army Form C. 2118.

WAR DIARY
or
INTELLIGENCE SUMMARY.
(Erase heading not required.)

Instructions regarding War Diaries and Intelligence Summaries are contained in F.S. Regs., Part II. and the Staff Manual respectively. Title pages will be prepared in manuscript.

Place	Date	Hour	Summary of Events and Information	Remarks and references to Appendices
WULVERGHEM.	7/4/16.		At 5 p.m. heavy bombardment in direction of ST. ELOI was heard. At 7 p.m. the enemy sent over about 20 Whiz-bangs in the vicinity of C.2. Our Artillery retaliated. Enemy Machine Guns inclined to be active on the Battalion on our left near C.2. At 11-30 p.m. our patrol went out from BOYLES FARM and patrolled the ground in front of the Diagonal for an hour and a quarter but no enemy patrols were seen or heard. Between 11 p.m. and 2 a.m. enemy working party were heard working on wire and parapet at ONTARIO FARM. WAS ALSO HEARD AT 1 a.m. Transport proceeding E. of MESSINES - STINKING FARM ROAD. Searchlight was also again seen playing on the MESSINES - STINKING FARM ROAD.	
	8/4/16.		Wind N.W. Weather fine. During the night parapets in 141 and 142 were rebuilt in places where broken down - together with a new traverse in 142. The parapets were also raised and strengthened. Situation during night - quiet. Morning quiet. Between 12-45 p.m. and 2-15 p.m. the enemy shelled trench 142 BOYLES FARM and FORT OSBORNE with heavy crumps, shrapnel etc knocking in the end of our Cellars and causing seven casualties. Retaliation seemed slow and ineffective. Enemy's attitude generally aggressive. Night quiet. Nothing of note occured.	
	9/4/16.		Weather fine. Wind N.E. Situation normal during morning. At 2.45 p.m. 10 Whiz-bangs were fired at a party filling sand bags behind one of our trenches but fortunately caused no casualties. At 4.0 p.m. about 20 shells were fired at FORT EBERLE and FLETCHERS FIELD. A patrol went out from 141 at 12-15 a.m. staying out for an hour and three quarters. No enemy patrols were seen or heard but working parties were heard in front of right sub sector and also at ONTARIO FARM. Evening and night exceptionally quiet. Our Aircraft very active.	

2353 Wt. W2544/1454 700,000 5/15 D.D.&L.   A.D.S.S./Forms/C.2118.

Army Form C. 2118.

WAR DIARY
or
INTELLIGENCE SUMMARY.
(Erase heading not required.)

Instructions regarding War Diaries and Intelligence Summaries are contained in F. S. Regs., Part II. and the Staff Manual respectively. Title pages will be prepared in manuscript.

Place	Date	Hour	Summary of Events and Information	Remarks and references to Appendices
WULVERGHEM.	10/4/16.		Wind N.E. Situation still quiet. Activity in the air during the morning and afternoon, several of our machines being observed reconnoitring in the afternoon. A Hun machine was driven off. The damage done by the enemy to our dug-outs at BOYLES FARM was repaired. Artillery seems very quiet. Brigade orders for the relief of the Battalion on night of 12/13th received. At 8-0 p.m. our Artillery bombarded Germans works at U.2.d.4.4.(Sheet 28). with good effct. The night was very quiet.	See Appendice No. 1.
	11/4/16.		Weather damp and fine rain. Wind - Slight N.W. Enemy inactive all day but some Artillery activity behind our Line. Brigade Operation Orders for relief tomorrow night received.	See Appendice No. 2.
	12/4/16.		Situation very quiet. Weather fine, but gusty wind. Artillery. Both sides inactive. Battalion relieved by 2nd.Leinsters and proceeded to KORTEPYP IN DIvisional Reserve. Lieut. Clarke hit in the foot on the road to NEUVE EGLISE. Work done during tour. Casualties during 6 days tour 1 Killed 8 Wounded.	
KORTEPYP	13/4/16		Morning spent in cleaning up Kit etc. All Leave cancelled after 18th by orders received from 24th Division. Working Party for R.E. of 200 supplied C.S.M.Marks of the Army Gymnastic Staff begins training N.C.O's in course of Bayonet Fighting and Physical Drill. 1 Officer and 6 N.C.O's in course of Bayonet Fighting and Physical Drill. Usual traning. Weather - changeable. Baths at NEUVE EGLISE allotted from 7-30 a.m. to 6 p.m. Similar working party to last night provided	

Army Form C. 2118.

WAR DIARY
or
INTELLIGENCE SUMMARY.
(Erase heading not required.)

Instructions regarding War Diaries and Intelligence Summaries are contained in F.S. Regs., Part II. and the Staff Manual respectively. Title pages will be prepared in manuscript.

Place	Date	Hour	Summary of Events and Information	Remarks and references to Appendices
KORTEPYP.	15/4/16.		Early morning run. Training as usual. Working party of 200 found for R.E.	
	16/4/16.		Weather fine. Divine Service held on parade Ground in Camp. Brigade Operation Orders No.9 for relief of 2nd Leinster on night of 18/19th received.	See Appendice No.3.
	17/4/16.		Training of Specialists. Physical Drill etc. Musketry. In the afternoon Boxing Contests were held. These were interrupted by rain and the remainder were postponed until tomorrow. 200 Working party for R.E. found. No Casualties on Working parties during period in Reserve.	
	18/4/16.		Parades - Inspection of Arms, Equipment, Ammunition, Gas Helmets etc. Bn relieved 2nd Leinsters in left sub-sector section trenches, first Company parading at 6-30 p.m. Night quiet. Two casualties caused by Rifle fire.	
WULVERGHEM.	19/4/16.		Weather wet and stormy. Wind W. Little activity during morning. Machine Guns rather active against DIAGONAL and 141 - 142. RATION FARM also shelled during morning. Artillery fairly active during morning, shelling ridge and Cross Roads over by line held by 8th. Sussex on our right. 141 - 142 heavily shelled with H.E. and Whizz-bangs during night. Damage comparatively slight. Work during night impeded by rain but two parapets and traverse built Sniping activity.	
	20/4/16.		Weather still cold and stormy. Morning quiet. Some shelling on the MESSINES - WULVERGHEM ROAD. At 9 p.m. our Artillery bombarded MESSINES and the MESSINES - GAPAARD ROAD searching for enemy Transport which has been seen and heard there lately. Casualties during day 3.	

Army Form C. 2118.

WAR DIARY
or
INTELLIGENCE SUMMARY.
(Erase heading not required.)

Instructions regarding War Diaries and Intelligence Summaries are contained in F.S. Regs., Part II. and the Staff Manual respectively. Title pages will be prepared in manuscript.

Place	Date	Hour	Summary of Events and Information	Remarks and references to Appendices
WULVERGHEM.	21/4/16.		GOOD FRIDAY. Weather fine and sunny. Wind S.E. Artillery quiet during morning and afternoon. At about 12 noon enemy shelled MORTAR FARM with Crumps where a platoon of C Company was situated, but caused no Casualties. Again at 7-25 p.m. MORTAR FARM was shelled together with the ground round about Headquarters with Whizz-bangs and Shrapnel. The Acting Adjutant (2nd Lt Hawthorne) was wounded in the leg by Shrapnel. Draft of One Officer (2nd Lt F.M.Hill) and 50 otherranks arrived midday and came up with Transport at 8-30 p.m. The wind changing to E. "Gas Alert" was received about 10-30 p.m. Working party of 100 for work at DIAGONAL.	
	22/4/16.		Weather damp. Wind N.E. Situation quiet. No Artillery activity during morning - one Solitary crump being put over to the right of MORTAR FARM. Draft of 5 officers. Lt. Bullock, 2nd Lt Holland, 2nd Lt Greenwood, 2nd Ly Beale, 2nd Lt Lloyd from 8th Battn arrived this evening. "Gas Alert" cancelled. Between 4 p.m. and 7 p.m., BOYLES FARM, DIAGONAL and Barrier on MESSINES ROAD were shelled withheavies and whizz-bangs and during the night at 8 p.m., 9-30 p.m., 11 p.m., 1 a.m. and 3 a.m. the enemy sent over whizz-bangs. Our Casualties were 3.	See Appendice No 4.
	23/4/16.		Weather fine. Wind N.W. to W. Aerial activity during morning. Brigade Operation Orders for relief by 2nd Leinsters on night of 24/25th. received. Situation quiet. B.G.C. 73rd Brigade made atour of our line in the afternoon. Artillery moderately quiet. At 11-45 p.m. half a dozen whizz-bangs were sent over F Company. Wind changed round to East.	

Army Form C. 2118.

WAR DIARY
or
INTELLIGENCE SUMMARY.
(Erase heading not required.)

Instructions regarding War Diaries and Intelligence Summaries are contained in F.S. Regs., Part II. and the Staff Manual respectively. Title pages will be prepared in manuscript.

Place	Date	Hour	Summary of Events and Information	Remarks and references to Appendices
WULVERGHEM.	24/4/16.		Great Aerial activity during early hours 5 a.m. and 9 a.m. One enemy Aeroplane was apparently hit by our A.A. and M.G. fire as he was seen to topple over and fall. 2nd Lt A.W.Heaton rejoined from Hospital today. During the afternoon Major General Capper made a tour of our front line. Situation quiet. Battalion relieved by 2nd Leinsters at 11-30 p.m. and returned to BRIGADE RESERVE at RED LODGE.	
RED LODGE.	25/4/16.		Leave re-opened today. Weather fine. Gas Alert. Working party for R.E. at night. Much aerial activity. HILL 63 shelled during day.	
	26/4/16.		Weather fine and hot. Gas Alert, still on. HILL 63 shelled during morning causing 2 slight casualties. Party of 3 Officers and 3 N.C.O's attended class of instruction by R.E. in wiring with screw pickets. Working party of 480 found. Tower Respirators issued to Machine Gunners, and inspected in the afternoon by B.G.C. 73rd. Brigade.	
	27/4/16.		At 1-15 a.m. this morning Gas Alarm was received and Battalion stood too for half an hour. Our Artillery meanwhile bombarded the German line heavily. Weather hot and fine. Wind W. 38 P.HG. Helmets issued to Battalion. Slight shelling on top of HILL 63.	
	28/4/16.		Weather hot and fine. Aerial activity during morning. Working parties on ridge shelled occasionally. Divisional Baths allotted this morning from 9-30 to 12-30 p.m. and 1-30 to 3-30 p.m. Working party as usual in evening.	

Army Form C. 2118.

WAR DIARY
or
INTELLIGENCE SUMMARY.
(Erase heading not required.)

Instructions regarding War Diaries and Intelligence Summaries are contained in F. S. Regs., Part II. and the Staff Manual respectively. Title pages will be prepared in manuscript.

Place	Date	Hour	Summary of Events and Information	Remarks and references to Appendices
RED LODGE.	29/4/16.		Weather fine. Artillery activity in morning on ridge. At 5 p.m. enemy shelled Batteries on right together with HILL 63 causing us 8 casualties. Remainder of evening quiet.	
	30/4/16.		At 12-45 a.m. the enemy sent over Gas in our sector followed by a heavy bombardment of HILL 63 and Reserve camps around. About 8 casualties were caused by this and a Y.M.C.A Hut adjacent was burnt down. About 1-30 a.m. the order was received to take action and the Battalion paraded and moved off taking up a Support line in the CAVALRY TRENCHES, Battalion Headquarters being at FORT BRANDON. The bombardment by our Artillery was very heavy and ceased about 2-30 a.m. afterwhich the situation calmed down. At about 4 p.m. the order was received to Stand down and the Battalion returned to RED LODGE. Our casualties during second bombardment were 1 Killed and 20 Wounded. Remainder of day quiet. Cleaning of Camp etc. Relief of 2nd Leinster Regt in L41 & L42 and C2. carried out. Situation Quiet. Gas reported on left of C.S. at 8-45 p.m. and a gas cloud was seen right over on left.	

Roger Rhodes Major
Comdg 1/5 Northum Fusiliers

SECRET.   　　　　　　　　　　　　　　　　　　　　　　　No 1   COPY NO: 9

73rd. INFANTRY BRIGADE.

OPERATION ORDER NO. 35.

H.Q. 73 I.B., April 10th., 1916.

1. The following reliefs will take place on the night of 12th./13th. April.

(a) 2nd. Leinsters will relieve 7th. Northamptons in Left Section.
2nd. Leinsters will pass road junction T.5.d.8.4. at 7.45 p.m.
On relief 7th. Northamptons will move to KORTEPYP (Divisional Reserve) via NEUVE EGLISE.

(b). 13th. Middlesex will relieve 9th. Royal Sussex in Right Section.
13th. Middlesex Regt. will not pass road junction T.18.a.6.7 before 10.45 p.m.
On relief 9th. Royal Sussex to RED LODGE (Brigade Reserve).

2. TRANSPORT.

7th. Northamptons will load on the WULVERGHEM Road at T.6.c. central and proceed to camp via NEUVE EGLISE. Tail of convoy to be clear of this point by 9.30 p.m.
2nd. Leinsters will proceed via NEUVE EGLISE to and off-load at T.6.c. central. Head of convoy not to reach this point before 10 p.m.
9th. Royal Sussex Regt. will load at RATION FARM proceeding via Road junction T.24.a.7.10, and on return journey will be clear of this point by 9.30 p.m.
13th. Middlesex Regt. will off-load at RATION FARM. Head of convoy not to pass Road junction T.24.a.7.10 before 10 p.m.

3. Completion of reliefs will be notified by Companies to battalion Headquarters, and by Battalions to Brigade Headquarters by orderly AND NOT BY TELEPHONE.

4. PLEASE ACKNOWLEDGE.

ISSUED AT 10 p.m.

R Hoohltt   Major,
Brigade Major, 73rd. Infantry Brigade.

Copy No. 1. File.
2. War Diary.
3. "G" 24 Div.
4. "Q" 24 Div.
5. 17 I.B.
6. 72 I.B.
7. 2nd. Leinsters.
8. 9th. R. Sussex.
9. 7th. Northamptons.
10. 13th. Middlesex.
11. 73rd. Coy. Machine Gun Corps.
12. 73/1 T.M. Battery.
13. 107th. R.F.A.
14. 129th. Fd. Coy. R.E.
15. B.T.O.
16. Bde. Sigs. Officer.

No 2

WORK DONE IN TRENCHES BY 7th. (S). Bn. NORTHAMPTONSHIRE REGIMENT

FROM APRIL 6th. to APRIL 12th.

C.2. Six Rifle racks made and put up in bays 1-5.
Three new dug-outs built and completed.
Six new traverses rebuilt.
Small dug-out for night signalling built.
Two new fire-steps made.
New latrine constructed at right od C.2.
Duck-boards relaid for 30 yards.
New traverse built at extreme left of trench.
Parapet built up in three places where it had been blown in.
75 yards of Apron wire put up in front of Diagonal.

141 & 142. Three new traverses built.
Two bays rebuilt.
Repairing parapet where it had been blown in.
Bomb store started in new island traverse.
These two trenches have been badly shelled and a lot of work had to be done in reclaiming them.

BOYLES FARM. Repairing side of cellar blown in by a shell.

BARBARY COAST. New Company Headquarters built to hold 4 Officers.
New Kitchen built for same.
New Trench dug from the right of C.2. to FORT LINDSAY and old trench reclaimed.

FORT LINDSAY. Partly drained and reclaimed.

BARRIER. New Parados built.

In the Field.
April 13th. 1916.

..................Major Commdg.
7th. (S). Bn. Northamptonshire Regiment.

Ref. Sheet 28.
1/10,000.

COPY No. 9

N° 3

73rd. INFANTRY BRIGADE ORDER NO.36.

H.Q. 73 I.B. April 16th. 1916

1 RELIEF.   The following reliefs will take place on the night of the 18th./19th. April, 1916.
(a).   9th. Royal Sussex will relieve 13th. Middlesex in
                                     Right Section.
   9th. Royal Sussex will pass road junction T.18.a.6.7 at 8 p.m.
   On relief 13th. Middlesex will move to KORTEPYP Huts. (Divisional Reserve) via SHRINE ROAD.
(b).   7th. Northamptons will relieve 2nd. Leinsters in
                                     Left Section.
   7th. Northamptons will move via NEUVE EGLISE and will not pass road junction T.5.d.8.4 before 11 p.m.
   On relief 2nd. Leinsters will move to RED LODGE (Brigade Reserve).

2 TRANSPORT.   13th. Middlesex Regt. will load at RATION FARM proceeding via Road junction T.24.a.7.10. When loaded will proceed to KORTEPYP Camp via NEUVE EGLISE, tail of convoy to be clear of road junction T.18.a.4.8 by 9.30 p.m.
   9th. Royal Sussex will off-load at RATION FARM proceeding via road junction T.24.a.7.10. Head of convoy not to pass road junction T.18.a.4.8 before 13th. Middlesex convoy is clear of this point at 9.30 p.m. Will return to camp via NEUVE EGLISE and will be clear of point T.18.a.4.8 by 11 p.m.
   2nd. Leinsters will load at RATION FARM proceeding via road junction T.24.a.7.10. Head of convoy not to pass road junction T.18.a.4.8 before 9th. Royal Sussex convoy is clear of this point at 11 p.m.
   7th. Northamptons will proceed via NEUVE EGLISE and off-load on WULVERGHEM Road at point T.6.c. central.

3. REPORTS.   Completion of relief will be notified by companies to battalion Headquarters and by battalions to Brigade Headquarters by orderly and NOT BY TELEPHONE.

   PLEASE ACKNOWLEDGE.

ISSUED AT 10 a.m.
                                    R Howlett
                                              Major,
                 Brigade Major, 73rd, Infantry Brigade.

```
Copy No  1.  File.
         2.  War Diary.
         3.  "G" 24 Div.
         4.  "Q" 24 Div.
         5.  17 I.B.
         6.  72 I.B.
         7.  2nd Leinsters.
         8.  9th Royal Sussex.
         9.  7th Northamptons.
        10.  13th Middlesex.
        11.  73rd Coy. Machine Gun Corps.
        12.  73/1 Trench Mortar Battery.
        13.  R.F.A. 107th Bde.
        14.  129th Field Coy. R.E.
        15.  B.T.O.
        16.  Brigade Signals.
```

SECRET. |No.4| COPY NO.

Ref Sheet   73rd. INFANTRY BRIGADE.
   28
1/40,000.   O P E R A T I O N O R D E R No. 37.

                                                    H.Q. 73rd.I.B. April 22nd. 19

1. RELIEF.   The following reliefs will take place on the night of the
                24th/25th. April, 1916:-

           (a) 13th. MIDDLESEX REGIMENT will relieve 9th. ROYAL SUSSEX
                REGIMENT in Right Section.
                13th. MIDDLESEX REGIMENT will pass road junction
                T.18.a.6.7. at 8.15 p.m.
                On relief 9th. ROYAL SUSSEX REGIMENT will move to
                KORTEPYP HUTS (Divisional Reserve).

           (b) 2nd. LEINSTER REGIMENT will relieve 7th. NORTHAMPTON-
                SHIRE REGIMENT in Left Section.
                2nd. LEINSTER REGIMENT will not pass road junction
                T.18.a.6.7. before 11.15 p.m.
                On relief 7th. NORTHAMPTONSHIRE REGIMENT will move
                to RED LODGE (Brigade Reserve).

2. TRANSPORT.   9th. ROYAL SUSSEX REGIMENT will load on WULVERGHEM Road
                at point T.6.c. central, proceeding via NEUVE EGLISE. When
                loaded will proceed to KORTEPYP HUTS via NEUVE EGLISE. Convoy
                to be clear of above point by 9.30 p.m.
                   13th. MIDDLESEX REGIMENT will off load at RATION FARM
                proceeding via road junction T.24.a.7.10, will return to Camp
                via NEUVE EGLISE. Tail of convoy to be clear of road junction
                T.18.a.4.8. by 9.30 p.m.
                   7th. NORTHAMPTONSHIRE REGIMENT will load at RATION FARM
                proceeding via road junction T.24.a.7.10. Head of convoy not
                to pass road junction T.18.a.4.8. before 13th. MIDDLESEX convoy
                is clear of this point at 9.30 p.m. When loaded will proceed
                to RED LODGE. Tail of convoy to be clear of road junction
                T.24.a.7.10. by 11.30 p.m.
                   2nd. LEINSTER REGIMENT will off load at RATION FARM,
                and will not pass road junction T.24.a.7.10. before 7th.
                NORTHAMPTONSHIRE REGIMENT are clear of this point at 11.30 p.m.

3. REPORTS.   Completion of relief will be notified by Companies to
                Battalion H.Q., and by Battalions to Brigade H.Q. by Orderly,
                AND NOT BY TELEPHONE.

                PLEASE ACKNOWLEDGE.

           ISSUED AT 10 a.m.   Capt.
                                                                  Major,
                                        Brigade Major, 73rd. Infantry Brigade.

                        Copy No. 1. File.
                                 2. War Diary.
                                 3. "G" 24th. Div.
                                 4. "Q" 24th. Div.
                                 5. 17th. I.B.
                                 6. 72nd. I.B.
                                 7. 2nd. Leinsters.
                                 8. 9th. Royal Sussex.
                                 9. 7th. Northants.
                                10. 13th. Middlesex.
                                11. 73rd. Coy. M.G. Corps.
                                12. 73/1.T.M. Battery.
                                13. 107th. Bde. R.F.A.
                                14. 129th. Field Coy. R.E.
                                15. B.T.O.
                                16. Brigade Sigs.

73rd Brigade.
24th Division.

7th BATTALION

NORTHAMPTONSHIRE REGIMENT.

May 1916

7th Northants
Vol 8

CONFIDENTIAL.

WAR DIARY.

of

7th SERVICE BATTALION NORTHAMPTONSHIRE REGIMENT.

FROM :- MAY 1st 1916.

TO :- MAY 31st 1916.

IN THE FIELD.

Instructions regarding War Diaries and Intelligence Summaries are contained in F. S. Regs., Part II. and the Staff Manual respectively. Title Pages will be prepared in manuscript.

INTELLIGENCE SUMMARY
(Erase heading not required.)

Place	Date	Hour	Summary of Events and Information	Remarks and references to Appendices
WULVERGHEM.	1/5/16.		Weather fine and hot. Enemy Machine Guns very active. Unusual number of flares sent up during night. Wind N. E.	
	2/5/16.		During afternoon 142 – end of DIAGONAL shelled for half an hour. Rifle Grenades sent over during night, but Machine Guns less active. Wind N.E. Weather changeable. Situation during day quiet. Thunderstorm and heavy showers in afternoon. Party of 10 other ranks proceeded on leave. Evening quiet.	
	3/5/16.		Machine Guns from ONTARIO FARM playing early morning. Artillery Quiet. 2 p.m. 30 Whiz-bangs fell in rear of 141 – 142. A troublesome sniper has today been silenced by our fixed rifle.	
	4/5/16.		Weather fine. Wind S.E. Artillery activity round NEIPPE. Enemy very quiet. One of our aeroplanes reconnoitring the enemy lines was seen to be hit and fall to the ground in flames. Draft of 25 O.R. arrived this evening.	
	5/5/16.		Weather fine. Wind S.E. Situation Normal.	
	6/5/16.		Weather stormy. Enemy Quiet. Their Artillery shelled WULVERGHEM. Battalion relieved by 2nd Leinsters at 9-30 p.m. Relief completed without casualties. Total casualties during tour Killed, One, Wounded, 8.	
KORTE PYP"	7/5/16.		Weather cold and stormy. Cleaning of equipment and clothing. Working party of 100 found for R.E. Dump in the evening.	

2449 Wt. W14957/M90 750,000 1/16 J.B.C. & A. Forms/C.2118/12.

INTELLIGENCE SUMMARY

(Erase heading not required.)

Place	Date	Hour	Summary of Events and Information	Remarks and references to Appendices
KORTEPYP.	8/5/16.		TRAINING. Physical Drill. Kit, Gas Helmet, Rifle inspections during morning. Lecture by N.C.O's who have attended Gas classes in the afternoon. Working party of 100 for burying cable found.	
	9/5/16.		TRAINING. Swedish Drill and Run. Specialists as usual. Bayonet Fighting. Baths at NEUVE EGLISE allotted and used.	
	10/5/16.		TRAINING. Physical Drill and Run. Inspection of Feet. Bathing at DIVISIONAL BATHS. No working party.	
	11/5/16.		Physical Training. Musketry. Training of Specialists. "STAND TO" sent form Brigade at 10-12 a.m. and the Battalion Stood to in twenty minutes. Draft of 40 O.R. arrived this afternoon.	
	12/5/16.		Run. Physical Drill. Company and Platoon Drill. Inspection of Draft by Commanding Officer. Cleaning up Camp etc. Battalion relieved 2nd Leinsters in 141, 142, and C.2 trenches at midnight. Relief completed without Casualties. Enemy Machine Guns rather active during night. "GAS ALERT".	
WULVERGHEM.	13/5/16.		Situation very quiet. Weather.- Rain-and wind.S.W. Gas Alert cancelled. No Artillery activity during morning. At 3-30 p.m. our Heavy Artillery opened fire on ONTARIO FARM OBTAINING 2 direct hits and several on Trench around, also exploding a bomb store. Enemy retaliated on 72nd Brigade front.	

INTELLIGENCE SUMMARY

(Erase heading if not required.)

Place	Date	Hour	Summary of Events and Information	Remarks and references to Appendices
WULVERGHEM.	13/5/16.		Parapets and parados strengthened in 141 and 142. Enemy's attitude quiet. Machine Guns active at about 8 p.m.. Throughout the night our Artillery opened on ONTARIO FARM with object of preventing the damage done in the pm afternoon from being repaired.	
	14/5/16.		Weather cold and misty. Wind N. 9 a.m. to 10 a.m. Artillery very quiet. At 2-30 p.m. Barbary Coast occupied by B Company and McBRIDES MANSIONS (Battalion Headquarters) were shelled by 4.2s, two direct hits being obtained on dug-outs in the former and one in the latter place on the Orderly Room. Total Casualties 4 wounded. Remainder of day quiet. 2nd Lieuts Mortimer, Butcher and Wright joined from 8th Battalion.	
	15/5/16.		Wind N.W. Weather damp. Artillery inactive during morning. At 2-30.p.m. about 20 4.2 Shrapnel burst close to North and South MIDLAND FARMS, also a few 5.9s fell near Battle O.P. in our lines. 9 p.m. Machine Guns very active during night on road etc, two men being wounded at Ration Dump. B and D Companies relieve C and D Companies in C.2., 141, and 142. this evening. No Casualties during relief.	
	16/5/16.		Weather fine and sunny. Wind S.W. Very much aerial activity in the morning. Artillery fairly quiet. Two Officers, 2nd Lieuts Debenham and Gotch joined from 8th Battalion.	
	17/5/16.		Situation very quiet. Aerial activity all day. Weather fine and sunny. New Orderly Room completed together with other dug-outs. Artillery shelled MIDLAND FARM, 141, and DIAGONAL during afternoon. Snipers active.	

Summaries are contained in F. S. Regs., Part II. and the Staff Manual respectively. Title Pages will be prepared in manuscript.

INTELLIGENCE SUMMARY

(Erase heading not required.)

Place	Date	Hour	Summary of Events and Information	Remarks and references to Appendices
WULVERGHEM.	17/5/16.		Gas Alert received about 6 p.m.. Wind N.E. Machine Guns very active during night. Operation Orders received from Brigade for relief.	
	18/5/16.		Weather fine. Wind N.E. Not much aerial activity or shelling during day. Battalion relieved by 2nd Battn. Leinster Regiment and returned to BRIGADE RESERVE at RED LODGE.	
RED. LODGE.	19/5/16.		Weather fine and hot. RED LODGE shelled with Shrapnel in the Morning causing 4 Casualties in B Company. Usual working parties found.	
	20/5/16.		Weather fine. Working parties as usual. beer Brigade Canteen opened here - being purchased from ARMENTIERES. Orders received from Brigade that tour of duty in the trenches would in future be 8 days. Draft of 20 O.R. arrived today. 2nd Lieut Durrant Swan rejoined.	
	21/5/16.		Weather fine. Aerial activity during early hours. Working parties as usual.	
	22/5/16.		Weather cooler. Thunderstorm in the afternoon. Working parties as usual.	
	Wednesday 23/5/16.		Weather fine. Nothing of note occurring. Usual Working parties. "GAS ALERT"	
	24/5/16.		Weather fine. Heavy shelling of artillery on left also HILL 63. Working parties as usual.	

INTELLIGENCE SUMMARY

(Erase heading not required.)

Place	Date	Hour	Summary of Events and Information	Remarks and references to Appendices
RED LODGE.	25/5/16.		Quiet today. Major E. R. Mobbs promoted Lieut. Col. dated 23/4/16.	
	26/5/16.		Quiet, again today. Battalion relieved 2nd Leinster Regt in the trenches tonight. Relief completed without casualties. Machine Gun active on road. 2nd Lt. D. W. Morris rejoined from Hospital.	
	27/5/16.		Wind N. W. B Coy and D Coy in front line. Situation quiet. German sniper seen to crawl out on parapet was fired on and hit by one of our snipers. Machine Gun and rifle fire heavy during the night.	
	28/5/16.		Situation quiet. Wind N. W. 2nd Lieut Gotch hit in head early in morning. Wind changes to N.E. and "Gas Alert" is issued.	
	29/5/16.		Wind N.E. Weather fine. Situation quiet.	
	30/5/16.		Situation Quiet. Artillery Activity at 5 p.m. B Coy and D Coy relieved tonight in front line by A Coy and C Coy. 1 Man of B Coy killed by rifle fire. Machine guns very active.	
	31/5/16.		Weather fine. Wind M. to N.E. Attitude quiet during morning. 8 Cadets arrive from Brigade Headquarters for 48 hours tour in the trenches and are taken up to C.3. and 141 - and 142. Day quiet with the exception of 50 Whiz-bangs falling near 141 - 142. Machine Guns not quite so vigorous. Casualties for the month. 1 Officer Wounded, 3 O.R. Killed, 24 Wounded 4 Slightly wounded still at duty.	

Commdg. 7th (S) Bn Northamptonshire Regiment

73rd Brigade.
24th Division.

7th BATTALION

NORTHAMPTONSHIRE REGIMENT.

June 1916

Army Form C. 2118.

WAR DIARY
or
INTELLIGENCE SUMMARY
(Erase heading not required.)

XIV 7th Northants Vol 9 June

CONFIDENTIAL.

WAR DIARY

of

7th (S). BN. NORTHAMPTONSHIRE REGIMENT.

for the period

June 1st 1916 - June 30th 1916.

In the Field.
July 1st. 1916.

Army Form C. 2118.

WAR DIARY
or
INTELLIGENCE SUMMARY

(Erase heading not required.)

Instructions regarding War Diaries and Intelligence Summaries are contained in F. S. Regs., Part II. and the Staff Manual respectively. Title Pages will be prepared in manuscript.

Place	Date	Hour	Summary of Events and Information	Remarks and references to Appendices
MILVERGHEM.	1/6/16.		Weather fine and warm. Wind safe (SW). Nothing of note occurring during day. Casualties 1 O.R. Killed. Enemy Machine guns very active after dusk.	
	2/6/16.		Situation very quiet. Weather fine. Wind N.W. Observation Balloon seen to break loose this evening and draft away well over German lines. Machine Guns less active tonight than usual. Draft of 30 O.R. arrive but remain in Transport lines as Battalion is being relieved tomorrow night.	
	3/6/26.		Weather fine - Wind N.W. Situation very quiet - practically no Artillery activity during day. Battalion relieved in left sector by 2nd Leinster Regiment and return to DIVISIONAL RESERVE at KORTEPYP. Relief completed by 12 midnight in order that all roads might be clear in preparation for raid to be undertaken by 72nd Brigade tonight. Casualties during the tour of 8 days are :- 1 Officer Wounded, 2 O.R. Killed, 3 O.R. Wounded including one still at duty. Work done during tour as per report annexed.	see appendix No 1.
KORTEPYP.	4/6/16.		Weather changeable. Working parties of 240 found for work on assembly trenches etc. Baths allotted to D Company till 12-30 p.m. Lieut P.S.HADLEY awarded the MILITARY CROSS and the undermentioned M.C.Os have been awarded the MILITARY MEDAL:- Sgt A. M. RUSTON. Cpl. R. MCMILLAN. L/Cpl. J. T. JACKSON. L/Cpl. C. FITCH. Sgt A. E. ALLEBONE has been awarded the DISTINGUISHED CONDUCT MEDAL.	
	5/6/16.		Battalion practiced in new method of wearing Gas helmets during a "Gas Alert" as shewn by classes recently held at BAILLEUL. Company etc drill. Working parties at night as usual. Weather fine.	

2449 Wt. W14957/M90 750,000 1/16 J.B.C. & A. Forms/C.2118/12.

Army Form C. 2118.

WAR DIARY
INTELLIGENCE SUMMARY
(Erase heading not required.)

Instructions regarding War Diaries and Intelligence Summaries are contained in F. S. Regs., Part II. and the Staff Manual respectively. Title Pages will be prepared in manuscript.

Place	Date	Hour	Summary of Events and Information	Remarks and references to Appendices
KORTEPYP.	6/6/16.	A.M.	Duration of Leave reduced to 7 days - allotment also reduced by about half. Weather stormy. All Waterproof capes withdrawn from Companies and returned to Ordnance. At 2 p.m. two shells were sent over dropping near the Buffs' Transport lines a little to one side of our Huts. 5 Officers arrived at 7 p.m., 2nd Lieuts Murray, Adderley, and Littlewood.	
	7/6/16.	A.M.	Weather showery. Baths at NEUVE EGLISE allotted from 8-30 a.m. to 12.30 p.m. 2nd Lieut C.D.Morgan rejoined from tour at 24 DIV. BASE DEPOT. Working parties of 240 supplied.	
	8/6/16.	A.M.	Weather fine. Baths at NEUVE EGLISE allotted from 7-30 a.m. to 12-30 p.m. Working parties of 240 supplied.	
	9/6/16.	A.M.	Weather showery. Training. Physical drill, Company and Platoon drill etc. Working parties of 240 supplied. Draft of 20 O.R. from 3rd Battalion arrived at 7 p.m.	
	10/6/16.	A.M.	Weather fine. Battalion Sports held in the afternoon. Working parties as usual at night. 2nd Lieut L.F.W.A.Mortimer returned to England today.	
	11/6/16.	A.M.	Day devoted to cleaning up Camp. Voluntary Service. Battalion parade at 6 p.m. - Brigadier General R.G.JELF presented Medal ribbons to the N.C.Os && who have won them. Battalion moved off at 10-15 p.m. and proceeded to trenches to relieve 2nd Leinster Regiment. - Casualty during relief.	

Army Form C. 2118.

WAR DIARY
or
INTELLIGENCE SUMMARY

(Erase heading not required.)

Instructions regarding War Diaries and Intelligence Summaries are contained in F. S. Regs., Part II. and the Staff Manual respectively. Title Pages will be prepared in manuscript.

Place	Date	Hour	Summary of Events and Information	Remarks and references to Appendices
HUIMECHEM.	12/6/16.		Weather showery and cold. Wind N.W. Enemy quiet all day. One O.R. Killed. 2nd Lieut I.H.Allport joined from 8th Bn. Northamptonshire Regiment.	
	13/6/16.		Weather stormy - Wind N.W. Situation very quiet. Artillery activity heard on our left in direction of HOOGE. Trench 141 - 142 shelled with 7, 7.5 and 4.2s between 10 and 11 a.m.	
	14/6/16.		2nd Lieut G.A.Williamson joined from 8th Bn.Northamptonshire Regiment. Situation quiet - Wind N.W. Between 2-30 and 3-30 p.m. enemy put over a few trench mortars.	
	15/6/16.		Situation Quiet - Wind N.W.	
	16/6/16.		Wind E. Gas Alert issued. Morning and afternoon Quiet. Major Dobbin from 1st Bn. Northamptonshire Regiment arrived today.	
	17/6/16.		At 12-30 a.m. the enemy released Gas on the 72nd Brigade front and opposite a portion of the 8th Royal Sussex Regiment. The wind blowing N.E., the Gas was blown over C.2.; missing 141 - 142 and catching BATTALION HEADQUARTERS. The enemy's heavy machine Gun fire which swept the whole of our line gave us an indication that Gas was intended and before the Gas was released practically everybody was fully prepared, eventually only 10 O.R. were gassed. This was succeeded by a heavy bombardment on the whole of the front, causing 33 casualties. Our Artillery replied very vigorously and prevented the enemy from leaving his trenches. Gas helmets were kept on for an hour and a half and were found very effective. The Bombardment ceased about 2-30 a.m. and the situation calmed down. The remainder of the day was very quiet. Total Casualties for this tour: 1 Officer Wounded, 7 O.R. Killed, and 55 Wounded.	

WAR DIARY
INTELLIGENCE SUMMARY

Army Form C. 2118.

Place	Date	Hour	Summary of Events and Information	Remarks and references to Appendices
WULVERGHEM.	17/6/16.	M.N.	Operation orders for move. 73rd Brigade relieved by 7th Australian Brigade. The Battalion was relieved by the 25th Bn. Australian Infantry at 11-30 p.m. and proceeded by to WULWERGHEM where 30 G.S. Wagons were waiting to convey them to new area. 450 all ranks were taken by these wagons.	See appendix No. 2.
HAPPENCOURT.	18/6/16.	M.N.	The remainder of the Battalion proceeded to the SIDING at 5 a.m. and were taken in 6 lorries to BAILLEUL where guides met them and conducted them to their billets at HAPPENCOURT, situated between BAILLEUL and METEREN. Battalion Headquarters at HAPPENCOURT. Remainder of the day the men were free. Transport arrived about 3 a.m.	
	19/6/16.	M.N.	Orders received for Battalion to move to new area and at 8 p.m. the Battalion paraded on main thoroughfare - BAILLEUL Road and marched via BAILLEUL to the WIELD HUTS near LOCRE a total distance of about 6 miles.	
LOCRE.	20/6/16.	M.N.	Day devoted to cleaning and resting. Commanding Officer, Company Commanders, Machine Gun Officers and Bombing Officer proceeded to reconnoitre our new line this afternoon. Advance party proceeded to new Camp at KEMMEL HILL to take over. At 4.0 p.m. the Battalion paraded and marched off to KEMMEL SHELTERS arriving there about 11 p.m.	
KEMMEL SHELTERS.	21/6/16.	M.N.	Weather fine. 100 men who were At the Gas attack paraded and proceeded to DRANOUTRE for inspection by General Plumer, 2nd Army Commander, at 8-50 a.m. 2nd Lieut. J.Caille joined from 8th Battalion today. Working parties found as usual.	
	22/6/16.	M.N.	Weather fine. Bath at LOCRE allotted to Battalion from 12 m.d. to 5 p.m. Working parties as usual.	

Army Form C. 2118.

WAR DIARY
or
INTELLIGENCE SUMMARY
(Erase heading not required.)

Instructions regarding War Diaries and Intelligence Summaries are contained in F. S. Regs., Part II. and the Staff Manual respectively. Title Pages will be prepared in manuscript.

Place	Date	Hour	Summary of Events and Information	Remarks and references to Appendices
KEMMEL SHELTERS.	23/6/16.		Weather stormy - Violent thunderstorm in the afternoon. Baths at LOCRE allotted. At 9.p.m. a heavy bombardment on our front took place and "Stand to" received about 10 p.m. At 11 p.m. order was received to "Stand down" by which time the situation seemed to have quietened down. Working parties as usual.	
	24/6/16.		Weather fine. Draft of 60 O.R. arrived from 6th Battalion. Usual working parties.	
	25/6/16.		"Gas Alert" received at 5-30 a.m. Situation very quiet. Working parties as usual.	
	26/6/16.		Weather Wet. No working parties tonight owing to minor enterprise being carried out by West Yorks Regt.	
	27/6/16.		Operation orders for relief of 2nd Leinster Regiment received. Lewis Gunners relieve Leinster Lewis Gunners. Battalion relieved in KEMMEL SHELTERS by 2 & 4th Middlesex. Parade 8-45 p.m. Battalion marched via KEMMEL to relief on 2nd Leinster in left Sector trenches (9th Sussex on our right). Battalion Headquarters at DOCTORS HOUSE, A Company, Support trenches, B Company, G.1. to 3.R.2 C Company, KEMMEL CHATEAU, D Company, G.4. Relief completed without casualties. Our Artillery and Trench Mortars very active during night Transport lines allotted and move completed by 6 p.m. today	See appendix No 3.
KEMMEL.	28/6/16.		Wind S.W. Weather Wet.	

Army Form C. 2118.

WAR DIARY
INTELLIGENCE SUMMARY

(Erase heading not required.)

Instructions regarding War Diaries and Intelligence Summaries are contained in F. S. Regs., Part II. and the Staff Manual respectively. Title Pages will be prepared in manuscript.

Place	Date	Hour	Summary of Events and Information	Remarks and references to Appendices
HEBUTERNE.	28/6/16		Considerable Artillery and Trench Mortar activity during the day. During the evening the enemy bombarded our lines heavily causing nearly 30 Casualties (including 2nd Lieut A.F.J.Burnham - Killed.). At 11-30 P.M. our Artillery retaliated vigorously damaging the enemy's wire and breaching his parapet. Leave cancelled from today.	
	29/6/16		Situation now normal. Wind S.W. Artillery active all round especially after dark.	
	30/6/16		"Gas Alert" received at 1.-30 a.m.. Between 2 - 3 a.m. a few whiz-bangs were fired on our trenches. Enemy attitude seems to be nervous. Wind S.W. Gas Alert cancelled at 6 a.m. Enemy retaliation below average. One of our Batteries when registering made several direct hits on our own parapet. Enemy wire still unrepaired. Casualties for the month:- KILLED, 1 Officer and 14 O.R., Wounded 20.R., 10.(including 4 Died of Wounds), Wounded slightly (still at duty) 4 O.R., Draft of 10 O.R. arrived today from 3rd Battalion.	

Confidential

Officer i/c A.G. Office at the Base.

Kindly attach the enclosed to my War Diary for June 1916.

[signature] Lieut and Adjutant
7th (S) Bn Northamptonshire Regt

ORDERLY ROOM
7th BATT. NORTHAMPTON

6.7.16

Nº 1

7th Service Battalion Northamptonshire Regiment

REPORT of WORK DONE during period 26th May to 3rd June 1916

MCBRIDES MANSIONS. Dug-outs rubbled and stengthened - duckboards raised and gangways drained. Wind vane erected.

FORBES TERRACE. Parados adjoining dug-outs raised

BARBARY COAST One new dug-out built, and one partially built completed.

C. 2. Foundations dug and work done on new Officers Dug-out. Two bays built up. Parados repaired in three places. Signallers dugout strengthened. Two new sniper plates put in. Observation Post in Bay 13 covered and built up. All duckboards raised and trench drained.

DIAGONAL AND BARRIER. Two traverses put up at Barrier - trench from Barrier to DIAGONAL cleared and sandbagged. Dugout on right of Diagonal completed. Right of DIAGONAL Sandbagged, and left of DIAGONAL drained.

SURREY LANE. Flying traverse erected, and parapet heightened

Trench 141-142 Parados traverses continued. Sniping plate re-set in 142. Parapet strengthened, and breaches repaired in 141. Trench overhauled and soak pits dug.

DRAGOON ALLEY. Clearing and revetting carried on.

FORT OSBORNE Cleaned generally - all duck boards taken up and refuse pits dug. Latrine heightened one foot. Wiring

N.B. WIRING. Listening post in front of Left end of C 2 wired, and wiring continued from L.P. to old line of wire (28 coils) New line in front of C 2 (12 coils) Twenty yards French wire in front of new DIAGONAL-repaired front line wire damaged by Minenwerfer. Parties out each night in front of 141-142 effecting minor repairs.

---------------------- Captain,
Commdg 7th Northamptonshire Regiment.   3rd June 16.

73rd. INFANTRY BRIGADE.
PRELIMINARY ORDER.

H.Q. 73 I.B., June 15th. 1916.

1. The 73rd. Infantry Brigade will be relieved on nights 16th./17th and 17th/18th June by the 7th. Australian Brigade. Operation Orders will be issued to-day.

2. The following Officers and Other Ranks of the 7th. Australian Brigade will arrive to-day. They will reach Brigade Headquarters at 6 p.m. and will be guided to Units Headquarters under Brigade arrangements.

They will bring rations for the 16th. and 17th. June.

<u>Front Line Battalions.</u> 26th. Batt. to 9th. Royal Sussex.
25th. " " 7th. Northamptons.

	Lewis Gunners.	1 Officer & 8 O.R. per batt. (2 O.R. to each front line gun).
	Grenadiers.	1 Officer and 1 Sgt. per batt.
	Signallers.	1 Officer, 1 N.C.O. and 5 men per bn. (1 man to each signal office).
	Scouts.	1 N.C.O. and 3 men per batt. (battalions to arrange for these men to go out on patrol along with their own.)
	Observers.	1 Officer and 6 men per battalion.
	Snipers.	1 Officer, 1 N.C.O. and 8 men per batt.
	Machine Gun Coy.	2 Officers, 3 N.C.O's & 24 men. Two men of above will be attached to each of the 12 guns at present in the front area.
	Trench Mortar Battery.	1 Officer and 1 N.C.O.
	Brigade Headquarters.	Bde. Signalling Officer. Bde. Intelligence Officer.
	RED LODGE.	1 Officer and 4 N.C.O's (adv.party 26th. battalion).
	KORTEPYP.	1 Officer and 4 N.C.O's (adv party 25th. battalion).

The Brigadier General Commanding feels sure that Unit Commanders will take a personal interest in ensuring that these Officers and Other Ranks are given every opportunity to make themselves acquainted with the ground with reference to their respective duties.

ISSUED AT 7 a.m.

Major,
Brigade Major, 73rd. Infantry Bde.

Copy No. 1. File.
2. "G" 24th. Div.
3. 7th. Australian Bde.
4. 2nd. Leinster Regt.
5. 9th. Royal Sussex Regt.
6. 7th. Northamptonshire Regt.
7. 13th. Middlesex Regt.
8. 73rd. Machine Gun Company.
9. 73rd. Trench Mortar Battery.

SECRET. COPY NO:- 11

73rd. INFANTRY BRIGADE.

OPERATION ORDER NO. 45.

H.Q. 73 I.B. June 15th. 1916.

1. The 73rd. Infantry Brigade will be relieved in the Centre Sector by the 7th. Australian Brigade as per attached tables.

2. One Officer per company and 1 N.C.O. per platoon of the 25th. and 26th. battalions of the 7th. Australian Brigade will go into the trenches tomorrow and stay there till the arrival of their battalion.
 Details of other advanced parties have already been notified.

3. The reliefs of the trench wardens of Forts BRANDON and EBERLE will be found by the 28th. battalion and will arrive with the 26th. Battalion tomorrow.

4. Units will hand over to corresponding units of the 7th. Australian Brigade:-
 All Trench Stores.
 Trench Maps (including Sheet 28 S.W.4 (1/10,000).
 Defence Schemes.
 Log Books.
 Intelligence Reports.
 Tables of work in hand and proposed.
 All documents and information which may be of value.

Lists of Trench Stores and documents handed over will be forwarded to Brigade Headquarters within 48 hours of relief being completed.

5. Arrangements for Transport of surplus stores and the position of refilling points will be notified later.

6. The command of the Centre Sector will pass to B.G.C., 7th. Australian Brigade on completion of Infantry Reliefs night 17th./18th. June.

7. Please acknowledge.

ISSUED AT 12 noon.
R Howlett
Major,
Brigade Major, 73rd. Infantry Brigade.

 Copy No. 1. File.
 2. War Diary.
 3. "G" 24th. Div.
 4. "Q" 24th. Div.
 5. 17 I.B.
 6. 72 I.B.
 7. 7th. Australian Brigade.
 8. 150th. I.B.
 9. 2nd. Leinster Regt.
 10. 9th. Royal Sussex Regt.
 11. 7th. Northamptons.
 12. 13th. Middlesex Regt.
 13. 73rd. Coy. Machine Gun Corps.
 14. 73rd. Trench Mortar Battery.
 15. A.P.M. 24 Div.

RELIEF OF THE 73rd. INFANTRY BRIGADE BY THE 7th. AUSTRALIAN BRIGADE.

7th. AUSTRALIAN BRIGADE.

DATE.	UNIT.	FROM.	TO.	ROUTE.	REMARKS.
16th. June.(1).	26th. Bn.	2nd. ANZAC Div. Area.	RED LODGE.	LE ROMARIN T.27.b.8.0 - T.28.b.5.9 - T.22.d.2.5 - RED LODGE.	Guides from H.Q. 73 I.B meet coys. at LE ROMARIN at 11.30 a.m.
	7th.Aus.M.G. Coy.	"	T.22.b.1.1.	LE ROMARIN.	Guides from 73rd. Coy. M.G.Corps meet coy. at LE ROMARIN at 12.noon.
	7th. Aus. T.M.Batt.	"	T.21.b.2.5.	"	Guides from 73 T.M.Battery meet battery at LE ROMARIN at 12.15 p.m.
	25th. Batt.	"	KORTEPYP.	B.1. central - T.20.c.3.0 - KORTEPYP.	Guides from 13th. Middlesex meet coys. at B.1. central 11.30 a.m.
Night 16th/17th. June. (2).	7th. Aus.M.G. Coy.(12 guns)	T.22.b.1.1.	Trench area.		All arrangements for relief to be made between O.S.C. M.G.Coys. direct.
17th. June. (3).	28th. Bn.	2nd. ANZAC Div. Area.	RED LODGE.	As in (1).	Guides from 73rd. Bde. H.Q. meet coys. at LE ROMARIN at 9.30 p.m.
	27th.Bn.	"	KORTEPYP.	As in (1).	Guides from 73rd. Bde. H.Q. will meet coys at B.1. central at 5 p.m.
Night 17th/18th. June. (4).	26th. Bn.	RED LODGE.	RIGHT SECTION TRENCHES(I36 - I46).	Via T.18.a.4.7.	First coy. to pass T.18.a.4.7. at 10 p.m. O.C. 9th. Royal Sussex to arrange direct with O.C. 26th. Bn. re guides. To be clear of KORTEPYP by 6 p.m. but not to pass NEUVE EGLISE till 9.45 p.m.
	25th. Bn.	KORTEPYP.	Left Section Trenches (I41 - C.2.).	Via NEUVE EGLISE - WULVERGHEM.	Guides for coys. from KORTEPYP to WULVERGHEM will be provided by 73rd. Bde. H.Q. O.C. 7th. Northamptons will arrange for guides from that point to trenches.

NOTE. UNITS OF THE 7th. AUSTRALIAN BRIGADE WILL MOVE WHEN IN THE 24th. DIV AREA WITH AN INTERVAL OF 5 MINS. BETWEEN COYS.

RELIEF OF THE 73rd. INFANTRY BRIGADE BY 7th. AUSTRALIAN BRIGADE.

73rd. INFANTRY BRIGADE.

DATE.	UNIT.	FROM.	TO.	ROUTE.	REMARKS.
16th. June.	2nd. Leinsters.	RED LODGE.	LOCRE (BADAJOZ HUTS.)	To B.1. central thence via S.27.a.6.7 - S.15.d.3.7½ - S.15.c.10.8 - S.9.b.3.8 - S.9.a.6.5 - LOCRE.	Not to leave until after arrival of corresponding battalions of 7th. Australian Brigade. These 2 battalions on arrival at LOCRE will come under tactical orders of G.O.C. KEMMEL DEFENCES (H.Q. at LOCRE) Advanced parties of 1 Officer & 4 N.C.O's per battalion will report at 150th. I.B. H.Q. at LOCRE by 12 noon 16th. inst.
	13th. Middlesex	KORTEPYP.	LOCRE (WAKEFIELD HUTS)	DO.	
17th. June.	73rd. M.G.Coy.	T.22.b.1.1.		Will be notified.	
	73rd. T.M.Batt'y.	T.21.b.2.5.		do.	
Night 17/18th. June.	9th. R. Sussex. Right Section Trenches.	ST.JANS CAPPEL.		B.1. central - BAILLEUL - ST.JANS CAPPEL.	Billetting parties will meet Staff Captain tomorrow morning at a place and time to be notified.
	7th. Northamptons. Left Section Trenches.	HAEGDOORNE.		B.1. central - S.27.a.6.7 - S.15.d.3.7½ - S.15.c.10. 8 - HAEGDOORNE.	do.

15.6.16.

SECRET.

B.M. 194.
15. 6. 16.

Officer Commanding

    2nd. Leinster Regiment.
    9th. Royal Sussex Regiment.
    7th. Northamptonshire Regiment.
    13th. Middlesex Regiment.

The 73rd. Infantry Brigade will relieve the 150th Infantry Brigade in the line nights 19/20 and 20/21st June, and the following will be the moves:-

<u>19th. June.</u>
7th. Northamptonshire Regt. from HAEGEDOORNE to LOCRE
                                        (WAKEFIELD HUTS)

<u>Night 19/20th June.</u>
13th. Middlesex Regt. from WAKEFIELD HUTS to Right
                                      Section Trenches.
2nd. Leinster Regt. from BADAJOZ HUTS to KEMMEL Shelters.

<u>20th. June.</u>
9th. Royal Sussex Regt. from ST. JANS CAPPEL to
                                      WAKEFIELD HUTS.

<u>Night 20/21 June.</u>
2nd. Leinster Regt. from KEMMEL Shelters to Left Section
                                              Trenches.
7th. Northamptonshire Regt from WAKEFIELD HUTS to
                                         KEMMEL Shelters.

Operation orders will be issued in due course.

R Howlett

H.Q. 73rd.I.B.   Major,
15. 6. 16.   Brigade Major, 73rd. Infantry Brigade.

Reference Operation Order No. 45 dated 15/6/16,
Units will be billeted, now, as under.

(1) 9th. Royal Sussex Regiment at S.1.d.1.7., taking over from West York Regiment.

(2) 7th. Northamptonshire Regiment at X.17.a.3.6., taking over from 13th. The Kings Regiment.

(3) 73rd. Coy. Machine Gun Corps will be billeted at M.24.d.3.6. (150 Coy. M.G. Corps).

   73rd. Trench Mortar Battery will be billeted at KEMMEL Shelters, (150 T.M. Battery).

   Guides will meet at DRANOUTRE CHURCH at 5 p.m. 17th. instant.

(4) Battalion billeting Officers will leave Brigade Headquarters at 9 a.m. to-morrow by Car (one per Unit).
   Battalion Billeting parties should proceed to their new billets on bicycles, so as to be there by 10 a.m. to meet their Officers.
   Guides from Battalion Billeting parties to meet their Units in the SQUARE at BAILLEUL to conduct them to their billets.
   Small advance parties may be sent by Battalions of 1 N.C.O. and 6 other ranks by march if desired.

(5) Brigade Headquarters will be at the Chateau, ST. JANS CAPPEL, from mid-night 17/18th. instant.

H.Q. 73rd. I.B.   Captain,
16. 6. 16.   Staff Captain 73rd. Infantry Brigade.

SECRET.

Ref. Sheets.
27 & 28
1/40,000.

COPY NO. 10.

73rd. INFANTRY BRIGADE.

OPERATION ORDER N0.46.

H.Q. 73 I.B. June 16th. 1916.

1. The 73rd. Infantry Brigade will relieve the 150th. Infantry Brigade in the line nights 19/20 and 20/21st. June as per attached table.

2. A thorough reconnaissance of the line will be made by C.O's, Company Commanders, and all specialist Officers of 2nd. Leinster Regt. and the 13th. Middlesex Regt. before going into the line. Guides will be provided by the 150th. Infantry Brigade Headquarters (LOCRE) to whom application should be made.
    O.C. 73rd. Coy. Machine Gun Corps and O.C. 73rd. T.M. Battery will arrange for their Officers and selected N.C.O's to reconnoitre the line before the 19th. inst.

3. (a). One Officer per Company and 1 N.C.O. per platoon of the 13th. Middlesex and 2nd. Leinsters will go into the line on early mornings of the 19th. and 20th. June respectively. Trench Stores will be taken over by these Officers.
   (b).. Grenadiers, Signallers and Lewis Gun detachments of 13th. Middlesex and 2nd. Leinsters will relieve those specialists of 4th. East Yorks and 4th. Yorks respectively 12 hours before battalion reliefs commence.

4. Battalions will send on advanced parties of one Officer, and one N.C.O. per company to take over billets or camps in daylight.

5. Battalions moving East of LOCRE in daylight will do so by companies at intervals of ½ mile.

6. Units will take over from corresponding units of the 150th. Infantry Brigade:-
    All trench stores.
    Defence Schemes.
    Log Books.
    Intelligence Reports.
    Tables of work in hand and proposed.
    All documents and information which may be of value.

7. A list of documents and trench stores taken over will be forwarded to Brigade Headquarters within 24 hours of relief being complete.

8. All other details to be arranged between O'S.C. direct.

9. 73rd. Infantry Brigade Headquarters will be at ST. JANS CAPPEL CHATEAU from midnight 17/18th. June. Further movements will be notified in due course.

10. PLEASE ACKNOWLEDGE.

R. Howlett

ISSUED AT 11 p.m.
Major,
Brigade Major, 73rd. Infantry Brigade.

P.T.O.

COPY NO. 1. File.
2. War Diary.
3. "G" 24 Div.
4. "Q" 24 Div.
5. 150th. I.B.
6. 149th. I.B.
7. 72nd. I.B.
8. 2nd. Leinsters.
9. 9th. R. Sussex.
10. 7th. Northamptons.
11. 13th. Middlesex.
12. 73rd. M.G.Coy.
13. 73rd. T.M.Battery.
14. 129th. R.E.
15. A.P.M. 24th. Div.
16. Bde. Sigs. Offr.
17. B.T.O. 73 I.B.

RELIEF OF THE 150th BRIGADE BY THE 73rd INFANTRY BRIGADE.

DATE.	UNIT.	FROM.	TO.	Unit to be relieved.	REMARKS.
19th June.	7th Northamptons.	X.17.a.3.6.	WAKEFIELD HUTS.	13th Middlesex.	To arrive after departure of 13th. Middlesex, hour of which to be notified to O.C. 7th Northamptons. by O.C. 13th Middlesex
	2nd Leinsters.	BADAJOZ HUTS.	KEMMEL SHELTERS (Bde. support).	5th Yorks Regt.	
Night 19/20 June.	13th Middlesex.	WAKEFIELD HUTS.	Right Section Trenches.	4th East Yorks.	
	73rd M.G.Coy.	M.24.d.3.6.	Trenches.	150th M.G.Coy.	
	73rd T.M.Battery.	KEMMEL SHELTERS.	Trenches.	150th T.M.Battery.	
20th June.	9th R.Sussex.	S.1.d.1.7.	WAKEFIELD HUTS.	7th Northamptons.	To arrive after departure of 7th. Northamptons., hour of which to be notified to O.C. 9th R. Sussex by O.C. 7th. Northamptons.
Night 20/21 June.	2nd Leinsters.	KEMMEL SHELTERS.	Left Section Trenches.	4th Yorks Regt.	Command of 150th Infantry Bde. Sector passes to B.G.C. 73rd. Infantry Brigade on completion of reliefs.
	7th Northamptons.	WAKEFIELD HUTS.	KEMMEL SHELTERS.	2nd Leinsters.	

Issued with 73rd. Infantry Brigade Operation Order No.46 dated 16. 6. 16.

SECRET.   COPY No. 9

73rd INFANTRY BRIGADE.
OPERATION ORDER No. 47.

H.Q. 73rd I.B. June 26th 1916.

1. The following reliefs will take place night 27/28th June:-

   (a) 9th Royal Sussex Regiment will relieve 13th Middlesex Regiment in Right Section Trenches.
   9th Royal Sussex Regiment will leave WAKEFIELD HUTS at 10 p.m. and proceed via DRANOUTRE.
   On relief 13th Middlesex Regiment to KEMMEL SHELTERS.

   (b) 7th Northamptonshire Regiment will relieve 2nd Leinster Regiment in Left Section Trenches.
   7th Northamptonshire Regiment will leave KEMMEL SHELTERS at 9.45 p.m.
   On relief 2nd Leinster Regiment to WAKEFIELD HUTS via KEMMEL.

2. Lewis Gun Detachments of 9th Royal Sussex Regt., and 7th Northamptonshire Regt., will relieve those of 13th Middlesex Regt., and 2nd Leinster Regt., respectively during the morning of the 27th June.

3. Brigade Transport Officer will make all arrangements for transport.

4. Completion of reliefs will be notified to Brigade Headquarters by orderly.

R Howlett

Issued at 10.15 a.m.   Major,

Brigade Major, 73rd Infantry Brigade.

Copy No. 1. File.
       2. War Diary.
       3. "G" 24th Div.
       4. "Q" 24th Div.
       5. 72nd I.B.
       6. 149th I.B.
       7. 2nd. Leinster Regt.
       8. 9th. Royal Sussex Regt.
       9. 7th. Northamptons.
      10. 13th. Middlesex Regt.
      11. 73rd Coy. Machine Gun Corps.
      12. 73rd Light. Trench Mortar Baty.

Secret   O.C.
7th Northamptons

No 3
HEADQUARTERS 73rd BDE.
No. BM490
Date 1/7/16

In continuation of 73rd Infantry Brigade Operation Order No. 48.-

Para 1.(a).

The 9th Royal Sussex Regiment on relief will become Brigade Reserve and move to Camp and Shelters as under:-

Headquarters and Two Companies - To KEMMEL SHELTERS.

Two Companies - To canvas shelters which will be pitched near KEMMEL SHELTERS under Brigade Arrangements.

Para 1.(b and c).

Headquarters Battalion in the Line (7th Northamptonshire Regiment) to FORT SASKATCHEWAN.

Headquarters Battalion in Brigade Support (13th Middlesex Regiment) to DOCTORS HOUSE.

The above moves to be completed by 11 p.m. Exact time to be arranged between O's Commanding concerned and notified to Brigade Headquarters.

R Howitt.

1. 7. 16.   Major,
                          Brigade Major, 73rd Infantry Brigade.

SECRET.   COPY NO. 17

73rd. INFANTRY BRIGADE.

Ref Trench   O P E R A T I O N   O R D E R   N O. 4 8.
Map 1/20,000   H.Q. 73.I.B. June 30th.1916.
Sheet 28 S.W.

1.   The following reliefs will take place:-

Night 1st./2nd. July.
(a). 1st. Royal Fusiliers relieve 9th. Royal Sussex in Right Section Trenches. Camp to which 9th. Royal Sussex will proceed on relief will be notified later.
(b). 13th. Middlesex Regt. relieve garrisons of 7th. Northamptons:-
    KEMMEL CHATEAU - 1 company.) To be completed as
    S.P.10.   - 1 platoon.) soon as possible
    FORT REGINA   - 1 section.) after dusk.

    FORT SASKETCHEWAN-15 N.C.O's) To be completed by
                           and men.) 3 p.m. 1st. July.
(c).7th. Northamptons. will relieve 7th. N.Fusiliers as far northwards as N.24.a.5.5. (Trench J.3.N. inclusive to 73rd. Infantry Brigade).
(d).17th. Trench Mortar Battery relieves 73rd. Trench Mortar Battery in Right Section.
(e).73rd. Company Machine Gun Corps relieves 149th. Coy. Machine Gun Corps in J.1. (1 gun).

Night 2nd./3rd. July.
(a). 17th. Coy. Machine Gun Corps relieves 73rd. Company Machine Gun Corps in Right Section (7 guns).
(b). 73rd. Trench Mortar Battery relieves 149th. Trench Mortar Battery in new area (1 Stokes gun).

3.   All other details of reliefs will be arranged between C.O's direct.

4.   All Trench Stores, Defence Schemes, Trench Maps, Log Books, Intelligence Reports, Tables of work in hand and proposed, and all documents and information which may be of value to relieving units will be handed over.
       Lists of Trench Stores and lists of documents handed or taken over will be forwarded to Brigade Headquarters within 48 hours of relief being completed.

5.   Completion of reliefs will be notified by wiring b the name of the present C.O.

6.   P L E A S E   A C K N O W L E D G E.

                R Howlett
ISSUED AT 10 a.m.   Major,
       Brigade Major, 73rd. Infantry Brigade.

    Copy No. 1. File.
          2. War Diary.
          3. "G" 24 Div.
          4. "Q" 24 Div.
          5. 17 I.B.
          6. 72 I.B.
          7. 149.I.B.
          8. A.P.M. 24 Div.
          9. 251 F.A.B.
         10. 2nd. Leinsters.
         11. 9th. R.Sussex.
         12. 7th. Northamptons.
         13. 13th. Middlesex.
         14. 73rd. M.G.Coy.
         15. 73rd. T.M.Battery.
         16. Bde. Sigs.
         17. B.T.O. 73 I.B.

H 2, H 3, 50 rifles, 1 Lewis gun.

J 1 + J 2 45 " (J 2 to J 3 to new J5 reinforcement

J 3 R 7 tankers by night go to J 2 by day.

H 5 by night 24, T 10 24 by night

73rd Inf.Bde.
24th Div.

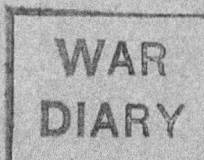

7th BATTN. THE NORTHAMPTONSHIRE REGIMENT.

J U L Y

1 9 1 6

Attached:

Appendices 1 to 4.

WAR DIARY
or
INTELLIGENCE SUMMARY.
(Erase heading not required.)

Army Form C. 2118.

1/7/1 73/M - 7/M - 24 July 9 Nortrants

Vol 10

CONFIDENTIAL.

WAR DIARY

of

7th (S). Battn. NORTHAMPTONSHIRE REGIMENT

for the month of J U L Y

1 9 1 6.

In the Field.

July 31st. 1916.

Army Form C. 2118.

WAR DIARY
or
INTELLIGENCE SUMMARY
(Erase heading not required.)

Place	Date	Hour	Summary of Events and Information	Remarks and references to Appendices
KEMMEL.	1/7/16.		Wind S.W. Orders received that a readjustment of the Brigade line will soon take place. From 9 to 10 a.m. the Hun shelled our front line with H.E. Shrapnel, Trench Mortars and Rifle Grenades. No damage done. Two enemy Aeroplanes observing during this shelling were repeatedly driven off by our A.A. guns. 2nd Lieut. Greenwood detailed to report to O.C. 73rd Trench Mortar Battery. Report on enemy wire attached. Operation Orders received at 10 a.m. Afternoon quiet. B Company in KEMMEL CHATEAU relieved by 13th Middlesex Regt and proceed to line to take over new trenches from 7th Bn. Northumberland Fusiliers as far North as N.24.a.5.5. (Sheet 28). Battalion Headquarters at DOCTORS HOUSE relieved by Headquarters, 13th Middlesex Regt and proceeded to new Headquarters at FORT SASKATCHEWAN. Only three dug-outs at present available there - others are being built under the supervision of R.E.	See appendix No 1. See appendix No 2
	2/7/16.		Trench Mortars very active all day most of them dropping behind our front line. Wind S.W. At 5 p.m. we sent over 3 Trench Mortars two of which made good, one being a "dud". Between 5 p.m. and 7 p.m. our Artillery retaliated on the enemy Trench Mortar Battery. The enemy wire cut by our bombardment on 28th prox. does not yet seem to have been repaired. Situation more or less quiet.	
	3/7/16.		Situation quiet. Wind S.W. Aeroplane activity during morning and afternoon.	

Army Form C. 2118.

WAR DIARY
or
INTELLIGENCE SUMMARY

(Erase heading not required.)

Instructions regarding War Diaries and Intelligence Summaries are contained in F. S. Regs., Part II. and the Staff Manual respectively. Title Pages will be prepared in manuscript.

Place	Date	Hour	Summary of Events and Information	Remarks and references to Appendices
KEMMEL.	3/7/16.		The enemy has repaired his wire now in several places. D Company relieved in line by 2nd Liensters (1 Coy) and return to KEMMEL SHELTERS.	
	4/7/16.		Wind S. Situation quiet. About 6 p.m. enemy Artillery opened on our Support line but was stopped by our retaliation. No casualties were caused. Battalion relieved by 2nd Leinster Regt in right sector and by 13th Middlesex in left sector and proceeded to KEMMEL SHELTERS. Total casualties for the tour - 1 Officer and 4 O.R. Killed, 1 39 O.R. Wounded (including 4 "slightly at duty"). No casualties on relief.	
KEMMEL SHELTERS.	5/7/17.		Weather fine. Working party of 200 found for 9 p.m. Situation quiet.	
	6/7/16.		Operation Orders for move to Divisional Rserve received this morning. Battalion relieved at KEMMEL SHELTERS by 9th Royal Sussex Regt. Paraded at 2.30 p.m. and marched to WAKEFIELD HUTS via LOCRE. Working parties of 200 found and taken to destination in wagons.	
LOCRE.	7/7/16.		Weather stormy. Inspection of Clothing, Arms etc. Working party of 200 paraded and 8.30 p.m. but were dismissed on order being received that all Divisional Working parties cancelled.	
	8/7/16.		Weather fine. Company Drill and usual parades. No working parties found. Operation Orders regarding relief of the Brigade received.	See appendices No 3
	9/7/16.		Weather fine.	

Army Form C. 2118.

WAR DIARY
or
INTELLIGENCE SUMMARY

(Erase heading not required.)

Instructions regarding War Diaries and Intelligence Summaries are contained in F.S. Regs., Part II. and the Staff Manual respectively. Title Pages will be prepared in manuscript.

Place	Date	Hour	Summary of Events and Information	Remarks and references to Appendices
LOCRE.	9/7/16.		Boxing Contests took place in the evening. No working parties.	
	10/7/16.		Operation Orders received from Brigade. At 9 p.m. our "Cutting out" party of 1 Officer and 24 O.R. paraded and were inspected by Major-General J.E.Capper C.B. Commanding 24th Division and proceeded to the trenches in G.S. wagons. At 12.55 a.m. the party left the front line from N.30.a.3.7. (Sheet 28) to effect a raid on the enemy front line trenches at N.30.a.4.8. On the party reaching the enemy wire it was discovered to be not completely cut through. At 12.58 a.m. our Artillery on the 17th Brigade front opened fire with the result that various flares were at once sent up all along the line. Two wire cutters who were busy cutting the remaining wire were discovered, and the enemy immediately manned his front line trench very thickly and reinforcements were heard hurrying to their front line. In spite of the heavy fire with rifles and grenades the wire was eventually cut and the party worked their way through and lay between the enemy wire and his front line parapet. As soon as the red and green lights were up the enemy opened a Minenwerfer and Artillery fire on our front line trenches making all communications with the party impossible As the element of surprise was missing and there was much congestion of German troops in their front line, it was thought that the greatest loss would be inflicted on the enemy by bombing into their congested trenches and L/Cpl Rogers, Ptes Smith, Gandell, and Brown crept to the top of their parapet and threw bombs into the trenches for a considerable time with good effect. The rest of the party remained where they were for about 40 minutes all in order and formed up in order their parties and when the fire slackened returned to our front line trench bringing their casualties (3 Wounded) with them, and returned to WAKEFIELD HUTS.	See appendices No 4
	11/7/16.		Cleaning up Camp. Battalion parades at 9.15 p.m. and marches via DRANOUTRE - NEUVE EGLISE to WULVERGHEM trenches 141 - C.3. relieving 8th Queens Regiment	

Army Form C. 2118.

WAR DIARY
or
INTELLIGENCE SUMMARY

(Erase heading not required.)

Instructions regarding War Diaries and Intelligence Summaries are contained in F. S. Regs., Part II. and the Staff Manual respectively. Title Pages will be prepared in manuscript.

Place	Date	Hour	Summary of Events and Information	Remarks and references to Appendices
WULVERGHEM.	11/7/16.		(9th Royal Sussex on our left). Battalion Headquarters at McBRIDES MANSIONS. A Company at BARBARY COAST, B Company in 141 and 141, C Company C.2 - C.3., D Company at FORBES TERRACE. Relief completed without casualties.	
	12/7/16.		Situation quiet. Enemy Artillery quiet. A few H.Es over Battery positions about 9 p.m. 1 B.R. seriously wounded.	
	13/7/16.		Situation quiet. Wind W. Enemy Artillery fairly quiet in this sector. Machineguns active after dark.	
	14/7/16.		Wind variable - W to N. Situation quiet. Our Artillery active during evening	
	15/7/16.		Wind W. Morning quiet. Enemy Aeroplanes over our lines driven off by our A.A.guns between 8 a.m. and 9 a.m. Between 1 p.m. and 2 p.m. C.2. and C.3. were whiz-banged. Our Artillery very active all day cutting the enemy wire and at 5.15 p.m. shelled the enemy front line At 11 p.m. first batch of 52 gas cylinders were carried up to C.3. and at 11.5 p.m. a second batch of 32 were taken up. This was completed without a hitch or casualty.	
	16/7/16.		Morning fine. Wind W. Our Artillery busy all the morning cutting wire. Enemy retaliation very weak. Carrying party provided for batch of 42 cylinders and taken up to C.4.	
	17/7/16.		Situation quiet. Our Artillery active during day. Orders for the proposed gas discharge in collaberation with the 17th Brigade's minor enterprise tonight issued to Companies.	

Army Form C. 2118.

WAR DIARY
or
INTELLIGENCE SUMMARY

(Erase heading not required.)

Instructions regarding War Diaries and Intelligence Summaries are contained in F. S. Regs., Part II. and the Staff Manual respectively. Title Pages will be prepared in manuscript.

Place	Date	Hour	Summary of Events and Information	Remarks and references to Appendices
WULVERGHEM.	17/7/16.		As the wind changed to N.N.E. gas could not be used. Enemy machine guns active during night.	
	18/7/16.		Wind variable N to N.N.E. Artillery still active during morning and afternoon shelling MESSINES. Wing unfavourable for discharging Gas. 2nd Lieuts Hartigan, Mattock, Harston, Lea, Page and Morton joined today from 8th Battalion.	
	19/7/16.		Wind variable NW. to N.E. Artillery active during morning but quiet later. Enemy shelled MORTAR FARM with a few H.E. Shrapnel this morning. A few whiz-bangs put into C.2. about 1 p.m. No damage done. Operation Orders for move to Rest Area received.	
	20/7/16.		Situation normal. Wind N.W. Artillery less active than previous days. Battalion relieved by the 12th Kings Liverpool Regt and marched back to BULFORD HUTS where Motor busses and G.S. wagons were waiting to take the party to GODEWAERSVELDE the Battalion billeting area. Transport followed later and arrived about 4 a.m.	
GODEWAERSVELDE.	21/7/16.		Troops rested and cleaned their equipment etc.	
	22/7/16.		Inspection of Iron Rations and equipment by Commanding Officer. All Companies issued with necessaries and clothing complete.	
	23/7/16.		Physical training and Company training. Preparations made for the move. All surplus Kit returned to store at BAILLEUL and all stores cut down to minimum.	
	24/7/16.		Battalion entrained at GODEWAERSVELDE by 7.30 a.m. and proceeded via HAZEBROUCK - BETHUNE - St POL - DOULLENS r AMIENS - to SALEAX where the Battalion detrained. Billetting parties were sent ahead from here on cycles.	

2449 Wt. W1957/M90 750,000 1/16 J.B.C. & A. Forms/C.2118/12.

Army Form C. 2118.

WAR DIARY
or
INTELLIGENCE SUMMARY
(Erase heading not required.)

Instructions regarding War Diaries and Intelligence Summaries are contained in F. S. Regs., Part II. and the Staff Manual respectively. Title Pages will be prepared in manuscript.

Place	Date	Hour	Summary of Events and Information	Remarks and references to Appendices
MOLLIENS-VIDAME.	24/7/16.		After an hours' halt the Battalion commenced to march to MOLLIENS-VIDAME marching through CLAIRY - PISSY - FLUY - and BOUGAINVILLE, arriving about 12 midnight.	
	25/7/16.		Day spent in cleaning up and resting.	
	26/7/16.		Training carried on.	
	27/7/16.		Training - Extended Order drill. Special classes at Bayonet Fighting held.	
	28/7/16.		Training - Bayonet fighting - Company and Platoon drill.	
	29/7/16.		Bathing of Companies at improvised baths at CHAU near OISSY.	
	30/7/16.		Training - Wood fighting. - Bayonet fighting. Operation orders for the move received.	
	31/7/16.		Battalion paraded at 4 a.m. Busses arrived at 5.30 a.m. and conveyed the Battalion to HANGEST where they entrained at 9 a.m. Detrainment at VECQUEMONT. Battalion then marched off proceeding via CORBIE to SAILLY le SEC where billets were already found.	

A P P E N D I C E S

1 to 4

SECRET.

HEADQUARTERS 73rd BDE.
No. C. 473.
Date 28. 6. 16.

Officer Commanding,
    2nd. Leinster Regt.
    9th. Royal Sussex Regt.
    7th. Northamptonshire Regt.
    13th. Middlesex Regt.
    73rd. Company Machine Gun Corps.
    73rd. Light Trench Mortar Battery.

No 1

    The following re-adjustments of the line will very shortly take place:-

    (a). 17th. Infantry Brigade will take over the section now held by the 9th. Royal Sussex.
    (b). The 73rd. Infantry Brigade will extend northwards as far as about N.24.a.4.7 (exact point will be notified later)

2.   Boundaries of the 73rd. Infantry Brigade will be:-

Northern Boundary.
    The road from LA POLKA through squares N.22.a., N.22.b., N.23.a., N.23.b.6.0. to a point in the front line trenches opposite the Northern end of PETIT BOIS.

Southern Boundary.
    The road from LINDENHOEK cross roads past SPY FARM to N.29.b.7.3, thence the road through point N.29.b.5½.7 to the front line trench (F.5.). The above road inclusive to Southern Brigade).

3.   (a). Reconnaissance by Battalions affected will be notified.
    (b). O's.C. 73rd. Company Machine Gun Corps and 73rd. Light Trench Mortar Battery will arrange with their opposite numbers of the 149th. Infantry Brigade for an early reconnaissance of the positions that now come within the new Brigade Area.

4.   Details will be issued in due course.

R Howlett

H.Q. 73 I.B.
28. 6. 16.
    Major,
    Brigade Major, 73rd. Infantry Brigade.

Secret.

7 Nakamkhwahe

HEADQUARTERS 73rd BDE.
No. C.173
Date 29/6/16

Ref attached, I have just heard from
149. I.B. that about 130 men at present
hold this part of the line. The B/G has
decided for the present to hold this
line with 3 coys. in front and 1 in
support at S.P.10. Will you be prepared
to carry this out at short notice? The
Officers of the Coy. selected to take over
this new part of the line should reconnoitre
it to-day.

You will be relieved of finding
Garrisons in full :-

    S. P. 10
    FORT REGINA
    " SASKATCHEWAN.

The B/G would be glad to receive
any remarks you may wish to make
on above, as soon as possible.

29/6/16.

R. Howlett Major
Bm, 73 I.B.

No 2

Report on Enemy Wire.

In front of H1A — Old wire: obscured by grass. Very bad on crest of hill on left. (MAEDELSTEDE Fm.)

G3 — Steel Post Pickets. Very bad. Posts knocked over & wire blown about.

G2 — D°. No attempt has been made to repair damage to wire or parapet here.

G2-1 — From Point 61 to Peckham Stakes wire blown about badly. Two large gaps about 6 feet across in enemy's main wire.

G1 (Glory Hole) — Wire here is considerably better & of good density. It appears to have been untouched by Shell fire but is rather low say from 3'6" to 4'.

30/6/16.

R W B Houghton
7th Northampton Regt Lieut

SECRET.

Ref.
Sheet 28
1/40,000.

No 3

COPY NO. 11

73rd. INFANTRY BRIGADE.
OPERATION ORDER NO. 50.

– 8 JUN 1916

1. The 73rd. Infantry Brigade will be relieved by the 150th. Infantry Brigade as per attached table.
   Transport Lines will remain as at present till further orders.

2. Battalions will send on advanced parties to take over billets or camps in daylight.

3. Units will hand over to corresponding units of the 150th. Infantry Brigade:-

   All Trench Stores.
   Defence Schemes.
   Log Books.
   Intelligence Reports.
   Tables of work in hand and proposed.
   All documents and information which may be of value.

   Lists of above will be forwarded to Brigade Headquarters within 48 hours of relief being complete.

4. All other details to be arranged between O.s.C. direct.

5. Completion of relief will be notified to Brigade Headquarters by wiring the word "PARTRIDGE".

6.   P L E A S E   A C K N O W L E D G E.

ISSUED AT 2 p.m.
                 R Howlett   Major,
         Brigade Major, 73rd. Infantry Brigade.

Copy No. 1. File.
       2. War Diary.
       3. "G" 24 Div.
       4. "Q" 24 Div.
       5. 17 I.B.
       6. 150 I.B.
       7. A.P.M. 24 Div.
       8. 24 Div. Art'y.
       9. 2nd. Leinsters.
     10. 9th. Royal Sussex Regt.
     11. 7th. Northamptonshire Regt.
     12. 13th. Middlesex Regt.
     13. 73rd. Coy. M.G.Corps.
     14. 73rd. Light T.M.Battery.
     15. 129th. Fd.Coy. R.E.
     16. 107th. Coy. A.S.C.
     17. B.T.O., 73 I.B.
     18. Bde. Sigs. 73 I.B.

RELIEF OF THE 73rd. INFANTRY BRIGADE BY THE 150th. INFANTRY BRIGADE.

DATE.	UNIT.	FROM.	TO.	RELIEVING UNIT.	REMARKS.
July 8th.	9th. R.Sussex.	KEMMEL SHELTERS.	DRANOUTRE.	6th. N.Fusiliers.	9th. R.Sussex to be clear of KEMMEL SHELTERS by 8.20/-
"	73rd. M.G.Corps.	Trenches.	M.24.b.1.1.	150th.M.G.Corps.	Relief to be completed by 8 p.m.
"	1 coy., 13th.Middlesex.	KEMMEL CHATEAU.	BADAJOS HUTS.	1 coy. 4th.East Yorks.	" " " " 9 p.m.
Night 8th/9th. July.	2nd. Leinsters.	Right Section Trenches.	DONCASTER HUTS.	4th. Yorks.	Relief commences at dusk.
"	13th.Middlesex.	Left Section Trenches.	BADAJOS HUTS.	4th. Yorks.	" " " "
"	73rd.T.M.Battery.	Trenches.	No.19.d.5.4.	150/- T.M.Battery.	
"	7th. Northamptons.				Remain at WAKEFIELD HUTS.
"	H.Q. 73 I.B.	N.20.d.2.5.	LOGRE (M.23.a.2.8.)		Command of Sector passes to B.G.C., 150th. Infantry Brigade on completion of reliefs in Trenches G.1. to J.3.R.

H.Q. 73 I.B.
8. 7. 16.

ISSUED WITH 73rd. INFANTRY BRIGADE OPERATION ORDER NO.50 dated 8. 7. 16.

SECRET.   No 4   COPY NO:- 17

Ref. Sheet 28. 1/40,000.

73rd. INFANTRY BRIGADE.
OPERATION ORDER NO. 51.

H.Q. 73 I.B., July 11th. 1916.

1. The following reliefs and moves will take place to-night 11th./12th. July.

(a). 7th. Northamptons will relieve 8th. Queens in trenches 141 to C.3 (both inclusive)
Battalion Headquarters will be at MC.BRIDES MANSIONS. BARBARY COAST will be taken over. STRATHCONA Terrace will remain in 72nd. Infantry Brigade area.

(b). 9th. Royal Sussex will relieve 12th. Royal Fusiliers in trenches C.4 to D.4 (both inclusive).
Battalion Headquarters will be at ST.QUENTINS CABERET. On relief 12th. Royal Fusiliers to WAKEFIELD HUTS.

(c). 2nd. Leinsters will move to BULFORD HUTS and be in Brigade Reserve. Time of move will be notified.

(d). 13th. Middlesex will move to DRANOUTRE and be in Divisional Reserve. Officer Commanding, 9th. Royal Sussex will notify Officer Commanding, 13th. Middlesex at what hour his battalions will be clear of DRANOUTRE.

(e). Arrangements for relief of Machine Gun Company and Light Trench Mortar Battery in the Sectors handed over will be made direct between the Commanders concerned. Personnel etc. not going into the forward area will be accommodated in camp to be notified.

2. Officer Commanding 9th. Royal Sussex and 7th. Northamptons will send one Officer per Company and one N.C.O. per platoon into the trenches during early afternoon to-day.
Advanced parties of units proceeding to camps, billets, etc., will be sent to take over during daylight. 13th. Middlesex will arrange with 9th. Royal Sussex direct.
Arrangements for other units will be notified.

3. All Trench Stores, Defence Schemes, Log Books, Intelligence Reports, tables of work in hand and proposed, and all documents and information which may be of value will be handed over.
Lists of Trench Stores and documents handed over will be forwarded to Brigade Headquarters within 48 hours of relief being completed.

4. Transport Lines will be as under:-

9th. Royal Sussex.)
13th. Middlesex Regt.) as at present.
7th. Northamptons.)
2nd. Leinsters.) T.27.d.6.2. (late transport lines of 2nd. Leinsters).

73rd. Coy. M.G.Corps.   To be notified.

Brigade Headquarters.   To be notified.

5. Boundaries have already been notified.

6. All other details will be arranged between O's.C. direct.

P.T.O.

2.

7. Brigade Headquarters will be at LOCRE till 10 p.m., and after that hour at place to be notified.

8. Completion of reliefs will be notified to Brigade Headquarters by wiring the word "APRICOT".

9. P L E A S E   A C K N O W L E D G E.

                                               Captain,
ISSUED AT 7 a.m.   for Major,
                      Brigade Major, 73rd. Infantry Brigade.

Copy No. 1. War Diary
          2. File.
          3. "G" 24 Div.
          4. "Q" 24 Div.
          5. C.R.A., 24 Div.
          6. A.P.M., 24 Div.
          7. C.R.E., 24 Div.
          8. 17 I.B.
          9. 72 I.B.
         10. 2nd. Leinsters.
         11. 9th. Royal Sussex.
         12. 7th. Northamptons.
         13. 13th. Middlesex.
         14. 73rd. Coy. M.G. Corps.
         15. 73rd. Light T.M. Battery.
         16. 129th. Fd. Coy. R.E.
         17. 197th. Coy. A.S.C.
         18. B.T.O., 73 I.B.
         19. O.C., Bde. Sigs.

73rd Brigade.
24th Division.

7th BATTALION.

NORTHAMPTONSHIRE REGIMENT.

August 1916.

Army Form C. 2118.

73
Vol 11

WAR DIARY
or
INTELLIGENCE SUMMARY.
(Erase heading not required.)

Instructions regarding War Diaries and Intelligence Summaries are contained in F. S. Regs., Part II. and the Staff Manual respectively. Title pages will be prepared in manuscript.

Place	Date	Hour	Summary of Events and Information	Remarks and references to Appendices
			CONFIDENTIAL. WAR DIARY of 7th (Service) Bn. NORTHAMPTONSHIRE REGIMENT FOR THE MONTH OF AUGUST 1916. ------------ In the Field.	

Army Form C. 2118.

WAR DIARY
or
INTELLIGENCE SUMMARY.

(Erase heading not required.)

Instructions regarding War Diaries and Intelligence Summaries are contained in F. S. Regs., Part II. and the Staff Manual respectively. Title pages will be prepared in manuscript.

Place	Date	Hour	Summary of Events and Information	Remarks and references to Appendices
SAILLY-LE-SEC.	1.8.16.		Day spent in bathing in the SOMME CANAL and Kit Inspection. Operation Orders for move tomorrow received.	Appendix No 1.
	2.8.16.		Weather hot and dry. Battalion paraded at 5.15 p.m. and marched to Reserve area at HAPPY VALLEY near BRAY SUR SOMME a distance of 6 miles arriving there about 8 p.m. Tents and bivouacs erected. Heavy bombardment all along the line during the night.	
HAPPY VALLEY.	3.8.16.		Weather hot and dry. Physical Training, Bayonet fighting etc.	
	4.8.16.		Weather fine but cool. Liaison between Infantry and Aeroplanes for Officers in the evening. Bayonet fighting, Kit inspections, etc.	
	5.8.16.		Weather fine. Company and Platoon drill. Bayonet fighting. Company distinguishing marks worn by all ranks.	
	6.8.16.		Weather fine and windy. Physical training etc. Voluntary services in morning and evening.	
	7.8.16.		Weather fine. Training carried on as usual.	
	8.8.16.		Physical drill and Bayonet fighting in the morning. Battalion paraded in marching order at 2.15 p.m. and moved off to new camp at F.21.b. Sheet 62D, formerly occupied by 99th Brigade. On arrival there bivouacs were made by the men.	
	9.8.16.		Orders received that the Battalion is relieving 55th Division tonight in the line. No training taking place. Commanding Officer and one Officer	

Army Form C. 2118.

WAR DIARY
or
INTELLIGENCE SUMMARY.
(Erase heading not required.)

Instructions regarding War Diaries and Intelligence Summaries are contained in F. S. Regs., Part II. and the Staff Manual respectively. Title pages will be prepared in manuscript.

Place	Date	Hour	Summary of Events and Information	Remarks and references to Appendices.
Nr. THE CITADEL.	9.8.16.		proceed up the line to reconnoitre. Move eventually cancelled.	
	10.8.16.		Weather misty and slight rain. Companies detailed for salvage work in collecting duck-boards, pickets etc, in this area.	
	11.8.16.		Battalion parade for practice attack in conjunction with the 13th Middlesex Regt at 9 a.m. and return about 12.30.	
	12.8.16.		Weather misty. Battalion parade at 9 a.m. for practice attack etc till 12 noon. Brigade distinguishing badges now received.	
	13.8.16.		Usual training 9-11 a.m. Voluntary services held in Camp.	
MONTAUBAN.	14.8.16.		Orders received to be ready to relieve 9th Royal Sussex at the CRATERS (A.8.c.). Further orders to carry out the relief received later. Battalion paraded at 5 p.m. and march via CARNOY to original British front line trenches. Battalion Headquarters and B & D Companies there, A & C Companies at MONTAUBON. Heavy shelling of gun positions between here and MARICOURT.	
	15.8.16.		Weather stormy. Working parties for digging Communication trenches through TRONES WOOD found by B & D Companies during morning. Two casualties in A Company caused by Shrapnel. Heavy shelling of gun positions during morning and early afternoon.	
	16.8.16.		Orders received to take over the line but were eventually cancelled.	

2353 Wt. W2544/1454 700,000 5/15 D.D.& L.   A.D.S.S./Forms/C. 2118.

Army Form C. 2118.

WAR DIARY
or
INTELLIGENCE SUMMARY
(Erase heading not required.)

Instructions regarding War Diaries and Intelligence Summaries are contained in F. S. Regs., Part II. and the Staff Manual respectively. Title pages will be prepared in manuscript.

Place	Date	Hour	Summary of Events and Information	Remarks and references to Appendices
MONTAUBAN.	17.8.16.		Issuing of Ammunition and Bombs in the morning. Operation orders received at 3.30 p.m. Battalion Operation orders issued. The Battalion moved forward at 4 p.m. and proceeded to the left Section trenches relieving the 8th Bn. Royal West Kents (72nd Brigade). Heavy shelling of rear area during night.	Appendix No 7. Appendix No 3
GUILLEMONT.	18.8.16.		Lieut & Q.M. Wall joined today. Major Murphy took over vice C.O. wounded. The Battalion attacked the QUARRY, GUILLEMONT at 3 p.m. and succeeded in reaching the left half of their objective, the right being driven back. Detailed Company reports :-	Appendix No 4
	19.8.16.		Battalion relieved by Royal West Kents and returned to the CRATERS (old German front line).	
MONTAUBAN.	20.8.16.		Battalion paraded and were addressed by the Brigadier General Commanding 73rd Brigade who complimented them on their conduct in the attack. Carrying party found at 3.10 p.m. Major Murphy rejoined the 2nd Leinster Regt and Captain H.B.King assumed command. Casualty Lists prepared and total casualties found to be :- Killed, Officers 5, O.R. 45, Wounded, Officers 15, O.R. 258, Missing, Officers 1, O.R. 49. Officers Casualties :- KILLED. 2/Lt.G.V.Nott. 2/Lt.H.Lloyd. 2/Lt.N.S.Beall. 2nd/Lt.A.C.D.Page. 2nd/Lt.M.B.Lea. WOUNDED. Lt.Col.E.R.Lobbs. Capt.H.Grierson. Lieut A.B.Cox. Lieut S.H.Notion. Lieut P.S.Hadley. Lieut R.T.R.Houghton. 2nd.Lt.E.G.Butcher. 2ndLt. H.Harris. 2nd Lt.C.D.Morgan. 2nd Lt. D.Morris. 2nd Lt. A.W.Holland. 2nd Lt. N.Mattock. 2nd Lt. A.Durrant Swaq. 2nd Lt. C.A.Debenham. 2nd Lt.C.F.Saunders. MISSING. 2nd Lt.T.J.Hartigan.	

Army Form C. 2118.

WAR DIARY
or
INTELLIGENCE SUMMARY.
(Erase heading not required.)

Instructions regarding War Diaries and Intelligence Summaries are contained in F. S. Regs., Part II. and the Staff Manual respectively. Title pages will be prepared in manuscript.

Place	Date	Hour	Summary of Events and Information	Remarks and references to Appendices
MONTAUBAN.	21.8.16.		Draft of 110 O.R. arrived today from Base. Operation orders for relief received at midnight.	
Nr. MEAULTE.	22.8.16.		Battalion area cleaned up. Billetting party sent on in advance. Battalion relieved by Kings Royal Rifles, 60th Brigade at 11.30 a.m. and proceeded to the Camp at the SAND-PIT area (E.8.c. Sheet 62D) via CARNOY arriving there at 2 p.m. Draft of 100 O.R. of the Essex Cyclists arrived today.	Appendices No 5.
	23.8.16.		Weather fine. Working party of 200 found for loading etc at EDGEHILL SIDING from 8.30 a.m to 5.30 p.m. New Drafts inspected by Brigadier General Commanding. Later received from Major Murphy 2nd Leinsters complimenting the Battalion on their conduct under fire. Major E.Lascelles, 11 Rifle Brigade arrived today and assumed temporary Command.	
	24.8.16.		Weather wet at first, fine later. Drafts inspected by General Officer Commanding 24th Division at 8 a.m. Draft of 40 O.R. arrived from the Northants Regt. Major E.Lascelles rejoined his Battalion today and Captain H.B.King reassumed command. Orders received at 4 a.m. that the Battalion would move at 8 a.m. to new area near DERNANCOURT. Orders issued to all concerned accordingly.	
	25.8.16.		Battalion paraded at 8 a.m. ready to move off with Transport on the road when orders received that move was cancelled till afternoon so the Battalion remained at the Camp and carried on with the training. Orders received at 2 p.m. that the move would take place at 5 p.m.. Battalion paraded at 5 pm and moved off marching via MEAULTE to Camping ground North of DERNANCOURT (E.13.c. Sheet 62D.). Weather very stormy and damp. Few tents available so bivouacs made.	

Army Form C. 2118

WAR DIARY
or
INTELLIGENCE SUMMARY.
(Erase heading not required.)

Instructions regarding War Diaries and Intelligence Summaries are contained in F. S. Regs., Part II. and the Staff Manual respectively. Title pages will be prepared in manuscript.

Place	Date	Hour	Summary of Events and Information	Remarks and references to Appendices
Nr. DERNANCOURT.	26.8.16.		Training of Specialists carried on. Company and Platoon drill, Bayonet fighting etc. Draft of 76 Other Ranks arrived at 6 p.m.	
	27.8.16.		Weather stormy. Battalion addressed by General Officer Commanding 24th Division at 10 a.m. Bayonet fighting, physical drill etc. Lecture by Assistant Instructor of Gymnasium at 3 p.m. today. Extra tents drawn from Brigade for the men.	
	28.8.16.		Weather fine. Physical drill. Bathing in afternoon in R. ANCRE. Bayonet fighting for drafts.	
	29.8.16.		Weather gusty. Training as usual. Orders received to shift Camp to a position on opposite side of valley. Just before camp was struck it commenced to rain very heavily. Move completed by 8 p.m. Orders received that Battalion would take over Support line tomorrow August 30th 1916.	
	30.8.16.		Weather wet. Battalion paraded at 10 a.m. and moved off towards new line. Relieved 2nd Bn. Argyle and Sutherland Highlanders in Savoy Trench (Support line) by 6 p.m. One casualty during relief.	
	31.8.16.		Battalion Transport moved to new Camp near FRICOURT. Enemy shelling our front line trench during the whole of the day. Casualties :- 5 Killed, 32 Wounded.	

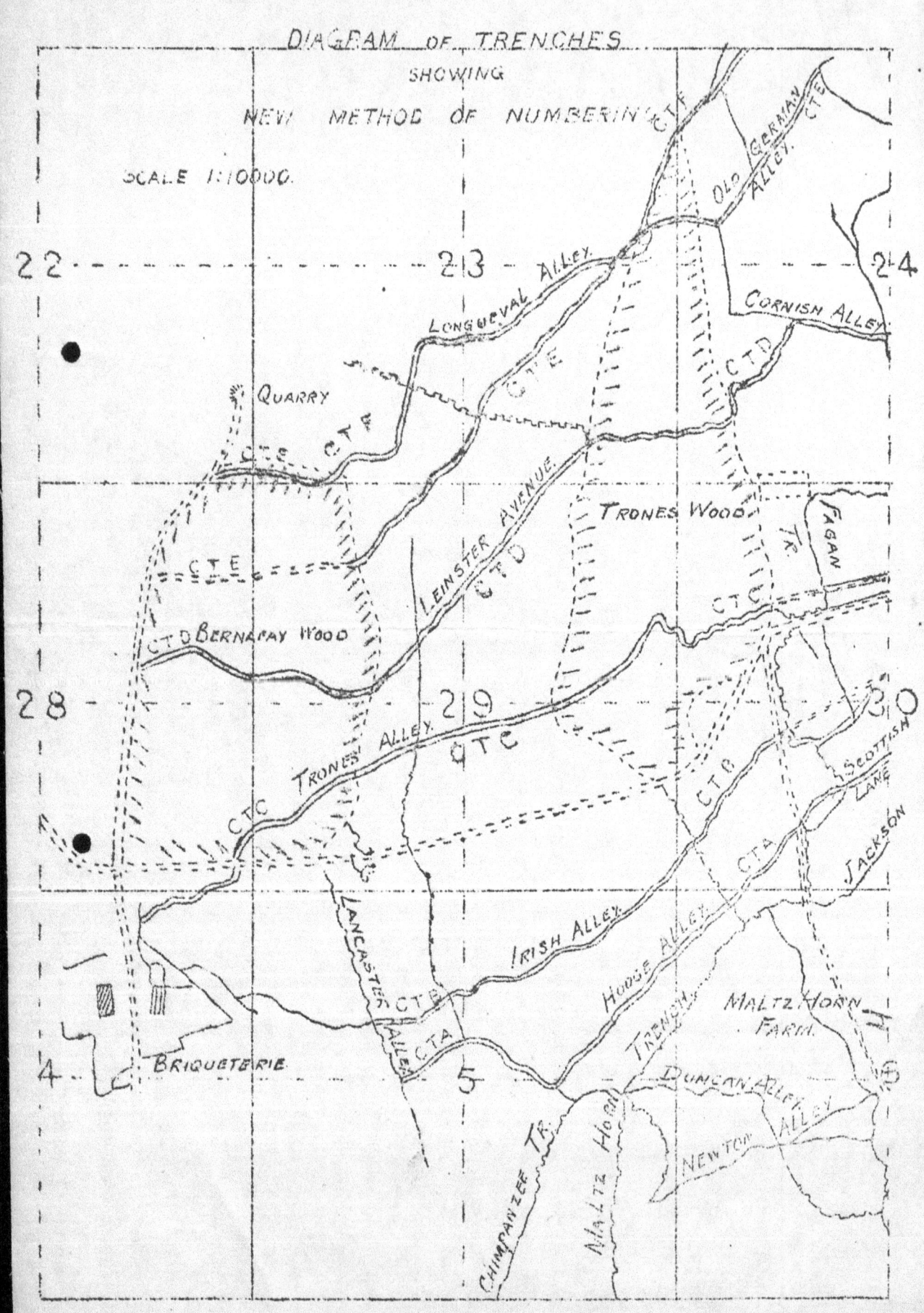

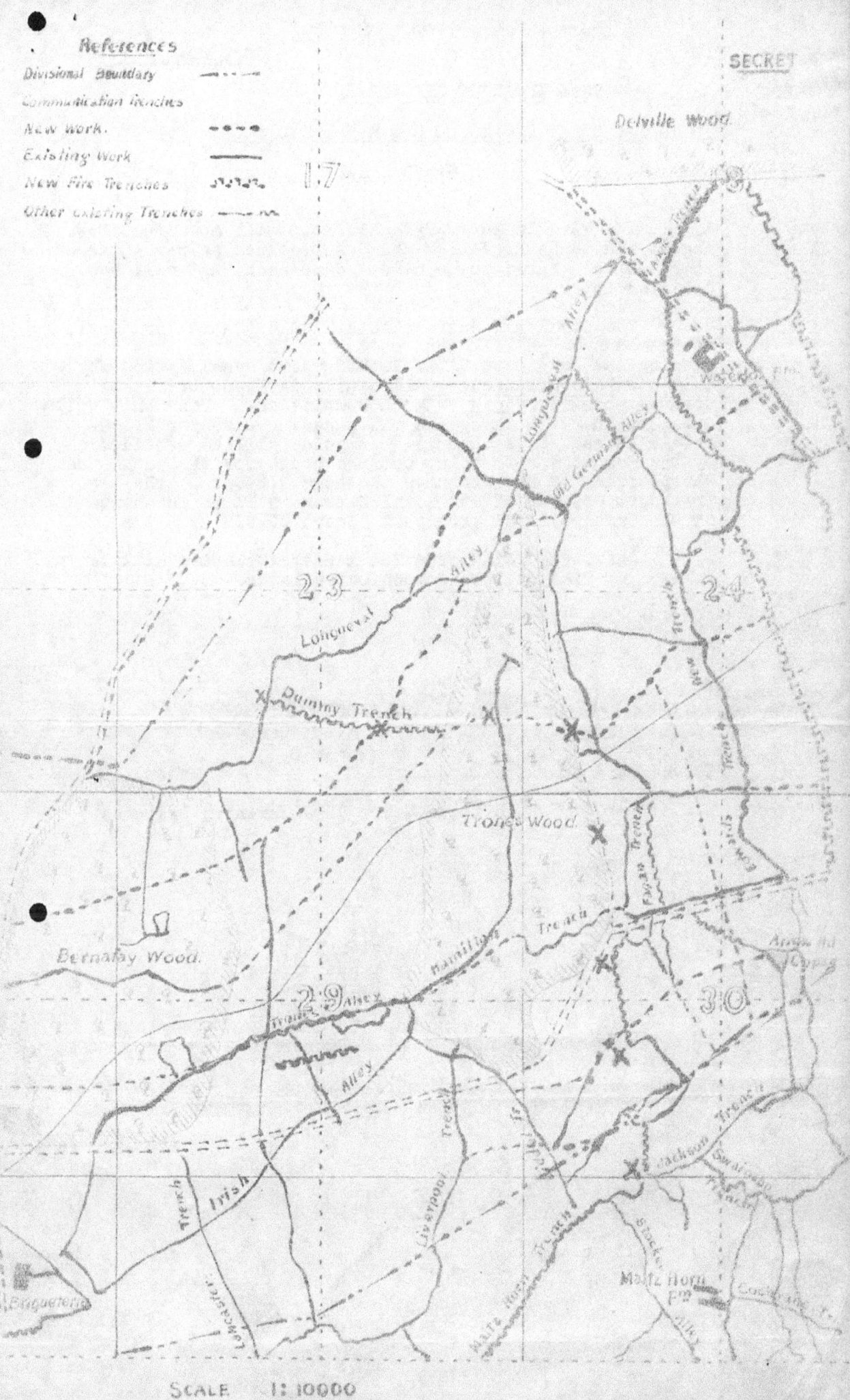

APPENDIX N° 1

SECRET.
Ref Sheet
62d
and 62d(N.E.)

COPY NO:- 7

73rd INFANTRY BRIGADE.

OPERATION ORDER NO 57.

H.Q. 73rd I.B.   August 1st 1916.

1. The 73rd Infantry Brigade Group will move tomorrow August 2nd to HAPPY VALLEY and Reserve Area as per attached time tables. Area to be allotted to each Unit will be notified later.

2. The 9th Royal Sussex, 13th Middlesex and 73rd Coy., Machine Gun Corps will send on their mens packs this evening 1st August to SAILLY-le-SEC where accomadation for them has been arranged. All available Transport to be used which will rejoin Unit on completion. Each Unit will detail a guard to safeguard the packs. A senior N.C.O. should be sent by each Unit. A guide will be provided by the Town Major to point out the house for the packs and the position of the bivouacs to these N.C.O's. The Transport Officer of 9th Royal Sussex will be in charge of the transport and arrange to leave CORBIE at 6 p.m.

3. Refilling point from 2nd August inclusive will be F.19.c.. Time will be communicated later.

R Howlett
Major,

Issued at 4 p.m.

Brigade Major 73rd Infantry Brigade.

Copy No. 1. File.
2. War Diary.
3. "G" 24 Div.
4. "Q" 24 Div.
5. 2nd Leinster Regt.
6. 9th Royal Sussex Regt.
7. 7th Northamptons.
8. 13th Middlesex Regt.
9. 73rd Machine Gun Coy.
10. 73rd L.T.M.Battery.
11. Bearer Div. (73rd F.Ambulance.)
12. 197th Coy. A.S.C.
13. 129th Coy. R.E.
14. Brigade Sigs.
15. B.T.O.

TABLE "A".

Date.	Unit.	From.	To.	Starting Point.	Time	Remarks.
2nd August.	13th Middlesex.	CORBIE.	SAILLY-LE-SEC.	Road Junction. I.36.a.5.5.	5 a.m.	These Units will bivouac at SAILLY - LE - SEC during the day. All Transport will accompany Units.
"	9th Royal Sussex.	"	"	"	5.20 a.m.	
"	73rd Coy. M.G.Corps.	"	"	"	5.40 a.m.	

TABLE "B"

DATE.	UNIT.	FROM.	STARTING POINT.	TO.	TIME.	ROUTE.	REMARKS.
2nd.Aug.	7th Northamptons.	SAILLY-le-sec.	J.18.c.8.2.	HAPPY VALLEY and Reserve Area.	6.10 p.m.	L.14.d.6.8. thence road running N.E. to destination	
"	9th R.Sussex Regt.	"	"	"	6.20 p.m.	"	
"	13th Middlesex Regt.	"	"	"	6.30 p.m.	"	
"	73rd.M.G.Company.	"	"	"	6.40 p.m.	"	
"	129th.Field Coy.R.E.	"	"	"	6.50 p.m.	"	
"	Bearer Divn. 73rd.Field Amb.	"	"	"	7.0 p.m.	"	
"	Brigade Signal Section.	VAUX.	J.27.c.3.6.	SAILLY	5.40 p.m.	SAILLY - le sec then as above.	To reach J.18.c.8.2 at 7.10 p.m.
"	2nd.Leinsters.	"	"	"	5.50 p.m.	"	To reach J.18.c.8.2 by 7.20 p.m.
"	73rd.T.M.Batty.	"	"	"	6 p.m.	"	To reach J.18.c.8.2 at 7.30 p.m.

(a) All Transport to march in rear of its respective Unit.

(b) Cross roads at K.13.d.6.2. must be cleared by tail of column at 8 p.m.

D.C.

APPENDIX No 2 / Abm 5

7th Northamptons

Zero hour on 18th August will be 2.45 pm.

Zero hour on 19th August will be 5.00 am.

Troops will shew their flares and mirrors at the following times:-

① On reaching each objective
② At 4.45 pm on Aug. 18th
③   "   6.00 am   "   "   19th
④   " 10.00 am   "   "   19th

Battalion HQ will communicate with the contact aeroplanes by panel.

R Hotblack

HQ 73rd B
18/8/16

Bde Major 7 Major
         73rd B Bde

Clg   A Co
H Coy   Lt Houghton
    B
    Capt Price
         D · Capt Brooks

SECRET.　　　　　　73rd. INFANTRY BRIGADE.

ELSIE
EE

Ref. Map.
LONGUEVAL　　OPERATION　ORDER　NO.59.(revised).
1/10,000.

1. **INFORMATION.**
The 24th. Division has been ordered to take GUILLEMONT and establish itself on a line East of the village. 73rd. Infantry Brigade and 1st. North Staffords on the right and the 17th. Infantry Brigade on the left.
Boundaries between Right and Left Brigades.
　　N.E. corner of copse at S.24.c. — road junction S.24.d.8.5. thence along BROMPTON ROAD (inclusive to 17th. Infantry Brigade)
　　S. Boundary of right brigade S.30.b.7.2. to T.25.b.1.4.

2. **OBJECTIVES.**
There will be four different objectives for the 73rd. Infantry Brigade:-
First Objective.　Enemy trench from S.30.b.7.3. to S.24.b.3.4.
Second Objective.　Enemy trench from T.25.a.3.3. to T.25.a.2.8. thence East to T.25.a.3.8. to T.19.c.3.2., thence round QUARRIES to T.19.c.2.5. thence S.24.d.8.3.
Third Objective.　Line of LONGUEVAL - GUILLEMONT road to junction of DOWN STREET & DOVER STREET thence to T.25.a.9.4.
Fourth Objective.　T.19.a.8.2. to T.19.d.3.4. thence to T.25.b.3.7. to road T.25.b.2.5.

　　On reaching first objective touch must be established with the 3rd. Division on right and 17th. Infantry Brigade on left.
　　On reaching second objective, a strong point must be established at the QUARRIES.
　　On reaching third objective, a strong post must be established at T.25.a.9.4.
　　On reaching fourth objective, strong points must be established at T.19.d.4.4. and T.19.a.9.1.
　　The work on these points will be improved by R.E. assistance as opportunity arises.

3. **CONSOLIDATION.**
　　The work of consolidation will be carried out with the greatest energy directly the objectives have been gained, and definite garrisons will be told off to each objective, who will remain and continue the work of consolidation after the troops have advanced to the next objective.
　　The advance of the 73rd. Infantry Brigade through the village of GUILLEMONT will be at the rate of 100 yards every 10 minutes.

4. **ATTACK.**
　　The attack of the 73rd. Infantry Brigade will be delivered on a frontage of two battalions as under:-
　　Right Attack.　　13th. Middlesex Regt.
　　Left Attack.　　 Vth. Northamptonshire Regt.

Right battalion. (Headquarters S.30.b.3½.0)
　　First objective enemy trench from S.30.b.7.2. to S.30.b.9.6.
　　Second objective, enemy trench from T.25.a.3.4. to T.25.a.2.8.

2.

24 D 10
S

Left Battalion. (Headquarters at S.30.a.7½.5.)
First Objective enemy trench from S.30.b.9.8. to S.24.d.7.4.
Second objective from T.25.a.2.8. to T.25.a.4.8., thence a line to point T.19.c.2.5. (including QUARRIES) to front line trench at S.24.d.8.4.

A small party of R.E. will accompany 7th. Northamptons for the purpose of blowing in entrance to the tunnel at the QUARRY. The R.E. party will report to Lt. Colonel MOBBS at S.30.a.7½.5. by 10 a.m. on the 18th. inst.

5. **ASSEMBLY TRENCHES FOR ATTACKING BATTALIONS.**
Right Battalion.
In front line trenches East of the ARROW HEAD COPSE and South of TRONES WOOD -- GUILLEMONT ROAD.
Left battalion.
In front line trenches opposite objective North of TRONES WOOD -- GUILLEMONT ROAD.

6. **ACTION OF MACHINE GUN COMPANY.**
Front line - four guns (two with each assaulting battalion)
Second line of six guns, to remain stationary during attack and give covering fire.
Brigade Reserve - six guns at Advanced Battle Headquarters.

7. **ACTION OF STOKES MORTARS.**
Two Stokes Mortars will accompany the 13th. Middlesex when they attack.
One Stokes Mortar will be in position to enfilade GUILLEMONT - MALTZ HORN FARM ROAD previous to assault.
One Mortar each will accompany 9th. Royal Sussex Regt. and the 2nd. Leinster Regt. for advance through village.
Three Mortars will be in Brigade Reserve at the BRICQUETERIE.

8. ~~ADVANCE TO THIRD OBJECTIVE OF THE 73rd. INFANTRY BRIGADE.~~

8. **SUPPORT BATTALIONS** (2nd. Leinster Regt. & 9th. Royal Sussex)
The 2nd. Leinster Regt. and 9th. Royal Sussex Regt. will move forward to occupy trenches vacated by the 13th. Middlesex and 7th. Northamptons respectively and be prepared to move forward under cover of darkness to a position of readiness in rear of first and second objectives and will assist in consolidation of both objectives.
On August 19th. at a time to be notified, both battalions will advance to third and subsequently to fourth objectives, clearing village in accordance with instructions issued in "Continuation of Operation Order No.59" (attached and revised).
Each man in these battalions will carry forward with him one of the following articles:-
One petrol can of water.
One box of Mills grenades.
Ten bandoliers of S.A.A.
One sand-bag containing ten rations.
One sand-bag containing eighty 1" Very Lights.
Two men. One box of "P" grenades.

in the proportion per battalion as follows:-
100 petrol cans of water, 40 bags of rations, 40 man loads of S.A.A., 200 boxes of Mills grenades, 20 boxes of "P" grenades and five sandbags of Very Lights, and will hand them over as required by battalions holding first and second objectives.
Details of drawing these stores will be communicated by the Staff Captain to units concerned.

9. **BATTALION IN DIVISIONAL RESERVE.**
   1st. North Staffords will be at the BRICQUETERIE and will be prepared to move at 15 minutes notice.

10. **R.E.**
   103rd. Field Coy. R.E. is allotted to the 73rd. Infantry Brigade to consolidate strong points at about T.25.a.9.4., the QUARRY, T.19.d.4.4. and T.19.a.9.1.
   Each Infantry battalion will detail 25 men and one N.C.O., and the 13th. Middlesex and 7th. Northamptons will each detail, in addition, one Officer (who can be drawn from Reserve Officers) to report to O.C., 103rd. Field Coy. R.E. at the cross roads CORNOY at 10 a.m. on the 18th. inst.
   The O.C., 103rd. Field Company, R.E. will report at Headquarters, 73rd. Infantry Brigade by 2 p.m. on 18th. inst.

11. **PIONEERS.**
   Two companies of Pioneers are allotted to the 73rd. Infantry Brigade and will dig the following Communication Trenches as opportunity occurs.
   1. Trench to be dug parallel to, and just North of, the TRONES WOOD - GUILLEMONT ROAD, from about S.30.b.4.7. to about T.25.a.0.8½. The O's.C. companies to report to Brigade Headquarters before starting work.

12. **ARTILLERY.**
   The attack will be preceeded and supported by the Heavy Artillery of the XIV and XV Corps, and by the Divisional Artillery of the 2nd. and 24th. Divisions.
   The artillery will lift, and the infantry will advance in accordance with the time table attached.
   IT IS ESSENTIAL THAT THE INFANTRY SHOULD ADVANCE AS CLOSE AS POSSIBLE UNDER THE BARRAGE, SO AS TO ENTER THEIR OBJECTIVES AS SOON AS THE DIVISIONAL ARTILLERY LIFTS ITS FIRE.

13. **ZERO HOUR.**
   This will be notified separately.
   "ZERO" is the time at which the artillery curtain comes down 100 yards in front of our trenches.

14. ROUTES, for "up" and "down" traffic will be in accordance with the sketch map issued to battalions to-day.

15. POLICE AND STRAGGLERS.
The 2nd. Leinster Regt. and 7th. Northamptons will each detail four police to form a control post at Western end of SCOTTISH TRENCH in order:-
   (a). To collect stragglers and send them back as the situation permits.
   (b). Direct wounded men to nearest Dressing Station.

16. EVACUATION OF PRISONERS.
All prisoners captured will be sent back under the necessary escort to the CRATERS (A.8.a.8.3.) where the A.P.M., 24th. Division will take them over.

17. DRESSING STATIONS.
Advanced Dressing Stations will be established at the BRICQUETRIE (A.4.b.) and the North West corner of BERNAFAY WOOD (S.28.b.9.9.)
Walking cases will proceed to BRANFAY FARM (F.29.b.)

18. DATE AND TIME OF OPERATIONS.
18th. August.
First objective – ZERO.
Second objective – ZERO + TWO HOURS.

19th. August.
Third objective – ZERO.
FOURTH " – ZERO + ONE AND A HALF HOURS.

Watches will be synchronised daily at 9 a.m., 1 p.m., and 5 p.m. till further orders.

19. RESERVE OF OFFICERS.
Five surplus Officers per battalion will report at Brigade Headquarters at 11 a.m. on the 18th. inst. and will be available to replace casualties.

20. COMMUNICATIONS.
1. The aeroplanes told off to communicate with us have a broad black band painted under each lower plane, and fly streamers from the end of both planes. Green flares will be burnt by the infantry, and mirrors will be flashed on reaching objectives and whenever our planes appear overhead. THE VITAL IMPORTANCE OF COMPLYING WITH THIS ORDER AND UTILISING EVERY OPPORTUNITY OF COMMUNICATING WITH OUR AEROPLANES AS WELL AS ORDINARY COMMUNICATION WILL AGAIN BE IMPRESSED ON ALL RANKS.
2. The positions of Report Centres and Visual stations will be as follows:-

Brigade Advanced Report Centre	S.30.c.6.3.
Right Advanced Report Centre.	S.30.b.8.6.
Left Advanced Report Centre.	S.24.d.9½.3½.
Right Battalion O.P. & visual Receiving station.	Just N. of ARROW HEAD COPSE.
Left battalion O.P. & visual receiving station.	Near junction of EDWARDS TRENCH WITH TRONES WOOD-GUILLEMONT ROAD.

One six foot periscope each will be supplied to the battalion visual receiving stations: slits 10 ft. – 11 ft. deep should be dug for these to accommodate one signaller and one observer.

5.

The positions of forward report centres must be decided by a close study of the ground, and notified to Brigade Headquarters as soon as possible by the two battalions concerned.

Half the pigeons allotted to each battalion will be kept at battalion headquarters, and the remainder will be sent forward in charge of the signallers attached to advanced or forward report centres.

3. Instructions about the installation of the I.T. set will be given by the Brigade Signalling Officer to the battalion Signalling Officer concerned.

4. The Right Battalion will arrange to send visual messages back to 24th. Division Station in PERRONNE AVENUE from a post just West of ARROW HEAD COPSE.

5. Each battalion will carry forward a telephone cable.

R Howlett
Major,
Brigade Major, 73rd. Infantry Brigade.

S E C R E T.

CONTINUATION OF OPERATION ORDER NO.59. (revised).

A. At "ZERO" 19th. inst. the third stage of the attack will be entered upon as follows:-
The 2nd. Leinster Regt. and 9th. Royal Sussex Regt. will move forward evading enemy barrage as much as possible and advance through the new front line to clear the village of GUILLEMONT, and form a line of Strong Points roughly on line HILL STREET across CHURCH SQUARE to junction of DOWN STREET and NORFOLK CRESCENT and joining up with Strong Post being formed at T.25.b.2.5.

INSTRUCTIONS FOR CLEARING VILLAGE.
The dividing line between battalions for purposes of clearing village will be the line of MOUNT STREET, 2nd. Leinsters taking South of this Street. It is suggested that two companies of each battalion be employed on this third stage, and definite tasks should be allotted to companies, platoons and sections by areas (after study of the large scale map) under the following headings:-
  (a). "Mopping up" parties.
  (b). Consolidating parties.

B. The final stage of the operation will be a further advance to East end of village, again allotting tasks as under (A) and the forming of strong points at T.19.a.9.1. (9th. Royal Sussex Regt), T.19.d.4.4.m T.25.a.9.4. and T.25.b.3.7. (2nd. Leinster Regt) and an advanced post at CEMETERY (by 2nd. Leinster Regt.) the whole covered by a screen of outposts.
Both A and B will be covered by a strong Heavy and Field Artillery barrage at intervals to be notified later.

---oOo---

1. The XIV Corps will renew the attack on GUILLEMONT on August 21st. at an hour to be notified later.
2. The 35th. Division will attack on the right and the 24th. Division on the left.
   The boundary between Divisions will be the road from TRONES WOOD to GUILLEMONT (inclusive to 35th. Division).
3. The objective for the attack by the 24th. Division on Aug. 21st. will be as follows:-

   South West corner of the Orchard at T.25.a.½.8 - trench junction at T.25.a.3½.8 - T.19.c.3.2.- road junction T.19.c.5.6 - T.19.a.5½.7 - T.19.a.½.6.
   Any tactical points in front of these objectives which can be seized must be at once occupied and consolidated.
   The objective of the 35th. Division will be the two lines of hostile trenches from the Strong Point at S.30.b.7.1½ to the S.W. corner of the ORCHARD at T.25.a.½.8.
4. The attack by the 24th. Division will be delivered as follows:-
   <u>Right Brigade.(72nd. Infantry Brigade)</u>
   The attack by this brigade depends on whether or not the enemy strong point at S.30.b.7.1½, which is being attacked to-day by the 35th. Division, has fallen.
   (a). <u>If Strong Point has fallen.</u>
      <u>Objective.</u> (attack to be made from the West)
      The enemy defences within the area North of DOWN STREET (inclusive) - T.25.a.3½.8.- road junction T.19.c.4½.6 - road junction S.24.d.8.5. and to connect with the 35th. Division on the right and 17th. Infantry Brigade on the left.
   (b). <u>If strong point has not fallen.</u>
      <u>1st. objective</u>(attack to be made from the west)
      The area North of MOUNT STREET from T.19.c.3.2 - road junction T.19.c.4½.6. - road junction S.24.d.8.5. and to form a defensive flank on the right along MOUNT STREET and to connect with 17th. Infantry Brigade on the left.
      <u>2nd. Objective.</u>(attack to be made from the North)
      The area between MOUNT STREET and DOWN STREET both inclusive and as far east as the line T.25.a.3½.8 - T.19.c.3.2.
      In the case of (b) operation above taking place, the attack on the 2nd. objective will commence 30 minutes after "Zero" time.
   <u>Left Brigade (17th. Infantry Brigade).</u>
   <u>Objective.</u> The area bounded by a line from road junction S.24.d.8.5.- road junction T.19.c.4½.6 - T.19.a.5½.7 - T.19.a. 0.7 and to connect with the 72nd. Infantry Brigade on the right.
5. Strong Posts will be established at:-
   T.25.a.0.8.)
   T.25.a.3½.8.) By the 72nd. Infantry Brigade.
   T.19.c.4½.6.)

   T.19.a.5½.½.) By the 17th. Infantry Brigade.

   The work of consolidation will be carried out with the greatest energy directly the objectives have been gained.

6. One Field Company R.E. is allotted to each of the attacking Infantry Brigades as under:-
   17th. Infantry Brigade   104th. F.Coy.R.E.
   72nd. Infantry Brigade.   129th. F.Coy. R.E.

   These companies will be used for establishing and consolidating strong points.
7. One company of Pioneers is allotted to each of the attacking Infantry Brigades. They will be used for connecting the captured position back to our present front line.
8. The Divisional Reserve will consist of:-

2.

8. The Divisional Reserve will consist of:-
    73rd. Infantry Brigade.
    12th. Sherwood Foresters (Pioneers) less 2 companies.
    103rd. Field Coy. R.E.

    The above will remain in their present positions and will be ready to move at 15 minutes notice.

9. The boundary between the 17th. and 72nd. Infantry Brigades will be:-

    From road junction S.24.d.8.5. - T.19.c.4½.6.

10. The attack will be preceded by a preliminary artillery bombardment commencing on the morning of August 21st.

11. All troops will wear "fighting kit", 220 rounds of S.A.A. per man will be carried.

12. Brigades will arrange to carry forward at least one telephone cable with each assaulting battalion.

13. Contact aeroplane patrols will be in observation from "Zero" to dark on 21st. August. Troops will notify their position by means of red flares and mirrors at the following times:-

    (1). On reaching each objective.
    (2). At 7.0 p.m.

14. All prisoners captured will be sent back under brigade escort to the Craters A.8.a.8.3., where the A.P.M., 24th. Division, will take them over.

15. The aeroplanes told off to communicate with us have a broad black band painted under each lower plane and fly streamers from the end of both planes.

Secret

2.

Sd. W.H.KAY, Lt.Colonel.
General Staff.

Officer Commanding,
    9th. Royal Sussex Regt.
    7th. Northamptonshire Regt.
    13th. Middlesex Regt.
    2nd. Leinster Regt.
    73rd. M.G.Coy.
    73rd. Light T.M.Battery.

HEADQUARTERS 73rd BDE.
A.B.M.71.
No ....
20. 8. 16.
Date ....

The above extracts from 24th. Divisional Operation Order No. 82 are forwarded for your information, and communication to all Officers.

Your attention is drawn to para 8. It must be borne in mind that this Brigade may be called upon to support either 17th. Infantry Brigade or the 72nd. Infantry Brigade.

Headquarters 17th. Infantry Brigade are at S.23.c.8.3.
Headquarters of the 72nd. Infantry Brigade are at LA BRICQUETERIE.

Routes to above must be known to all Officers.

H.Q. 73 I.B.
20. 8. 16.

R Hoblitt
Major,
Brigade Major, 73rd. Infantry Brigade.

with the Northamptonshire Regiment.

Operation Order No
  by
Lieut Col E.R. Mobbs.

No 3

Ref. Map. LONGUEVAL 1/10000.

(1) <u>Information</u>.   The Battalion has been ordered to attack the enemy's front line from T.25.a.0.8 to S.25.d.8.5

(2) <u>Attack</u>
  "A" Company will attack on the right in two waves 100 yards apart, the Lewis Guns going with first wave and one machine gun will go forward with the second wave.
  "C" Company will attack on the left in two waves with the Lewis Guns going over with the first, and one machine gun with the second, this to be on the left flank covered by Bombers.
  "B" Company will attack in one line with the Headquarter Bombers and "B" Company Bombers in the centre. The flank platoons of this Company will push forward over the attacked trench about 30 yards & dig in and form a

2. protective screen.

"D" Company will be in reserve for carrying parties and digging a CT to new line.

A small party of RE will accompany the Battalion for the purpose of blowing in entrance to tunnel.

Companies will at once start to consolidate and signal back to Battalion Headquarters as soon as this is finished. Every endeavour must be made to dig back a Communication Trench. The position will be selected tomorrow.

The QUARRY is to be taken and held at _all costs_.

The barrage on the QUARRY will lift at the same time as the one on the front trench.

(3) <u>Formation for assault</u>.

In front line trench opposite objective N of TRONES WOOD – GUILLEMONT RD.

(4) <u>Traffic</u>.

The following are <u>up</u> routes:—
JACKSON TRENCH – FAGAN TRENCH.
"down traffic" SCOTTISH TRENCH.

(5) <u>Prisoners</u>.

These must be sent under the least possible escort to Battalion Headquarters.

These will be synchronised daily at 9 a.m., 2·30 p.m., & 6 p.m. till further notice.

(7) ZERO HOUR.

The attacking troops will at once leave the assembly trenches in successive waves, keeping as close as possible to line of barrage which will also give the general line of attack.

(8) At ZERO + 2·15 the 2nd Leinsters and one Battalion of the 97nd I.B. will go through our line and clear the village and dig in on the other side.

(9) BATTALION HEADQUARTERS will be at S·30·A·7½·5.

Auj Ad 1/1 Northamptonshire R.

APPENDIX.
No 4.

7th (S). Bn. NORTHAMPTONSHIRE REGT.

"A" Company movements in Attack.

The Company advanced on right of QUARRY in line No 1 Platoon on left, No 4 on right.

Very few casualties occurred in the advance except No 3 Platoon in the centre between the QUARRY and the GUILLEMONT ROAD.

No opposition was met but when they started consolidating many casualties were caused by Machine Gun fire front left and right and also by Snipers.

Then a bombing attack started on right flank and most of men went to repulse it. At 5 oclock more bombing came from a Sap running along the side of the GUILLEMONT ROAD under the hedge nearest the QUARRY. Most of the men had been killed or wounded and all the Officers had become casualties.

At 5.30 p.m. the men saw the Middlesex on the right had retired and they fell back in shell holes half way across "NO MAN'S LAND".

At dusk the men returned to KNOTT TRENCH and reported to the Adjutant and were sent on stretcher bearing.

There was no enemy shelling. The casualties caused by shell fire were from our own guns.

7th (S). Bn. NORTHAMPTONSHIRE REGT.

"B" Company movements in Attack.

The whole Company formed the third assaulting wave covering the whole front.

The right half Company on reaching the right half of the German front line merged itself into "A" Company and came under command of Lieut. Houghton.

The position being threatened by the retirement of the troops on the right, this party, then much reduced by Machine Gun fire withdrew with "A" Company. As the casualties were very heavy it is impossible to find out further details of this half Company.

The left half Company reached the first line with little opposition and half dug in in front of this line according to Operation orders.

At 4.45 p.m. the remainder pushed on to second objective with "C" Company but got too far and were caught by our own Artillery. When this lifted however, they returned and dug in and consolidated.

No counter attack was attempted on night of 18/19th.

7th (6) Bn. NORTHAMPTONSHIRE REGT.

"C" Company movements in Attack.

At ZERO "C" Company moved in two waves on the left of the Battalion sector and attacked on a frontage of 100 yards. Very few casualties were suffered until the first wave arrived withing 20 yards of the enemy trench. The enemy then offered much resistance, throwing a considerable number of bombs. The trench was rushed and the enemy was seen to be retiring towards th Station. Much trouble was caused by bombers from a small strong point about 40 yards to the left of the QUARRY and also by snipers from the mound directly behind the QUARRY. The latter were killed by bombers.

By this time all the Company Officers were casualties and the Company was under the command of a Corporal.

There was no shelling by the enemy. Casualties were caused by our own guns.

The work of consolidation was then begun the Company digging in about 50 yards beyond the enemy trench on a small ridge Lewis guns were pushed out to cover this work.

Shortly afterwards reinforcements arrived under an Officer wh took command.

By 7 p.m. everything was fairly normal.

7th (S). Bn. NORTHAMPTONSHIRE REGT.

"D" Company movements in Attack.

Night of 17th.   2 Platoons, 1 Machine Gun. TEAL TRENCH.

                        2 Platoons, 1 Machine Gun. FAGAN TRANCH.

MORNING OF 18th.   Party of 40 and N.C.Os sent to Brigade Hdqrs

                       Party of 25 and 1 Sgt sent to 103 Coy R.E.

                       This completed the Company except for a few Machine Guns, a few N.C.Os and other details.

Midday, 18th.   All men left and a machine gun moved to C.D.3 and were joined by first fatigue party.

1.30 - 2-45 p.m.   Bombing party for Mopping up sent to report to "B" Company under 2nd Lieut Hartigan (9men). Another party sent to take "P" Bombs to Battalion Bombers (about 10 men).

2.45 - 4 p.m.   Company moved to KNOT TRENCH. Sussex already here so extended to left. 2nd Lieut Wright received here a message for reinforcements and at once took over 30 men near him. I was buried by shell and remainder were taken over by Sussex (about 25 men) and attached to them.

Night of 18th.   Party of 25 came back with 103 Coy R.E. and remainder remained in captured trenches.

Night of 19th.   Relieved by Royal West Kents.

Appendice No 5

Aug. 21st

Dear King,

On leaving your battalion after my few days in command I want to express my appreciation of the good work done on the 18th and 19th and of the fine spirit of all ranks which helped to carry this through.

I feel sure the battalion has a great future before it.

Thank you and all for your most loyal support.

Wishing you all the best of luck

Yours sincerely
A D Murphy

73rd Brigade.
24th Division.

7th BATTALION.

NORTHAMPTONSHIRE REGIMENT.

September 1916.

Army Form C. 2118.

WAR DIARY
or
INTELLIGENCE SUMMARY
(Erase heading not required.)

CONFIDENTIAL.

WAR DIARY

OF

7th SERVICE BATTALION NORTHAMPTONSHIRE REGIMENT.

FROM :- SEPTEMBER 1st 1916

TO :- SEPTEMBER 30th 1916.

IN THE FIELD.
SEPTEMBER 30th. 1916.

Certified true copy
[signature]
Capt.
A/Adjutant
7th Northamptonshire Regt.

Army Form C. 2118

WAR DIARY
or
INTELLIGENCE SUMMARY

(Erase heading not required.)

Instructions regarding War Diaries and Intelligence Summaries are contained in F. S. Regs., Part II. and the Staff Manual respectively. Title pages will be prepared in manuscript.

Place	Date	Hour	Summary of Events and Information	Remarks and references to Appendices
DELVILLE WOOD.	1/8/16.		2nd Lieuts. C.R.G.Hawkins, L.H.Halliday, and G.P.Rathbone joined from 8th Bn. Northamptonshire Regiment today.	
	2/8/16.		Major T.H.S.Swanton, 1st Bn. East Surrey Regiment joined for duty today and assumed Command. The Battalion relieved the 8th Bn. Royal Sussex Regt and the 2nd. Bn. Leinsters in the front line. C Company returned to SAVOY TRENCH. One Lewis Gun team was knocked out on the way up. No other casualties during relief. D Company accounted for 2 Germans on left of TEA LANE. Night quiet except for our own Artillery that constantly fired short.	
	3/8/16.		At 12 noon the 8th Bn. The Buffs and the 12th Bn. Royal Fusiliers on our left attacked a strong point. Operation Orders arrived just in time to allow warning to be sent to our front line. Another 100 yards of TEA TRENCH was reclaimed on the left and at night our patrols were busy. One German came into TEA LANE and was dealt with.	
	4/8/16.		Weather fine in morning and afternoon but wet at night. This spell in the trenches was by far the worst the Battalion has spent, the difficulty of getting food and water up was much greater than usual. Battalion relieved by 7th Bn. The Kings Regiment of the 55th Division, and returned to Camp near FRICOURT - MEAULTE ROAD. 56 O.R. casualties during this tour.	
NR.FRICOURT.	5/8/16.		Weather damp. Operation Orders No. 66 received for move today. Battalion moved off at 5 p.m. and marched to BERNANCOURT via MEAULTE arriving there at 7.30 p.m. where Billets were arranged. Operation Orders for move to back area received at 11.30 p.m.	

Army Form C. 2118.

WAR DIARY
or
INTELLIGENCE SUMMARY.
(Erase heading not required.)

Instructions regarding War Diaries and Intelligence Summaries are contained in F. S. Regs., Part II. and the Staff Manual respectively. Title pages will be prepared in manuscript.

Place	Date	Hour	Summary of Events and Information	Remarks and references to Appendices
DERNANCOURT.	6/8/16.		Weather damp. Battalion paraded and moved off at 6.30 a.m. and marched to EDGE HILL Station where it entrained at 10 a.m. Arrived at LONGPRE STATION at 1.30 p.m. and marched via L'ETOILE - BOUCHON - to VILLERS -sous- ALLIX. into billets.	
VILLERS-sous-ALLIX.	7/8/16.		Cleaning of clothing, arms, equipment etc. Billets cleaned out which were in a very bad condition.	
	8/8/16.		Training commenced. Efforts made to reform all specialists. Bombers under 2nd.Lt.R.E.Duchesne - Lewis Gunners under 2nd.Lt.G.A.Williamson. Weather fine.	
	9/8/16.		Weather fine. G.O.C. and B.G.C visit billets and inspect Companies training. All roads near billets cleaned up. Transport gets ready for Show on 12th. All specialists training hard - bombing pits dug.	
	10/8/16.		Weather fine. Church Parade at 11 a.m. Training of Companies all the morning. Rifle range constructed. 2nd.Lieuts Harston and Allport rejoin from 4th Army School	
	11/8/16.		Weather fine. B.G.C visits Companies during training. Captain R.Gurney and 2nd.Lieut E.Wright proceed to PARIS on 48 hours leave Trenches prepared for Bombing. The improvement in smartness of the Battalion is very noticeable.	

Army Form C. 2118

WAR DIARY
or
INTELLIGENCE SUMMARY

(Erase heading not required.)

Instructions regarding War Diaries and Intelligence Summaries are contained in F. S. Regs., Part II. and the Staff Manual respectively. Title pages will be prepared in manuscript.

Place	Date	Hour	Summary of Events and Information	Remarks and references to Appendices
VILLERS-sous-AILLY.	12/9/16.		Weather cloudy but no rain. Training as usual. Party of 5 Officers and 150 O.R. proceed at 7.30 a.m. to march to AILLY thence by wagons to ABBEVILLE, thence by train to WOINCOURT – detrain there and march to 4th Army Rest Camp at AULT. The Camp is situated on top of the cliff overlooking the Sea. Men were not called upon to do any work and a very enjoyable time was spent by all ranks.	
	13/9/16.		Leave party at AULT made the most of their time and money. Training proceeds.	
	14/9/16.		Weather fine but overcast. Leave party returns at 9 p.m.. Their arrival arouses the village that pictures hoards of Uhlans.	
	15/9/16.		Weather fine. Training proceeds. Usual visits from Generals. These are now of daily occurrence.	
	16/9/16		Route march arranged and Advance Guard out when orders were received to be ready to entrain at short notice. A Company found and brought back. Later on in the morning G.O.C. Division found touring the Country in search of the Battalion which is expected to findout on the march.	
	17/9/16.		Weather fine. Divine Service at 10 a.m. followed by celebration of Holy Communion. No training takes place by order of Brigadier.	
	18/9/16.		Weather wet. Training continued but hindered by rain. All trenches have to be filled in which means whole Battalion gets soaked through.	

Army Form C. 2118.

WAR DIARY
or
INTELLIGENCE SUMMARY.
(Erase heading not required.)

Instructions regarding War Diaries and Intelligence Summaries are contained in F.S. Regs., Part II. and the Staff Manual respectively. Title pages will be prepared in manuscript.

Place	Date	Hour	Summary of Events and Information	Remarks and references to Appendices
VILLERS-sous-AILLY.	19/9/16.		Weather unsettled. Battalion starts at 5 a.m. for LONGPRE STATION where it entrains at 5.30 a.m. and proceeds to FOUQUEREUIL where it detrains in recordtime and marches to BRUAY where it is billeted in empty houses and barns. This is the first town of any size in which the Battalion have been billeted since it came out.	
BRUAY.	20/9/16.		Weather showery. Training continues.	
	21/9/16.		Weather showery. Battalion busy cleaning up billets and generally tidying up. Commanding Officer and Officers Commanding all Companies proceed to reconnoitre the new line held by South African Brigade in 9th Division. Following MILITARY MEDALS awarded in Divisional Routine Orders :- No.14803 CPL. L. E. BUNYAN. No.7265 PTE H. E. BARDY. No.20093 PTE. J. BLAKE. No.18769 PTE F. WARLEY. No.12856 PTE. S. CHILDS. No.15751 PTE E. CARR. No.14737 PTE W. WEST. 2nd Lieuts Evans and Knight joined today from 8th Bn. Northamptonshire Regiment.	
ESTREE-CAUCHIE.	22/9/16.		Weather fine. Battalion marches to ESTREE CAUCHIE where it is billeted for night. 6 Officers reconnoitre new line.	
	23/9/16.		Weather fine. Battalion moved up to line and relieved 2nd South African Battalion. C and D Companies billeted in cellars in CARENCY - A and B Companies in MAROELLE TRENCH. Headquarters at TALYS. Relief completed by 4.30 p.m. Battalion marches up by Platoons at 500 yards distance. Captain R.C. TOWER wounded by Archie Shell.	Appendix No 1.

Army Form C. 2118.

WAR DIARY
or
INTELLIGENCE SUMMARY

(Erase heading not required.)

Instructions regarding War Diaries and Intelligence Summaries are contained in F. S. Regs., Part II. and the Staff Manual respectively. Title Pages will be prepared in manuscript.

Place	Date	Hour	Summary of Events and Information	Remarks and references to Appendices
CARENCY.	23/9/16.		Draft of 10 O.R. join today - all old 7th men.	
	24/9/16.		Weather fine. A quiet day. Battalion very busy with carrying and working parties. Trenches surveyed by 2nd.Lt. Evans and map produced. 103 O.R. and 2nd.Lt.Greenwood attached to R.E. for Tunnelling purposes.	
	25/9/16.		Weather fine. Quiet day - no shelling. Battalion busy on carrying and working parties. Medical Officer effects a gallant rescue of a Major from bottom of a 180 ft. well. Two new Officers join this evening - 2nd Lieuts Hall and Laycock. Anniversary of Battle of LOOS.	
	26/9/16.		Weather fine. Battalion busy on carrying and working parties. Draft of 13 O.R. join today - all old 7th men, returned from Hospital and Base.	
	27/9/16.		Weather fine. Working parties as usual.	
	28/9/16.		Weather fine. Working parties as usual.	
	29/9/16.		Weather overcast and showery. Working parties as usual. Front line reconnoitred by all Company Commanders ready for relief on October 1st.	
	30/9/16.		Weather fine. Working parties as usual.	

SECRET.   COPY NO:- 10

Ref.Map   73rd. INFANTRY BRIGADE.
36.B.S.E.
1/20,000   OPERATION ORDER NO.70.
and Trench
Maps.   H.Q., 73 I.B., September 22nd., 1916.

1.   The 73rd. Infantry Brigade will relieve the 1st. South African Infantry Brigade on September 23rd. as per attached table.

        Every precaution will be taken to conceal movement on the way to and during reliefs. C.O's are responsible that adequate stops are taken to ensure that an interval of 500 yards is maintained between platoons.

2. ROUTES. For all excepting M.G.Coy and 73rd. T.M.Battery.
        IN - W.18.a.3.7. - CARENCY + Hospital Corner -
             Caberet Road - Ersatz Avenue.
        OUT- Redoubt Road - 130 road - 130 Alley.

        M.G.Coy and T.M.Battery may use Redoubt Road - 130 road - 130 Alley for both ingoing and out-going.

3.   Commanders of relieving units will personally ensure that all defences held by the 1st. South African Brigade are taken over and garrisonned. A certificate that this has been done will be forwarded to Brigade Headquarters by unit Commanders after completion of reliefs.

4. TRANSPORT.
        No Transport is to be nearer the trenches by day than the West End of CARENCY.

5.   The 9th. Divisional Artillery will continue to cover the front after completion of reliefs.

                                        Trench Stores
6.   All Defence Schemes, maps, log books, tables of work in hand and proposed, etc. will be taken over. Lists of articles taken over will be forwarded to Brigade Headquarters within 24 hours of completion of reliefs.

7.   The following officers and men will be detailed for attachment to the 176th. Tunnelling Company R.E. They will be required to join by 12 noon September 24th. and will be administered by the Tunnelling Company:-

        7th. Northamptons.   2 Officers and 101 O.R.
        2nd. Leinsters.   25 O.R.
        13th. Middlesex.   25 O.R.

        Further orders re joining will be notified.

8.   Brigade Headquarters will be in ARRAS ALLEY.
        All routine correspondence will be sent to Back Brigade Headquarters (VILLERS- AU - BOIS, Y.19.a.5.2.)

9.   Completion of reliefs will be notified by wiring the name of the O.C. unit concerned.
        B.G.C., 73rd. Infantry Brigade will assume Command of the Left (CARENCY) Section on completion of relief.

                                P.Hewitt
ISSUED AT 2 p.m.   Major,
                        Brigade Major, 73rd. Infantry Brigade.
PLEASE ACKNOWLEDGE.
                                                P.T.O.

2.

Copy No. 1. Filo.
2. War Diary.
3. "G" 24 Div.
4. "Q" 24 Div.
5. 17 I.B.
6. 72 I.B.
7. 1st. S.A. Inf. Bde.
8. A.P.M. 24 Div.
9. 9th. Royal Sussex
10. 7th. Northamptons.
11. 13th. Middlesex.
12. 2nd. Leinsters.
13. 73rd. M.G.Coy.
14. 73rd. Light T.M.Battery.
15. Supply Officer, 73 I.B.
16. B.T.O.
17. Bde. Sigs.
18. 129th. Fd.Coy.R.E.

TABLE ISSUED WITH 73rd Infantry Brigade OPERATION ORDER No.70. dated 22.9.16.

UNIT.	UNITS TO BE RELIEVED.	PLACE AND HOUR AT WHICH GUIDES WILL MEET.	REMARKS.
73rd Machine Gun Coy.	28th M.G.Company.	HOSPITAL CORNER (X.16.d.3.4.) at 9 a.m.	2 guns to be relieved after dark.
73rd Lt.T.M.Battery.	S.A.Light T.M.Battery.	" at 9.30 a.m.	
13th Middlesex Regt.	1st South African Inf.Btn.	" at 10 a.m.	Left Sub-Section Trenches (THIERET ALLEY inclusive to SOUCHEZ River). Left Picquet to be relieved after dark.
2nd Leinster Regiment.	4th S.A.Inf.Battn.	" at 12.30 p.m.	Right Sub-Section Trenches. (GOBRON ALLEY inclusive to THIERET ALLEY).
7th Northamptonshire Regt.	2nd S.A.Inf.Batn.	West end of CARENCY at 2.30 p.m.	Battalion in Support.
9th Royal Sussex Regiment.	3rd S.A.Inf.Battn.		Battalion in Reserve at VILLERS au BOIS. Relief to commence at 3 p.m.

Battalions will move by Platoons at 6 minutes interval from billets.

73rd Brigade.
24th Division.

7th BATTALION.

NORTHAMPTONSHIRE REGIMENT.

October 1916.

Army Form C. 211

Vol 13

WAR DIARY
INTELLIGENCE SUMMARY.
(Erase heading not required.)

CONFIDENTIAL.

WAR DIARY

OF

7th (Service). Battn. NORTHAMPTONSHIRE REGIMENT.

FROM :- OCTOBER 1st. 1916.

TO :- OCTOBER 31st. 1916.

IN THE FIELD.

OCTOBER 31st. 1 9 1 6.

Army Form C. 2118

WAR DIARY
INTELLIGENCE SUMMARY.
(Erase heading not required.)

Instructions regarding War Diaries and Intelligence Summaries are contained in F. S. Regs., Part II. and the Staff Manual respectively. Title pages will be prepared in manuscript.

Place	Date	Hour	Summary of Events and Information	Remarks and references to Appendices
SOUCHEZ.	1.10.16.		Battalion relieved 2nd Bn. Leinster Regiment in the right sub-section of the 73rd Brigade line. Battalion Headquarters in ZOUAVE VALLEY. Relief completed by 4 p.m. Enemy fairly quiet. Brigade Operation Orders No.71 attached. Defence Scheme drawn up.	Appendices No 1. Appendices No 2.
	2.10.16.		About 2 a.m., 50 7.7 and 4.2 were fired on WILSON STREET and trenches in rear - very little damage done. Our Stokes Mortars were active at 2.30 p.m.	
	3.10.16.		Morning quiet - weather wet. A few Trench Mortars fired at our left Company (C) about 1 p.m. Our Trench Mortar Batteries opened out about 2.30 p.m. cutting the enemy's wire. About 5.15 p.m. enemy sent about 6 heavy trench Mortars at WILSON STREET. Our patrols bombed KENNEDY CRATER during the night.	
	4.10.16.		Weather wet. Much activity on the part of our Stokes Guns and Trench Mortars to which the enemy replied with heavy Trench Mortars. Several 4.2's fired at ZOUAVE VALLEY during the morning. Day fairly quiet on the whole. Night also quiet. Scheme for small raid on enemy trenches drawn out.	Appendices No 3.
	5.10.16.		Weather changeable. Enemy rather more active and strongly retaliated to our trench mortar shelling about 11.30 a.m. During afternoon trench mortars again active on both sides. Captain H. B. King proceeded on Leave today.	

2353 Wt. W2514/1454 700,000 5/15 D.D.&L. A.D.S.S/Forms/C. 2118.

Army Form C. 2118.

WAR DIARY
INTELLIGENCE SUMMARY.
(Erase heading not required.)

Instructions regarding War Diaries and Intelligence Summaries are contained in F. S. Regs., Part II. and the Staff Manual respectively. Title pages will be prepared in manuscript.

Place	Date	Hour	Summary of Events and Information	Remarks and references to Appendices
SOUCHEZ.	6.10.16.		Weather fine. Enemy trench mortars active to which we retaliated with rifle grenades. One of the trench mortar bombs fell in WILSON STREET exploding two bomb stores but wounding nobody. Our heavy trench mortars bombarded the enemy front line and wire during the morning. After dinner the enemy trench mortars were exceedingly lively bombarding BRISSON, CHALK STREET, SOUCHEZ ALLEY, and ZOUAVE VALLEY.	
	7.10.16.		Weather changeable. Not so much activity today, both morning and afternoon quiet. Between 5 p.m. and 8 p.m. our Artillery sent over about 50 shells and from 5.30 p.m. to 7 p.m. our Stokes Guns successfully bombarded the enemy wire between KENNEDY and IRISH CRATERS to which the enemy replied with Trench Mortars. Operation Orders No.73 for relief in afternoon of 10th inst received.	Appendice No H
	8.10.16.		Morning quiet - weather fine. During afternoon trench mortars very active and our Artillery sent over a few shells. A raid on the enemy trenches carried out by 2nd.Leinsters Regt. at 10 p.m. from our Section resulting in the capture of one Hun (wounded). 2nd.Lt.R.E.DUCHESNE killed whilst examining our wire during night. Lieut C.L. CLARKE killed while patrolling in "No Mans Land" early morning.	
	9.10.16.		During the night enemy has been much more lively, his sentries and machine guns firing continuously. An enemy working party was dispersed by our Lewis Gun fire. Trench mortars again active during the morning. Artillery inactive.	

Army Form C. 2118

WAR DIARY

INTELLIGENCE SUMMARY.

(Erase heading not required.)

Instructions regarding War Diaries and Intelligence Summaries are contained in F.S. Regs. Part II. and the Staff Manual respectively. Title pages will be prepared in manuscript.

Place	Date	Hour	Summary of Events and Information	Remarks and references to Appendices
SOUCHEZ.	10.10.16.		At 3.40 a.m. a raiding party under Lieut Shankster and 2nd.Lieut B.Wright entered the enemy trenches and inflicted several casualties on them. Lieut Shankster was unfortunately shot dead, he being our only casualty. (See detailed report). Trench Mortars active during morning. 2nd.Lieut B.Wright wounded in leg today but remains at duty. The Battalion was relieved in the afternoon by the 3rd Rifle Brigade. and proceeded to DIVISIONAL RESERVE at CAMBLAIN L'ABBE, a distance of about 6 miles, into Huts. Congratulations received from Divisional Commander on result of raid. Total Casualties during tour of 9 days :- KILLED - 3 Officers. " - 4 O.R. WOUNDED - 1 Officer. " - 15 O.R.	Appendix No 5. Appendix No 6.
CAMBLAIN L'ABBE.	11.10.16.	noon.	Companies bathe at the Divisional Baths during morning and afternoon. Major Swanton proceeds on leave today. Inspection of clothing etc.	
	12.10.16.		Weather fine and windy. Bathing of Companies at Divisional Baths. Draft of 10 B.R. joined today - all original 7th men. Company and Platoon drill. - Bayonet fighting etc.	
	13.10.16.		(Sheet 36 B.) Battalion practiced the attck on model German trenches at U.10.b. proceeding in Motor busses from Divisional Headquarters and returned about 5 p.m.	

WAR DIARY
or
INTELLIGENCE SUMMARY.

(Erase heading not required.)

Army Form C. 2118.

Place	Date	Hour	Summary of Events and Information	Remarks and references to Appendices
CAMBLAIN L'ABBE.	14.10.16.	nil.	Usual training carried on.	
	15.10.16.	nil.	Church Parade in the morning. Working party of 150 men for work in ZOUAVE VALLEY provided returning at 3 a.m.	
	16.10.16.	nil.	Usual training. Company and Platoon drill, etc.. Notification in TIMES of the undermentioned being awarded the MILITARY MEDAL. No.15216 L/Sgt. W.Redley. No.15720 L/Cpl. W.A.Cotton. No.12788 Cpl. C.H.Filkins. No.17109 L/Cpl. W.L.Drage. No.18535 Cpl. C.V.Blythe. No.15285 L/Cpl. G.Jinks.	
	17.10.16.	nil.	Gas Helmets inspected by Medical Officer. Physical training, Bombing etc.. Orders for relief on 18th received.	
	18.10.16.	nil.	Battalion paraded at 7.15 a.m. and moved off in Platoons via VILLERS-AU-BOIS to BERTHONVAL WOOD and CABARET ROUGE relieving the 8th Bn.The Queens Regiment (72nd Infantry Brigade). Working parties as per Appendice found immediately on relief.	Appendice No 1
BERTHONVAL WOOD.	19.10.16.	nil.	Working parties as per Table.	
	20.10.16.	nil.	Working parties as per Table.	
	21.10.16.	nil.	Working parties as per Table.	
	22.10.16.	nil.	Working parties as per Table.	
	23.10.16.	nil.	Major Swanton rejoins from Leave and Captain Millard assumes position of 2nd in Command. Working parties as usual.	

Army Form C. 2118

WAR DIARY
or
INTELLIGENCE SUMMARY.

(Erase heading not required.)

Instructions regarding War Diaries and Intelligence Summaries are contained in F.S. Regs., Part II. and the Staff Manual respectively. Title pages will be prepared in manuscript.

Place	Date	Hour	Summary of Events and Information	Remarks and references to Appendices
BERTHONVAL WOOD.	24.10.16.	—	Working parties as usual. A pouring wet day.	
	25.10.16.	—	Working parties as usual. Lieut. Colonel E.R. Mobbs rejoined and resumed command of the Battalion. Major Swanton transferred to 9th East Surreys with temporary Command.	
	26.10.16.	—	Weather wet - Working parties as usual.	
GOUY SERVINS	27.10.16.	—	Battalion relieved by 14th Canadian Battalion and marched back to GOUY SERVINS for the night. There were no casualties during this tour in the Reserve line although the working parties were often "minnied".	
MAZINGARBE.	28.10.16.	—	Battalion marched from GOUY SERVINS to MAZINGARBE where it spent the night in huts. This march of 8 or 9 miles was accomplished without anyone falling out except one "non-starter".	
LOOS.	29.10.16.	—	Battalion left MAZINGARBE at 10 a.m. and met guides of 17th Welsh Regiment at GRENAY CHURCH. Relief completed by 2 p.m.	
	30.10.16.	—	At 12 noon enemy blew a Camouflet near SOUTH CRASSIER (NORTH) damaging one of our Galleries. Afternoon-enemy active with Trench Mortars. Our Casualties - NIL. 2nd.Lt. Crompton joined the Battalion today.	
	31.10.16.	—	Brigadier General Commanding 73rd Infantry Brigade visits trenches. Enemy very quiet during the day.	

SECRET.   No 1   COPY NO. 10

Ref.Map   73rd INFANTRY BRIGADE.
36 B.S.E.
1/20,000   OPERATION ORDER No. 71.
& Trench
Maps.
                              H.Q. 73rd I.B. September 29th 1916.

1. The following reliefs will take place on 1st Oct. and night 1st/2nd October:-
   (a) 9th ROYAL SUSSEX REGT will relieve 13th MIDDLESEX REGT in Left Sub-section trenches. (THIERET ALLEY inclusive to SOUCHEZ RIVER)
       On relief 13th MIDDLESEX REGT to VILLERS-AU-BOIS (Brigade Reserve).

   (b) 7th NORTHAMPTONSHIRE REGT, will relieve 2nd LEINSTER REGIMENT in Right Sub-section Trenches. (GOBRON ALLEY inclusive to THIERET ALLEY).
       On relief 2nd LEINSTER REGIMENT to the BAJOLLE LINE and CARENCY (Brigade Support).

2. Battalions will move from their present billets, dug-outs etc., by platoons at intervals of 500 yards.
   The leading platoon of the 9th ROYAL SUSSEX REGT will reach HOSPITAL CORNER at 9.30 a.m.
   The leading platoon of 7th NORTHAMPTONSHIRE REGT will move at 12 noon.
   All other details to be arranged between Os.C. concerned.

3. The Main Communication Trenches will be used for ingoing ~~traffic~~ and outgoing traffic as already ordered.

4. 13th Middlesex Regiment will detail 1 Officer and 50 men for attachment to 9th Royal Sussex Regt.
   The detachment of 27 men of 7th Northamptonshire Regiment attached to Left Battalion for work with 176th Tunnelling Coy. R.E. will remain there till further orders.

5. The handing and taking over of work in hand and proposed must be very thorough.
   Return showing Trench Stores etc., handed or taken over will be forwarded to Brigade H.Q. within 24 hours of relief being completed.

6. Completion of relief will be notified by wiring to Brigade Headquarters the name of the O.C. concerned.

7. PLEASE ACKNOWLEDGE.

                                        R Howitt
ISSUED AT 7.30 a.m.
                                        Major,
                              Brigade Major, 73rd Infantry Brigade.

Copy No. 1. File.
        2. War Diary.
        3. "G". 24th Div.
        4. "Q". 24th Div.
        5. 17th I.B.   No.19. 176th.Coy.
        6. 72nd I.B.   R.E.
        7. 63 I.B.   20. 17th Sherwood
        8. A.P.M. 24th Div.   Foresters
        9. 9th Royal Sussex.   21. 50th Div.R.F.A.
       10. 7th Northants.   22. 52nd Bde. R.F.A.
       11. 13th Middlesex.
       12. 2nd Leinsters.
       13. 73rd M.G.Coy.
       14. 73rd Lt.T.M.Bty.
       15. 129th Field Coy. R.E.
       16. B.T.O.
       17. Brigade Signals.
       18. Supply Officer 73rd I.B.

1/7th S Bn Northamptonshire Regt.
DEFENCE SCHEME

No 2

CARENCY 1. or right sub-section of CARENCY section

DISTRIBUTION The front and support lines are held by three Coys. One Coy is in Reserve in HEATON ROAD and SOUCHEZ ALLEY

RIGHT COY. Front line from GOBRON inclusive to UHLAN inclusive - including defences of TWIN, MOMBER, and LOVE CRATERS - Two Platoons with three Lewis Guns.

    <u>Close support line</u> JESMOND ROAD - One Platoon

    <u>Second Support line</u> HEATON RD - One Platoon

CENTRE COY. From line From UHLAN exclusive to ARNAU inclusive - including defences of NEW and KENNEDY CRATERS. Two Platoons with Two Lewis Guns

    <u>Close support line</u>. LIME STREET. Two Platoons

LEFT COY. From line From ARNAU exclusive to THIRIET exclusive - Two Platoons with Two Lewis Guns

    <u>Close support line</u> CHALK ST. One Platoon
    SECOND SUPPORT LINE. SOUCHEZ ALLEY. 1 Platoon

RESERVE COY. HEATON RD. and right of SOUCHEZ ALLEY. - One Coy with one Lewis Gun.

BATTN HQ. ZOUAVE VALLEY. between UHLAN and
COBURG. where 130 ALLEY meets ZOUAVE
VALLEY

BY NIGHT.   The supporting Platoons of the 3
Front line Coys are employed for work in or
near their own front line in two reliefs
thus providing a reinforcement for the forward
garrisons by night whilst leaving always
a nucleus in support trenches.
    The Reserve Coy is almost entirely
employed on mining fatigue working
night and day in three continuous reliefs
⅔rds of the Coy is therefore always in
hand as a reserve.

Action in   The front trenches are held lightly
Case of   and the defence of the line depends chiefly
attack   on a series of advanced saps which
are being made with T shaped heads.
    These give more command than
the main front line and they offer good
opportunities for enfilade fire in both
directions.   Most of them have
Lewis Guns installed to assist their
garrisons.   The Craters are
similarly defended by short advanced
trenches along the nearer lip All
these advanced posts are in touch with
each other.

In the event of attack on our front all advanced posts will hold their ground supported by remainder of front line garrisons (and working parties) in the main front line KING ST - WILSON ST.

If the enemy should reach and occupy any portion of the main front line he will be immediately counter-attacked and driven out by the Support Platoon of the Coy concerned from the Close Support line. This immediate Counter-attack will be assisted by bombing parties from both flanks of the lost portion of the trench. The place vacated in the Close support line by the Counter-attacking party will be occupied at once by the Platoon of the Company concerned from the Second Support line. [All these movements will be made across the open whether by day or by night.] O.C. Centre Coy is responsible that a garrison is maintained in LIME ST until this trench is taken over by other Troops.

The Reserve Coy will occupy and hold the line HEATON ROAD - SOUCHEZ ALLEY where it will be at the disposal of O.C. Battalion.

If the attack is preceded by a heavy bombardment all ranks, with the exception of the sentries, and the Officers and NCOs on duty in each Coy will seek refuge during the bombardment in deep dugouts or such other cover as is available in their own trenches. A sentry must be posted at the entrance to each dug out to give warning of attack or of the cessation of the bombardment and these sentries must be in touch with the look out sentries. As soon as the bombardment ceases or an attack is reported all men will move to their fire positions at full speed

Action in Case of a hostile mine explosion } In the event of a mine being sprung under or near our parapets, it is the duty of the Commander nearest to the spot to take instant action. If the explosion has destroyed any portion of our front line the outer lip of the crater must be occupied by the troops nearest at hand and held until the arrival of the Coy *"Crater jumping party" (* 1 Platoon to be detailed by each Coy from the close support line. In addition to above 1 Platoon to be detailed from close support or second support line to bring up consolidating materials from the Emergency dumps. If a mine is sprung in front of our trenches and within reach the "Crater Jumping Party" of the Coy on whose front the explosion has occurred will immediately rush over and occupy the near lip of the new crater, consolidating parties being sent up immediately after as above.

Action of working parties — In the event of attack all working parties in the Bn sub-section will stand fast and the Officer i/c will report to the nearest Coy HQ for instructions

Artillery Support — A50 Batty covers the Bn front South of KENNEDY CRATER
B50 Batty covers the Bn front North of KENNEDY CRATER
D50 Howr Batty covers whole Bn front
Both Field Battys are connected by telephone with Bn HQ and the three from Corps have a separate artillery hot wire to Bn HQ for use in an emergency.
These Battys are liable to be changed

Trench mortars — There are two 2" Trench Mortars in the Bn sub-section and four Stokes guns. The Officers in charge of both live close to Bn HQ

Bombs. — Bombs are distributed as follows:
FRONT LINE — 1410 bombs.   CLOSE SUPPORT LINE — 1962 bombs.
SECOND SUPPORT LINE — 2032.   BN RESERVE — 6060
Numbers liable to alteration

Rations. — There are 3720 reserve rations and a reserve of water in the sub-section

Maxim Guns — There are two Vickers Maxims in the Section under the orders of the OC Section

APPENDIX No. 3.

Ref. Aeroplane Map 16A - 84

Scheme for a small raid to be carried out by the 7th Northamptonshire Regiment about 7pm on evening 9/10th October 1916.

———

I. It is intended to enter enemy's front line trench between KENNEDY and IRISH CRATERS, with the intention of ~~bombing~~ one of the enemy's advanced posts on KENNEDY CRATER and of obtaining as many prisoners as possible

II. Two parties each of one Officer and 12-16 O.R. will each enter the enemy's trench at a point approximately in line with our B3 advanced post and will work outwards towards IRISH and KENNEDY CRATERS. At the same time a party of 1 NCO and 8 O.R. will make a demonstration against enemy's post on KENNEDY CRATER from No MANS LAND, assisted by our advanced posts in A3 on KENNEDY CRATER.

III. The party working towards IRISH CRATER will not proceed further than the enemy communication trench leading to IRISH CRATER

The party working towards KENNEDY

CRATER will not proceed further than the enemy's communication trench leading to their support line.

IV Should artillery support be needed it should be directed on hostile communication trenches at their junction with the support line.

V Each party will return independently after capturing some half dozen prisoners. Tracing tapes will be laid down by connecting files to guide the return.

Two Lewis Guns will be detailed to assist on the flanks

Sniping and rifle grenades will engage the enemy's front line between KENNEDY and LOVE CRATERS.

Wire has been previously cut.

Major
Commdg
7th Service Bn Northamptonshire Regt.

4/10/16

RAID

The raiding party will consist of 2 officers and 28 other ranks and will be divided into two parties A and B.

A party under Lt Wright consists of
1 officer 4 NCOs 16 men

B party under Lt Chanter consists of
1 officer 2 NCOs 7 men

Both parties will leave B.I. sap at the same time and make for the point X where a gap has previously been made in the enemy's wire.

On entering the German trench A party

will turn to the right. This party has previously been divided into four groups each consisting of 1 NCO and 4 men.

These groups are organised as follows
(1) Bayonet man with rifle and bandolier
(2) N.C.O. with revolver and knobkerry
(3) Bomber with 10 bombs "   "
(4) 2nd Bomber   "   "
(5) 2nd Bayonet man   "   "

The last group will halt about 15 yds to the right of the point of entry or at the mouth of any dug out which may be found between the points X and V (see sketch).
Of the 3 remaining groups, the rear one will halt at the point V to prevent the approach of any Germans from the communication trench; the other two will proceed up the sap, the first one turning to the right to the point Y, the second one turning to the left to the point W. The officer will go with the first group.
B party will similarly be organised in two groups, the first consisting of 1 officer 1 NCO and 3 men, the second of 1 N.C.O. and 4 men. This party, on entry

the German trench will turn to the
left. The second group will halt
about 20 yds to the left of X or at the
mouth of any dug-out between X and
Z; the first party will proceed to
the point Z.

A covering party of 1 NCO and 4 men
will stay on the parapet at the
point X to see that no Germans approach
the trench over the open, to mark the
point of entry and to take back
prisoners.

Each group after fulfilling its programme
will return by the way it came,* the
group at V will be the last group of
A party to retire.

The officer in charge of B party will
wait until every man has retired

* reporting itself all present to the NCO
in charge of the covering party at X.

The attention of enemy posts at Y and W will
be engaged by a small bombing demonstration
from our lip of the crater.

SECRET.
Art Mats.
36.B.S.E.
1/20,000
+ Trench
Maps.

N° 4   COPY NO. 10

73rd INFANTRY BRIGADE.

OPERATION ORDER No. 73.

H.Q. 73rd I.B. Oct. 7th, 1916.

1. The 73rd Infantry Brigade (less 73rd Machine Gun Company) will be relieved by 17th Infantry Brigade on 10th October and night 10/11th October as per attached table.

   The 17th Machine Gun Company will relieve the 73rd Machine Gun Company on 11th October and night 11/12th October under arrangements to be made between Os.C. direct.

   Every precaution will be taken to conceal movement. Os.C. are responsible that an interval of 500 yards is maintained between platoons.

2. Routes as under:-

   IN - W.18.a.3.7. - CARENCY - HOSPITAL CORNER - REDOUBT ROAD - 130th ROAD - 130th ALLEY.

   OUT - ERSATZ ALLEY - CABARET ROAD.

3. No transport is to be nearer the trenches by day than the West end of CARENCY.

4. All Defence Schemes, Maps, Log Books, Tables of work in hand and proposed, Trench Stores will be handed over. Lists of articles taken over will be forwarded to Brigade H.Q. within 24 hours of relief being completed.

5. (a) The parties required for work by 176th Tunnelling Coy. will be carefully handed over. The party of 27 O.R. of 7th Northamptonshire Regiment attached to Left Sub-Section will be considered as belonging to 9th Royal Sussex Regiment for purposes of handing over.

   Above does not refer to permanent parties detailed in 73rd Infantry Brigade Operation Order No. 70.

   (b) The parties attached permanently to 129th Field Coy. R.E. remain with that Unit.

6. Completion of reliefs will be notified by wiring the name of the O.C. concerned.

7. B.G.C. 17th Infantry Brigade will assume command of the CARENCY SECTION on completion of Infantry Reliefs.

ISSUED AT 7.30 a.m.

R. Howlett
Major,
Brigade Major, 73rd Infantry Brigade.

Copy No. 1. File.
2. War Diary.
3. "G" 24th Div.
4. "Q" 24th Div.
5. 17th I.B.
6. 72nd I.B.
7. 63rd I.B.
8. A.P.M. 24th Div.
9. 9th Royal Sussex.
10. 7th Northants.
11. 13th Middlesex.
12. 2nd Leinsters.
13. 73rd M.G.Coy.
14. 73rd Lt.T.M.B.
15. 129th Fld.Coy.R.E.
16. B.T.O.
17. Bde. Signals.
18. S.O. 73rd I.B.
19. 176th Coy. R.E.
20. 12th S.Foresters.
21. Left Group Arty.

TABLE ISSUED WITH 73rd INFANTRY BRIGADE OPERATION ORDER No.73.

DATE.	UNIT.	RELIEVING UNIT.	PLACE AT WHICH GUIDES WILL MEET.	TIME.	BILLET AT.	REMARKS.
Oct.10th.	73rd Lt.T.M.Bty.	17th Lt.T.M.Bty.	HOSPITAL CORNER. (The personnel of 17th Lt.T. Bty. will arrive in rear of 12th.R.F. and 3rd R.Bde. for respective Sub-Sections).	To be notified.		Number of guns to be brought out will be notified later.
"	9th Royal Sussex. (Lt.Sub-Section).	12th R.Fusiliers.	HOSPITAL CORNER.	9.30 a.m.	H.Q. and 2 Coys CAMBLAIN L'ABBE. 2 Coys.VILLERS - AU-BOIS. (12th.R.F)	Left Picquet to be relieved after dark.
"	7th Northants. (Rt.Sub-section)	3rd.Rifle Bde.	"	12 noon.	CAMBLAIN L'ABBE HUTS (1st R.F)	
"	2nd Leinsters. (Support Battn)	8th Buffs.	West end of CARENCY.	2.30 p.m.	GOUY SERVINS.	
"	13th Middlesex. (Reserve Battn)	1st R.Fusiliers.			ESTREE-GAUCHIE. (3rd R.Bde.)	Relief to commence at 3 p.m.
"	73rd Bde.H.Q.	H.Q.77 I.B.			CHATEAU DE LA HAIE.	On completion of Infantry Relief.
Oct.11th.	73rd M.G.Coy.	17th M.G.Coy.			CAMBLAIN L'ABBE.	

1 Guide per Platoon will be found by Battalions in the front line. These will assemble at Battalion Headquarters and move to rendezvous under an Officer.

APPENDIX. N°5.

REPORT ON MINOR ENTERPRISE CARRIED OUT BY THE 7th. BATTALION
NORTHAMPTONSHIRE REGIMENT ON THE EARLY MORNING
OF 10. 10. 16.

(Reference plan and scheme attached)

ACTION BY PARTIES.
1. The parties left Sap B.1. at 3.55 a.m., and though a few stray shots were fired at them as they left, both parties got well forward into "NO MAN'S LAND"; and when within a few yards of the German front line, it became obvious to all ranks that the enemy were not only on the alert, but were actually manning their fire steps, and in considerable force.
    Lt. G.SHANKSTER, in command of the parties, showed a fine offensive spirit in at once deciding to carry out his task, though he would, under the circumstances, certainly have been justified in abandoning the enterprise, as the element of surprise would obviously be wanting. This fine young officer (who unfortunately was killed) obviously decided to take his men into the trench, do as much damage as he could, and to come out as quickly as possible; and the front line trench was entered at 4 a.m.. The parties entered the trench at point arranged, and were met with instant opposition by a much superior force. The parties chanced to enter the German trench just at a point where there was a large dugout entrance, with another entrance a few yards further on. "P" bombs were thrown into both these entrances, and three Germans, who attempted to come out of them, were shot dead at point blank range. Meantime, unfortunately, Lt. SHANKSTER had been shot immediately on reaching the trench; and his body was not recovered. The trench at this point was at least seven feet deep, and I consider that any organised attempt to bring in his body would have undoubtedly resulted in serious losses to the raiders, as the moon was still up. As it was, the whole party, excepting Lt. SHANKSTER, returned to our trenches in safety, in spite of close range machine gun and rifle fire; the result, I consider, of the bold action taken by the raiders. 2/Lt. B.WRIGHT assumed command of the party when Lt. SHANKSTER was killed, and showed a splendid example of courage and coolness to his men. The parties were all back in our front line trench by 4.22 a.m..

ENEMY TRENCHES.
2. These were at least seven feet deep, well fire stopped, and revetted. At the point entered, the parados appeared to be much lower than the parapet, and had a hedge growing on it, through which some enemy riflemen kept firing.

ACTION BY ARTILLERY AND TRENCH MORTARS.
3. As arranged in scheme; and, taking into account that the enemy were manning and holding their trenches thickly, considerable loss must have been caused to them.

WIRE.
4. Enemy wire had been well cut by 2" Trench Mortars.

COMMUNICATIONS.
5. The wires to all supporting units and to Headquarters, worked without a hitch

NOTE.

NOTE.
6. It has been established without doubt that three whistles is the signal for the enemy to man his front line and his support trenches, and, under present circumstances, good results would be obtained by our blowing three whistles in "NO MAN'S LAND", and having as many Stokes guns and 2" Trench Mortars laid in readiness to fire on above points a few minutes after the signal is given.

RETALIATION. 7. Enemy retaliated with Trench Mortars and "Minnies" and rifle grenades; the signal for them to open being, in this instance, three green rockets.

CASUALTIES. 8. <u>Enemy</u> - three men killed.

<u>Raiding party's.</u> - One officer killed.

H.Q. 73 I.B.
10. 10. 16.

Brigadier General,
Commanding 73rd. Infantry Brigade.

KENNEDY CRATER.

W

Y

B.1.

X

N

GERMAN TRENCH.

BRITISH TRENCH.

POINT X = S. 9. c. 1½. 4.

"C" Form (Original).
MESSAGES AND SIGNALS.

Army Form C, 2123.

Prefix	Code	Words	Received From	Sent, or sent out At	Office Stamp
		51		11.7 a.m.	AT 10/10/16
Charges to collect			By	To SK	
Service Instructions (BB) AT				By Charlton	

Handed in at .... Office 10.32 a.m. Received 11.10 a.m.

TO OC B Coy ~~FLUITE~~ App No 6

Sender's Number: BM 182   Day of Month: 10   In reply to Number: AAA

Message from Condy begins aaa Please convey the divisional commander's congratulations to Fluite on the results obtained in their raid this morning aaa The divisional commander deeply regrets to hear of the loss of 2/Lt SHANKSTER aaa Ends aaa Please let all ranks know this aaa

FROM: ~~Fluite~~
PLACE & TIME: FLUITE 11.35 am

This line should be erased if not required.

Wt. 432—M437 500,000 Pads. HWV 5/16 Forms C.2123.

App No 7

WORKING PARTIES TO BE DETAILED FOR WORK UNDER THE 104th FIELD COY. R.E.

PARTY	R.E. Officer I/C of WORK.	RENDEZVOUS.	LOCALITY OF WORK.	No. of MEN.	HOURS OF WORK.	UNIT SUPPLYING WORKING PARTY.
"A"	2/Lt. NICHOLLS.	CENTRAL DUMP.	SMALL CAVE TOTTENHAM.	36 in 3 Shifts.	5.a.m.-1.p.m. 1.p.m.-9.p.m. 9.p.m.-5.a.m.	7th. Northants. Rgt. " " "
"B"	2/Lt. WATSON.	-do-	-do-	40. 40.	9.a.m.-1.p.m. 1.p.m.-5.p.m.	" "
"C"	2/Lt. WATSON.	R.E.Advance H.Q's 100 yds.S.of where BOYAU 123 meets ARRAS-BETHUNE Road.	"	4. 4.	9.a.m.-1.p.m. 1.p.m.-5.p.m.	" "
"D"	2/Lt. FRANCIS	"	GRANBY AVENUE.	25.	2/Lt FRANCIS to arrange time and rendez-vous direct with O.C.UNIT.	"
"E"	2/Lt. FRANCIS	"	SNARGATE STREET DUG-OUT No.2 (W)	9.	Time and rendezvous to be given to unit by 2/Lt. FRANCIS.	13 Middlesex
"F"	2/Lt. FRANCIS.	"	HARTUNG DUG-OUT.	15.	-do-	9th Royal Sussex
"G"	2/Lt. NICHOLLS.	CENTRAL DUMP.	CAVALIER.	30.	9.a.m.-5.p.m.	"
"H"	-do- -do-	-do-	BIG CAVE TOTTENHAM. 66	30 men in 3 shifts.	5.a.m.-1.p.m. 1.p.m.-9.p.m. 9.p.m.-5.a.m.	" " "
"I"	2/Lt. WATSON.	-do-	"	12.	6.30.p.m.-10.30.p.m.	"
"J"	-do- -do-	Railway end of International.	"	30. 30.	9.a.m.-1.p.m. 1.p.m.-5.p.m.	" "

-2-

BATY.	R.E. OFFICER I/C OF WORK.	RENDEZVOUS.	LOCALITY OF WORK.	No. of MEN.	HOURS OF WORK.	UNIT SUPPLYING WORKING PARTY.
"K".	2/Lt. FRANCIS.	-	ERSATZ ALLEY.	20.	2/Lt FRANCIS to arrange time and rendezvous direct with O.C. UNIT.	9th R. SUSSEX Rg
"L".	2/Lt. NICHOLLS.	CENTRAL DUMP.	SOMBARD.	20.	6.p.m.	2nd. LEINSTER RGT.
"M"	-do-	-do-	COMPANY H.Q's.	16 men in 4 shifts.	5.a.m.-9.a.m. 9.a.m.-1.p.m. 1.p.m.-5.p.m. 5.p.m.-9.p.m.	" "
"N"	Lt. ROBERTS.	POINT G.	CABARET TRENCH.	10.	-	7th NORTHANTS RGT
"O"	"	GRANBY DUMP	-	10.	7.p.m. unloading R.E. Material.	9th. R. SUSSEX.

73rd Brigade.
24th Division.

7th BATTALION

NORTHAMPTONSHIRE REGIMENT.

December 1916.

Army Form C. 2118.

WAR DIARY
or
INTELLIGENCE SUMMARY.
(Erase heading not required.)

CONFIDENTIAL

WAR DIARY

OF

7th SERVICE BATTALION NORTHAMPTONSHIRE REGIMENT.

FROM :— DECEMBER 1st. 1916.
TO :— DECEMBER 31st. 1916.

In the Field.

DECEMBER 31st. 1916.

WAR DIARY

INTELLIGENCE SUMMARY.

(Erase heading not required.)

Instructions regarding War Diaries and Intelligence Summaries are contained in F. S. Regs., Part II. and the Staff Manual respectively. Title pages will be prepared in manuscript.

Place	Date	Hour	Summary of Events and Information	Remarks and references to Appendices
MAROC.	1.12.16.		A very foggy day. Every available man in the Battalion employed on working parties. In addition 100 men of A and B Companies to LES BREBIS to Divisional Baths.	
	2.12.16.		A frosty day. C.O. inspected draft of 12 men (all men of this Battalion), which arrived yesterday.	
	3.12.16.		A fine day. Found the usual large working parties.	
	4.12.16.		Captain Gurney left the Battalion to be attached to 72nd Infantry Brigade for instruction as Staff Captain.	
	5.12.16.		At 1.30 a.m. the Battalion "Stood To" on account of a Hun raid on our trenches at present held by 2nd.Leinster Regiment. The raid was beaten off leaving one prisoner (wounded) and one dead. The Battalion stood down at 3 a.m. During the day the enemy shelled MAROC.	
	6.12.16.		Relieved 2nd.Leinster Regiment in right sub-sector. Relief complete at 10 a.m. Since our last tour the Canadians on our right have taken over the Southern Crassier and Seventh Avenue. A draft of 6 men (all of this Battalion) arived this morning.	
	7.12.16.		A foggy day. Two patrols went out about 4 a.m. to search for signs of the raiding party which raided our lines on December 5th. Nothing was discovered. Enemy very quiet.	

INTELLIGENCE SUMMARY.

(Erase heading not required.)

Instructions regarding War Diaries and Intelligence Summaries are contained in F.S. Regs., Part II. and the Staff Manual respectively. Title pages will be prepared in manuscript.

Place	Date	Hour	Summary of Events and Information	Remarks and references to Appendices
MAROC.	8.12.16. wet		A wet day. The Commanding Officer confined to his bed with a temperature. 2nd.Lieuts Twigg, Hammond, and Goodwin with a draft of 44 men joined from the Base. Most of the men with about 3 months training and the majority aged between 35 and 40. Two patrols went out. A very quiet day. Pte Temple Sniped and Killed in CRASSIER SAP.	
	9.12.16. wet		As the Commanding Officer was still confined to his bed Major Millard inspected the draft all of whom were afterwards fitted with Small Box Respirators and passed through the gas chamber. A very wet day. The Commanding Officer has to go back sick and Major Millard takes over Command.	
	10.12.16. wet		A very wet day. Our guns including heavies had an organised shoot on the enemy's trenches. He did not retaliate. Pte Culverhouse was Killed and one man wounded by a minenwerfer in QUEEN STREET. 2nd.Lieut G.A.Williamson proceeded on Leave.	
	11.12.16 wet		A fine day. Issued Operation Orders for relief tomorrow.	
	12.12.16. wet		Snow early, followed by rain. Battalion was relieved by 2nd Leinster Regiment and went into Reserve. A and B Companies to MAROC and C and D Companies to LES BREBIS. Lieut Dryland Joined the Battalion. Total casualties during tour - 2 Killed., 2 Wounded.	

Instructions regarding War Diaries and Intelligence Summaries are contained in F.S. Regs, Part II and the Staff Manual respectively. Title pages will be prepared in manuscript.

INTELLIGENCE SUMMARY.
(Erase heading not required.)

Place	Date	Hour	Summary of Events and Information	Remarks and references to Appendices
MAROC.	13.12.16.		A draft of 174 men arrived amongst them being 11 men who were previously with this Battalion. A and B Companies find working parties and C and D Companies proceed with training including use of range at FOSSE 6. 200 men to Baths at LES BREBIS	
	14.12.16.		The draft was inspected by Colonel Lucas (Acting Brig.General) in the afternoon. R.S.M.Carter rejoined after his month's leave. 100 men bathed.	
	15.12.16.		39 men of the draft all of whom had been in France before were allotted to Companies. The remaining 135 men were sent to Training Camp at NOEUX LES MINES. Lieut Marshall proceeded in charge of the draft with 2nd.Lieuts Webb and Cameron, and R.S.M.Carter. Tea and a concert were provided for the men of C and D Companies in the Church Army Hut, LES BREBIS. The refreshment and entertainment were provided by the REV. E. U. EVITT.	
	16.12.16.		A fine day. Church Parade under the REV. E. U. EVITT at Church Army Hut, LES BREBIS was attended by C and D Companies.	
	17.12.16.		A fine day. Relieved 2nd. Leinster Regiment in the right sector. Relief complete by 10.30 a.m. Sgt Chapman hit by sniper in BARRIGADE SAP. A small camouflet was blown about 6 p.m. under the SOUTHERN CRASSIER but the Tunnelling Coy. report that very little damage was done and no casualties Good news arrived from VERDUN and this was posted on a board in view of the German trenches in front of our right Company. CAPTURED AT VERDUN. 11300 Prisoners. 116 Guns. 69 Machine Guns.	

INTELLIGENCE SUMMARY.

(Erase heading not required.)

Place	Date	Hour	Summary of Events and Information	Remarks and references to Appendices
MAROC.	19.12.16.		A cold day with snow in the afternoon. The new Brigadier (General DUGAN) visited the trenches in the morning.	
	20.12.16.		A draft of 20 men arrived from Divisional Training Camp. 2nd Lieut Knight returned from Divisional School.	
	21.12.16.		A bright frosty day. A draft of 10 men (8 old 7th) arrived this evening. 2nd. Lieuts Barton and Crompton were wounded by explosion of rifle grenade which they were firing. Heavy Artillery fire about 2 miles South of us during the afternoon which later information revealed as a very successful Canadian raid.	
	22.12.16.		A wet morning. About 1.30 a.m. heavy trench mortaring on our immediate left. This was connected with a Hun raid on Canadians which was beaten off.	
	23.12.16.		A very wet day. Enemy shelled out support and front lines vigorously at 8 p.m. and we called for retaliation which immediately silenced him.	
	24.12.16.		A very wet day and trenches getting into a bad state. Nothing to report.	
	25.12.16.		A bright day. Battalion relieved by 2nd Leinster Regiment and went into Brigade Reserve, B Company to DUKE STREET, A Company to O.G.1, and C and D Companies to billets in MAROC. Relief complete by 11 a.m. The men were issued with extras of plum pudding, sausages, oranges and apples, cigars, bloaters and beer. Only a few small working parties were required so the Battalion had a rest. Captain H.E.R. Warton went sick.	

INTELLIGENCE SUMMARY.

(Erase heading not required.)

Instructions regarding War Diaries and Intelligence Summaries are contained in F. S. Regs., Part II. and the Staff Manual respectively. Title pages will be prepared in manuscript.

Place	Date	Hour	Summary of Events and Information	Remarks and references to Appendices
MAROC.	26.12.16.		Colonel MOBBS returned to the Battalion.	
	27.12.16.		Every available men on working parties. Conference of Commanding Officers in our Battalion Headquarters. Baths were allotted to Battalion and men bathed.	
	28.12.16.		Working parties as usual.	
	29.12.16.		Weather wet. - Working parties as usual. Company Commanders conference prior to relieving 2nd Leinster Regiment in the line.	
	30.12.16.	morning.	Weather wet. Wind S.W. Battalion relieved the 2nd Leinster Regiment in the line this Trenches in a very bad state owing to the rain, mud in places 3 feet deep. Working parties busy all night draining and cleaning. Enemy artillery active in the afternoon on SOUTH STREET. Practice "Gas Alarm" was made at 5 p.m. and all stood to with respirators on.	
	31.12.16.		Weather fine but still damp. Everything quiet.	

2353 Wt. W2544/1454 700,000 5/15 D. D. & L. A.D.S.S./Forms/C. 2118.

73rd Brigade.
24th Division.

7th BATTALION

NORTHAMPTONSHIRE REGIMENT.

November 1916.

Army Form C. 211

WAR DIARY
or
INTELLIGENCE SUMMARY.
(Erase heading not required.)

Vol 14

CONFIDENTIAL.

WAR DIARY

OF

7th SERVICE BATTALION NORTHAMPTONSHIRE REGIMENT.

FROM :- NOVEMBER 1st 1916.

TO :- NOVEMBER 30th 1916.

:-:-:-:-:-:-:-:-:-:-

In the Field.
NOVEMBER 30th 1916.

Army Form C. 2118.

WAR DIARY
or
INTELLIGENCE SUMMARY.
(Erase heading not required.)

Instructions regarding War Diaries and Intelligence Summaries are contained in F. S. Regs., Part II. and the Staff Manual respectively. Title pages will be prepared in manuscript.

Place	Date	Hour	Summary of Events and Information	Remarks and references to Appendices
MAROC.	1.11.16.	AMcl	Enemy very quiet by day and night.	
	2.11.16.	AMcl	G.O.C. and B.G.C. inspect the line from 9 a.m. to 12.30 p.m. Certain Trench Mortar activity during afternoon. About 11.45 p.m. a hostile patrol approached BARRIER SAP but was driven off.	
	3.11.16.	AMcl	B.G.C. visits trenches. Enemy inactive during day.	
	4.11.16.	AMcl	Enemy inactive until evening when more active with Trench Mortars and aerial darts. Casualties - 3 Killed, 3 Wounded.	
	5.11.16.	AMcl	Very clear day. Enemy secure direct hit on new work in CRASSIER TRENCH. B.G.C. visits the line in the morning.	
	6.11.16.	AMcl	Battalion relieved in line by 2nd.Leinsters and returned to Support Billets, A and B Companies in Trenches, C and D Companies in MAROC. Rain all day.	
	7.11.16.	AMcl	Rain all day. Large working parties busy in line which is falling in all over.	
	8.11.16.	AMcl	Rain all day. Working parties all night repairing trenches.	
	9.11.16.	AMcl	Rain all day. Working parties as usual repairing front trenches	
	10.11.16.	AMcl	Finer weather. A dug-out in O.G.1 falls in during the night killing one man.	

Army Form C. 2118

WAR DIARY
or
INTELLIGENCE SUMMARY.
(Erase heading not required.)

Instructions regarding War Diaries and Intelligence Summaries are contained in F. S. Regs., Part II. and the Staff Manual respectively. Title pages will be prepared in manuscript.

Place	Date	Hour	Summary of Events and Information	Remarks and references to Appendices
MAROC	11.11.16.		Weather fine. Winter clothing issued, leather coats and thick undervests. G.O.C. Division and G.S.O. 1st Corps visit Battalion.	
	12.11.16.		Relieved 2nd.Liensters in Right Loos Sector. Relief completed 11 a.m	
	13.11.16.		Weather fine. Day very quiet. Snipers claim a hit opposite Sap H. Lieut A.W.Heaton rejoined.	
	14.11.16.		Weather fine. Our trench mortars active against the enemy front and support line in TRIANGLE.	
	15.11.16.		Weather fine. B.G.C. visits trenches.	
	16.11.16.		Weather fine. An Officers Patrol went up to enemy's line and found it unoccupied. Three Trench Mortars scored direct hits on our front line trench but there were no casualties.	
	17.11.16.		Weather fine and frosty. Lieut Berridge took out a patrol to reconnoitre enemy sap near NORTHERN GRASSIER with the object of securing a prisoner. Sap was found unoccupied. G.O.C. visits the trenches. Lieut Marshall rejoined from a course and 2nd.Lieut Pennycook joined the Battalion. A test with S.O.S. Rockets was carried out but owing to the rockets being damp was not very successful.	

Army Form C. 2118

WAR DIARY
or
INTELLIGENCE SUMMARY.
(Erase heading not required.)

Instructions regarding War Diaries and Intelligence Summaries are contained in F. S. Regs., Part II. and the Staff Manual respectively. Title pages will be prepared in manuscript.

Place	Date	Hour	Summary of Events and Information	Remarks and references to Appendices
MAROC.	18.11.16.		Battalion relieved by 2nd.Leinsters in Right Loos Sector and went into Brigade Reserve Billets in MAROC. Relief completed by 11 a.m.	
	19.11.16.		Party of 80 men under the Commanding Officer attended Church Parade at NOEUX LES MINES afterwards the Army Commander distributed decorations to men of the Division. The following Northamptons received decorations:-	
			Captain B.WRIGHT. MILITARY CROSS.	
			L/Sgt V.M.COLTON. D.C.M.	
			Sgt E.E.BUNYAN. MILITARY MEDAL.	
			L/Sgt C.BLYTHE. MILITARY MEDAL.	
			Cpl.W.A.COTTON. MILITARY MEDAL.	
			L/Cpl W.WEST. MILITARY MEDAL.	
			Pte W.L.DRAGE. MILITARY MEDAL.	
			Pte K.E.BARBY. MILITARY MEDAL.	
			Pte E.CARR. MILITARY MEDAL.	
			2nd.Lieut W.H.Cawston joined today. 140 men issued with new gas helmets and tested in gas chamber. 100 men went to Divisional Baths at LES BREBIS.	
	20.11.16.		Weather fine. In addition to large working parties, 200 men went to baths at LES BREBIS and 260 men were fitted with gas helmets.	
	21.11.16.		Weather fine. Company Kit inspections and gas drill.	
	22.11.16.		Usual large working parties. Over 100 men bathed.	
	23.11.16.		The Regimental Football team played a match with the 12th Sherwood Foresters who were beaten by 2 - 1.	
	24.11.16.		Battalion relieved the 2nd.Leinsters in right Loos Sector. Relief commenced at 7.45 a.m. and completed by 10.15 a.m.	

Army Form C. 2118.

WAR DIARY
or
INTELLIGENCE SUMMARY.
(Erase heading not required.)

Instructions regarding War Diaries and Intelligence Summaries are contained in F.S. Regs., Part II. and the Staff Manual respectively. Title pages will be prepared in manuscript.

Place	Date	Hour	Summary of Events and Information	Remarks and references to Appendices
MAROC.	24.11.16.		Our front has been slightly extended on the left since last tour. Two direct hits on ENGINEER TRENCH with enemy Trench Mortars.	
	25.11.16.		Weather wet. B.G.C. visits the line in the morning. A quiet day.	
	26.11.16.		G.O.C. visits the line.	
	27.11.16.		Weather fine. 2nd.Lieut I.M.Allport hit on the chin while in ENGINEER SAP by a sniper. Enemy dropped some Minnies in MIDDLE ALLEY. Enemy sniping unusually active. 2nd.Lieut C.R.G. Hawkins returned from Hospital and remained in LES BREBIS under arrest pending Court Martial. Company relief took place at 8 a.m., A and D Companies going into the line.	
	28.11.16.		Weather fine but very misty. 2nd.Lieut Bennett, Royal Engineers was hit by a sniper in ENGINEER SAP and died shortly afterwards. Lieut Veasey, Leicestershire Regiment attached to us for instruction.	
	29.11.16.		At Midnight we exploded a Bangalore Torpedo opposite RUSSIAN SAP under enemy's wire and followed this with fire fr m Machine Guns and Trench Mortars. The Artillery also fired a few salvoes on the enemy's trenches at the point of TRIANGLE. The enemy retaliated with Trench Mortars and Machine Guns. We had no casualties.	

2353 Wt. W2514/1454 700,000 5/15 D.D.&L. ADSS./Forms/C. 2118.

WAR DIARY

INTELLIGENCE SUMMARY.

(Erase heading not required.)

Army Form C. 2118

Place	Date	Hour	Summary of Events and Information	Remarks and references to Appendices
MAROC.	30.11.16.		Battalion was relieved at 8 a.m. by 2nd.Leinsters and went into Support, A and B Companies in MAROC and the other two Companies D and C in the KEEPS and DUKE STREET respectively. Court Martial of 2nd.Lieut Hawkins was held in LES BREBIS under the presidency of Brigadier General MITFORD. 2nd.Lieut Hawkins was acquitted. Captain H. MILLARD becomes Acting Temp. Major while Second in Command.	

SECRET.　　　　　　　　　　　　　　　　　　　　　　　COPY No. 10
Ref.Sheet　　　　73rd INFANTRY BRIGADE.
36.B.1/40,000.
　　　　　　　　OPERATION ORDER No.80.
　　　　　　　　　　　　　　H.Q. 73rd I.B. Nov. 16th 1916.

1. The following reliefs in the LOOS SECTION will take place on November 18th 1916:-

   (a) 2nd Leinsters will relieve 7th Northamptons in Right Sub-Section. First platoon to move at 8 a.m.
   On relief 7th Northamptons will become battalion in Reserve (D.Battalion).
   PICCADILLY WILL not be used by either of these Battalions.

   (b) 13th Middlesex will relieve 9th Royal Sussex in Left Sub-Section. First Platoon to move at 11 a.m.
   On relief 9th Royal Sussex will become Battalion in Support (C.Battalion).
   13th Middlesex will proceed via PICCADILLY.

   All movements will be by platoons or detachments at 200 yards interval.

2. 　　Reference Defence Scheme Appendix "L".
   (a) Working parties on the 18th instant will be found as under:-
   C Battn. All parties　　　　　　　　　　　:- 9th Royal Sussex.
   D Battn.　"　"　up to 2 p.m. inclusive - 2nd Leinsters.

   After these hours the parties will be supplied by the relieved battalions.
   (b) Party No.6(Permanent, during tour of duty) will be relieved by 12 noon under arrangements between Os.C. 2nd Leinsters and 7th Northamptons.
   (c) The Os.C. 13th Middlesex and 2nd Leinsters will arrange to leave sufficient guides to guide first parties of 9th Royal Sussex and 7th Northamptons respectively for 173rd Tunnelling Coy.R.E. to rendezvous. Arrangements to be made between Os.C concerned.

3. List of Trench Stores taken or handed over will be forwarded to Brigade Headquarters within 24 hours of relief being complete.

4. Reports on work completed during tour of duty(including 73rd M.G.Coy. and 73rd Lt.T.M.Battery) and work proposed during ensuing tour, will reach Brigade H.Q. by 9 a.m. 19th instant.

5. Completion of reliefs will be notified to Brigade H.Q. by wiring the word "APPLE".

6. PLEASE ACKNOWLEDGE.

　　　　　　　　　　　　　　　　　　　R. Howlett
　　　　　　　　　　　　　　　　　　　　　　Major,
Issued at 6 p.m.　　　　　　Brigade Major, 73rd Infantry Brigade.

Copy No. 1. File.　　　　　　　No.11. 13th Middlesex.
　　　　 2. War Diary.　　　　　　12. 2nd Leinsters.
　　　　 3. "G" 24th Div.　　　　　13. 73rd M.G.Coy.
　　　　 4. "Q" 24th Div.　　　　　14. 73rd Lt.T.M.Battery.
　　　　 5. A.P.M. 24th Div.　　　 15. 129th Fld.Coy.R.E.
　　　　 6. 17th I.B.　　　　　　　16. 173rd Tun.Coy.R.E.
　　　　 7. 72nd I.B.　　　　　　　17. Rt.Group Arty.
　　　　 8. 4th Can.I.B.　　　　　 18. S.O.73rd I.B.
　　　　 9. 9th R.Sussex.　　　　　19. B.T.C.
　　　　10. 7th Northants.　　　　 20. Bde.Signals.
　　　　　　　　　　　　　　　　　　21. S.O, TM's

CONFIDENTIAL.

WAR DIARY

OF

7th SERVICE BATTALION NORTHAMPTONSHIRE REGIMENT.

FROM - JANUARY 1st. 1917.

TO - JANUARY 31st. 1917.

In the Field.

JANUARY 31st. 1917.

Army Form C. 2118.

WAR DIARY
INTELLIGENCE SUMMARY.
(Erase heading not required.)

Instructions regarding War Diaries and Intelligence Summaries are contained in F. S. Regs., Part II. and the Staff Manual respectively. Title pages will be prepared in manuscript.

Place	Date	Hour	Summary of Events and Information	Remarks and references to Appendices
MAROC.	1.1.17.		Weather fine. Enemy Artillery very active during the morning and his attitude seems more alert.	
	2.1.17.		We exploded a Bangalore Torpedoe at 5.50 a.m. successfully blowing a gap in the enemy wire. Remainder of day quiet.	
	3.1.17.		Weather fine. Artillery activity during the whole of the day. Notification appears in the times that the Commanding Officer has won the D.S.O.	
	4.1.17.		Weather damp. Preparations made to explode another Bangalore Torpedoe early tomorrow morning.	
	5.1.17.		Bangalore Torpedoe exploded at 3 a.m. Battalion relieved by 2nd Leinster Regiment in the line. B Coy. and Headquarters return to LES BREBIS (DIVISIONAL RESERVE), A Coy and C Coy remain at MAROC while D Company remain in SOUTH STREET under the Command of the Leinster Regiment to act as Support owing to a Company of the Leinster Regiment preparing for a Raid. A Company returned to MAROC this evening.	
	6.1.17.		Usual Working parties. Lieut.Col. E.R.Mobbs detailed as Member of Court of Enquiry and is away all day. A little training carried out.	

Army Form C. 2118.

WAR DIARY
INTELLIGENCE SUMMARY.
(Erase heading not required.)

Instructions regarding War Diaries and Intelligence Summaries are contained in F. S. Regs., Part II. and the Staff Manual respectively. Title pages will be prepared in manuscript.

Place	Date	Hour	Summary of Events and Information	Remarks and references to Appendices
MAROC.	7.1.17.		Weather fine. Training of A and B Companies carried on with	
	8.1.17.		Draft of 21 O.R. from Training Battalion arrive. Working party of 150 for burying cable is found and proceed at 3 p.m. 7 p.m., and 11 p.m.	
	9.1.17.		2nd.Lieut. I.M. ALLPORT is killed during the last hour of the above Working party by a Machine Gun bullet in the forehead and is buried in MAROC. Commanding Officer visits the Divisional Training Battalion. Draft from Davisional Training Battalion inspected by Commanding Officer. Lieut A.W.Heaton returnns from Leave.	
	10.1.17.		Commanding Officer visits the trainingGrounds of A and B Companies and addressed B Company.	
	11.1.17.		A and B Companies were provided with a Tea and Concert in the Church Army Hut, LES BREBIS. Battalion relieved 2nd Leinster Regiment, relief being completed by 11 a.m. Three casualties during the day, none serious. Snow and Sleet during the day.	
	12.1.17.		The B.G.C went round the line with the C.O. At about 8.45 p.m. the enemy, having probably observed our patrol and immashing a raid, sent up two red rockets and his artillery and trench mortars opened a heavy fire on our front and support lines. Our artillery took the enemy rockets for our S.O.S. and retaliated. The firing lasted about half an hour during which all Companies and Hdqrs. stood to. Our casualties were 4 of which 3 were slight. Total casualties for the day - 7.	

2353 Wt. W2544/1454 700,000 5/15 D.D.&L. A.D.S.S./Forms/C. 2118.

Army Form C. 2118.

WAR DIARY
~~INTELLIGENCE SUMMARY.~~
(Erase heading not required.)

Instructions regarding War Diaries and Intelligence Summaries are contained in F. S. Regs., Part II and the Staff Manual respectively. Title pages will be prepared in manuscript.

Place	Date	Hour	Summary of Events and Information	Remarks and references to Appendices
MAROC	13.1.17.		Snow with frost at night. A very quiet day. Rations were very late.	
	14.1.17.		A fine day with fog and frost during the morning.	
	15.1.17.		Snow. A quiet day. A draft of 47 men from the Training Battalion arrived this evening.	
	16.1.17.		A fine frosty day. At 4.30 p.m. the enemy commenced to shell our front chiefly on the left and we retaliated and stood to. Everything was quiet again in half an hour. A draft of 6 men arrived this evening.	
	17.1.17.		The Canadians on our right raided the enemy on a large scale and took 102 prisoners and a mine was blown under the Southern Crassier. This led to some retaliation on our trenches. Owing to above, our relief was postponed until 2 p.m. and was completed by 4.30 p.m. Snow and thaw during the day. Total casualties during tour - 2 killed - 13 wounded.	
	18.1.17.		Snow and frost. Over 100 men to Divisional Baths at LES BREBIS.	
	19.1.17.		Frosty with snow on ground.	
	20.1.17.		Frosty with snow on ground. A party of 40 men from A Company to CINEMA at LES BREBIS to see the SOMME film.	
	21.1.17.		Very cold. Middlesex raided on our left and took 3 prisoners one of whom was sent	

2353   Wt. W2544/1454 700,000 5/15   D. D. & L.   A.D.S.S./Forms/C. 2118.

WAR DIARY or INTELLIGENCE SUMMARY.

(Erase heading not required.)

Army Form C. 2118.

Place	Date	Hour	Summary of Events and Information	Remarks and references to Appendices
MAROC.	23.1.17.		To our Headquarters for examination by Corps Intelligence Officer. 2nd.Lieut.Fitzhugh joined the Battalion from the 1st Battalion.	
	24.1.17.		Very cold. A large number of men to Baths at LES BREBIS. A party of 40 men from D Company to CINEMA at LES BREBIS to see SOMME film.	
	25.1.17.		Hard frost. Relieved 2nd Leinster Regiment in line. Relief complete by 10 a.m. A quiet day.	
	26.1.17.		Frosty. At 3 oclock this morning the enemy commenced a heavy bombardment on our lines, chiefly with trench mortars especially directed against KING ST. and BARRICADE SAP held by D Company. He attacked in a party about 80 strong, but only one Officer and 12 men reached our trenches entering both BARRICADE SAP and KING ST. close to their junction. Of these, the Officer and 5 men were killed and the remainder quickly driven off taking with them one of our men who was wounded as prisoner but he managed to escape when near the enemy wire and returned to our line. One of the raiding party got lost on his way back and ran into the wire opposite the 9th Royal Sussex Regiment and was taken prisoner by them. The enemy left 2 heavy Mobile charges near our wire and these were brought in by Patrols. Our casualties were 4 killed and 14 wounded, chiefly in preliminary bombardment.	
	27.1.17.		Hard frost. A quiet day. Officers of 9th K.O.Y.L.I. who are relieving us visited the line.	

Army Form C. 2118.

WAR DIARY
or
INTELLIGENCE SUMMARY.
(Erase heading not required.)

Instructions regarding War Diaries and Intelligence Summaries are contained in F. S. Regs., Part II. and the Staff Manual respectively. Title pages will be prepared in manuscript.

Place	Date	Hour	Summary of Events and Information	Remarks and references to Appendices
MAROC	26.1.17.		Clear and frosty. At 8 oclock this morning the enemy bombarded our left company front with Minnies and Aerial darts. Artillery retaliation was called for and the enemy stopped. Pte. Boyson was killed by a sniper. 2 Killed and 3 wounded during the day.	
	27.1.17.		A quiet day. We were visited by 2 Officers of the Swedish Army. Owing to some delay on the Railway, rations were very much delayed. Capt. & Adjt Hobbs of the Lancashire Fusiliers attached to us for instruction.	
	28.1.17.		Rations only reached the line at 9 a.m. and consisted only of reserve rations and an issue of Rum.	
	29.1.17.		Very cold. Battalion was relieved by 2nd Leicester Regiment and proceeded to Division Reserve Billets at LES BREBIS. Relief completed by 11.30 a.m.	
	30.1.17.		D Company, 2 Platoons of B Company and 2 Lewis Gun teams, all concerned in the Raid on our trenches on the 24th inst were inspected by General ANDERSON, 1st Corps Commander in the CINEMA, LES BREBIS. After General ANDERSON had addressed them they were also addressed by General CAPPER.	
	31.1.17.		Snowing.	

Vol 17

CONFIDENTIAL.

WAR DIARY

OF

7th SERVICE BATTALION NORTHAMPTONSHIRE REGIMENT.

FROM :- FEBRUARY 1st. 1917.

TO :- FEBRUARY 28th. 1917.

:0:0:0:0:0:0:0:0:0:0:0:

IN THE FIELD.

FEBRUARY 28th. 1917.

Army Form C. 2118.

WAR DIARY
INTELLIGENCE SUMMARY.
(Erase heading not required.)

Instructions regarding War Diaries and Intelligence Summaries are contained in F. S. Regs., Part II. and the Staff Manual respectively. Title pages will be prepared in manuscript.

Place	Date	Hour	Summary of Events and Information	Remarks and references to Appendices
LES BREBIS.	1.2.17.		Captain H.B.King returned from leave.	
	2.2.17.		Musketry and Physical Drill during morning.	
	3.2.17.		All arms inspected by Brigade Armourer. 500 men taken to entertainment in the Cinema in the evening. The "Snipers" provided the programme.	
MAROC.	4.2.17.		Relieved 2nd Leinster Regiment this morning, "A" and "D" Companies in front line. A quiet day.	
	5.2.17.		B.G.C. visited the line.	
	6.2.17.		A "minnie" dropped amongst a party of "C" Company in CORDIALE AVENUE, killing 2 and wounding 7.	
	7.2.17.		Inter-Company relief this morning, B and C Companies relieving D and A Companies in front line.	
	8.2.17.		The line was visited by Officers of the 8th East Lancs who are relieving us. Received Operation Orders for relief on 11th inst. Lieut.Col E.R.Mobbs D.S.O. proceeded on leave to England and Major Millard assumed command.	
	9.2.17.		A quiet day.	
	10.2.17.		A quiet day.	
PETIT SAINS.	11.2.17.		Battalion was relieved by the 8th East Lancs and moved to billets in PETIT SAINS. Relief complete by 12 noon.	

2353 Wt. W2544/1454 700,000 5/15 D.D.&L. A.D.S.S./Forms/C. 2118.

Army Form C. 2118.

WAR DIARY

INTELLIGENCE SUMMARY.

(Erase heading not required.)

Instructions regarding War Diaries and Intelligence Summaries are contained in F.S. Regs., Part II. and the Staff Manual respectively. Title pages will be prepared in manuscript.

Place	Date	Hour	Summary of Events and Information	Remarks and references to Appendices
LAPUGNOY.	12.2.17.	A.D.	Battalion marched at 8.30 a.m. by Platoons as far as NOEUX LES MINES where it formed into column and proceeded via VAUDRICOURT, HESDIGNEUL, and LABEUVRIERS to rest billets at LAPUGNOY. It was inspected en route between VAUDRICOURT and HESDIGNEUL by Field Marshal Sir Douglas Haig. The Battalion marched well and reached its billets about 2.30 p.m.	
	13.2.17.	A.D.	No work was done but all men in "A" and "B" Companies were inoculated and examined for-scabies. General Dugan and Col. Kay visited the Billets.	
	14.2.17.	A.D.	C and D Companies were inoculated and examined for Scabies. The O.C. and Company Co.manders attended a conference on the new organisation at Brigade Headquarters.	
	15.2.17.	A.D.	The O.C. inspected all Companies during the morning. 2nd.Lt. P.Knight was evacuated Sick.	
	16.2.17.	A.D.	A bright frosty morning. The Brigade was inspected at HESDIGNEUL by General Nivelle commanding the French Armies. The Battalion.paraded at 7.30 a.m. and marched to HESDIGNEUL the inspection taking place at 10.35 a.m. The thaw set in this afternoon.	
	17.2.17.	A.D.	A warm day. The Companies carried on with inspections.	
	18.2.17.	A.D.	40 men from each Company attended Church Parade in the Divisional Canteen, LAPUGNOY.	
	19.2.17.	A.D.	The Battalion began its training programme today with Physical training, Bombing and Bayonet Fighting.	

Army Form C. 2118.

WAR DIARY
INTELLIGENCE SUMMARY.
(Erase heading not required.)

Instructions regarding War Diaries and Intelligence Summaries are contained in F.S. Regs., Part II and the Staff Manual respectively. Title pages will be prepared in manuscript.

Place	Date	Hour	Summary of Events and Information	Remarks and references to Appendices
LAPUGNOY.	19.3.17.		Draft of 13 men arrived from Base and 65 from Training Battalion which is now closed.	
	20.3.17.		A very wet day and training had to be stopped about 10.30 a.m.	
	21.3.17.		Fine and warm. "A"Company was allotted the range at ALLOUAGNE and M&N other Companies various small ranges in sand pits. B Company to Baths at FOUQUIERES during the afternoon. The Commanding Officer returned from leave this evening. The Battalion Team played the 73rd Machine Gun Coy in the first round of the Brigade Football competition and won 5-0.	
	22.3.17.		All Companies continued shooting except "A" which proceeded to Baths at FOUQUIERES. We won the match against the 73rd Light Trench Mortar Battery in second round of Brigade Football competition 11-0.	
	23.3.17.		A Brigade Field Day for Officers was held near LA BEUVRIERE and after lunch in the Cinema, a conference was held on the day's proceedings. The Commanding Officer acted as Referee and Major Millard acted in Command.	
	24.3.17.		Companies continued training with Bombing and Musketry. The Battalion Team won its semi-final round against 8th Royal Sussex Regt by 12 goals to 2.	
	25.3.17.		Church Parade attended by 60 men per Company. An Officers Revolver competition was held. The Divisional Band visited the Battalion area and played from 6 p.m. to 7.30 p.m.	

WAR DIARY
INTELLIGENCE SUMMARY.
(Erase heading not required.)

Army Form C. 2118.

Instructions regarding War Diaries and Intelligence Summaries are contained in F.S. Regs., Part II. and the Staff Manual respectively. Title pages will be prepared in manuscript.

Place	Date	Hour	Summary of Events and Information	Remarks and references to Appendices
LAPUGNOY.	25.2.17.	A.M.	2nd.Lieut Wright returned from a course and 2nd.Lieut Twigg took over Command of C Company, Capt. Warton being transferred to B Company as 2nd. in Command.	
	26.2.17.	A.M.	The Battalion went for a route march parading at 9 a.m. and proceeded to CHOCQUES and LA BEUVRIERE where a lecture on Bayonet Fighting was given by Capt. Anderson. In the afternoon a Divisional Cross Country race was run. The race started from ALLOUAGNE and finished at LAPUGNOY. The Battalion Team finished 4th, Capt. Elliman being 5th man in and Cpl Moore 8th.	
	27.2.17.	A.M.	During the morning Companies continued training in Bayonet Fighting and Musketry. In the afternoon the final round of the Brigade Football Competition was played on the C.C.S. ground. The Battalion beat the 73rd Brigade Headquarters Team by 4-1 and after the game, General J.E.Capper C.B. presented the winners with a Silver Cup. The Divisional Band was allotted to the Battalion for the day and played during the match.	
	28.2.1917.	A.M.	One Platoon per Company paraded at 9 a.m. and marched to the Bois des Dames where a scheme was carried out for practice in liaison between Infantry and Aircraft. The remainder of the Companies continued training. C Company to baths at EOUQUIERES.	

CONFIDENTIAL.

WAR DIARY

OF

7th SERVICE BATTALION NORTHAMPTONSHIRE REGIMENT.

FROM :- MARCH 1st. 1917.

TO :- MARCH 31st. 1917.

In the Field.
MARCH 31st. 1917.

Army Form C. 2118.

WAR DIARY
or
INTELLIGENCE SUMMARY.
(Erase heading not required.)

Instructions regarding War Diaries and Intelligence
Summaries are contained in F.S. Regs., Part II.
and the Staff Manual respectively. Title pages
will be prepared in manuscript.

Place	Date	Hour	Summary of Events and Information	Remarks and references to Appendices
LAPUGNOY.	1.3.17	7 A.M.	Training in Bombing and firing rifle Grenades. The Battalion football team played the 1st Batn. North Staffords in the afternoon and lost 4-1. Owing to an outbreak of measles, No.13 Platoon has had to be isolated.	
	2.3.17	7 A.M.	The Commanding Officer inspected transport and presented prizes for the best turn-outs. The B.G.C. arrived during the inspection. The Battalion team played the 12th Sherwood Foresters in the afternoon and beat them 2-0.	
HALLICOURT.	3.3.17	7 A.M.	The Battalion left its rest billets, paraded at 9.30 a.m. and marched to HALLICOURT. It was inspected during the march by General GATTER. The weather during the rest period has been exceptionally good there having been only one wet day.	
ABLAIN ST. NAZAIRE.	4.3.17	2 P.M.	The Battalion paraded at 2 p.m. and marched via BARLIN, HERSIN, PETIT SAINS, GRAND SERVINS to ABLAIN ST. NAZAIRE where it relieved the 2nd Bn. Leinster Regiment in Support lines. Relief complete by 9 p.m.	
	5.3.17	7 A.M.	Snow during the night followed by a quick thaw. At 6.15 p.m. a "Stand To" was practised, all Companies and Headquarters moving to Battle positions.	
	6.3.17	7 A.M.	A bright day with great aerial activity, 3 British and one German planes being brought down.	
	7.3.17	7 A.M.	Drill and extremely cold with a strong wind. A quiet day. The G.O.C. visited the line and lunched at Headquarters.	

Army Form C. 2118.

WAR DIARY
of
INTELLIGENCE SUMMARY.
(Erase heading not required.)

Instructions regarding War Diaries and Intelligence Summaries are contained in F. S. Regs., Part II. and the Staff Manual respectively. Title pages will be prepared in manuscript.

Place	Date	Hour	Summary of Events and Information	Remarks and references to Appendices
ABLAIN ST. NAZAIRE.	8.3.17.	A.M.	Extremely cold with snow during the night and in the morning. A quiet day. 2nd Lieuts. Pasmore, Morris, and Morgan rejoined from England today.	
	9.3.17.	A.M.	Cold with snow at times. A quiet day. B.G.C. visited the area.	
	10.3.17.	A.M.	A quiet day. The Battalion was relieved at ABLAIN ST. NAZAIRE, and LORETTE SPUR by the 73rd Canadian Regiment and went forward and relieved the 2nd Bn. Leinster Regiment in the Right SOUCHEZ Sector. Very dark early in the evening with fog.	
SOUCHEZ.	11.3.17.	A.M.	About 5.15 a.m. the enemy began to shell our Support lines very heavily and there was also some Machine Gun fire. We obtained retaliation which was very effective and after 25 minutes the enemy stopped without making any attempt to come over. Otherwise a quiet day.	
	12.3.17.	A.M.	A quiet day. One man killed in NORTHUMBERLAND POST by a Sniper.	
	13.3.17.	A.M.	A quiet day with some rain. Inter-Company reliefs this evening, B Company relieving C Company on the left, and A Company relieving D Company on the right.	
	14.3.17.	A.M.	A quiet day with rain. Working parties cancelled at night owing to darkness and wet.	
	15.3.17.	A.M.	A fine day.	

WAR DIARY
or
INTELLIGENCE SUMMARY.
(Erase heading not required.)

Army Form C. 2118.

Place	Date	Hour	Summary of Events and Information	Remarks and references to Appendices
BOUCHER.	5.3.17.		G.O.C. visited the line. Working parties again cancelled. The Red Ensign, being the only flag available was hoisted on Lone Tree this evening by 2nd Lieut Berridge.	
	6.3.17.		A fine day. At 3.45 this morning the Canadians on our right carried out a Raid on VIMY RIDGE. This led to a little shelling of our line, 3 men being wounded. We were relieved by the 2nd Bn Leinster Regiment relief being complete at about 4 p.m. The Battalion became Divisional Reserve, A and B Companies being at PETIT SAINS, and C and D Companies and Headquarters in SAINS-EN-GOHELLE. Total casualties of tour 4 Killed and 4 Wounded.	
SAINS-EN-GOHELLE.	7.3.17.		A bright day. No work was done.	
	8.3.17.		A fine day. Church Parade at 10.30 a.m. in front of the CHATEAU conducted by the Rev. E.U.EVITT. The Battalion Team played the 12th Royal Fusiliers at Football and drew 3 all.	
	9.3.17.		Dull with 4 spots rain. The Companies carried on with training of Platoons in Attack. The Germans raided our Right Company Trench (now occupied by 2nd Bn. Leinster Regiment) at 5 a.m. but failed to secure any identifications.	
	10.3.17.		A very wet cold day. C and D Companies moved from SAINS-EN-GOHELLE to BOUVIGNY HUTS with Brigade Major Command.	

Army Form C. 2118.

WAR DIARY
or
INTELLIGENCE SUMMARY.
(Erase heading not required.)

Instructions regarding War Diaries and Intelligence Summaries are contained in F. S. Regs., Part II. and the Staff Manual respectively. Title pages will be prepared in manuscript.

Place	Date	Hour	Summary of Events and Information	Remarks and references to Appendices
SAINS-EN-GOHELLE.	20.3.17.		At 6.30 p.m. there was a Battalion Concert in the Canteen SAINS-EN-GOHELLE. C and D Companies Bathed in the Brewery.	
	21.3.17.		A cold day with rain.	
	22.3.17.		A cold day with snow showers. The Battalion relieved the 2nd Bn. Leinster Regiment in the trenches, the first Platoon moving off at 6.15 p.m., and relief being complete by 10 p.m. A and B Companies in front line with C and D Companies in Support.	
BOUVIGNY.	23.3.17.		A quiet day till 8.45 p.m. when our left Company (B) was shelled and manned heavily apparently in retaliation for our Stokes fire as MX they appeared to be searching for the Stokes emplacement. KILLER TRENCH was damaged and entrance to Company Headquarters was blown in, one man being killed.	
	24.3.17.		Enemy shelled KILLER TRENCH in the afternoon doing considerable damage. A draft of 10 O.R. (all but 1 being old 7th men) arrived today.	
	25.3.17.		A wet day. Inter-Company relief took place, C and D Companies going into front line. 2nd Lieut Barridge and two daylight patrols of enemy's wire and old front line.	
	26.3.17.		Snow and rain during day. The enemy shelled KILLER TRENCH during the afternoon but did no damage. He also shelled BRIXTON TRENCH and ARRAS ROAD.	

WAR DIARY
or
INTELLIGENCE SUMMARY.
(Erase heading not required.)

Army Form C. 2118.

Place	Date	Hour	Summary of Events and Information	Remarks and references to Appendices
BOUCHEZ.	27.3.17.		A wet day with some showers of hail. Enemy shelled HEADQUARTER TRENCH on the right occupied by A Company at intervals during day but did no damage. At 8.55 p.m. the enemy opened a heavy bombardment on our front chiefly left Company (C) and communication trenches. He also shelled the left Battalion heavily. Our Artillery opened fire very promptly and effectively, and after ½ hour everything settled down. Again at midnight the enemy opened fire but this stopped after a few minutes. Our casualties were 1 Killed and 2 Wounded.	
	28.3.17.		Bright at first changing to dull and rain later. About 5.30 p.m. a heavy bombardment on our lines and on VIMY RIDGE opened and our Artillery retaliated. This lasted about an hour. The enemy opened again about 9.45 p.m. but all was quiet again by 10 p.m. 2nd Lieut G.P.Rathbone was wounded. Casualties :- O.R. Killed 3 - Wounded 10 (including 2 slightly, still at duty).	
	29.3.1917.		A very wet day. At dusk a Canadian patrol came across to BOUCHEZ POST and reported that they were expecting to be attacked during the night. BOUCHEZ POST was reinforced but no attack developed. A whizz-bang knocked out 7 men at BOUCHEZ POST & 1 was killed.	
	30.3.17.		Changeable during day, fine at night. Battalion was relieved by 2nd Bn. Leinster Regiment and proceeded into Brigade Reserve at ABLAIN ST. NAZAIRE and LORETTE SPUR. B Company in ABLAIN LANE, A Company in BAJOLLE LINE, C Company in DUG-OUT LANE, and D Company in MAISNIL LINE. At about 10 p.m. (during relief), the enemy started whizzbanging and minnying our Right Company. Retaliation was	

Army Form C. 2118.

WAR DIARY
INTELLIGENCE SUMMARY.
(Erase heading not required.)

Instructions regarding War Diaries and Intelligence Summaries are contained in F.S. Regs., Part II and the Staff Manual respectively. Title pages will be prepared in manuscript.

Place	Date	Hour	Summary of Events and Information	Remarks and references to Appendices
	30.3.17	A/01	obtained and after half an hour the activity ceased. Relief was completed just after midnight one man of B Company being wounded on way out. During the tour we had 7 men killed, 2 died of wounds, and 22 wounded (including 3 slightly), an army.	
	31.3.17	A/01	We sniped with men at intervals. At 9.30 p.m. the Cameronians on the right of our line raided the enemy and took 8 prisoners.	

7th BATTN. NORTHAMPTONSHIRE REGIMENT

73rd INFANTRY BRIGADE

24th DIVISION

APRIL 1917

Vol 19

CONFIDENTIAL.

WAR DIARY

OF

7th SERVICE BATTALION NORTHAMPTONSHIRE REGIMENT.

FROM - APRIL 1st. 1917.
TO   - APRIL 30th. 1917.

In the Field.
APRIL 30th. 1917.

Army Form C. 2118.

WAR DIARY

INTELLIGENCE SUMMARY.

(Erase heading not required.)

Instructions regarding War Diaries and Intelligence Summaries are contained in F. S. Regs., Part II. and the Staff Manual respectively. Title pages will be prepared in manuscript.

Place	Date	Hour	Summary of Events and Information	Remarks and references to Appendices
ABLAIN ST NAZAIRE	1.4.17.		A wet day and very cold. B Company bathed at Baths in ABLAIN ST NAZAIRE.	
	2.4.17.		Heavy snow all day. A wiring party of 200 men from C and D Companies under Major Millard wired NOULETTE SWITCH. D and B Companies bathed.	
	3.4.17.		A wet day. Same wiring party as last night. 2nd.Lieuts Evans and Knight rejoined this evening. Received orders that the Battalion returns to the line tomorrow night - this was unexpected as after 8 days in the line we had been promised 8 days out. Capt Seys, Heavy Machine Gun Corps attached to us for instruction.	
	4.4.17.		A dull day. Battalion was relieved in LORETTE DEFENCES by 1st Royal Fusiliers, relief being completed by 11.15 p.m. The Battalion then moved forward and took over the SOUCHEZ SECTOR from the 2nd Leinster Regiment. This relief completed at 1.30 a.m. No casualties during relief.	
SOUCHEZ.	5.4.17.		A bright day. Heavy bombardment by our guns of VIMY RIDGE and enemy trenches in BOIS EN HACHE all day. We intended raiding the enemy during the night but the attempt had to be postponed owing to the moon being very bright.	
	6.4.17.		A pouring wet day and night. Bombardment continues. One of our guns continually fired short and about 11.30 p.m. landed a shell in HEADQUARTER TRENCH killing Pte Hines, the Commanding Officers Runner.	

Army Form C. 2118.

WAR DIARY

INTELLIGENCE SUMMARY.

(Erase heading not required.)

Instructions regarding War Diaries and Intelligence Summaries are contained in F. S. Regs., Part II. and the Staff Manual respectively. Title pages will be prepared in manuscript.

Place	Date	Hour	Summary of Events and Information	Remarks and references to Appendices
SOUCHEZ.	6.4.17.		The enemy very windy all night and opened several times with short bursts of Artillery fire. One of these bursts opened just as raiding party was leaving our trenches and the raid had to be again postponed.	
	7.4.17.		A fine day. Received Operation Orders for attack by 2nd Leinster Regiment and 9th Royal Sussex Regiment opposite BOIS EN HACHE in conjunction with Canadian attack on VIMY. This Battalion is Support. Enemy artillery active with repeated short bursts. Our heavies shelling all day.	
	8.4.17.		A fine day. Our artillery shelled enemy heavily all day. He retaliated at intervals during the night.	
	9.4.17.		A fine day. We shelled the enemy trenches heavily from 2 a.m. to 4.10 a.m. this morning. At 5.30 a.m. our artillery opened on VIMY RIDGE to cover the Canadian attack on the ridge, south of the PIMPLE. News has been received that this was very successful. 2nd Lieut Passmore wounded in face by a whizz-bang. The 2nd Leinsters were to have taken over the front line and attacked the BOIS EN HACHE tonight but at 6.30 p.m. (all arrangements being complete), the attack was cancelled.	
	10.4.17.		A bright day with snow during the afternoon. The Middlesex on our right (South of SOUCHEZ RIVER) sent up the S.O.S about 4 p.m. The PIMPLE was heavily shelled by us. O.Ps report enemy massing opposite us about a mile behind his line. A quiet night.	
	11.4.17.		A bright cold day with heavy snow at night. Major Millard was hit in the head about 10 a.m. by a whizzbang in HEAD-QUARTER TRENCH.	

WAR DIARY

INTELLIGENCE SUMMARY.

(Erase heading not required.)

Army Form C. 2118.

Place	Date	Hour	Summary of Events and Information	Remarks and references to Appendices
SOUCHEZ.	11.4.17.		2nd Leinster Regiment took over left front line and we withdrew B and C Companies to ABLAIN LANE, A Company in right front and D Company in right support.	
	12.4.17.		Snowed heavily during morning. A shell dropped in No.1 Post, killing 2nd.Lt.Hammond and 6 others and wounding 5. At 5.30 a.m. the 2nd Leinster Regiment attacked from the BOIS EN HACHE and the 9th Royal Sussex Regiment attacked on their left. The attack succeeded in capturing the enemy front line but the Leinster casualties were heavy. At the same time the Canadians attacked and captured THE PIMPLE, immediately South of our line. We were to have attacked this evening on a front of about 200 yards immediately adjoining and North of the river but at the last moment this was cancelled.	
	13.4.17.		A fine day. It became apparent during the morning that the enemy had withdrawn and patrols were pushed out at 3.30 p.m. Orders were received to "Stand To" and be ready to move forward in support.	
	14.4.17.		A fine day. Battalion left the trenches and moved forward in support of 12th Royal Fusiliers at 1.30 p.m. Headquarters were established in Hammerhead of old German line until 4.30 p.m. and then moved forward to RED MILL at ROLLENCOURT the Companies being in position on the river line between Cite de l'Abattoire and LEIVIN, C and D Companies in front line and A and B in support. 2 British planes brought down XM near our lines. Signs that Country has been hurriedly evacuated by enemy.	
ROLLENCOURT.	15.4.17.		A very wet day. C and D Companies sent up to support 13th Middlesex (who had taken over front line from 12 Royal Fusiliers) to West of BOIS de RIAUMONT in evening	

Army Form C. 2118.

WAR DIARY
or
INTELLIGENCE SUMMARY.
(Erase heading not required.)

Instructions regarding War Diaries and Intelligence Summaries are contained in F. S. Regs., Part II. and the Staff Manual respectively. Title pages will be prepared in manuscript.

Place	Date	Hour	Summary of Events and Information	Remarks and references to Appendices
ROLENCOURT.	15.4.17.		but were recalled after 2 hours.	
	16.4.17.		Fine morning - wet later. A quiet day. We took over the line at night from the 13th Middlesex Regiment, D Company on right and A Company on left on Eastern edge of BOIS de RIAUMONT and C Company on N.E. edge of CITE de RIAUMONT. Headquarters in CITE des BURFAUX. 17th Brigade on our left and 5th Division on our right. A Company had 14 casualties chiefly from shelling. Enemy shelled us heavily from midnight till 4 a.m.	
CITE des BURFAUX	17.4.17.		Windy and wet. During the afternoon, G.O.C., B.G.C., B.M., and C.R.E., visited the line and when in BOIS DE RIAUMONT were suddenly confronted by 3 Huns. Having no revolvers they hastily withdrew and called for an instant counter attack, 2 Companies of the Middlesex being sent up in Support. Two of our platoons searched the wood but could discover no signs of the enemy who had been able to enter the wood owing to the fact that two A Company posts established to protect that corner of the wood had both been blotted out by shell fire. A Company again had heavy casualties. At dusk under Brigade orders our line was drawn back from CITE de RIAUMONT to eastern edge of wood. During the afternoon one of the posts of this advanced line was attacked by a rifle and bombing party which was driven off leaving 5 dead and taking with it 4 wounded. Our casualties were 2 Killed and 2nd Lt. Cawston slightly wounded.	
	18.4.1917.		A wet day. Our attack on some houses on edge of BOIS de RIAUMONT from which enemy snipers had been active was organised for 5 a.m. The signal for attack was the opening of artillery fire but the Artillery failed to open and the attack was postponed. We were ordered to re-occupy our posts in the CITE de RIAUMONT and C Coy. did this about midnight.	

Army Form C. 2118.

WAR DIARY
or
INTELLIGENCE SUMMARY.
(Erase heading not required.)

Instructions regarding War Diaries and Intelligence Summaries are contained in F. S. Regs., Part II. and the Staff Manual respectively. Title pages will be prepared in manuscript.

Place	Date	Hour	Summary of Events and Information	Remarks and references to Appendices
CITE DES BUREAUX	19.4.17	A.M.	Wet day. C Company posts in CITE de RIAUMONT were pushed forward during the morning under party led by 2nd Lieuts Berridge and Morris and all the houses North of road from rENS to BOIS de RIBUMONT (8 rows of houses in all) were occupied by us. Battalion was relieved by 46th Division, the 6th Sherwood Foresters taking over our right and the 8th Sherwood Foresters taking over our left. A good relief completed by 11 p.m. After relief on way back 2 men of C Coy were killed and 4 wounded. Battalion proceeded into billets at PETIT SAINS. Total casualties during tour since April 14th - 61 of whom 17 were killed.	
PETIT SAINS	20.4.17	A.M.	A fine day. Battalion remained at PETIT SAINS.	
MARLES LES MINES	21.4.17	A.M.	A fine day. Battalion marched off at 10.30 a.m. to MARLES LES MINES, route PERSIN, - BARLIN, - HATTICOURT.	
FEBVIN PALFART	22.4.17	A.M.	A fine day. Battalion marched off at 6.30 a.m. via FOZINGHEM, AUCHEL, COUCHY-a-la-TOUR - FONTAINE les HERMANS to FEBVIN PALFART where it arrived about 2.30 p.m. and went into billets this being its training area.	
	23.4.17	A.M.	A fine day. Nothing was done except Company inspections of Kit, etc...	
	26.4.17	A.M.	A fine day. B.G.C. inspected the Battalion at 9 a.m. and addressed the men. He also presented medals given by himself and by the Commanding Officer to the members of the football team which won the 73rd Brigade Football Cup at LAPUGNOY.	
	24.4.17	A.M.	A fine day. C.O. inspected all Coys. during the morning.	

Army Form C. 2118.

WAR DIARY
or
INTELLIGENCE SUMMARY.
(Erase heading not required.)

Instructions regarding War Diaries and Intelligence Summaries are contained in F. S. Regs., Part II. and the Staff Manual respectively. Title pages will be prepared in manuscript.

Place	Date	Hour	Summary of Events and Information	Remarks and references to Appendices
CAMBLAIN CHATLAIN	26.4.17		A fine day. Orders were received at 1.30 a.m. that the Battalion would march back to the NOEUX LES MINES area by stages. At 1 p.m. the Battalion marched off via FONTAINE les HERMANS - COUCHY a-la-TOUR to CAMBLAIN - CHATLAIN where it arrived about 6 p.m. and went into billets.	
NOEUX LES MINES	27.4.17		A fine day. Battalion marched off at 9 a.m. via DIVION - BRUAY - RUITZ - and HEUCHIN to NOEUX LES MINES where it arrived at 1.30 p.m. and went into hutment camp.	
	28.4.17		A fine day. Nothing was done beyond Company inspections.	
	29.4.17		A fine day. Church Parade in Y.M.C.A. Hut taken by Rev. E.U. Evitt. A Company bathed at Divisional Baths in NOEUX LES MINES.	
	30.4.17		A fine day. Companies began training in Bayonet Fighting, Physical Training and Musketry. B Company bathed.	

Vol 20

CONFIDENTIAL.

WAR DIARY

OF

7th SERVICE BATTALION NORTHAMPTONSHIRE REGIMENT.

FROM MAY 1st. 1917.
TO MAY 31st. 1917.

:-:-:-:-:-:-:-:-:-:-:

IN THE FIELD.
MAY 31st. 1917.

Army Form C. 2118.

WAR DIARY

INTELLIGENCE SUMMARY.

(Erase heading not required.)

Instructions regarding War Diaries and Intelligence Summaries are contained in F.S. Regs., Part II. and the Staff Manual respectively. Title pages will be prepared in manuscript.

Place	Date	Hour	Summary of Events and Information	Remarks and references to Appendices
NOEUX LES MINES.	1.5.17.		Fine. Company training.	
	2.5.17.		Fine. Company training. NOEUX LES MINES was shelled during the morning.	
	3.5.17.		Fine. Company training.	
	4.5.17.		Fine. Company training. 2nd Lieut L.E.Barnes and draft of 32 men arrived this evening.	
LAPUGNOY.	5.5.17.		Fine. Battalion left NOEUX LES MINES at 9.30 a.m. and marched via VAUDRICOURT and HESDIGNEUL to LAPUGNOY dinner being taken en route. Arrived LAPUGNOY at 2 p.m. and went into billets.	
	6.5.17.		Fine. Church Parade in the morning on No.18 C.C.S. Football ground was taken by Rev. E.U.Evitt.	
	7.5.17.		Fine. Two Companies in BOIS DES DAMES practising scheme.	
	8.5.17.		Wet morning. Draft of 49 men arrived.	
L'ECLEME.	9.5.17.		Fine. Battalion marched off at 10 a.m. via CHOCQUES and GONNEGHEM to L'ECLEME where it arrived about 12.30 p.m. and went into billets.	
THIENNES.	10.5.17.		Fine. Battalion marched off at 9.45 a.m. via BUSHES, ST. VENANT, and HARVERSKERQUE to THIENNES where it arrived about 2 p.m. and went into billets.	
	11.5.17.		Very hot. Battalion remained at THIENNES and was inspected with the 9th Royal Sussex in afternoon by G.O.C. (Major Genl. Capper) who bade us farewell before leaving to take up his new appointment. At 5 p.m. Swimming competition was held in the Canal.	

Army Form C. 2118.

WAR DIARY
INTELLIGENCE SUMMARY.
(Erase heading not required.)

Instructions regarding War Diaries and Intelligence
Summaries are contained in F. S. Regs., Part II
and the Staff Manual respectively. Title pages
will be prepared in manuscript.

Place	Date	Hour	Summary of Events and Information	Remarks and references to Appendices
STEENVOORDE.	12.5.17.		Very hot. Battalion marched off at 8.30 a.m. via HAZEBROUCK and STEENVOORDE to billeting area between GODEWAERSVELDE and the Belgian frontier. Dinner and tea were taken en route. Battalion arrived at destination at 6 p.m. after a very trying march.	
	13.5.17.		A very hot day. The Battalion rested.	
	14.5.17.		A fine day with a few showers. Battalion marched off at 6 p.m. via ABEELE, RENINGHELST and OUDERDOM to VANCOUVER CAMP arriving at 10 p.m. A good march.	
VANCOUVER.	15th, 16th, 17th.		Working parties. - every available man being sent.	
	18.5.17.		Received sudden orders to move from VANCOUVER CAMP to TORONTO CAMP and moved off at 8.45 p.m. Working parties cancelled.	
	19.5.17.		Very hot. Large working parties.	
	20.5.17.		Very hot. Usual working parties. Church Parade of 50 men per Company at 5.15 p.m.	
	21/24th/5.17.		Usual large working parties.	
	25.5.17.		2nd Lieut C.A.Debenham was wounded on working party.	
	26.5.17.		2nd Lieut P.Knight was killed and Sgt Colton wounded on working party.	
	27/28.5.17.		Usual large working parties.	

Army Form C. 2118.

WAR DIARY

INTELLIGENCE SUMMARY.

(Erase heading not required.)

Instructions regarding War Diaries and Intelligence Summaries are contained in F. S. Regs., Part II. and the Staff Manual respectively. Title pages will be prepared in manuscript.

Place	Date	Hour	Summary of Events and Information	Remarks and references to Appendices
TORONTO.	29.5.17.		The Battalion received sudden orders to move at 6 p.m. to HEKSKEN where it went under canvas. The usual working parties were found, one party of B Company having 2 Killed, 1 Missing, and 5 wounded by shell fire.	
	30/31.5.17.		Working parties as usual.	

CONFIDENTIAL.

WAR DIARY

OF

7th SERVICE BATTALION NORTHAMPTONSHIRE REGIMENT.

FROM :- JUNE 1st, 1917.
TO :- JUNE 30th, 1917.

:-:-:-:-:-:-:-:-:-:-:

IN THE FIELD.
JUNE 30th, 1917.

Army Form C. 2118.

WAR DIARY

INTELLIGENCE SUMMARY.

(Erase heading not required.)

Instructions regarding War Diaries and Intelligence Summaries are contained in F.S. Regs., Part II. and the Staff Manual respectively. Title pages will be prepared in manuscript.

Place	Date	Hour	Summary of Events and Information	Remarks and references to Appendices
HEKSKEN.	1/6/17.		80 men and 2 Officers from each Company were sent up to SWAN CHATEAU to work on dug-outs and remain there. A Battalion Concert was given in the evening.	
	2/6/17.		Working party remained at SWAN CHATEAU.	
	3/6/17.		Working party returned from SWAN CHATEAU this evening.	
	4/6/17.		Battalion moved to Camp at G.19.b.8.8. (Sheet 28) this evening.	
"	5/6/17.		Battalion moved to HALIFAX Camp H.14.c.2.5. (Sheet 28) at 10.30 pm. this evening.	
"	6/6/17.		The Camp was shelled by a heavy gun during the morning but no damage was done. The Battalion left Camp at 11.45 p.m. for SWAN CHATEAU (I.19.d. Sheet 28), "C" Company remaining behind to find fatigues.	
	7/6/17.		The Battalion was shelled en route for SWAN CHATEAU and the neighbourhood of the Chateau was particularly heavily shelled with Gas shells which caused a few casualties and made things very uncomfortable. The Battalion got in about 2 a.m. The attack on St. ELOI and MESSINES started about 3.10 a.m. and the Battalion remained at the Chateau until 2 p.m. when it moved forward to ECLUSE Trench (between VOORMEZEELE and the CANAL) and about 5 p.m. to Old French Trench just North of St. ELOI. The Commanding Officer was struck over the heart by a piece of shell and severely bruised.	

WAR DIARY

INTELLIGENCE SUMMARY.

(Erase heading not required.)

Place	Date	Hour	Summary of Events and Information	Remarks and references to Appendices
	8/6/17.		About 2.30 a.m. Battalion moved forward across DAMMSTRASSE and occupied "BLACK LINE" from DENYS WOOD to RAVINE WOOD (including parts of both), Headquarters being in DENYS WOOD. A Battalion in Support. Relief complete by 4 a.m. Trenches had been completely destroyed by our shell fire but the men worked well and soon provided good cover. About 10 p.m. the enemy guns opened and he counter-attacked but was unable to reach our front line owing to our barrage. All was quiet by midnight. Casualties were 5 O.R. Killed, 19 B.R. Wounded.	
	9/6/17.		The enemy was fairly quiet but at 9.30 p.m. shelled RAVINE WOOD heavily. 8th Bn. Buffs relieved B Company in DENYS WOOD and they moved to OBSCURE ALLEY.	
	10/6/17.		At 10.30 p.m. S.O.S. went up on our right and our barrage opened promptly. Both sides shelled very heavily until mid-day. The Commanding Officer was again hit by a piece of shell in the neck.	
	11/6/17.		After a quiet day the Battalion was relieved about 5 p.m. by 2 Companies of the 32nd Royal Fusiliers (41st Division) and returned to DOMINION CAMP (G.23,b,9,8, Sheet 28). A good relief with no casualties. Total casualties during operations - 1 Officer Wounded - 7 men Killed - 1 Man Missing - (afterwards reported Wounded) - 42 O.R. Wounded.	
	12/6/17.		Battalion remained in Camp. Our 2nd Bn. encamped near us.	
	13/6/17.		At 7 p.m. the Battalion moved to MICMAC CAMP H.31,b.2,5.	
	14/6/17.		Battalion remained in Camp. Lieut Col E R Mobbs went on leave and Major T.Foster of 9th Royal Sussex Regt took over Command.	

WAR DIARY

Army Form C. 2118.

Place	Date	Hour	Summary of Events and Information	Remarks and references to Appendices
	15/6/17.		Battalion left MICMAC CAMP at 6-45 p.m. and proceeded up the line and relieved 12th Royal Fusiliers in front line of HILL 60 sector; "A" and "C" Companies in front line, "B" Company in support and "D" Company in Reserve. Front was held by 6 Strong Points from the Railway at I.36.c.3.0. to KLEIN ZILLEBEKE (Sheet 28) 2nd Lieut Fitzhugh was wounded during relief;	
	16/6/17.		Relief complete about 3 a.m. A fairly quiet day but out support line, IMPARTIAL TRENCH I.36.c.2.6. to I.36.a.9.2. was heavily shelled all night, 2nd Lieut Adderly being Killed, 2nd Lieut Underwood, Wounded, and 9 O.R. Killed and 25 O.R. Wounded (includes 7 Slightly Wounded -still at duty).	
	17/6/17.		Our front was heavily shelled again throughout the day. Casualties 4 O.R. Killed - 12 O.R. Wounded (includes 3 slightly wounded - still at duty);	
	18/6/17.		Owing to Battalion Boundary being changed, Battalion Headquarters were moved South of the Railway to IMPACT SUPPORT I.35.c.4.2. A German Artillery officer who was on forward observation duty with his Orderly walked into our lines by mistake at dawn and surrendered to the Brigadier and Capt Marshall. During the afternoon 2nd Lieut Berridge and 2nd Lieut Laycock took 4 prisoners from a dug-out in a Communication Trench which ran from the German lines to our own. Our lines were again heavily shelled.	
	19/6/17.		Battalion relieved this evening by 9th Royal Sussex Regt and went into Support in Old German and British front lines. Heavily shelled during relief.	
	20/6/17.		Desultory shelling all day. Large working and carrying parties found;	

Army Form C. 2118.

WAR DIARY

(Erase heading not required.)

Instructions regarding War Diaries and Intelligence Summaries are contained in F. S. Regs. Part II. and the Staff Manual respectively. Title pages will be prepared in manuscript.

Place	Date	Hour	Summary of Events and Information	Remarks and references to Appendices
WARHEM.	21/6/17.		Rather quieter today.	
	22/6/17.		Desultory shelling during day.	
	23/6/17.		Battalion was relieved by 1st North Staffords, relief commencing at midnight.	
	24/6/17.		Owing to heavy shelling of our lines and of Artillery in our rear with Gas shells, relief was considerably delayed and was not completed till 4 a.m. 2nd Lieuts Wright, Callie, and Bury were wounded during relief. Battalion went into Camp at MICMAC CAMP near OUDERDOM. Total Casualties on tour - 1 Officer Killed - 5 Officers Wounded - 25 O.R. Killed - 90 O.R. Wounded including 28 Slightly Wounded - still at duty. 2nd Lieut Lucas who was attached to 129th Field Coy R.E. was wounded today.	
	25/6/17.		The Corps Commander - General Morland - visited the Camp.	
	26/6/17.		Lieut Col E.R.Mobbs returned from leave and Major T.Foster rejoined his Battalion.	
	27/6/17.		Battalion entrained at BUSSEBOOM siding at 1 p.m. and detrained at LUMBRES about 6.30 p.m. and marched to BAYENGHEM being caught in heavy thunderstorm just before it arrived Battalion went into billets.	
BAYENGHEM	28/6/17.		Brigadier General Commanding visited Battalion during the morning.	
	29/6/17.		A wet day. No work was done.	
	30/6/17.		Captain Jackson joined the Battalion, also Lieut George and 2nd Lieuts Hawthorne and Chapman.	

CONFIDENTIAL.

WAR DIARY

OF

7th SERVICE BATTALION NORTHAMPTONSHIRE REGIMENT.

FROM :- JULY 1st, 1917.

TO :- JULY 31st, 1917.

IN THE FIELD.
JULY 31st, 1917.

WAR DIARY

INTELLIGENCE SUMMARY.

(Erase heading not required.)

Army Form C. 2118.

Instructions regarding War Diaries and Intelligence Summaries are contained in F.S. Regs., Part II. and the Staff Manual respectively. Title pages will be prepared in manuscript.

Place	Date	Hour	Summary of Events and Information	Remarks and references to Appendices
BAYENGHEM.	1/7/17.		Church Parade was taken by Rev.E.U.EVITT at 11 a.m.	
	2/7/17.		The G.O.C. 24th Division visited the Battalion during the morning. Major. D.W.Powell and 2nd/Lt. L.H.Halliday joined the Battalion. A concert was held in the evening.	
	3/7/17		A very wet day. Company inspections only.	
	4/7/17.		Companies trained their Platoons in attack formations.	
	5/7/17.		2nd Lieuts Nicholson, Gorringe, Wheeler and Litchfield joined from England today with a draft of 14 men.	
	6/7/17. and 7/7/17.		Battalion continued training Platoons in attack. Capt A.J.W.Cunningham R.A.M.C. left to join 73rd Field Ambulance and Capt T.O.Williams joined in his place.	
	8/7/17.		A wet morning and Church Parade was cancelled in consequence.	
	9/7/17.		Battalion continued training and bathed. Arrangements had been made for the Battalion to march down to the seaside on the 10th inst., but were cancelled. Five Military Medals awarded to N.C.Os and men of the Battalion. Draft of 17 O.R. joined.	
	10/7/17.		Battalion continued training - "A" Company having use of the range. Capt & Adjt A.W.Heaton proceeds on leave, Capt H.W.Jackson appointed Acting Adjutant.	
	11/7/17.		Training continued. Battalion held Aquatic Sports in the Lake at Headquarters during the afternoon.	

WAR DIARY

INTELLIGENCE SUMMARY

(Erase heading not required.)

Army Form C. 2118.

Instructions regarding War Diaries and Intelligence Summaries are contained in F. S. Regs., Part II. and the Staff Manual respectively. Title pages will be prepared in manuscript.

Place	Date	Hour	Summary of Events and Information	Remarks and references to Appendices
BAYENGHEM.	12/7/17.		Inspection of all arms by Brigade Armourer Sergt.. Testing of Box Respirators by Brigade Gas N.C.O.. Battalion held Athletic Sports during the afternoon. All Officers and senior N.C.Os. visit the MODEL of the ground over which forthcoming operations are to take place.	
	13/7/17.		Battalion practices attack on "Flagged" ground. All Officers attend lecture at the MODEL by G.O.S.1 24th Division. Heats of Brigade Sports run off during the afternoon.	
	14/7/17.		All Companies visit the MODEL. Draft of 12 men join. Brigade Sports were held during the afternoon.	
	15/7/17.		Church Parade during morning. C Company played "D" Company & 1st North Staffords at football in the evening. Object - To create an Entente between neighbouring Companies in forthcoming operations.	
	16/7/17.		Battalion practiced a combined attack with 2nd Leinster Regiment on "Flagged" Course. Divine Service for Roman Catholics in the evening.	
	17/7/17.		Battalion again practiced combined attack with 2nd Leinster Regiment of "Flagged" Course. Contact Aeroplanes take part. Tactical situations created. Field Marshall Sir Douglas Haig present.	
RENESCURE.	18/7/17.		Battalion moved 15 miles by march route to RENESCURE starting at 4.40 am. New billets good but a long distance apart. Packs carried by motor lorry- no men fell out.	

WAR DIARY
INTELLIGENCE SUMMARY

(Erase heading not required.)

Army Form C. 2118.

Instructions regarding War Diaries and Intelligence Summaries are contained in F.S. Regs., Part II and the Staff Manual respectively. Title pages will be prepared in manuscript.

Place	Date	Hour	Summary of Events and Information	Remarks and references to Appendices
LA KREULE.	19/8/17.		Battalion moved at 8 a.m. from RENESCURE, 9 miles to Camp ½ mile North of LA KREULE. Accommodated in tents.	
EECKE.	20/7/17.		Battalion left camp at 8.15 a.m. and marched 4 miles to Billets in EECKE. Men carried packs and wore steel helmets. Very hot marching. The Commanding Officer was complimented by the B.G.C. on the excellent marching of the Battalion.	
RENINGHELST.	21/7/17		Battalion left EECKE at 6 a.m. and marched 9 miles to bivouacs 1 mile West of RENINGHELST (Staging Area 6"). No men fell out during the march.	
	22/7/17.		Draft of 34 O.R. arrived this evening. Battalion Cricket Team played team from 6th Battalion Northamptonshire Regiment who are encamped near by.	
	23/7/17.		Companies inspections. Battalion Football Team visited the 6th Battalion and played them. Battalion moved off at 6.40 p.m. via RENINGHELST and OUDERDOM to Camp near MICMAC CAMP at MXX. N.1.a. Central (Sheet 28) a distance of about 3½ miles.	
	24/7/17.		An uneventful day. Weather hot and fine.	
	25/7/17.		Baths at DICKEBUSCH BREWERY allotted to the Battalion from 1 p.m. to 5 p.m., but owing to the wet weather only "A" Company bathed.	
	26/7/17.		"C" and "D" Companies bathed at the Baths from 8 a.m. to 12 noon today.	

Army Form C. 2118.

WAR DIARY
or
INTELLIGENCE SUMMARY.
(Erase heading not required.)

Instructions regarding War Diaries and Intelligence Summaries are contained in F. S. Regs., Part II. and the Staff Manual respectively. Title pages will be prepared in manuscript.

Place	Date	Hour.	Summary of Events and Information	Remarks and references to Appendices
	27/7/17.		Companies paraded under their own arrangements. Company Commanders under Major D.W.Powell reconnoitred the line this morning starting at 5 a.m. During the night enemy aeroplanes flew over and dropped bombs - a few in the vicinity of the Camp.	No 1
	28/7/17.		Companies parade as yesterday. Operation Orders No.41 for the forthcoming attack issued this afternoon (See Appendix No.1.)	
	29/7/17.		Operation Orders received from 73rd Brigade re the move to the line tonight. Battalion moved up by Companies commencing at 2 p.m. with the exception of "A" Company.	
	30/7/17		"A" Company moved up today.	

	31/7/17		The Battalion ("B" and "C" Companies) attacked the enemy line at SHREWSBURY FOREST at 3.50 a.m. this morning during which the Commanding Officer (Lieut Colonel E.R.Mobbs D.S.O.) was killed. Our casualties were :-
			   Lieut. Col. E.R.Mobbs. D.S.O. Killed
			   2nd Lieut. T.P.Litchfield. Killed;
			   2nd Lieut L.H.Halliday. Missing;
			   2nd Lieut T.Ward. Missing.
			 Capt A.O.Marshall. Wounded. 2nd Lieut F.L.Franklin. Wounded
			 Blieut S.H.Motion. Wounded. 2nd Lieut L.J.Laycock. Wounded
			 LieutA.F.R. George. Wounded. 2nd Lieut A.H.Webb. Wounded.
			 2nd Lieut W.H.Cawston. Wounded. 2nd Lieut C.D.Morgan. Wounded;
			 Other Ranks. Killed 37, Wounded 162, Missing 47. Total 246.
			 See APPENDIX "A" for report on the action;
			 Congratulatory Memo received from B.G.C. 73rd I.B. (see APPENDIX "B"	

2353 Wt W2544/1454 700,000 5/15 D.D.&L. A.D.S.S./Forms/C. 2118.

REF. SHEET 28.N.W. ZILLEBEKE.   SECRET.

App. No 1   Copy No. 14

OPERATION ORDERS No. 4.

BY

LIEUTENANT COLONEL E. R. MOBBS D.S.O.
COMMANDING 7th BATTALION NORTHAMPTONSHIRE REGIMENT.

JULY 28th, 1917.

---

1. **INTENTION.**

    (A). The 24th Division will co-operate in the forthcoming operations which will commence on ZERO DAY at an hour to be notified. The 24th Division is the right attacking Division of the II Corps of the 5th Army. The 30th Division is on our left and the 41st Division of the 10th Corps on our right.

    (B). The 73rd Brigade is the centre attacking Brigade of the 24th Division, the 17th Brigade on the Left and the 72nd Brigade on the Right.

    (C). The Battalion is the Right assaulting Battalion of the Brigade.
    The 2nd Leinster Regiment is the left assaulting Battalion.
    The 13th Middlesex Regt is in Reserve.

2. **OBJECTIVE.**

    (A). The capture and consolidation of the BLUE LINE.
    (B). The capture and consolidation of the BLACK LINE.

3. **PRELIMINARY DISPOSITIONS AND ACTION OF COMPANIES.**

    On ZERO DAY Companies will be disposed in or near our present front line. The formations have already been explained to Companies.
    The dispositions and action of the Companies in the two different phases of the attack have also been explained to everyone.

4. **BOUNDARIES.**

    The Boundaries between Companies are as under :-

    In the BLUE LINE. The point of junction of Companies will be about the T in TRENCH.

    In the BLACK LINE. The point of junction of Companies will be about J.26.d.9.3.

    The Boundaries between Battalions and Brigades are shewn on the special map issued to all Companies.

5. ARTILLERY BARRAGES.

(A). At ZERO HOUR the barrage will be put down 200 yards in front of the assembly positions. At ZERO plus 4 it will move forward at the average rate of 100 yards in 4 minutes until it reaches the BLUE LINE on which it will pile up.

(B). At ZERO plus 32 minutes it will lift off the BLUE LINE and advance at a similar rate as before until it forms a protective barrage 300 yards in front of the BLUE LINE where it will stop until ZERO plus 83 minutes.

(C). At ZERO plus 83 minutes the barrage will advance again at the rate of 100 yards in 4 minutes until it reaches the BLACK LINE on which it will pile up.

(D). At ZERO plus 99 it will lift off the BLACK LINE and advance at a similar rate as before until it forms a protective barrage 200-300 yards in front of the BLACK LINE where it will stop until ZERO plus 140 minutes.

(E). At ZERO plus 140 minutes the barrage will move forward again until it forms a new protective barrage about 400-500 yards in front of the BLACK LINE where it will remain.

This is to enable leading Companies to push forward patrols well forward.

The Barrage timings for Brigades on either flank are slightly different and men must be warned not to be misled by them.

6. FLARES.

"A" and "C" Companies will light flares (in groups of 3) when called upon by the Contact Aeroplanes at about the following hours:-

(a) 15 minutes after reaching the BLUE LINE.
(b) 30 minutes after reaching the BLACK LINE.
(c) ZERO plus 8 hours.
(d) ZERO plus 9 hours.

Every man will carry one flare but only the most advanced line of the Battalion will light them.

Contact Aeroplanes will be marked by Two Black Plates fixed to the rear of the planes.

The call for the flares is a succession of "A's" on a KLAXON HORN. If this fails to produce an answer the aeroplane will fire a WHITE LIGHT as a further call.

7. PRISONERS OF WAR.

A collecting station will be established at about T.30.d.20.90 as soon as possible after ZERO HOUR. This will be under the Provost Sergeant who will arrange for escorts to conduct prisoners to the Divisional Cage at H.30.d.5.1 He will obtain a receipt for all prisoners handed over and will keep a record of the numbers sent down.

Prisoners captured by Companies will be collected into batches and sent back to the Battalion Collecting Station. Men returning with messages and slightly wounded men will be used for escort duty.

8. **MEDICAL**   The Battalion AID POST will be at CANADA STREET TUNNELS. Walking Wounded will proceed direct to Divisional Collecting Post at LARCH WOOD TUNNEL. No one but stretcher bearers will leave the fighting area to conduct Wounded to the rear

9. **LIAISON.**   During the operations all Companies will keep the closest touch with Platoons and Companies on their flanks. The following are the Battalion Liaison Officers:-
   2nd Lieut. How   : 2nd Leinsters
   Lt. Dryland   : 1st North Staffs.

10. **DUMPS**   The Battalion Dump for S.A.A. Bombs Tools etc will be at I.30.d.20.90. After the capture of the BLACK LINE a forward dump will be established in the BLUE LINE. Officer commanding B Company will be responsible for forming these and for keeping them replenished.

11. **MACHINE GUNS AND LIGHT TRENCH MORTARS**   A subsection of the 73rd Machine Gun Company will be attached to the Battalion, and will move forward with D Coy and select positions for the defence of the BLACK LINE.
    Two guns of the 73rd L. Trench Mortar Batty are attached to the Battalion, and will move forward with D Company, and select a position behind the BLUE LINE and move forward again when the BLACK LINE is consolidated.

12. **COMMUNICATIONS.**   Brigade Report Centre - CANADA TUNNELS
    1st Relay Station - I.30.b.7.7.
    2nd Relay Station - J.25.d.0.0.
    Advanced Report Station - J.25.d.4.9.
    Report centres will be marked by a BLUE & WHITE FLAG and by a BLUE LAMP at night.

13. **OBSERVATION POSTS.**
    An Observation Post will be established at I.30.a.90.90 under the Battalion Intelligence Officer. It will consist of 1 N.C.O. and 3 men supplied by "B" Company.

14. **BATTALION HEADQUARTERS.**
    Battalion Headquarters will be at I.30.d.80.90 MOUNT SORREL and will not move forward till after the capture of the BLACK LINE.

JULY 28th, 1917.   ....Lieut. Colonel.

Commanding 7th Battalion Northamptonshire Regiment.

          Copy No. 1.   File.
          "   "   2.   O.C. A Coy.
          "   "   3.   O.C. B Coy.
          "   "   4.   O.C. C Coy.
          "   "   5.   O.C. D Coy.
          "   "   6.   1st North Stafford Regt.
          "   "   7.   2nd Leinster Regt.
          "   "   8.   H.Q. 73rd Inf. Bde.
          "   "   9.   H.Q. 72nd Inf. Bde.
          "   "   10. 73rd Machine Gun Company.
          "   "   11. 73rd Light Trench Mortar Battery.
          "   "   12. O.C. 13th Middlesex Regt.
          "   "   13. R.S.M.
          "   "   14. Intelligence Officer.

APPENDIX A

7th SERVICE BATTALION NORTHAMPTONSHIRE REGIMENT.

NARRATIVE OF OPERATIONS IN SHREWSBURY FOREST 31st JULY 1917.

29th JULY 1917.

Battalion Headquarters, "C", "D", and "B" Companies went up to the forward area on the afternoon and evening of 29th July 1917 ("A" Company was ordered to remain in Camp on account of the trenches it was to occupy being flooded).

"C" Company relieved part of the 9th Royal Sussex Regiment in 5 front line posts of the trenches and about IMAGE TRENCH.

"D" Company took CANADA STREET TUNNELS.

"B" Company in LARCH WOOD TUNNELS.

"B" Company suffered 5 Other Rank casualties through enemy gas shells on the march to the forward area and Lieut Cawston was wounded. Other Companies had no casualties.

Owing to the heavy rain and many shell holes the ground was in a very bad condition.

Battalion Headquarters were established in CANADA STREET TUNNELS which were very wet and crowded with troops making progress through the Tunnels very slow.

30th JULY 1917.

Situation normal throughout the day except that enemy heavily shelled IMAGE SUPPORT, ILLUSIVE SUPPORT and CENTRAL AVENUE at 1.45 a.m. and 4 p.m. Enemy split red lights preceded the former shelling.

"A" Company marched from Camp and occupied METROPOLITAN Left at 4 p.m., where they rested until night time and had tea.

A Conference of Company commanders was held at Battalion Headquarters at 5 pm and notification that ZERO hour for the attack on the following morning was to be at 3.50 am was received before the conclusion of the Conference - also correct time for synchronization.

About 9.30 pm Lt Colonel Mobbs D.S.O. (Commdg) went forward with Lt. Col Murphy D.S.O. M.C. (O.C. 2nd Leinster Regiment) and 2nd Lt. F.R. Berridge, M.C. (Intllgce Officer 73rd I.B.) to ascertain the position of the stakes which had previously been put out by the 9th Royal Sussex Regt. to mark the outer flanks of the assaulting Companies of the two Battalions in their forming up positions. These were found by moonlight, and 2/Lt Berridge remained out to put out tape to mark the line upon which the Coys would form up.

During this time Battalion Headquarters were moved to another part of CANADA STREET TUNNELS A and C Companies with D Company in support were formed up behind the tape line by 3.30 am. This operation was begun at midnight as it was necessary to allow plenty of time for the Companies to find their positions without noise, and also for D Company to get out of CANADA STREET TUNNELS

Previous to ZERO (3.50 am.) the Germans were shelling moderately in "NO MANS LAND" causing some casualties amongst our troops who were forming up for the attack. A German barrage fell 50 to 100 yards in front of our forming up line less than three minutes after ZERO causing rather heavy casualties, including one or two officers. At the same time enemy shells fell 100 to 150 yards behind our own front line, but this could not be described as a barrage. The rapidity with which the enemy barrage opened would appear to show that he was expecting the attack.

Owing to the darkness the assaulting Companies were unable to keep a correct line, and also the men were inclined to "bunch" which it was difficult to prevent until daylight.

However owing to the same cause, i.e. the darkness direction was undoubtedly lost from the beginning of the advance.

It appears that German Machine Guns were brought forward from JEHR TRENCH into shell holes in front of it before our barrage reached them. They were thus quite while our barrage was piling up on JEHR TRENCH.

Our assaulting troops being held up were unable to keep up with the barrage, lost direction, and became disorganized. The machine guns already referred to were dealt with enabling a further advance to be made across JEHR TRENCH, but again German Machine Guns enfiladed us from LOWER STAR POST, which was then on our left flank and to our rear, which the enemy still continued to hold.

The line reached is shewn on the attached map.

The assaulting Companies at this time were highly disorganised - had no connection with their left - and had no Officers. It was then that the Commanding Officer (Lt Col. E.R. Mobbs D.S.O. and 2/Lt Berridge M.C. arrived in the front line. The former with a handful of men charged an enemy Machine gun post, and was seriously wounded. Before dying he wrote out a message to his Battalion Headquarters, for reinforcements to be sent forward, and stating that he was seriously wounded - an act shewing his devotion to duty at the last. The message however was never delivered.

It must be stated here that the capture of the first objective or blue line had been reported. This was correct as far as the Battalion front was concerned - but LOWER STAR POST, on our left, had not been captured. It had however been reported by walking wounded that the second objective, (or the Black Line) had been captured. It was then that Col. Mobbs decided to go forward to ascertain the situation.

Lt. Col. Mobbs daring and extraordinary courage being known he was restrained from leaving his Headqrs for half an hour, but at the end of that time he definitely decided to go forward with a view to personally supervising the consolidation of the ground captured and of selecting a position for advanced Battalion Headquarters.

Before doing so he ordered B Company (in reserve) to advance, occupy and consolidate JEHR TRENCH.

In a most critical situation, when the two assaulting Companies had lost all their Officers, 2/Lt F. R. Berridge M.C. with the assistance of C.S.M. Alford and Sgt. Twentyman reorganized the line and sent in a report to Battalion Headquarters. Upon receipt of this report D Company of the 13th Middlesex Regt. was sent forward to JEHR TRENCH with special instructions to gain connection on the flanks. This Company suffered heavy casualties in going forward and is reported to have crossed JEHR TRENCH and later to have withdrawn and "dug in" between ILLUSIVE DRIVE and ILLUSIVE RESERVE believing that none of our troops were in front of them.

The Trench Mortar Subsection also withdrew to that line from J.35.c.55.25., a German Trench Mortar position they had occupied believing it to be the one shown in aeroplane photographs about J.35.d.00.68., but owing to LOWER STAR POST being still held by the enemy it was decided to withdraw our advanced troops to about the line of ILLUSIVE AVENUE and to consolidate strong posts on that line, and establish communication with a Northampton strong point at J.31.a.5.7, and a Leinster Strong Point at J.35.a.4.4.

An amended Order was sent to O.C, D Company 13th Middlesex Regiment.

2/Lt Berridge again went forward to effect this with--drawal which he successfully accomplished, shewing the utmost gallantry and dash, establishing a line of strong posts under heavy machine gun and shell fire. Several messages he sent back during the time he was forward did not reach Battalion Headquarters the runners having lost their way. He reported personally afterwards. 2/Lt. Berridge's work cannot be overestimated, and it was due to his efforts and devotion to duty that the situation was cleared.

A carrying party was organized to take wire, sandbags water and ammunition to the posts which had been established but it took many hours to find the way.

Stretcher bearers had sufferred heavy casualties so that 12 reserve stretcher bearers were sent for from the back area, and in the meantime, on account of the large numbers of wounded who were lying out, stragglers (men who had lost their way etc) were collected and placed at the disposal of the Medical Officer. Many of these men did most excellent work, and the greater portion of the area was cleared by nightfall.

The relief of the Battalion, partly by the 1st North Staffs and partly by the 13th Middlesex Regt was ordered on ZERO evening. Runners were sent forward to bring in guides from the posts. This was just before dark. The runners failed to find the posts and the guides never arrived.

It being considered inadvisable to carry out the relief by night it was not commenced until about 4 am the following day 1st August 1917.

Great credit is due to 2/Lts Gorringe, Williams, and Wild, and the N.C.O.s and men with them in holding these posts during the night under heavy shell fire, and in the most trying circumstances.

During the morning of the 1st August the 1st North Staffs relieved the three right posts of the Battalion and the 13th Middlesex Regt relieved five posts on the left.

The former had been formed on the 72nd Brigade front, when direction had been lost. The relief was completed by 11.45 am.

A dump of barrage rations water and rum was formed at CANADA STREET TUNNELS for the men on their way back to Camp.

It had rained incessantly throughout the operations and the men were thoroughly exhausted, wet through, and covered with mud.

....

LOWER STAR POST   LOWER STAR POST proved to be the key of the situation, and undoubtedly was the cause of holding up the attack, and preventing the final objective being taken.

It is considered that the boundary between two Units should not have passed so close to such a strong point but that special assaulting troops should have been detailed to envelope the post.

ZERO

ZERO HOUR If ZERO HOUR is during darkness it is extremely difficult for the assaulting troops to keep proper direction and a correctly extended line. To ensure a successful operation from the start it would seem advisable that ZERO HOUR should be during daylight.

REPORTS A line of objective should not be reported as captured until it is ascertained that the flanks have been secured and communication obtained on the right and left. It is dangerous to base reports on the statements of Wounded.

STATE OF GROUND Operations were undoubtedly handicapped by the bad condition of the ground owing to the severe weather which existed previous to and on the 31st July 1917. This also to a certain extent withheld the assaulting troops from keeping close in to our barrage, the rate of advance of which is considered to have been too fast under the circumstances.

MAP READING The question of map reading generally, knowing one's way position and finding the way, especially at night, proved exceedingly difficult. This was principally due to the similarity of the ground and lack of landmarks. The use of the compass with a large scale clearly contoured map would appear to have been the only safe method to adopt. It is not considered that the large SHREWSBURY FOREST map was adaptable to the circumstances.

SANITATION Latrine accommodation in CANAL STREET TUNNELS was practically nil. No special latrine could be claimed and looked after by any one Battalion, because troops in the TUNNELS belonged to several Regiments. It would have been advantageous if a Brigade Sanitary Section had been organised to make and look after latrines. This would have probably decreased the large amount of urinating in the TUNNELS.

....

Captain
6/8/17. 7th Northamptonshire Regiment.

Vol 23

CONFIDENTIAL

7th Service Battalion Northamptonshire Regiment
-:-:-:-:-:-:-:-:-:-:-:-:-:-:-

W A R   D I A R Y

for

the period from 1st August 1917 to 31st August 1917.

@:@:@:@:@:@:@:@

In the Field
2/9/17.

Army Form C. 2118.

WAR DIARY
of
INTELLIGENCE SUMMARY.
(Erase heading not required.)

Instructions regarding War Diaries and Intelligence Summaries are contained in F.S. Regs., Part II. and the Staff Manual respectively. Title pages will be prepared in manuscript.

Place	Date	Hour	Summary of Events and Information	Remarks and references to Appendices
Line.	1/8/17		The Battalion was relieved by the 1st North Staffords and the 13th Middlesex Regiment this morning and returned to "J" Camp at DICKEBUSCH H.27.d.9.7. During the day parties of men continually rejoined. Major D.W. Powell assumed Command from today.	
DICKEBUSCH	2/8/17		The whole day devoted to resting the men and cleaning up kit etc. The vicinity of the camp was shelled during the night.	
do	3/8/17		Rifle inspection held by Company Commanders. The remainder of the day left for the men.	
do	4/8/17		Physical training and Company inspections during the morning.	
do	5/8/17		The Battalion has been reorganised into two Companies under Command of Captain Twigg (No.2.Company) and Lieut Passmore (No.1.Company)	
do	6/8/17		Major H.Grant Thorold joined the Battalion from the 3rd Batyn. Reorganisation under two Company system continued with, Company inspections - re-equipment of men etc carried out. By the 2nd Leinsters and ourselves would take over the line and orders issued accordingly. Orders received that a composite Battalion formed	
do	7/8/17		Preparing for the line - the Battalion moved off in the afternoon and proceeded towards the line but before arriving at JAKSON'S Dump orders were received that the operation order was cancelled and accordingly turned back and returned to DICKEBUSCH CAMP.	
do	8/8/17		Physical training carried on.	
do	9/8/17		Usual training - Company inspections etc.	

Army Form C. 2118.

WAR DIARY
or
INTELLIGENCE SUMMARY.
(Erase heading not required.)

Instructions regarding War Diaries and Intelligence Summaries are contained in F. S. Regs., Part II. and the Staff Manual respectively. Title pages will be prepared in manuscript.

Place	Date	Hour	Summary of Events and Information	Remarks and references to Appendices
DICKEBUSCH	10/8/17		Orders received that the Battalion would relieve the 3rd Battn Rifle Brigade in the line tomorrow and Operation Orders issued accordingly.	
LINE	11/8/17		Relief of 3rd Bn Rifle Brigade in the trenches carried out. Relief complete 2-30.a.m. without casualties.	
do	12/8/17		Battalion heavily shelled but majority of shells fell short of or over our front line and supports. Enemy active during the 24 hours except from 5.a.m. to 9.a.m.	
do	13/8/17		Enemy shelling as above - as night No.1.Company relieved No.2. in front and support lines - relief completed in 2 hours with 1 casualty - Quiet hours as above.	
do	14/8/17		Usual hostile artillery active.	
do	15/8/17		Usual artillery activity - relieved by 8th Royal West Kents night of 15/16 relief completed by by 11-30.p.m. which was very good. Brigade very pleased with relief - casualties during relief NIL. During this tour a system of relays of runners was organised between front posts and Brigade Headquarters. This proved very satisfactory and saved much labour for the runners concerned. Casualties during tour 6 other ranks Killed and 9 other ranks Wounded.	
MICMAC	16/8/17		Battalion at C Camp MICMAC. Day spent in cleaning up xxxx	
do	17/8/17		Companies engaged in training specialists.	
do	18/8/17		Parades as usual. 2nd Lieuts J.C.Pike, H.F.C.Lobb, G Graham-Green joined today.	
do	19/8/17		2nd Lieut A.E.Barton rejoined today. Training as usual.	

Army Form C. 2118.

WAR DIARY
or
INTELLIGENCE SUMMARY.
(Erase heading not required.)

Instructions regarding War Diaries and Intelligence Summaries are contained in F.S. Regs., Part II and the Staff Manual respectively. Title pages will be prepared in manuscript.

Place	Date	Hour	Summary of Events and Information	Remarks and references to Appendices
MICMAC.	20/8/17		Battalion moved to BREWERY CAMP "J" at 3.p.m.	
DICKEBUSCH	21/8/17		CAMP "J" shelled at 6.a.m. - 7.30.a.m. One man slightly wounded and one horse killed.	
do	22/8/17		Training as usual.	
do	23/8/17		Battalion proceed up the line to relieve 6th Royal West Kents in the right sector - very good relief - complete by 10-15.p.m. No casualties during relief - night very quiet.	
LINE	24/8/17 25/8/17		Very quiet - showers at intervals - ground that had improved becomes very bad again.	
do	26/8/17		Day and night very quiet - S.O.S. goes up at 3.30.p.m. on left of Division.	
do	27/8/17		Battalion relieved in the line by 3rd Bn Rifle Brigade - relief finished by 10.40.p.m. Battalion returns to "C" CAMP, MICMAC, in pouring rain. Casualties during tour 3 other ranks killed, and 4 other ranks Wounded.	
MICMAC	28/8/17		Major Storey from 8th Queens joins today and takes over position of 2nd in Command. Lieut R.W.Gates joins today from 3rd Battn.	
do	29/8/17		Training interrupted by storms. Lieut R.B.Fawkes joined today.	
do	30/8/17		Training as usual. Lieut-Col D.W.Powell proceeds to PARIS on 48 hours leave and Major Storey assumes Command. Following officers joined today:- 2/Lt W.E.Boulter V.C. 2/Lt L.Bostock. 2/Lt M.S.Gotch.	
do CAMP "J"	31/8/17		Battalion moved to "J" CAMP, BREWERY, DICKEBUSCH. Aeroplane bombs fall near during march - casualties NIL. 2/Lt E.W.Cockerill joined today.	

Headquarters.

24th Division.

No: M/188.

CONFIDENTIAL.

D.A.G. 3rd: Echelon.

BASE.

Herewith "Appendix "B", to War Diary of 7th Northants Regt: which was omitted from the Diary when forwarded under my M.188 dated 17th instant.

[signature]
Major General.
Commanding 24th Division.

21st: Aug: 1917.

APPENDIX B

S P E C I A L   O R D E R

I would like to place on record my very high appreciation of the splendid fighting qualities and gallantry of the Officers, N.C.O's and men who took part in the action of the 31st. July, 1917.

The enemy did his best to break up our attack and prevent us from gaining our objective. He employed his best troops for this purpose. His Artillery and machine gun fire was heavy and intense during the advance - the ground was boggy and ploughed up with shells. In spite of all these difficulties and opposition the 7th. Battalion Northamptonshire Regiment and the 2nd. Battalion Loinster Regiment drove the enemy from his position on the high ground which the Brigade had been ordered to seize. Many Officers were either killed or wounded and the fight resolved itself into a soldiers' battle which was won by extraordinary pluck and determination.

This was a performance of which the troops may very well feel more than proud.

H.Q. 73 I.B.
6. 8. 17.

Brigadier General,
Commanding, 73rd. Infantry Brigade.

Appendix "B"

SPECIAL ORDER

I would like to place on record my very high appreciation of the splendid fighting qualities and gallantry of the Officers, N.C.O's and men who took part in the action of the 31st. July, 1917.

The enemy did his best to break up our attack and prevent us from gaining our objective. He employed his best troops for this purpose. His Artillery and machine gun fire was heavy and intense during the advance - the ground was boggy and ploughed up with shells. In spite of all these difficulties and opposition the 7th. Battalion Northamptonshire Regiment and the 2nd. Battalion Leinster Regiment drove the enemy from his position on the high ground which the Brigade had been ordered to seize. Many Officers were either killed or wounded and the fight resolved itself into a soldiers' battle which was won by extraordinary pluck and determination.

This was a performance of which the troops may very well feel more than proud.

H.Q. 73 I.B.
6. 8. 17.

Brigadier General,
Commanding, 73rd. Infantry Brigade.

Vol 24

7TH BATTN NORTHAMPTONSHIRE REGIMENT

WAR DIARY

FOR THE PERIOD 1ST TO 30TH SEPTEMBER 1917.
-:-:-:-:-:-:-:-:-:-

Army Form C. 2118.

WAR DIARY
or
INTELLIGENCE SUMMARY.
(Erase heading not required.)

Instructions regarding War Diaries and Intelligence Summaries are contained in F. S. Regs., Part II. and the Staff Manual respectively. Title pages will be prepared in manuscript.

Place	Date	Hour	Summary of Events and Information	Remarks and references to Appendices
DICKEBUSCH.	1/9/17.		Battalion engaged during morning in improving camp and building sandbag protection around tents. Captain H.W.Jackson is ordered to report to "Q" 24th Division for attachment.	
do	2/9/17.		Erection of sandbag walls continued and general improvement of Camp.	
do	3/9/17.		Orders received for the Battalion to take over the line in the neighbourhood of the MENIN ROAD. Battalion proceeded up the line as Support Battalion to the 73rd Infantry Brigade. Tracks were shelled during relief. Relief complete by 10-45.p.m. 1 O.R. Wounded relief.	
LINE.	4/9/17.		Day quiet. Work carried on during night on new trenches.	
do	5/9/17.		Day quiet. At 8-30.p.m. enemy heavily shelled support lines and left of our Division and attacked the Division on our left. Battalion "stood to" but all was quiet by 9-45.p.m. We had no casualties. Work was carried as usual during the night on our new trenches.	
do	6/9/17.		Day quiet. A few gas shells (probably mustard) fell around Battalion Hqrs and "C" Company, resulting in 6 casualties - no killed. During the day our heavy artillery dropped about 12 shells short in our lines. Work as usual on our new trenches.	
do	7/9/17.		Day quiet. One man wounded by our shells dropping short. Battalion relieved by 8th Royal West Kent Regiment and 1st North Staffordshire Regt. Relief complete by 4-30.p.m. Battalion returned to C Camp MICMAC. All in without casualties by 6-30.p.m.	
MICMAC.	8/9/17.		Cleaning up - clothing, rifle and equipment inspections.	
do	9/9/17.		Training - Company and platoon drill, musketry etc.	

Army Form C. 2118.

WAR DIARY
or
INTELLIGENCE SUMMARY.
(Erase heading not required.)

Instructions regarding War Diaries and Intelligence Summaries are contained in F.S.Regs., Part II. and the Staff Manual respectively. Title pages will be prepared in manuscript.

Place	Date	Hour	Summary of Events and Information	Remarks and references to Appendices
MICMAC.	10/9/17.		Training - Company drill under Major Storey. Orders for move to DICKEBUSCH received.	
DICKEBUSCH.	11/9/17.		The Battalion moved to "K" Camp near DICKEBUSCH at 2-30.p.m.	
do	12/9/17.		Working party of 75 O.R. for the R.E's proceeded at 3.a.m. and returned about 10-30.a.m. No casualties. Work - carrying duckboards to the forward area.	
do	13/9/17.		Working party of 75 O.R. for the R.E's same as yesterday. Casualties 1.O.R.Wounded. The Battalion moved to field near HALLEBAST CORNER and erected bivouacs and tents, staying there for one night.	
RENINGHELST.	14/9/17.		Battalion moved at 11.20.a.m. and marched via LA CLYTTE and WESTOUTRE, to huts between REHINGHELST and WESTOUTRE. Orders received for the move by bus tomorrow. Major S.S.Hayne joined and assumed duties of Second in Command.	
do	15/9/17.		Battalion moved off at 6-25.a.m. and marched to busses via RENINGHELST and embussed there. From there the convoy proceeded via RENINGHELST - LOCRE - BAILLEUL - to billets near STEENWERCK.	
STEENWERCK.	16/9/17.		No Church parades.	
do	17/9/17.		The Battalion was inspected by the G.O.C.24th Division - Major General A.C.Daly, in the field adjoining the transport field at 10-15.a.m. this morning	
do	18/9/17.		Training - Platoon drill, bomb throwing, Physical and Bayonet training, anti gas instruction. Major F.B.Storey reported to the 8th Queens Regt.	
do	19/9/17		Usual training. Major Haynes practiced all Companies in entraining. Orders received that the Battalion would entrain to BAPAUME area tomorrow 20th. Operation orders issued accordingly.	

Army Form C. 2118.

WAR DIARY
or
INTELLIGENCE SUMMARY.
(Erase heading not required.)

Instructions regarding War Diaries and Intelligence Summaries are contained in F.S. Regs., Part II. and the Staff Manual respectively. Title pages will be prepared in manuscript.

Place	Date	Hour	Summary of Events and Information	Remarks and references to Appendices
BAPAUME	20/9/17.		The Battalion paraded at 4.p.m. and marched to BAILEUL entraining there at 6.p.m. Arrived at BAPAUME station at 3.a.m. 21/9/1917.	
BARASTRE	21/9/17.		On detraining the Battalion marched via BAPAUME - HAPLINCOURT and BARASTRE to camp near the latter place, arriving there about 7-30.a.m. Draft of 42 O.R. arrived today.	
do	22/9/17.		Company inspections and drill.	
do	23/9/17.		Orders received that the Battalion would move tomorrow and O.O.s issued accordingly. Company and platoon drill carried out by Companies in the morning.	
HAUT ALLAINES.	24/9/17.		Battalion moved off at 8-30.a.m. and marched via MOLAINS - HAPLINCOURT - ALLAINES to Camp at HAUT ALLAINES.	
do	25/9/17.		Battalion moved off at 8.a.m. and embussed at HAUT ALLAINES at 8-20.p.m. from there via HAMEL - ROISEL to BERNES.	
BERNES.	26/9/17.		Battalion moves off at 6-30.p.m. via MONTIGNY - HERVILLY - HESBICOURT and HARGICOURT and takes over the trenches from 21st Battn Northumberland Fusiliers on the right sub-sector of the Brigade front. Dispositions - A and B Companies in the front line - D Company in Support and C Company in Reserve. Relief completed without casualties by 11.p.m. Very quiet night.	
LINE	27/9/17.		Enemy sent over a few "Minnies" in the afternoon otherwise situation quiet.	
do	28/9/17.		At "stand to" this morning enemy artillery was fairly active on front line and Battalion Hqrs. Casualties - "B" Company 1.O.R. Killed 3.O.R.Wounded.	
do	29/9/17.		"B" Company was "Minnied" rather heavily at 2.a.m. but no casualties were sustained. Remainder of day fairly quiet. B.G.C. visited the line today.	

Army Form C. 2118.

WAR DIARY
or
INTELLIGENCE SUMMARY.
(Erase heading not required.)

Place	Date	Hour	Summary of Events and Information	Remarks and references to Appendices
LINE.	30/9/17.		2/Lieut M.S.Gotch and Pte Varnham reconnoitre new trench in No Mans Land under construction by the enemy but find same unoccupied. Inter Company relief during the night - C Company relieving B Company who goes into reserve and D Company relieves A Company who take over Support Line. Enemy artillery very active during relief causing A Company 1.O.R. casualty. Nothing however came of this. Both artilleries very busy throughout the night.	

Vol 25

CONFIDENTIAL.

WAR DIARY

OF

7th SERVICE BATTALION NORTHAMPTONSHIRE REGIMENT.

FROM - OCTOBER 1st. 1917.
TO - OCTOBER 31st. 1917.

:-:-:-:-:-:-:-:-:-:

IN THE FIELD.
OCTOBER 31st. 1917.

Army Form C. 2118.

WAR DIARY

INTELLIGENCE SUMMARY.

(Erase heading not required.)

Instructions regarding War Diaries and Intelligence
Summaries are contained in F. S. Regs., Part II.
and the Staff Manual respectively. Title pages
will be prepared in manuscript.

Place	Date	Hour	Summary of Events and Information	Remarks and references to Appendices
	1/10/17.		G.O.C. visited the line.	
	2/10/17		Day Quiet. Artillery not very active on enemy side. 2nd.Lieut.A.M.Hoare joined today.	
	3/10/17		2nd.Lieut. J.W.Tetley joined today. Day fine. Artillery more active on both sides. Orders received that Battalion would be relieved tomorrow night.	
	4/10/17		Battalion relieved by 2nd Leinster Regiment. Relief completed without casualties. Battalion then returned to billets at HERVILLY. Total casualties during tour, 1 O.R. Killed, 4 O.R. Wounded.	
HERVILLY.	5/10/17.		Day spent in cleaning up after the tour in the trenches. Kit and Rifle inspections etc..	
	6/10/17.		Party of 50 O.R. provided for work under III Corps R.E.Park from 9 am to 5 p.m. Company inspections etc.. Party of 1 N.C.O. and 15 O.R. provided for work under R.E. at ROISEL.	
	7/10/17.		Baths at ROISEL allotted for the afternoon. Party of 1 N.C.O. and 15 O.R. again provided for 104th Coy R.E. at ROISEL. Orders issued for relief of 2nd Leinster Regiment in the line by us.	
LINE.	8/10/17		The Battalion relieved the 2nd Leinster Regiment in the line this evening. Relief completed without casualties. Weather bad and the trenches are fallen in inparts and are in a sodden state.	
	9/10/17.		Weather now fine. Enemy artillery quiet during the day - only a few shells being sent into HARGICOURT. Condition of trenches very bad, pumps no use as mud is so thick.	

Army Form C. 2118.

WAR DIARY

INTELLIGENCE SUMMARY.

(Erase heading not required.)

Instructions regarding War Diaries and Intelligence Summaries are contained in F.S. Regs., Part II. and the Staff Manual respectively. Title pages will be prepared in manuscript.

Place	Date	Hour	Summary of Events and Information	Remarks and references to Appendices
LINE.	10/10/17		Weather improved but trenches require a lot of cleaning. Scoops come up and better progress is made. Enemy quiet.	
	11/10/17.		Orders issued for relief of A and B Companies by C and D Companies. Shortly after C Company's relief, the enemy tried to bomb one of our saps (the right sap on this Company front) - about 15 bombs being thrown. Our sentries replied with rapid fire and nothing more occurred.	
	12/10/17		Enemy quiet tonight. Short bursts of fire were directed against HARGICOURT and VILLERET during the day.	
	13/10/17		G.O.C. III Corps presented Medal Ribbons to N.C.Os. and men who had been awarded medals, at BERNES this morning at 10 a.m. Usual inactivity on the part of the enemy during the day.	
	14/10/17		Orders for relief tonight. Battalion was relieved by 2nd Leinster Regiment in front line and returned to Brigade Support at L.10.a (Sheet 62 C.) Relief completed by 11.30 p.m. Total casualties - for tour - 2 O.R. wounded.	
	15/10/17		Day occupied with rifle and feet inspections and cleaning up after the tour.	
	16/10/17		Working parties amounting to 210 O.R. were found for work under R.Es on Support lines, new Brigade Headquarters, etc.,	
	17/10/17.		Baths at ROISEL allotted during the day from 9 am to 11 am. Working parties as yesterday were found today by the Battalion. Weather fine.	
	18/10/17.		Working parties practically the same as yesterday. Weather fine but colder.	

Army Form C. 2118.

WAR DIARY

INTELLIGENCE SUMMARY.

(Erase heading not required.)

Instructions regarding War Diaries and Intelligence Summaries are contained in F.S. Regs., Part II. and the Staff Manual respectively. Title pages will be prepared in manuscript.

Place	Date	Hour	Summary of Events and Information	Remarks and references to Appendices
	19/10/17		Baths at ROISEL allotted from 2 p.m. to 3 p.m. to-day. Usual working parties found.	
	20/10/17		Battalion relieved 2nd Leinster Regiment in the line without casualties. Enemy unusually quiet during relief.	
	21/10/17		Enemy shelled backward areas. D Company sustained 1 O.R. Killed and 3 O.R. Wounded	
	22/10/17		Enemy attitude quiet. Weather became rainy. Trenches in better condition than last tour.	
	23/10/17		Enemy active in early part of the day with Trench Mortars. Weather continued rainy. Relief postponed till 27th.	
	24/10/17		Enemy more active with artillery. A few shells close to Battalion H.Q. probably in retaliation for Heavy Trench Mortar (Flying Pig). Weather still bad. B and D Companies relieved A and C Companies in the front line. Battalion relief put back to 26th. Pte Bowler wounded.	
	25/10/17		Weather drier but very high wind. Day quiet. At 1.40 a.m. 1st Battn. North Staffordshire Regiment (Brigade on our right) raided enemy trenches and obtained identification. Artillery and Trench Mortars took part. Enemy retaliated with Trench Mortars and Artillery on raided front and our front. All quiet by 3.15 a.m. Casualties nil. Relief put forward to 27th. On evening of this day, all reliefs were cancelled. Final orders issued that evening for relief is 27th/28th.	
	26/10/17		Enemy artillery active. Battn.H.Q. shelled between 9.30 a.m. and 10 a.m. Otherwise quiet.	

Army Form C. 2118.

WAR DIARY
or
INTELLIGENCE SUMMARY.

(Erase heading not required.)

Instructions regarding War Diaries and Intelligence Summaries are contained in F. S. Regs., Part II. and the Staff Manual respectively. Title pages will be prepared in manuscript.

Place	Date	Hour	Summary of Events and Information	Remarks and references to Appendices
HERVILLY.	27/10/17.		Enemy artillery active on same areas during the afternoon. Battalion relieved in line by 2nd Leinster Regt.. Relief completed by 7.50 p.m. Right Battalion H.Q. moved to L.5.b.3.2. at 7 p.m. Casualties Nil. Battalion moved to Divisional Reserve at HERVILLY.	
	28/10/17.		Cleaning up etc.. Football match during the afternoon. G.O.C. Corps (Lt.Genl.Sir T.D'O Snow K.C.B., K.C.M.G. visited the Battalion this morning	
	29/10/17		Working parties improving and constructing billets, horse standings, etc.. Special party under 2nd Lieut Gotch digging practice trenches. Battalion Concert Party give their first concert at Y.M.C.A. ROISEL under the management of 2nd Lieut Evans.	
	30/10/17		Working parties same as yesterday. Inspection of rifles etc by Bde. Armourer Sergt. Battalion team played 73rd Field Ambulance during afternoon and won 2-1.	
	31/10/17		Working parties - training of Lewis Gunners etc.. Inspection of cycles by Bde. Armourer Sergt. Lecture by Commanding Officer to raiding party during the evening.	
	1/11/17.		Working parties,- training, etc.. Battalion team played 18th Sherwood Foresters during the afternoon and lost 1-0.	

Operation Orders No 70.
by
Major. S. S. HAYNE.
Commanding - 7th Bn Northamptonshire Regt

In the Field   9-10-17.

1. The Battalion will relieve the 2nd Bn. Leinster Regt in the line tomorrow 10th inst.

2. Companies will be disposed as follows:-
   "A" Company. - Left front.
   "B" Company - Right front.
   "D" Company - Support. (COLOGNE RESERVE)
   "C" Company - Reserve.

3. "A" Company will move at   4-30. P.M.
   "B" Company   "   "   "   4-30. P.M.
   "D" Company   "   "   "   5. P.M.
   "C" Company   "   "   "   5. P.M.
   Headquarters   "   "   "   5-15. P.M.

4. "D" Company will attach one platoon to move with "A" Company, and one platoon will be at the Gum boot store HARGICOURT at 4-45. P.M. and will join "B" Company and proceed up the line with it.
200 yards distance will be maintained between platoons.

5. Officers and Coy kits for Transport lines will be ready at Coy. Hqrs by 4 P.M.

6. Tpt Officer will arrange for Tpt proceeding up the line with Companies, to report at 4. P.M.

7. Gum boot arrangements will be notified later.

8. Water. - Each Coy will be issued during the day with 15 cans of water which will be taken up the line in Company limbers.

                       W. Heaton
                       Capt & Adjt
                 7th Northamptonshire Regiment

Copy No 1   "A" Coy
       2   "B" Coy
       3   "C" Coy
       4   "D" Coy
       5   "T&O"
       6   "Q.M."
       7   2nd Brigade
       8   File

73/pt Vol 26

Confidential.

War Diary
of
7th (S). Bn Northamptonshire Regiment

From :- Nov 1st 1914
To :- Nov 30th 1914.

In the Field
Nov 30- 1914.

WAR DIARY
or
INTELLIGENCE SUMMARY.
(Erase heading not required.)

Army Form C. 2118.

Place	Date	Hour	Summary of Events and Information	Remarks and references to Appendices
HERVILLY	1/12/17		Working parties during day. Battain Football team played 12th Sherwood Foresters during the afternoon & lost 1-0.	
	2/12/17		The Battalion paraded at 8am for Divine Scheme but owing to the bad weather it was abandoned. No working parties found.	
	3/12/17		Orders for the relief in the line of 2nd Lincoln Regt issued. Battalion relieved 2nd Lincoln Regt in line without casualty. Relief completed by 3.30 pm.	
HARGICOURT	4/12/17		Day quiet. At dawn this morning enemy raised Division on left obtaining identification. L/C Bransion wounded today.	
	5/12/17		Day quiet. Later- Company relief took place tonight. B Coy relieved MIDDROFF and C Coy took over old line on Back. Relief complete by 6pm. Pte Dixon wounded. 1 new Officer (2/Lt CARRUTHERS) arrived attached for instruction today.	

WAR DIARY or INTELLIGENCE SUMMARY

Army Form C. 2118.

Place	Date	Hour	Summary of Events and Information	Remarks and references to Appendices
	4/4/17		Weather became rainy. Enemy Artillery much more active on back areas and front line. At 6.00 a.D. MURPHY DSO, MC, 2nd Lincolns Regt. hit on head by shell in Bryant Support. Dr. Lauder accidentally injured.	
	4/4/17		Enemy active with Minenwerfer in morning. At 1352 2/Lt Lawson I was hurried & never by a moment. Weather has all day but improved in evening. Condition of trenches very bad owing mud and duckboards. Enemy snipers more active.	
	5/4/17		The Battalion carried out night patrols between A.25 c & O.3 and safe running out safe from BOWER LANE and MALAKOFF SUPPORT and HINDON. I am two parties on the left crawled on the right flank (2/Lt GREY 2/Lt SHAW 2/Lt CLARK and Sergts. 2/Lt SHELTON) on the were near the junctions of the right top with the German line and entered the top. They found two Germans on a sentry approach on the left side of the top as you look West. One man was left at the entrance. A couple sentry took care two famt. in the top near the sentries after our escorts. The crowds thereupon shot both sentries	

WAR DIARY
or
INTELLIGENCE SUMMARY.
(Erase heading not required.)

Army Form C. 2118.

Place	Date	Hour	Summary of Events and Information	Remarks and references to Appendices
	July 10 (cont)		The wood around the dug-outs to the rear of the entrance there is a Mr Grenon which rolled all these occupants. On hearing the shots the party on the right crop mode forward but found that the men each group were more difficult to negotiate than had been supposed. Before they could secure the woods the enemy had reinforced in such numbers as to render the chances of success very small. The arrival of their reinforcements had comprised the escape to entertain after removing as safe from 6 to 8 wounded. In these circumstances the O.C. party decided to withdraw. Several hand grenades were thrown by the enemy but no casualties occurred. In the meantime the crowd of the left party had rushed forward but were seen and fired on before they reached the enemy wire and were compelled to withdraw. The left attacking party made several attempts to get through between keep up by M. Gun grenades and rifle fire. At 2.45 am the parties were withdrawn. The enemy artillery were quiet but before and after the raid throughout the day.	

WAR DIARY or INTELLIGENCE SUMMARY

Army Form C. 2118.

Place	Date	Hour	Summary of Events and Information	Remarks and references to Appendices
	9/4/17		Enemy quiet. Battalion were relieved by 2nd Leinster Regt in the line. Relief complete without casualty by 7.30 p.m. A & C Coys proceeded to TEMPLEUX QUARRIES. B & D Companys to neighbourhood of L.10.a.	
	10/4/17		Working parties of 220 found covering at 1 pm Kitsons	
	11/4/17		Working parties found as yesterday	
	12/4/17		Usual working parties found.	
	13/4/17		Usual working parties. Baths at TEMPLEUX available to A, C & D Coys	
	14/4/17		Usual working parties. One casualty	
	15/4/17		Only one party of 20 O.R. found today owing to the Battalion relieving the 2nd Leinster Regt in the line. Battalion relieved 2nd Leinster Regt in the line. Relief complete by 4.45 p.m. Casualties NIL. Trenches dont fair - practically unimpeded	
	16/4/17		Enemy Artillery more active shelling POND TRENCH and FERRET. Weather still fine.	

WAR DIARY or INTELLIGENCE SUMMARY

Army Form C. 2118.

Place	Date	Hour	Summary of Events and Information	Remarks and references to Appendices
	14/4/17		Cavalier - 17331 B/C Wood J (Commander of raid) Circular was warnessed. The Battalion carried out a raid early this morning on enemy trenches between A.25.d.0.3. and top running out between BUNKER and SUNNY (the same trench as raid of Jan 6th) 60 men led by 2 Officers (2nd Lts GRAVES and PEARSON) divided into 2 parties of 30 each carried out the raid. The school was put as in last raid. The raid was started at 1.35 am. At 2.30 am men went into left party were unable to enter trench and that enemy wire strong and firing. At 2.20 am very sharp bombing took place and at 2.55 am both parties withdrew. At 3.6 am everything quiet. The organization and execution of the raid were good but new parties were unable to enter trench or obtain identifications. This was due to the fact that the enemy was on the alert and patrols and warning of our attempt, removing him to increase his garrison. Neither side was of October or James McCaw Campbell was wounded.	

WAR DIARY or INTELLIGENCE SUMMARY

Army Form C. 2118.

Place	Date	Hour	Summary of Events and Information	Remarks and references to Appendices
	28/7/17		Day quiet on our front. Occasional activity of Artillery on our left. At 5.30 am violent bombardment took place reaching from left of Division on our left to our right. Shell fire was practically confined to Division on our left. Enemy were very active with Minenwerfer on our Sector. He also threw a few menageant hand grenades. No attack took place on our front. At dawn activity gradually died away (6.30 am) all the morning our F.A. flew at a very low altitude up and down our front. Apparently RFC and A.A. guns were unable to cope with the enemy aircraft about and very nervous. Day and evening quite a little shown on the line. Intr. Company relief took place by and D Coys relieving A and C Coys on the front line. A bty being relieved by D bty and B bty by C bty. Relief complete without casualty.	
	29/7/17		At 6.30 am our Artillery opened and turning oil was discharged on the Decauville on our left attacks but withdrew later to their original line. At the same time reading parties of both Lancaster Regt & 9th North Surrey Regt	

Army Form C. 2118.

WAR DIARY
or
INTELLIGENCE SUMMARY.
(Erase heading not required.)

Instructions regarding War Diaries and Intelligence Summaries are contained in F.S. Regs., Part II. and the Staff Manual respectively. Title pages will be prepared in manuscript.

Place	Date	Hour	Summary of Events and Information	Remarks and references to Appendices
	29/11/17 (cont)	A.M.	up our trenches to raid enemy lines. The 2nd Leinster Regt found front trench's and increased and blowing in dug-outs had obtained no information. The 9th East Surrey Regt met with some resistance. The enemy Artillery was active on left of Division and on our front confined its activity to Minenwerfer. Coys. 2nd Lieut W.C. TOSDEVIN was reted. by at staff during the morning. Orders as to action in case of German retirement received during the morning. Weather became rainy during the afternoon.	
	2/11/17	A.M.	Day quiet. Battalion relieved in the line by 2nd Leinster Regt. Relief completed without casualties by 4pm.	
HERVILLY	22/11/17	A.M.	Cleaning up etc. Battalion team played 43rd Field Ambulance during afternoon. Battalion Concert Party gave concert at YMCA Roisel during evening.	
	23/11/17	A.M.	All tex respirators of Battalion were tested by Bar. Gas NCO in the morning. Parade - training etc. with Company arrangement. Lt Col DeCourcey Parries on leave. Major S.S. Haynes assuming command.	
	24/11/17	A.M.	Working parties etc. Battalion team played 73rd Bde. HQs during afternoon.	

WAR DIARY
or
INTELLIGENCE SUMMARY.

Army Form C. 2118.

(Erase heading not required.)

Place	Date	Hour	Summary of Events and Information	Remarks and references to Appendices
	23/11/17	a.m.	Working parties. Voluntary Divine Service for men not on working parties. Musketry Competition with 2nd D.A.C. commenced today. 2nd Lieut S.H. Marton	
	24/11/17	a.m.	Training :- A and B Coys carried out a Platoon Lecture Scheme under direction of Major S.S. Hayes. Battalion Scout parcel 17th Reserve Fourteen during the afternoon. Battalion Guard Party gave a show at Forest during the evening.	
	25/11/17	a.m.	Wet day - Coys paraded for Senior Inspector. Feeting of our entertainers to box reproduced to Bn. the 10.0. Battalion moved into the line to relieve 2nd Bn Lincoln Regt. Relief complete by 9.45 pm. Night quiet. Enemy very alert and nervous of attack our right coy when he however the own were about 8 pm. Trenches have fallen in very badly.	
HARGICOURT	26/11/17	a.m.	M.Gs active along road during early morning. Spires moved about hut during the day. Sergeants' and the ridge on to north were shelled intermittently until 5 p.m. The forward area was watched. One or two enemy snipers were very active to this Company. About 9pm an enemy aeroplane	

2353 Wt W2544/1454 700,000 5/15 D.D.&L. A.D.S.S./Forms/C. 2118.

WAR DIARY
or
INTELLIGENCE SUMMARY.
(Erase heading not required.)

Army Form C. 2118.

Place	Date	Hour	Summary of Events and Information	Remarks and references to Appendices
	28/11/17 (cont)		own our lines and few bombards and foreward later he was joined by 5 others. Our M.Gs and L.Gs failed to drive them off. Just after midnight 28th/29th two patrols were sent out, one from right company consisting of 1 Officer and 4 O.Rs. and one from left company of 1 Officer & 5 O.Rs. The right patrol reached enemy trench near an old sap and found a gap at the junction of the sap and front line. They were seen and fired upon but returned without casualties. The left patrol went from MINNOW TRENCH to the enemy wire and heard working parties busy clearing WOOD TRENCH. This party also returned safely.	
	29/11/17		Enemy very quiet. A few shells (4.2"ems) fell behind SUGAR TRENCH and BOWER LANE about 10 a.m. A sniper was active opposite right company during morning but ceased when our sniper killed one of his companions. Slight movement in BELLICOURT and along road to HARGICOURT. Active M.Gs. active at "Stand to".	

WAR DIARY or INTELLIGENCE SUMMARY

Army Form C. 2118.

Place	Date	Hour	Summary of Events and Information	Remarks and references to Appendices
	29/11/18	11 A.M.	Two large parties of the enemy were observed moving at about 5.45 p.m. by our patrols who were in touch by the enemy, who returned to their trench and afterwards emerged as two fighting patrols and attempted to work round our patrols. The patrols withdrew and our Lewis Guns opened out and dispersed the party.	
	30/11/18	11 A.M.	Enemy very quiet except in BELLICOURT where much movement was seen. Enemy attacked the 55th Division and captured the villages of VILLERS GUISLAIN and GONNELIEU. This did not affect our front. Orders for the relief of the Division by the Cavalry Division were cancelled. Information was received that the enemy might possibly attack and precautionary measures taken - B Company occupying COLOGNE RESERVE and standing to during the night. A stand to by trench mortars took place at 6.15 am 1/12/18. No enemy action resulted from this.	

Copy No 5

7TH NORTHAMPTONSHIRE REGIMENT.

ORDER NO 1.
BY
LIEUT COL D. KIRKWOOD, COMMANDING

In the Field. —:—:—:—:—:—:—   .....19.

Reference Map S.O. 1/40,000.

1. The Battalion will carry out a tactical scheme tomorrow (2nd Nov 1917) in accordance with orders issued as-under.

2. Companies (as strong as possible) will assemble in column of route on the road leading S.W. through NEUVILLY, in order A - B - D - C. – the head of the leading Company being at Cross Roads at 8-15.a.m.

3. Dress – Fighting order (steel helmets). Mounted Officers will be mounted.

4. Breakfasts will be at 7-15.a.m.

Sd................Lt Col Comdg,
7th Northamptonshire Regiment.

Copy No.1. "A" Company.   Copy No.5. Coy.Comdr.
  "   2. "B" Company.   "   6. File.
  "   3. "C" Company.
  "   4. "D" Company.

OPERATION ORDER NO.5. BY LIEUT COL D.W.POWELL, COMMANDING
7TH BATTN. NORTHAMPTONSHIRE REGIMENT.

IN THE FIELD.   3RD NOV. 1915.

1.   The Battalion will relieve the 2nd Leinsters in the
     line tonight 3/4 November 1915.

          B Coy will be on the Left.
          D Coy "   "   "   " Right.
          C Coy will be in Support at VALLEY POSTS with
               one platoon in RIFLE PIT TRENCH.
          A Coy will be in Reserve.

2.   Companies will move in the following order - 200 yards
     interval to be maintained between Sections :-

          B Coy.   3.p.m.
          C Coy.   3.30.p.m.
          D Coy.   3.45.p.m.
          A Coy.   4.p.m.
          HQrs.   4.30.p.m.

     If the enemy observation balloons are up relief will
     be postponed till dusk.   The platoon of C Coy for
     RIFLE PIT TRENCH will move off with D Company and
     one platoon of C Company which is attached to the
     Right Company at night will move off with D Company.

3.   The Transport Officer will arrange for Transport for
     SAA and Lewis Guns to move with Companies. Mess Cart and
     Maltese Cart also transport for Orderly Room stores and
     Officers' kit will be at Batt. Hqrs. at 3 - ?.p.m.
     Pack horses to be at Batt. Hqrs. at 2.30.p.m.

4.   All Spare kit to be stacked outside billets before
     Companies move off.

5.   Gum boots will be drawn from the Gum boot store
     HARGICOURT as follows:-

          B Coy   45 prs.
          D Coy   45 prs.
          C Coy   45 prs.
          A Coy   40 prs.
          HQrs.   20 prs.

                                   ────────── Capt. and Adjt.,
                                   7th Northamptonshire Regiment.

SECRET

[illegible header] Northamptonshire Regt
[illegible] by Lieut D W [illegible] Comdg

Copy No. 6   Nov 4/1917

1. The Southern boundary of the 13th IB
will be adjusted on night of 4th Nov 1917
to run as follows:—
   Left line (exclusive to 13th IB)
L.6.c.9.5 L.5.c.9.5 and hence along
present boundary.

2. The 9th Royal Sussex Regt will extend
its front to the South taking over as far
as sap at A.25.d.00.90 inclusive and
will move to relief of B & C Coys at
11.30 pm.

3. B Coy on relief will proceed to dug-
outs at SLAG HEAP L.5.d.5.2 and will
find one Platoon by night for SUGAR
TRENCH and one for FOREST TRENCH.
These to report immediately their Platoons
relieved. [illegible] of each of these Platoons
the Officers may be withdrawn at
morning stand down.

4. C Coy on relief will take over from
the 9th East Surrey Regt between IVER
LANE and FISH LANE and will send
forward advance party on morning
of the 5th instant.

5. The start will be made from a ZERO HOUR. The leader of each party will start independently at ZERO.

6. SIGNAL FOR WITHDRAWAL. The "Cookhouse" call will be sounded. Three buglers will be found by Battalion HQrs. for this purpose.

7. MACHINE GUNS. D Coy will provide two Lewis Guns with teams. These will take up a position near the Listening Post East of the centre of BOWER LANE. They will give covering fire in the event of enemy counter-attack.

8. COOPERATION OF OTHER UNITS. These arrangements will be in accordance with extracts from Brigade Orders issued separately.

9. A Beacon fire will be lit in the neighbourhood of MALAKOFF FARM ten minutes after the signal for withdrawal has sounded.

10. All concerned will be in position half an hour before ZERO.

11. Hour of ZERO will be notified later.

12. SYNCHRONISATION OF WATCHES. The watches of all concerned will be synchronized at x pm and half an hour before ZERO at Advanced Battn. HQrs.

13. PRISONERS.   Prisoners will be conducted to Advanced Bn. H.Q.

14. EVACUATION OF WOUNDED   Advanced Medical Aid Post will be in dug-out on MALAKOFF TRENCH at F.30.c.6.5.

15. Battalion H.Q. will move to the Company dug-out in BOWER LANE from one hour before ZERO until one hour after the signal of withdrawal has been given.

L W Powell Lieut Col
Commanding
7(S) Bn Northamptonshire Regt

11-11-1917.
Issued at 6 pm.

Copies to O's C. All Companies
        73rd Inf. Bde
        2/Lt L E Barnes
        2/Lt R Pearson.

7th (X) Bn Northamptonshire Regt.
[illegible] by [illegible] F.C. Daniel Company
C.S.M.[?]

1. The Battalion will be relieved by the 2nd [illegible] Battalion [illegible] the night of 4/5th [illegible] and [illegible] relief will become a Battalion in support.

2. The Battalion will be disposed as follows after relief:
   HQ, A Coy, C Coy, [illegible] at [illegible]
   B Coy & D Coy at Old Brigade HQ
   L.10.A.
   Capt [illegible] will be in command of the two Companies at L.10.A.

3. KIT & TRANSPORT. All Coy and Officers Kits and cooking utensils will be at [illegible] at 5 pm. A/C K.C. will be ready outside Bn HQ at 5 pm. Ration [illegible] will be [illegible] Ration at the [illegible] [illegible] will be at [illegible] [illegible]

4. Coys will send 1 NCO and [illegible] 1 NCO will be sent for Mess [illegible] Ration Party to arrive at Bn HQ at 12 noon tomorrow 4th inst.

Capt Adjt
7th Northamptonshire Regt.

Operation Orders by [?] [?]
to 6th [?]
commanding [?] [?]

1. The Battalion will relieve the 2nd
Canadian [?] in the line tonight 15/16 Nov 17
A Coy on left will relieve [?] B Coy
[?] A Coy
" " right " " [?] B Coy
reserve [?] C Coy
[?] Coy will move at [?] [?]
and at 30 min of clear [?] [?] to
clear will be sent to all Companies
from HQ at 3 bm.
Companies will move as follows:-
A Coy 4 [?]
B Coy 4.15 pm
C Coy 4.30 pm
D Coy 4.45 pm
Bn HQ 6 pm.

2. [?] will be carried out over the
[?] as far as possible owing to the
condition of the trenches. Coys will
detail [?] NCO per platoon to protect an
advance party during the afternoon
under Company arrangements.
All spare kit must be ready for

Transport at 3.15pm. Transport Officer will arrange Transport for Companies' Lewis Guns and kit going up the line.

Captain & Adjt
7th Northamptonshire Regt

13/8/1917.
 Issued at 11.30am

 Copies to O.C. Companies
  RSM.

Operation Order No 60 by Lt Col D.W. Powell - Commanding.
7th Bn Northamptonshire Regt

The Field — 18-11-17

1. An inter-company relief will take place tonight 18/19 Nov.

2. B Coy will relieve C Coy which will become Company in Reserve.

   D Coy will relieve A Coy, which will become Company in Support.

3. D Coy will move at 4-45 pm
   B Coy will move at 5-15 pm

   Relief will be carried out over the top as far as possible

4. Coys will send forward NCO's during the day to take over.

M Heaton
Capt. Adjt
7th Northamptonshire Regt

Copy No 1 A Coy   No 3 C Coy
     No 2 B Coy   No 4 D Coy
                   No 5 File

1st (8) Bn Northamptonshire Regt
Operation Order No 63.

Ref Sheet 0 1/10,000.

1. The Battalion will carry out a raid on the enemy's line between A.25.d.1.3. and A.25.d.15.15. on the night of 16th/17th Nov. with the object of obtaining identification.

2. The raiding party will consist of 30 O.R. from A Coy and 30 O.R. from C Coy. 2nd Lieut Barnes will command the party. 2nd Lt Pearson will assist him.

3. FORMATION. The raiding party will be organized in two attacking parties of 14 O.R. with a support of 10 O.R. to each party. 12 men specially trained as crawlers will be allotted, 6 to each attacking party.

4. METHOD OF EXECUTION. The attacking parties will work as follows:—
The left party along the Sap which leaves MINNOW SUPPORT at A.25.d.0.3.
The right party along the Sap which leaves the junction of MINNOW TRENCH & with BOWER LANE.

BJO

5. C Coy's cooking utensils will be transferred to B Coy at SLAG HEAP under arrangements to be made by Sergt Duffield.

A.P. Stenton
Capt Adjt
R[?]

24-11-1904

Copy No 1 - A Coy
2 - B
3 - C
4 - D
5 - Sgt Duffield
6 - File

7th Service Bn Northamptonshire Regt.
Operation Order No. 67.

In the Field.   26th November 1915

The Battalion will relieve the 2nd Bn The [Surrey?]
Regiment in the line tomorrow 27th November 1915.
    C Company will be on the right
    D Company   "   "   " left
    B Company   "   " in support
    A Company   "   " in reserve

Companies will move as follows:-
    C Company at 3 pm.
    D Company at 3.15 pm.
    B Company at 3.30 pm.
One Platoon of B Company will move with each
front line Company.
    A Company will move at 3.45 pm.
    Headquarters "   "   " 4 pm.
Route via YEMPLEUX. 200 yds intervals will be
maintained between Platoons.

Advance parties of 1 NCO per Platoon and 1 for Bn
Headquarters will report at the Orderly Room at 10 am.

Transport Officer will arrange for transport to move with
each Company.
    All surplus kit & stores must be dumped outside billets
by 3 pm.

Completion of relief will be notified by O.C. Companies
using their runners.
    Maps of trenches will be forwarded without
delay to Bn Headquarters.

                                        [signature]
                                        Captain & Adjutant.
                                7th Service Bn Northamptonshire Regiment.

26-11-1915

Copies to
A.C. Companies
T.M.
R.S.M.

CONFIDENTIAL.

WAR DIARY

OF

7th SERVICE BATTALION NORTHAMPTONSHIRE REGIMENT.

FROM - DECEMBER 1st. 1917.
TO - DECEMBER 31st. 1917.

IN THE FIELD.
DECEMBER 31st 1917.

Army Form C. 2118.

WAR DIARY
or
INTELLIGENCE SUMMARY.

(Erase heading not required.)

Instructions regarding War Diaries and Intelligence Summaries are contained in F. S. Regs., Part II. and the Staff Manual respectively. Title pages will be prepared in manuscript.

Place	Date	Hour	Summary of Events and Information	Remarks and references to Appendices
HARGI-COURT.	1/12/17.		Enemy quiet. A little shelling of Support trenches - about 30 shells between 2 a.m. and 3 p.m. No unusual movement. Enemy shelled his own front line about 3 pm. Lights were sent up splitting into two greens and two whites - shelling then ceased. Continous patrols kept watch of enemy front that night - but it was very bright that they could not get far enough. No unusual movement was observed.	
	2/12/17.		5th Guards Division reported opposite to us intending attack. Preparations for immediate counter attack - Support Company moved to COLOGNE RESERVE permanently while Reserve Company moved there each morning at 4 a.m. and stood to until 8 am.	
	3/12/17.		13th Middlesex Regiment who had been moved from Divisional Reserve at HERVILLY to positions in reserve behind Division on our left returned to HERVILLY. 2nd Lieut Evans reported from course.	
	4/12/17.		Battalion was relieved in line by 2nd Leinster Regiment. Relief completed by 7.15 pm. Casualties during tour - 1 O.R. Killed. "A" and "D" Companies moved to Brigade Reserve at L.10.a. "B" and "C" Companies moved to TEMPLEUX QUARRIES near Battalion Headquarters.	
	5/12/17.		"A" and "D" Companies stood to from 5 a.m. to 8 am. in HARGICOURT TRENCH. "B" and "C" Companies stood to in billets. The remainder of the day was spent in cleaning up. Rifle inspections by Companies. 2nd Lieuts. Butlin, Hoare, and Tetley reported from variouscourses.	
	6/12/17.		Stand To arrangements as usual. In addition two Platoons were sent as permanent garrison of TOINE - ORCHARD TRENCH.	
	7/12/17.		Working parties as usual	
	8/12/17.		Working parties as yesterday.	
	9/12/17.		Usual working parties.	

Army Form C. 2118.

WAR DIARY
or
INTELLIGENCE SUMMARY.
(Erase heading not required.)

Instructions regarding War Diaries and Intelligence Summaries are contained in F. S. Regs., Part II. and the Staff Manual respectively. Title pages will be prepared in manuscript.

Place	Date	Hour	Summary of Events and Information	Remarks and references to Appendices
HARGI-COURT.	10/12/17.		Battalion relieved 2nd Battalion Leinster Regiment in the line. Left TEMPLEUX QUARRIES commencing at 4 pm. Relief was completed without casualties by 7 pm. Trenches were in a slightly better condition being hardened by the frosts. Two officers patrols reported enemy clearing his trenches and strengthening his wire.	
	11/12/17.		Captain M.H.Mattock was attached to Battalion Headquarters during absence on leave of Captain A.W.Heaton.	
	12/12/17.		Artillery active but individual movement below normal.	
	13/12/17.		Hostile relief suspected. 20th Landsturm Regiment had been in line up till tonight.	
	14/12/17.		Increase of Artillery. Reserve positions shelled by 4.2.s and 5.9.s for 3 hours during day. Aircraft observed for the enemy batteries which fired chiefly from direction of BONY. French Division on our right attacked by Gas projectors. Many casualties.	
	15/12/17.		About same Artillery activity. All men were warned to be in readiness for gas attack but none was attempted.	
	16/12/17.		Artillery much quieter. Battalion was relieved in the line by 2nd Battalion Leinster Regiment and proceeded to Divisional Reserve at HERVILLY. Relief was completed by 10 pm.	
	17/12/17.		Working parties out clearing roads of snow.	
	18/12/17.		Battalion moved to BERNES.	
	19/12/17.		Day spent in clearing up. Working parties employed on hutting at BOUVINCOURT and HANCOURT.	
	20/12/17.		Working parties as above and also clearing snow at HERVILLY.	

Army Form C. 2118.

WAR DIARY
or
INTELLIGENCE SUMMARY.
(Erase heading not required.)

Place	Date	Hour	Summary of Events and Information	Remarks and references to Appendices
BERNES.	21/12/17.		Parades and inspections.	
	22/12/17.		Parades as usual.	
	23/12/17.		Parades and working parties.	
	24/12/17.		Church Parades (cancelled last moment.) All arms inspected by Brigade Armourer Sergeant.	
	25/12/17.		Cleaning up and games.	
	26/12/17.		Parades as usual.	
	27/12/17.		Proceed to line taking over from 3rd Battn. Rifle Brigade. Relief complete by 7.30 pm. Line now held from FISH LANE (exclusive) to CARBINE TRENCH (inclusive).	
	28/12/17.		Day very quiet. Artillery Nil.	
	29/12/17.		Day quiet. Hostile aircraft fairly active. A few shells on right Company.	
	30/12/17.		Day quiet. A few shells on front and support lines. Enemy aircraft not very active. Enemy machine guns active at night.	
	31/12/17.		Day quiet as before. Enemy machine guns active at night on HARGICOURT – BELLICOURT ROAD. Battalion relieved in line by 9th Battn. Royal Sussex Regiment. Relief complete by 7.30 pm. Battalion on relief was disposed as follows :– Battn. Hdqrs., "A" and "B" Companies – TEMPLEUX QUARRIES. "C" and "D" Companies – L.10.a. and SLAG HEAP QUARRIES respectively.	

Instructions regarding War Diaries and Intelligence Summaries are contained in F. S. Regs., Part II. and the Staff Manual respectively. Title pages will be prepared in manuscript.

Operation Orders No. 64
by
Major S. S. Hayne. Comdg 7th Northamptonshire Rgt

In the Field.   3-12-1917

1. The Battalion will be relieved tomorrow Decr 4th by the 2nd Leinster Regt. and after relief will become Battn in Brigade Reserve.

2. A & D Coys will go to Old Bde Hqrs at L.13.A. Hqrs — B and C Coys will go to TEMPLEUX QUARRIES. Relief will commence about 4-30 P.M — 1. N.C.O. per Company as Advance Party will report to Bn. Hqrs at 12 noon.

3. All Officers and Company kits to be at Cookhouse by 5 pm. Coys limbers will be at Cookhouse at 5-30 P.M.

4. After relief 2/Lts Williams and Wheeler will remain with B Company and 2/Lt Norman will rejoin D Company.

5. Gumboots will be returned to store.

6. Offrs Coys will ensure that all empty petrol cans are brought out of the line and taken with them to their new quarters where they will be required for drawing water from the water cart.

A. P. Seaton
7 Northampton Regt

Operation Orders No. 72. by
Major S. S. Moore Commanding
7th (S) Bn Northamptonshire Regt

1. The 2nd Bn Leinster Regt will relieve the 7th Bn Northamptonshire Regiment on the evening of 16th and night of 16th/17th inst.

2. Relief will commence as soon as possible after dusk.

3. ROUTE - L.10.H. - HESBECOURT - HERVILLY.

4. All Gum Boots will be returned to the Bde. Gum Boot Store at HARGICOURT, and receipts forwarded to the Orderly Room by 11 am 17th inst.

5. Advance party consisting of 1 N.C.O. from each Company and 2 N.C.O.s from Bn. HQ will report at Bn HQrs at 12.30 pm and proceed to HERVILLY to take over.

6. MG Kits will be outside HQrs by 4.15 pm. Limbers for Lewis Guns and Officers Mess Kits will be outside cookhouse. Companies will be responsible for having their own water tins on their

cook house.

Companies will be responsible
for having their own water tins
on their respective Coy. limbers.

~~On completion of relief Companies will wire name of their Coy and code.~~

Completion of relief will be reported
by sending letter of company
followed by code word "CLOSED".

Station Orders No 41
by Captain J. S. Harvey commanding
4th Battalion Hampshire Regiment

1. The Company which will be carrying
out guards the 13th inst. and after
the Companies will be disposed as follows:—
    Firing line (Right section)   C Coy
              (Left   "   )   D Coy
    Supports (Cologne Rd)   A Coy
    Reserve   B Coy

2. A Coy will send one Platoon under an
   Officer to C Coy and one Platoon under an
   Officer to D Coy.

3. Reliefs will commence at 4.30 pm.

4. Advance parties will be sent in under
   Company arrangements.

5. [illegible] B Coy will take over 55
   [illegible] of guns held by C Coy.
   The two Platoons of A Coy will on the
   line will hand over their gun boats
   to the Platoons of B Coy relieving them
   if required.

6. Companies will be responsible for their own water cans

7. 2/Lieut Horner will join to-day on arrival

B.H. Mattock. Capt for O.C.
1/ Northamptonshire Regiment.

12-12-1914

Copies to All Coys
Q.M.
T.O.
file

1st (S) Bn Northamptonshire Regt

Operation Orders by Lieut Col D. W. Powell, Commdg

No 73   Copy No 8   Dec 11/1914

1. MOVE   The Battalion will move to new's Coy lines
             11th December 1914.
             Companies will move off independently at
             the following times:-
               A Coy   - 1.30 pm
               C   - 1.45 pm
               D   - 2.00 pm
               B Coy   - 2.15 pm
               HQ   -

2. TRANSPORT ARRANGEMENTS.   Transport will move off
             with Companies etc.
                              All kits and stores will
             be ready in each billet by 11 am tomorrow.

3. DINNERS.   Dinners will be at 12 noon.

4. ADVANCE PARTIES. O.C. Coys & MG will detail advance
             parties, to act as guides to precede main
             body for billeting etc arrangements.

5. CLEANLINESS OF BILLETS.   Special attention will be paid
             to ensure that all billets are left in a clean
             and sanitary condition.

                                          D. H. Mattock. Capt & Adjt
                                          1st (S) Bn Northampton Regt

11/12/1914
                    Copy No 1 - OC A Coy
                           2 - " B Coy
                           3 - " C Coy
                           4 - " D Coy
                           5 - MG
                           6 - TO
                           7 - RSM
                           8 - File

OPERATION ORDERS NO.74
BY
MAJOR S.S.HAYNE, COMMANDING 7TH BN NORTHAMPTONSHIRE REGT.

IN THE FIELD.   -*-*-*-*-*-*-   26-12-1917.

Reference Sheet 62.C. 1/20.000.

1. The Battalion will relieve the 3rd Bn Rifle Brigade on the night of 27./28th December, and on completion of relief will occupy the centre Sector.
   Companies will be disposed as follows:-

   "B" Company   - Right Subsector.
   "A" Company   - Centre Subsector.
   "C" Company   - Left Subsector.
   "D" Company   - Support (COLOGNE RESERVE)
                    interval

2. Companies will move by platoons, at 200 yds/ in the following order :-

   "B" Company   - 2.p.m.
   "A" Company   - 2-15.p.m.
   "C" Company   - 2-30.p.m.
   "D" Company   - 2-45.p.m.
   Bn Headqrs   - 3.p.m.

3. Route will be via HERVILLY - K.12.d.2.4. - TEMPLEUX - HARGICOURT. In case of hostile shelling in TEMPLEUX, the track L.7.b.35.75. - L.3.c.70.75. will be used.

4. Guides (1 per platoon) will meet Companies at Bn Hqrs L.5.b.3.2. at 4.p.m.

5. Advance party of 2 N.C.O.s per Company and 2 N.C.O.s from Hqrs will parade at the Orderly Room at 10-30.a.m. under Sgt Duffree.

6. Transport. All kits stores etc will be outside billets by 1-30.p.m. Limbers for Lewis Guns and Officers Mess kits will proceed with Companies.

7. Gumboots will be drawn by Companies from Gumboot Store HARGICOURT as under :-

   B.Coy.25 prs - A.Coy.40 prs - C.Coy.40 prs - D.Coy.20 prs - Hqrs.15prs

Copy No.1. A Coy.
"   No.2. B Coy.
"   No.3. C Coy.
"   No.4. D Coy.
"   No.5. R.S.M.
"   No.6. T.O.
"   No.7. Q.M.
"   No.8. 3rd R.B.
"   No.9. File.

_____Captain and Adjt,
7th Northamptonshire Regiment.

Vol 28

CONFIDENTIAL.

WAR DIARY

OF

7th SERVICE BATTALION NORTHAMPTONSHIRE REGIMENT.

FROM - JANUARY 1st. 1918.
TO   - JANUARY 31st. 1918.

IN THE FIELD.
JANUARY 31st. 1918.

Army Form C. 2118.

WAR DIARY
or
INTELLIGENCE SUMMARY.

(Erase heading not required.)

Instructions regarding War Diaries and Intelligence Summaries are contained in F. S. Regs., Part II. and the Staff Manual respectively. Title pages will be prepared in manuscript.

Place	Date	Hour	Summary of Events and Information	Remarks and references to Appendices
TEMPLEUX QUARRIES.	1/1/18.		Battalion in Support. Working parties found by A, B, and C Companies for work with the R.E's. etc...	
	2/1/18.		Working parties as yesterday. Captain W.F.Mattock proceeds on leave and 2nd.Lieut.A.F.Barton assumes duties of Adjutant.	
	3/1/18		Working parties as usual. Advance parties of 8th Bn.Queens Regiment who relieve us tomorrow were shewn round the various Company billets, etc...	
	4/1/18.		Battalion relieved in Brigade support by 8th Bn. Queens Regiment and proceeded to BERNES. No casualties have occurred in the Battalion during the whole of this tour.	
BERNES.	5/1/18.		Baths at BERNES allotted.	
	6/1/18.		Large working parties found by the Battalion. Several working parties found.	
	7/1/18.		Divine Service etc.. Several working parties. Junior N.C.O's. class under R.S.M." Advance parties proceed to take over Camp at VRAIGNES.	
	8/1/18.		Battalion relieved by 12th Bn. Royal Fusiliers and moved to VRAIGNES and became Divisional Reserve. Relief complete by 5.30 pm.	
VRAIGNES.	9/1/18.		Training etc. A very cold day with a heavy fall of snow during the afternoon.	
	10/1/18.		Training as usual. Company Officers and N.C.Os. reconnoitre route to VERMAND.	
	11/1/18.		Training as usual.	
	12/1/1918.		Battalion provides large working parties for work on Support lines etc..	
	13/1/18.		Voluntary Divine Service. Large working parties again found today.	
	14/1/18.		Practically all the Battalion engaged on working parties - no training carried out.	

Army Form C. 2118.

WAR DIARY
or
INTELLIGENCE SUMMARY.
(Erase heading not required.)

Instructions regarding War Diaries and Intelligence Summaries are contained in F. S. Regs., Part II. and the Staff Manual respectively. Title pages will be prepared in manuscript.

Place	Date	Hour	Summary of Events and Information	Remarks and references to Appendices
VRAIGNES.	15/1/18.		Working parties chiefly engaged in constructing Strong Points in the vicinity of VRAIGNES.	
	16/1/18.		Work continued on construction of Strong Points for the defence of VRAIGNES.	
	17/1/18.		Pouring rain. Work on Strong Points postponed. Captain A.W. Heaton rejoins from leave and is attached to 73rd Infantry Brigade Headquarters.	
	18/1/18.		Working parties engaged on Strong Points and on erecting mud walls around huts as a protective measure against aeroplane bombs.	
	19/1/18.		Training etc.. Company teams play off first round in Brigade Football Competition during the afternoon. Three companies successful.	
	20/1/18.		Battalion entrains at VRAIGNES siding at 12.45 p.m. on Light Railway and proceeds to ROISEL. Detrained about 2 p.m. and had dinners after which the Battalion proceeds to the line by march route and relieves 12th Bn. Royal Fusiliers in Centre Sector - Relief complete by 7 p.m. without casualties.	
LINE.	21/1/18.		Day passed quietly. Enemy retaliated during the afternoon for our Trench Mortars.	
	22/1/18.		Our aeroplanes showed much more activity, going well over the Bosch lines. Right Front shelled during the afternoon.	
	23/1/18.		Enemy very quiet. No artillery fire except during the latter part of the afternoon.	
	24/1/18.		Battalion was relieved in the line by 9th Bn. Royal Sussex Regiment. Relief complete by 6.45 p.m. Battalion moved to Support. Positions - One Company at L.5.b., One Company at L.10.a., and two Companies at TEMPLEUX QUARRIES.	
TEMPLEUX QUARRIES.	25/1/18.		Working parties found by Companies at for work in Support Area, etc..	
	26/1/18.		Working parties as yesterday.	

Army Form C. 2118.

WAR DIARY
or
INTELLIGENCE SUMMARY.
(Erase heading not required.)

Place	Date	Hour	Summary of Events and Information	Remarks and references to Appendices
TEMPLEUX QUARRIES.	27/1/18.		Working parties - Voluntary Non-Conformists Service in BAKERLOO TUNNEL.	
	28/1/18.		Working parties as usual.	
	29/1/18.		Battalion relieved by 1st Bn. North Staffordshire Regiment and moved to BERNES - Divisional Support Area.	
BERNES.	30/1/18.		Cleaning up, inspections, etc.	
	31/1/18.		Practically all men of the Battalion employed at work on the GREEN LINE.	

OPERATION ORDERS NO.1.
BY
MAJOR S.S.HAYNE, COMMANDING 7TH BN NORTHAMPTONSHIRE REGIMENT.

IN THE FIELD.   **********   3/1/1918.

1. The Battalion will be relieved by the 8th QUEENS Regiment on January 4th, and on relief will proceed to BERNES and become Divisional Support.

2. Our Companies will be relieved by the corresponding Companies of the QUEENS Regiment.

3. Guides will be required as under and will report to Battalion Headquarters TEMPLEUX QUARRIES at 1-15.p.m. on the 4th instant :-

   1 guide per platoon.
   1 for each Company Hqrs.
   2 for Battalion Hqrs.

   R.S.M. to detail guides as under:-

   1 guide to conduct guards to
   (a) Gumboot Store HARGICOURT.
   (b) Brigade bomb Store HARGICOURT.

   1 guide to guide parties to
   (a) Traffic Control Post L.4.d.2.3.
   (b) Traffic Control Post L.5.d.2.3.

   to report at Battn Headquarters at 1-15.p.m.

   O.C."A" Company to detail one officer to be in charge of guides who will report to Battn Hqrs for detail at 10-30.a.m. tomorrow.

   O.C."B" Company will give orders for one representative from each post for which he is finding an escort to Vickers guns to report at Battn Hqrs at 1-15.p.m. to act as guides to parties of relieving Units.

3. All kits etc to be packed outside dumps ready for loading by 2.p.m. The Transport Officer will arrange to collect these and convey them to BERNES. "D" Company's limbers will be at Dressing Station HARGICOURT.

4. Companies on being relieved will march off independantly to billets at BERNES with platoons at 300 yds distance. Relief complete to be telephoned to Bn Hqrs at TEMPLEUX QUARRIES by sending O.C.Coy's name. O.C."D"Company to forward this via 9th Royal Sussex Hqrs.

5. O.C. "D" Company will hand in all gumboots to gumboot store by 11.a.m. 4th inst, obtaining receipts for same.

6. O.C.s Coys to hand over all stores etc to incoming Units and obtain receipts for these. All receipts and lists of these to be forwarded to the Orderly Room by 11.a.m. 5th inst.

7. The Senior N.C.O. of these two guards will send by telephone to Battn Hqrs the word "Complete" on the Brigade gas and bomb store guards being relieved.

8. All detached guards and posts will on relief proceed to BERNES independently.

Copies Nos 1-4. Coys.
         5. R.S.M.
         6. T.O.   --------------2/Lt A/Adjt,
         7. Q.M.   7th Northamptonshire Regiment.
         8. 8th Queens.
         9. File.

Copy No.....

OPERATION ORDER No. 2

BY

MAJOR S. S. HAYNE COMMANDING

7th SERVICE BATTN. NORTHAMPTONSHIRE REGT.

****

REFERNCE MAP 62 C.1/40,000.

1. The Battalion will be relieved by the 12th Battn. Royal Fusiliers Regiment on afternoon of the 8th instant and on relief will march to billets at VRAIGNES and will become Divisional Reserve.
Distance - 3 miles.

2. Route - BERNES - HANCOURT. Companies will march with platoons at 200 yards distance.

3. The order of Companies leaving this area will be notified later. Probable hour of first Platoon leaving - 4 p.m.

4. All kits to be stacked ready for loading by 3 p.m.

5. Officers Commanding Companies will detail one guide per platoon to parade under the R.S.M. outside the Orderly Room at 2.15 p.m. These guides will be march off in one party to VRAIGNES under Sergt. Rubens.

6. Blankets will be rolled in bundles of ten labelled and securely tied under supervision of one Officer per Company and will be stacked inside billets until called for.

7. Transport Officer will arrange to collect all kits and blankets at 3 p.m. and convey them to VRAIGNES.

8. Lewis Gun limbers to follow immediately behind last platoon of each Company.

9. Officers Commanding Companies will inspect their respective billets before marching off.

10. Jerkins will be packed in bundles under Company arrangements and will be conveyed by Transport to destination.

11. Teas will be ready on arrival.

12. Officers Commanding Companies will report personally at Battalion Headquarters when their Companies have been billetted.

Jany. 7th 1918.   ....A R Barton........2nd. Lieut A/Adjutant.
                                   7th Service Battalion Northamptonshire Regiment.

Copy No.1 - Hdqrs.   Copy No.5 - D Coy.   Copy No.9 - Sgt George.
     2 - A Coy.   6 - Q.M.   10 - Sgt Rubens.
     3 - B Coy.   7 - T.O.   11 - War Diary.
     4 - C Coy.   8 - R.S.M.   12 - File.

7th S. Bn. Northamptonshire Regiment.

Reference Sheet
62 C.

OPERATION ORDER NO. 5 .... 19/1/1918
==============================

1. The Battalion will relieve the 12th Bn Royal Fusiliers in the Centre Sector on the night of 20/21st Jany. 1918.
2. On relief the Battalion will hold the line as under
    A Company..... Right Sub-sector,
    C   "   ..... Centre Sub-sector,
    D Company..... Left Sub-sector,
    B Company..... Support - COLOGNE RESERVE
3. Companies etc will march off at 12.15 pm in the following order to VRAIGNES Siding for entrainment by light Railway to ROISEL.
    Advance Party - A Coy - C Coy - D Coy - B Coy - Bn Headquarters.
200 yards distance will be maintained between Coys and parties.
    Lewis Guns will be carried to place of entrainment.
    Lewis Gun limbers will convey them from ROISEL to the line.
4. Dinners will be at ROISEL. The train is due to arrive at 2 pm. Guides will meet the Battalion at place of detrainment.
5. Officers commanding Companies will arrange that advance parties have dinners before entrainment. These parties on arrival at ROISEL will be formed up by Sgt. Rubens and marched to the trenches. Officers commanding Companies must ensure the N.C.O.s of their respective Companies know the particular sector their Companies are taking over
    Strength. 1 N.C.O. per Platoon
    Sgt. Rubens. Bn HQ.
6. The Battalion will march from ROISEL to the trenches as under, maintaining two hundred (200) yards between Platoons. The same distance applies to every six transport vehicles. Lewis Gun limbers to follow immediately in rear of the last platoon of each Company.
    A Company - C Company - D Company - B Company - Bn Headquarters.
Officers commanding Companies to parade their respective Companies to conform with the leading platoon of A Company starting at 5/15 pm.
    ROUTE: ROISEL to Road Junction TEMPLEUX L.2.d.2.8 North to Road Junction L.2.b.8.8, South-east to HARGICOURT
Officers commanding Companies must use their discretion regarding proceeding across country if TEMPLEUX is being shelled.
    Distance : Four miles.
    Dress : Fighting order with packs, steel helmets to be worn.
7. All Defence Schemes, schemes of work in hand, and proposed aeroplane photographs, trench stores, etc.. will be taken over and lists forwarded to Bn. HQ. by 10 am 21st instant. All A.A., Lewis and Vickers Gun Positions will be carefully over.
8. Gum-boots will be drawn at HARGICOURT Gum-boot store Numbers for each Company will be notified tomorrow.
    Whale oil can be obtained from our advanced Dressing Station, if required.

9. Blankets to be rolled in bundles of ten, labelled and securely tied, under the supervision of an Officer, and be stacked ready for loading by **9.30 am.** All other kit not for the trenches to be stacked ready for loading by **10.15 am.**

All trench kit to be ready for loading by **11.15 am.**
Sgt. Wilford to arrange transport for above.
Mess Cart and Medical Cart to collect kits at **11.15 am**
Cookers will proceed to ROISEL immediately after breakfast.   Dinners to be ready on arrival of Battalion.

10. Relief Complete will be reported by wiring the Code Word " W E T "

A.R.Barton.

2nd Lieut., A/Adjutant,
19/1/18   7th Service Bn Northamptonshire Regiment.
Issued at 9/30 pm.

Copies to :-   All Companies.
Bn Headquarters.
R&S.M.
Cook Sgt.
Sgt. Rubens
Quartermaster
Sgt. Wilford
****

To
O.C.
Commanding 7th Northampton[shire]
23.1.1918   Reg[t]

1. The Battalion will be relieved by the
7th R[oyal] Sussex Regiment on the night of
the 24th/25th Jan[uar]y 1918 and after relief
Companies will be disposed as follows:—
    B[attalio]n H[Q]. C and D Coy. — REMIEUX [QUARRY]
    A Company   L.10.A
    B Company   L.S.B.4.3 and dug-
                                 out behind SLAG HEAP

2. Reliefs will commence as soon as
possible after dusk.
    A Coy 7th R. Sussex R. will relieve A Coy
                                        7th North[ants]
    D Coy 7th R. Sussex R.   "   "   D Coy   "
    B Coy   "   "   "   "   C Coy   "
    C Coy   "   "   "   "   B Coy   "

3. The following guides will be
provided by D Coy to meet A Coy 7th
R. Sussex Reg[t] at L.6.A.5.1 at 5.15 p.m.
or as soon as it is sufficiently dark
    1   Guide from PIN SAP GROUP
    1   "   " RUBY LANE GROUP
    1   "   " Coy. HQ

4. Advance parties as under will report to Bge Hdqrs at Bn HQ at 10.30 am tomorrow. A and B Companys guides to proceed to Bn HQ at dawn.
    1 NCO for Coy HQ.
    1 NCO per Platoon
    1 NCO from Bn HQ.

5. OC C Coy will detail 1 Officer to report to OC 9th R. Sussex Regt at TEMPLEUX QUARRIES by 10am tomorrow to take over Lewis Gun Positions, defence scheme etc. C Company will take over Lewis Gun Positions as relief.

6. All kits will be ready by 5.45 pm. Limbers for Lewis Guns, Officers Mess kit etc will meet Companies at the Regimental Aid Post.

7. All gumboots will be returned to the Brigade store HARGICOURT and receipts forwarded to the Orderly Room by Noon 25th instant.

8. All dixies, food carriers etc will be handed over to the 9th R. Sussex Regiment and a receipt obtained. Advance parties will take over corresponding stores

from the 9th Royal Sussex Regt.
9. All Companies will be responsible for their own water cans.
10. Handing over and taking over statements will be forwarded to the Orderly Room by 12noon 25th instant.
11. Relief complete will be reported by wiring the code word "MUD"

W.K.xxxxx. Captain
A/Adjutant
7th (Service) Bn Northamptonshire R

23-1-18
Copies to:— All Companies
Bn HQ
Quartermaster
Transport Officer
OC 9th R Sussex Regt.

Lyncal

Vol 29

Confidential.

7TH (SERVICE) BATTALION NORTHAMPTONSHIRE REGIMENT.

WAR DIARY

FOR

THE MONTH OF FEBRUARY 1918.

WAR DIARY
or
INTELLIGENCE SUMMARY.

(Erase heading not required.)

Army Form C. 2118.

Place	Date	Hour	Summary of Events and Information	Remarks and references to Appendices
BERNES	1/2/18		Large working parties found for work on the GREEN LINE.	
"	2/2/18		Working parties as usual. Battalion concert party gave a show in the evening.	
"	3/2/18		Voluntary Divine Services. Large working parties as usual.	
"	4/2/18		Working parties as usual. Battn team plays 120 Co.R.E. during afternoon.	
"	5/2/18		Working parties. Draft of 17 O.R. joined from Corps Reinforcement Camp.	
"	6/2/18		Working parties. Football match during afternoon.	
"	7/2/18		Working parties. 2/Lt Webb proceeds to England for 6 months tour of duty.	
"	8/2/18		Working parties.	
"	9/2/18		Working parties as usual.	
"	10/2/18		Working parties. Orders received for the Battalion to relieve 8th Queens Regt in the Right Sector on night of 11/12th.	
"	11/2/18		Battalion moved from BERNES and relieved 8th Queens Regt. Taking over front from RUBY LANE to CLUBS LANE. Relief complete by 8.p.m. without casualties. Enemy very quiet by day. Machine guns active by night.	
LINE.	12/2/18		Day misty and quiet. Our snipers killed seven Bosches. Pte Houghton killed by enemy sniper.	
"	13/2/18		At 12-10.a.m. troops on our right raided the enemy line, under a heavy barrage. Bosche retaliation on our front slight. All quiet by 1-30.a.m. Morning quiet.	
"	14/2/18		Enemy artillery more active. Our "Pip" retaliated for "Minnies" on COLOGNE RESERVE. During the morning Cpl Berrisford, L.opl Warnham and Pte Humphrey crawled out and bombed Bosche Post at end of PIT SAP, wounding one, two ran away and were shot down.	

Army Form C. 2118.

WAR DIARY
INTELLIGENCE SUMMARY.
(Erase heading not required.)

Instructions regarding War Diaries and Intelligence Summaries are contained in F. S. Regs., Part II. and the Staff Manual respectively. Title pages will be prepared in manuscript.

Place	Date	Hour	Summary of Events and Information	Remarks and references to Appendices
LINE	15/2/18		Slight T.M. activity - no aerial activity.	
"	16/2/18		Enemy very nervous. Slight increase in artillery fire. Patrol out last night, no Bosche found.	
"	17/2/18		Enemy artillery active during the morning, otherwise quiet.	
"	18/2/18		Great artillery activity, our own during the night on Battalion Hqrs and neighbourhood. Bosche retaliated during afternoon.	
"	19/2/18		Battalion relieved in the line by 8th Queens Regt. Relief complete by 7-50.p.m. without casualties. on relief Batn marched to BERVES.	
BERVES.	20/2/18		Clearing up.	
HERVILLY	21/2/18		Battalion moved to HERVILLY. 210 men on working party.	
"	22/2/18		210 men on working parties.	
"	23/2/18		Working parties same as yesterday.	
"	24/2/18		Presentation of decorations etc by Lieut General G.T. McN Kavanagh V.C. B. C.M.C. D.S.O. Commanding Cavalry Corps. Working parties as yesterday.	
"	25/2/18		Working parties. Bayonet fighting refresher course for 4 officers and 5 N.C.O.s under C.S.M.I. Packford.	
"	26/2/18		Working parties, training etc.	
"	27/2/18		Working parties as usual. Preparations commenced for move to BOVES area.	
"	28/2/18		Working parties. Advance party leaves for BOVES area. Notification received during afternoon that rest, owing to threatened enemy attack is cancelled. C Company ordered to proceed to TEMPLEUX to take up a position in support.	

Copy No. 7

[illegible header] By Major W.S. [?]
                                   Commanding
In the Field.   February 14th 1918

1. Inter-company reliefs will be carried
out on the night of the 15/16
February, & on completion of relief
companies will be disposed as
follows:—
        Front Line.   A Coy. Right Sector
           "   "   C "   Left   "
        L.10.A.   D "   Position now
                              occupied by A Coy
                       B "   Position now
                              occupied by C Coy

2. Advance parties will be sent on under
Company arrangements.
B & C Company's parties will move
before dawn.
If necessary guides will be arranged
for by Coys.

3. All stores, reserve rations, maps,
defence schemes, A.A. Gun positions
etc. will be carefully handed over,
and lists forwarded to the orderly

position by 12 noon, 16th inst.

4. B. Coy will move off at 5 p.m. and
C. Coy at 5.145 p.m.
Companies will move in platoons at
300 yards interval.

5. All officers' Kits will be packed and
stacked at dumps by 3 p.m.
The T.O. will arrange to collect them
for return to stores.
L.G limbers will proceed with Coys.
L.G limber for B. Coy. will be at A'.P
HARGICOURT. Limber for D. Coy at
CRATER DUMP.

6. A & C Coys will each draw 35 pairs
of Gum Boots from gum boot store.
Anymore gum boots required will be
taken over from D & B Coys & receipt
given.

7. All water cans will be left at the
dumps.

8. Relief complete will be reported by
wiring the code word SON. P.T.O

14/2/1918 H. H. Holroyd Captain a/Adjutant
Issued at.   1st Service Batt. Northamptonshire Regt.

Copy No 1 — A. Coy
" " 2 — B. Coy
" " 3 — C. Coy
" " 4 — D. Coy
" " 5 — QM & TO
" " 6 — Bn HQ

Operation Orders No. 9
by
Lt. Col. O.D. Bennett, Commanding, 7th Northamptonshire Regt.

In the Field.   19/2/1918.

1. The 7th Northamptonshire Regiment will be relieved by the 8th Bn Queens (R.W.Surrey) Regiment in the Right sub-section on the night of 19/20th Feby 1918.

2. On relief the 7th Northamptonshire Regiment will move to BOUZES and will come under the Command of the B.O.C. 17th Infantry Bde.

3. Advance party if one N.C.O. per Company and one for Battalion Hqrs will leave Battn Hqrs at 8.a.m. 19th Feby, under Sgt Penberg and will report to R.S.M. G. Hitch at HEVILLY at 10.a.m.   The party will then proceed to BOUZES and take over billets from 8th Queens. 2/Lt Gerrings will accompany this party and take over all A.A.posts, guards, defence schemes, particulars of work etc.

4. O.C."C" Coy will detail the following guides to meet "C" Coy 8th Queens at the R.A.P. SAUCICOURT at 6-30-p.m.
    1 guide for Right group.
    1   "   " Left group.
    1   "   " for BOUZES.
    1   "   " for Coy. HQRS.

5. All officers mess kits etc will be at dumps by 3-30.p.m.
L.G.Limber for A Coy will be at Crater Dump.
L.G.Limber for C Coy will be at R.A.P.SAUCICOURT.

6. All movement East of HEVILLY will be by platoons at 200 yards interval.

7. All Trench Stores, Maps, Defence Schemes, Aero photos, details of Reserve Rations water etc., will be carefully handed over and lists forwarded to the Orderly Room within 12 hours of relief.

8. All gumboots will be returned to Gumboot Store SAUCICOURT and receipts forwarded to the Orderly Room by 12 noon 20th inst.

9. Companies will be responsible that all water cans are returned to the Q.M.Stores.

10. Relief complete will be reported by wiring the Code Word "WHAT HO"

Copy No.1.   A Coy.
     2.   B Coy.   N.H.Mitch............Captain and Adjt,
     3.   C Coy.   7th Northamptonshire Regiment.
     4.   D Coy.
     5.   C.O.
     6.   T.O.
     7.   8th Queens.
     8.   Bn Hqrs.
     9.   File.
    10.   Hqrs Mess.

73rd Brigade.

24th Division.

7th BATTALION

NORTHAMPTONSHIRE REGIMENT

MARCH 1918

Vol 30

7TH (SERVICE) BATTALION NORTH HAMPSHIRE REGIMENT.

WAR DIARY
for
THE MONTH OF MARCH 1918.

Army Form C. 2118.

WAR DIARY
or
INTELLIGENCE SUMMARY.
(Erase heading not required.)

Instructions regarding War Diaries and Intelligence Summaries are contained in F. S. Regs., Part II. and the Staff Manual respectively. Title pages will be prepared in manuscript.

Place	Date	Hour	Summary of Events and Information	Remarks and references to Appendices
HERVILLY	1/3/19		Orders received that the Battalion will be moved to the VRAIGNES area in Reserve - Advance leaves to take over billets.	
HANCOURT	2/3/19		Battalion moved to HANCOURT and was accommodated in huts. As Battalion now formed part of the Corps Reserve we were held at half-hours notice to move.	
"	3/3/19		Divine services etc.	
"	4/3/19		Commanding Officer and O.C.s Companies reconnoitre the BROWN LINE.	
"	5/3/19		Working parties etc.	
"	6/3/19		Working parties etc. Coy Commanders reconnoitre new Sector being taken over by us.	
"	7/3/19		Training etc. Working party found at night.	
"	8/3/19		Working parties - training etc.	
"	9/3/19		Working parties.	
"	10/3/19		Divine services - Brigade Armourer inspects all small arms.	
"	11/3/19		Training etc.	
"	12/3/19		Training etc - Brigade runners competition.	
"	13/3/19		Training etc.	
"	14/3/19		Training - Brigade Signal competition in which this Battn came out top.	
"	15/3/19		Training etc.	
"	16/3/19		Training etc. Brigade Cross country run - Battn coming out second.	

A6945 Wt.W1422/M180 150,000 12/16 D.D.&L. Forms/C./2118/14.

Army Form C. 2118.

WAR DIARY
or
INTELLIGENCE SUMMARY.
(Erase heading not required.)

Instructions regarding War Diaries and Intelligence Summaries are contained in F. S. Regs., Part II. and the Staff Manual respectively. Title pages will be prepared in manuscript.

Place	Date	Hour	Summary of Events and Information	Remarks and references too Appendices
HANCOURT.	17/3/18		Divine services etc.	
"	18/3/18		Working party of 200 found - training etc.	
"	19/3/18		Working parties - training etc.	
"	20/3/18		Commanding Officer, Company Commanders and Coy officers reconnoitre the positions Battalion is to occupy in the event of an enemy attack. Owing to news being received of an impending enemy attack the Battalion is held in especial readiness to move up to support.	
JEANCOURT.	21/3/18		At about 4-40.a.m. enemy opened up an intense bombardment on the forward zone. At about 5-40.a.m. orders were received to move forward to support and within half an hour the last Coy had left. Companies were disposed in four redoubts covering the villages of JEANCOURT and VENDELLES and so supporting the troops of the 17th Infantry Brigade who were holding the line in front of LE VERGUIER and also the right flank of the 66th Division who joined up with the left of the 17th Infantry Brigade. Owing to a thick mist observation was rendered impossible. Enemy attack developed during the morning and drove in the forward posts of the 17th Infantry Brigade to LE VERGUIER and forcing back the 66th Division on our left front. Situation was very obscure and very little news could be obtained. By dusk the Right of the 66th Division had fallen back on to our B Company who held the left Redoubt. The 17th Infantry Brigade to our front and Right front held their positions in front of LE VERGUIER. This line was maintained throughout the night.	
"	22/3/18		At about 8.a.m. news was received that enemy had renewed his attack and had succeeded in taking LE VERGUIER. Troops on our left and right were falling back steadily. At about 1.p.m. the C.O. went over to 17th Infantry Brigade Headquarters next to get news of the situation but found that they had retired and also the troops to our Right, leaving our Right flank in the air. Our left Company reported the enemy advancing on their left flank. At 1-25.p.m. a message was despatched to 73rd Infantry Brigade Hqrs Beames stating that both our flanks were in the air and that we were apparently isolated and that if compelled to retire we should take up a position on the VENDELLES - HERVILLY Ridge. At 1-35.p.m. owing to the rapid advance of the enemy on our flanks and to avoid being surrounded, the C.O. ordered Companies to withdraw. This withdrawal was effected in good order but with some difficulty owing to our isolated position. The Battn withdrew through the 50th Division who had been brought up and were holding the GREEN LINE in front of BERNES. After concentrating at HANCOURT we proceed to HERBECOURT and rested there for the night.	

WAR DIARY
INTELLIGENCE SUMMARY.
(Erase heading not required.)

Army Form C. 2118.

Place	Date	Hour	Summary of Events and Information	Remarks and references to Appendices
FLEZ.	23/3/19		At about 4.a.m. the Battalion moved to FLEZ and took up positions in the open west of that village. At about 8.a.m. the troops to our left front were seen retiring and the enemy was also seen advancing on our Right flank. Orders were received that in the event of a general retirement becoming necessary we should proceed due west and take up positions on the high ground East of FALVY. The 3rd Rifle Brigade who were in front of us commenced to withdraw and the Battalion took up positions to cover this withdrawal. The enemy had meantime brought field guns into action and was enfilading our Right Flank with Machine Guns. After the 3rd R.B.s had passed through the Battalion was gradually withdrawn to the high ground in front of FALVY and East of the SOMME River. We were constantly engaged with the enemy throughout this withdrawal. Owing to the situation on our Right Flank all troops were withdrawn over the SOMME River and the bridges were blown up. The 8th Division were in position on the west bank of the River and the Battalion moved back through them and concentrated at LICOURT - afterwards being disposed in positions to support the 8th Division.	
LICOURT.	24/3/19		At about 8.a.m. the Brigade was relieved by a Brigade of the 8th Division and moved back to CHAULNES where the troops were rested and had dinner. Orders were received about 2.p.m. to move up to support the Division on our Right and to hold the line FONCHES - FONCHETTE, which position we held all night. We were not in touch with the enemy who was about 3 miles in front.	
FONCHES.	25/3/19		At 2.45.a.m. the Battalion was ordered to co-operate in a counter attack delivered by the French on our Right and the 8th Division on our left. We came into contact with the enemy East of CURCHY and owing to the French attack on our Right not taking place we formed a defensive line together with the remnants of another Division. Owing to our Right flank being in the air the enemy got round our flank and behind CURCHY in considerable force, causing us many casualties and forcing us to withdraw to our original line FONCHES - FONCHETTE about 2.p.m. Troops on both our flanks withdrew too far leaving both our flanks in the air, but they came up into position again about 4.p.m. Our advanced posts were continually engaged with the enemy throughout the afternoon. We also repulsed a strong German patrol between us and the 72nd Infantry Brigade. About 7.p.m. we withdrew our left flank to conform with the the 9th Royal Sussex Regt and the 13th Middlesex Regt who had been forced out of a village on our left.	
"	26/3/19		At 5.a.m. a silent withdrawal was ordered and was successfully carried out to the HALLU - CHAULNES line where the Battalion was in support to the Brigade. 100 men from the Reinforcement Battalion were attached to us at this point. About 8-30.a.m. the 72nd Infantry Brigade on our Right had their Right flank (which was already in the air) turned, forcing the whole line to withdraw to a line in front of "ARVILLERS". continued over leaf.	

WAR DIARY
or
INTELLIGENCE SUMMARY.

(Erase heading not required.)

Army Form C. 2118.

Place	Date	Hour	Summary of Events and Information	Remarks and references to Appendices
WARVILLERS	26/3/18		Continued. About 4.p.m. the enemy suddenly started to withdraw and a patrol of 2/Lt Shaw and 6 O.R. were immediately sent out through the village of MEHARICOURT and on the Eastern side encountered a German patrol, which it engaged and captured two who were slightly wounded. At 11.p.m. the enemy attempted a strong reconnaisance with about 300 men against our B Company and the left of the 8th R.Sussex Regt who were on our Right. They were heavily fired on at 300 yards range with rifles and Machine Guns and were completely annihilated.	
MEHARICOURT	27/3/18		At 8.a.m. the enemy delivered a strong attack on the 12th Sherwoods and the Division on our left, from the village of MEHARICOURT. The attack was repulsed by the Battalion with strong enfilade fire, and this enabled the Division on our left who had retired, to come up again into their original line. The 12th Sherwoods who had also retired to conform with the Division on the left, also came forward again and occupied a line in front of their original position. At 11-30.a.m. an attack on the 72nd Brigade on our Right forced them to withdraw, leaving th is Brigades Right flank in the air - About 1.p.m. after several unsuccessful attempts at turning our Right flank the enemy succeeded in entering our trench with a bombing party, covered by a Machine Gun behind his flanks - the situation was rendered impossible owing to the Machine Guns on his flanks. It was found possible however to form a block in our trench sufficiently far to be out of bombing range - the straight part of this trench being then covered with a Lewis Gun and an attack across the open by the enemy made impossible by placing a Machine Gun on either side of the trench thereby covering our flank. The 17th Middlesex Regiment were ordered forward to join up with the 62nd Infantry Brigade and form a defensive flank.	
"	28/3/18		At 2.a.m. a silent withdrawal was ordered through the 17th Middlesex Regt who were holding the village of WARVILLERS. B and D Companies assisted in covering the withdrawal of the Brigade to the CAIX line which we reached at 11-30.a.m. The situation at this time was most critical - both flanks having been turned. At 4.p.m. the Brigade was ordered to withdraw - both flanks round our flanks, and a hasty retirement was necessary. We withdrew through the French who held the line at BOUCOURT. During the whole time we were subjected to continuous and heavy Machine Gun fire from our Right flank, rendering our retirement most difficult. The Brigade concentrated at VILLERS AUX ERABLES where busses should have been waiting for us, but owing to the enemy pressing so closely on our retirement we were compelled to retire by route march across country by compass, across the river to CASTEL wood, where we bivouaced for the night.	
CASTEL	29/3/18		At 7-30.a.m. we were ordered forward to defend the bridgehead at CASTEL. At 2-30.p.m. three Companies were withdrawn and placed in position in front of CASTEL wood, leaving C Coy to defend the Bridgehead.	

WAR DIARY
or
INTELLIGENCE SUMMARY.

(Erase heading not required.)

Army Form C. 2118.

Instructions regarding War Diaries and Intelligence Summaries are contained in F. S. Regs., Part II. and the Staff Manual respectively. Title pages will be prepared in manuscript.

Place	Date	Hour	Summary of Events and Information	Remarks and references to Appendices
	20/3/18. Continued.		At 7.p.m. the Brigade was ordered to concentrate just South of HALLES and from there the Ba^{tn} marched to billets in TREZY GILMONT.	
TREZY-GILMONT.	30/3/18.		The Battalion was ordered to hold the Bridges at BERTRANCOURT AND THIEVRES. xExRax Companies were disposed as follows :- B Coy at BERTRANCOURT, D Coy at THIEVRES, C and A Companies in Support. Cavalry made a counter attack during the afternoon and drove the enemy out of the wood on the high ground N.E. of BERTRANCOURT.	
"	31/3/18.		During the morning the enemy attacked and drove the 8th Division who were taking over from the Cavalry out of the wood.- Cavalry attacked again at 5.30.p.m. retaking the high ground and the front edge of the wood. The Battalion was relieved at 7.30.p.m. and returned to billets in TREZY GILMONT.	
			Attached are copies of Congratulatory messages received.	

MAB DIGBY

1. From Lieut General Sir C.T. McM.Kavanagh, K.C.B. C.V.O. D.S.O.
   Commanding the Cavalry Corps.

My dear Daly,

A line of congratulation on the way the 24th Division have been, and still are fighting. I am delighted to hear it from all sides, especially as I said to the Army Commander that they would.

                                    Yours sincerely,
                                    (sd) C.T.Kavanagh

2. Telegram from G.O.C. XIX Corps.
   To. G.O.C. 24th Division.

Congratulations and thanks and convey to all ranks my warmest congratulations and thanks for your splendid efforts during the last 15 days. The fighting spirit and powers of endurance shown are beyond all praise and have been of vital importance in maintaining the front of the 19th Corps.

                                    (sd) H.E. Watts. Lieut Genl,
                                    Commanding 19th Corps.

3. From Major General Sir J.E. Capper. K.C.B.
   Commanding the Tank Corps.
   (late G.O.C. 24th Division)

                                    9 Regent St,
                                    London.
                                    24/4/18.

Dear Daly,

I was overjoyed to see that the 24th Division had won special commendation from the Chief for its conduct during the first rush of the German offensive.

Will you allow me to congratulate you and the Division on its behaviour. It still holds a particularly warm place in my heart and I would most gladly be with it instead of being here where fighting is not part of my job. The best of good wishes and luck to the best Division in the British Army, and therefore in the world.

                                    Yours sincerely,
                                    (s) J.E.Capper.

4. From Major General Sir I.J. Bols, K.C.B. C.M.G. C.B. D.S.O.
   (late G.O.C. 24th Division.)

Telegram.

CAIRO. 27/3/18.

Well done to the 24th Division.

                                    (signed) BOLS.

73rd Inf.Bde.
24th Div.

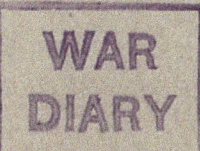

7th BATTN. THE NORTHAMPTONSHIRE REGIMENT.

A P R I L

1 9 1 8

7th (SERVICE) BATTALION NORTHAMPTONSHIRE REGIMENT.

WAR DIARY

for

The month of APRIL 1918.

Army Form C. 2118.

WAR DIARY
or
INTELLIGENCE SUMMARY.
(Erase heading not required.)

Instructions regarding War Diaries and Intelligence Summaries are contained in F. S. Regs., Part II. and the Staff Manual respectively. Title pages will be prepared in manuscript.

Place	Date	Hour	Summary of Events and Information	Remarks and references to Appendices
THEZY GLIMONT.	April 1st. 1918.		The Battalion takes over defensive positions about THENNES and BERTEAUCOURT from 9th Royal Sussex Regiment - A Coy. being in THENNES, C Coy. in BERTEAUCOURT - B Coy. in Support, and D Coy. in Reserve.	
THEZY GLIMONT.	April 2nd. 1918.		Orders received from Brigade to withdraw our A Company from defensive positions about THENNES - this was completed by 1-30 p.m. and the Coy. returned to billets in THEZY GLIMONT. After dusk C Coy. was relieved in BERTEAUCOURT by a Coy. of the 9th Royal Sussex Regt. and returned to billets in THEZY GLIMONT.	
THEZY GLIMONT.	April 3rd. 1918.		At 7a.m. D Coy. was relieved by a Coy. of the 13th. Middlesex Regt. and returned to THEZY GLIMONT. At 4-30 a.m. A Coy. relieved B Coy. in support, and B Company returned to THEZY GLIMONT. At 4 p.m. C Coy. relieved a Coy. of the 9th. Royal Sussex Regt. in Support.	
BOIS DE GENTELLES	April 4th. 1918.		Battalion Headquarter A & B Coys. moved off at 4-30 a.m. and marched to BOIS DE GENTELLES. - A & B Coys. were disposed in battle positions to the South East of BOIS DE GENTELLES. C & D Coys were relieved at 12 Noon and arrived at BOIS DE GENTELLES about 1 p.m. where they remained for the night.	
BOIS DE GENTELLES	April 5th. 1918.		C & D Coys. relieved A & B Coys. in positions in front of BOIS DE GENTELLES at about 8 p.m. Battalion proceeded by march route to LONGEAU where we billetted for the night.	
LONGEAU.	April 6th. 1918.		Battalion embussed at 6-30 a.m. and proceeded to SALEUX. Battalion entrained at SALEUX at 8-30 p.m. for ST. VALERY-SUR-SOMME.	
ESCARBOTIN.	April 7th. 1918.		Arrived ST. VALERY AND DETRAINED AT ABOUT 3 a.m. Coys and Headquarters disposed in various billets for short rest and breakfast. At 10 a.m. Battalion proceeded by march route to ESCARBOTIN, arriving at 1-30 p.m. Billetting party had proceeded in advance and met Coys. and guided them to billets.	
ESCARBOTIN.	April 8th. 1918.		Day spent in cleaning up, etc. 1st. Line Transport who had proceeded by road arrived about 12-30 p.m.	
ESCARBOTIN.	April 9th. 1918.		Kit Inspection. Reorganization of Companies etc. Inspection of all Small Arms by Armourer Sgt. Refitting men with clothing etc.	

A6953 Wt. W14422/M1180 350000 12/16 D.D. & L. Forms/C./2118/14.

Army Form C. 2118.

WAR DIARY
or
INTELLIGENCE SUMMARY.
(Erase heading not required.)

Instructions regarding War Diaries and Intelligence Summaries are contained in F.S. Regs., Part II. and the Staff Manual respectively. Title pages will be prepared in manuscript.

Place	Date	Hour	Summary of Events and Information	Remarks and references to Appendices
ESCARBOTIN	April 10th 1918		Training etc. Battalion Parade during morning.	
ESCARBOTIN	April 11th 1918.		B.C. inspected Battalion and congratulated men on their behaviour during recent operations. Lewis Gun classes under Instructors from C.W.C. Lewis Gun School. Draft of 7 officers and 396 O.R. joined.	
ESCARBOTIN	April 12th 1918		Training, etc.	
ESCARBOTIN	April 13th 1918		The Battalion (less the Draft) proceeded by march route to AULTE and spent the day on the beach, returning at 6 p.m. in the evening.	
ESCARBOTIN	April 14th 1918		Divine Services etc. (SUNDAY).	
ESCARBOTIN	April 15th 1918		Training Classes under special instructors from C.W.C. Notification received from Brigade that Brigade will probably move tomorrow 16th inst. to the ARRAS Area.	
ESCARBOTIN	April 16th 1918		Orders received that Brigade would be transferred to First Army Area. O.Os. issued to Coys etc.	
HOUDAIN.	April 17th 1918		Transport parade 12 midnight and Battalion less C Coy. at 1 a.m.; and proceeded to WOINCOURT. Entrained at WOINCOURT about 5 a.m. for PERNES, arriving about 5-30 p.m. proceeded by march route to HOUDAIN arriving about 7 p.m. where Battalion was accomodated in billets.	
"	April 18th		"C" Company arrive at about 10.a.m. Hqrs A,B,and D Companies inspected by the C.O.	
"	April 19th		Training etc. "C" Company inspected by the C.O. Draft of 5 Officers and 33 O.R. join.	
"	April 20th		Training etc. Lecture by C.O. to all Officers and N.C.Os in the morning.	
"	April 21st.		M.Clemenceau, President of the French Council, visits the Battalion area during the morning. Training Classes under instructors from Corps school during afternoon. C Coy allotted range.	

Army Form C. 2118.

WAR DIARY
or
INTELLIGENCE SUMMARY.
(Erase heading not required.)

Instructions regarding War Diaries and Intelligence Summaries are contained in F. S. Regs., Part II. and the Staff Manual respectively. Title pages will be prepared in manuscript.

Place	Date	Hour	Summary of Events and Information	Remarks and references to Appendices
HOUDAIN	22/4/1918		Training, etc. D Coy allotted range.	
"	23/4/1918		Training as usual. At 6-15.p.m. enemy aeroplanes dropped five bombs in the Battalion area causing the following casualties :- 7 O.R. Killed. 19 O.R. wounded. 5 horses killed and 3 wounded.	
"	24/4/1918		Training as usual. Football match during the afternoon.	
"	25/4/18		Training as usual.	
"	26/4/1918		Training under Company arrangements - O.C. and Company Commanders go through a tactical scheme with the B.C.C.	
"	27/4/1918		Training under Company arrangements. C Coy allotted range.	
"	28/4/1918		Training etc as usual.	
"	29/4/1918		Training as usual. Notification received at midnight that the Battalion would probably move to-morrow.	
"	30/4/1918		Orders received at 3.a.m. for the Battalion to proceed by march route to SAINS EN GOHELLE area. Battalion moved off at 8-30.a.m. And on arrival at BRUAY, en route, orders were received to return to HOUDAIN owing to a German attack further North. We arrived at HOUDAIN at 1-30.p.m and remained there for the night.	

CONFIDENTIAL.

7th Service Battalion Northamptonshire Regt.

WAR DIARY

for the month of MAY. 1918.

Army Form C. 2118.

WAR DIARY
or
INTELLIGENCE SUMMARY.
(Erase heading not required.)

Place	Date	Hour	Summary of Events and Information	Remarks and references to Appendices
HOUDAIN	1/5/18		At 1.20 p.m. orders were received that the Battalion would move off at 2 p.m. to march to LES BREBIS - via BARLIN and SAINS-EN-GOHELLE. Arrived at LES BREBIS at 6 p.m.	
LES BREBIS	2/5/18		Orders received that the Battalion would take over the line from the 4th Canadian Mounted Rifles. Battalion marched off at 8 p.m. and proceeded via MAROC and LOOS to our position. "A" "C" and "D" Companies in front line - "B" Company in Support. Relief very late owing to some guides losing their way - not being completed until 5 a.m. Night very quiet.	
HILL 70 SECTOR.	3/5/18		Enemy very quiet in this sector - the trenches are good on the whole. Nothing of excitement occurred during the day. 1 Other Rank wounded.	
- do -	4/5/18		Slight enemy artillery activity today. Orders received that the 11th Division would discharge GAS on their front together with Gas Projectors at a time to be notified later. Time eventually received being 10.30 p.m. and 12.30 a.m. respectively. Detailed instructions issued for Companies to be ready standing to in their Dig-outs. Operation eventually cancelled by wire.	
- do -	5/5/18		Orders received that the Gas Attack ordered for yesterday would take place providing the conditions were favourable - time to be notified. In view of the drizzle that commenced it was however postponed once again.	
- do -	6/5/18		Orders for relief by 9th Bn: Royal Sussex Regiment issued. Relief commenced at 8.30 p.m. and on relief the Battalion became Battalion in SUPPORT - being distributed around the VILLAGE LINE - HARTS and HARRISONS CRATERS and GUN SWITCH TRENCH and PEP TRENCH. Lieut. W.L. MAYNE wounded during relief together with 1 O.R. killed and 1 O.R. wounded by Shell fire. Battalion Headquarters established in VILLAGE LINE.	
- do -	7/5/18		Working Parties found by all Companies for working in this area. Situation very quiet during the day.	

Army Form C. 2118.

WAR DIARY
or
INTELLIGENCE SUMMARY.
(Erase heading not required.)

Instructions regarding War Diaries and Intelligence Summaries are contained in F. S. Regs., Part II. and the Staff Manual respectively. Title pages will be prepared in manuscript.

Place	Date	Hour	Summary of Events and Information	Remarks and references to Appendices
HILL 70 SECTOR.	8/5/18		Working Parties as yesterday. Enemy very quiet on our front. Orders received at night giving particulars of a proposed enemy attack on this front. From information received it is believed the enemy is attacking tomorrow night on a front between LENS and ROBECQ. Orders issued that everybody will "stand to" in Battle Positions from 8.30 p.m. to 7.0. a.m.	
- do -	9/5/18		No Working Parties today in view of tonights' impending attack. All Companies "stand to" at 8.30 p.m. The Division on left (11th DIVISION) sent over 8,000 gas projectors about 8 p.m. and our Artillery heavily bombarded the enemy lines. During the night no enemy activity developed and dawn broke without the expected attack coming. "Stand down" was at 8 a.m.	
- do -	10/5/18		Working Parties commenced again today. Enemy still very quiet.	
- do -	11/5/18		Working Parties as usual today. Orders for the relief of 9th Bn: Royal Sussex Regiment received. Relief probably taking place tonight and Operation Orders issued accordingly. Later - relief postponed until tomorrow.	

- do -	12/5/18		Relief took place today - new dispositions as follows :-
			 "A" Company. Two Platoons ... HYTHE TUNNEL.
			                         Two Platoons ... BLUE LINE.
			 "D" Company. Two Platoons ... BLUE LINE.
			                         One Platoon ... HUSLEY TRENCH.
			                         One Platoon ... O.G.Y.
			 "B" Company. Two Platoons ... O.G.1.
			                         One Platoon ... LOOS TRENCH.
			                         One Platoon ... LOOS
			 "C" Company. ... VILLAGE LINE.
			
			 Battalion Headquarters at "HATCHETS" in LOOS.
			
			 Orders received that the 11th DIVISION would discharge gas on their front together with Gas Projectors. Time 10.30 p.m. and 12.30 a.m. respectively. Gas was successfull discharged.	

Army Form C. 2118.

WAR DIARY
or
INTELLIGENCE SUMMARY.
(Erase heading not required.)

Instructions regarding War Diaries and Intelligence Summaries are contained in F. S. Regs, Part II. and the Staff Manual respectively. Title pages will be prepared in manuscript.

Place	Date	Hour	Summary of Events and Information	Remarks and references to Appendices
HILL 70 SECTOR.	13/5/18		Enemy very quiet. One Platoon of "C" Company isolated. Working Parties found by "C" Company - three platoons at HYTHE TUNNEL. One Platoon of "B" Company for carrying Ammunition for 73rd Light Trench Mortar Battery.	
- do -	14/5/18		Working Parties as usual. Enemy Artillery active during morning firing on LOOS CRASSIER. Good observation and large number of our own and enemy Balloons up. Our own Heavy Artillery active during the night.	
- do -	15/5/18		Enemy very quiet. Working Parties as usual.	
- do -	16/5/18		Everything still quiet on our Front.	
- do -	17/5/18		Enemy artillery more active during the day. A few gas shells dropped in vacinity of LOOS about 9.30 p.m. 2/Lieut. BEARUP rejoined Battalion from Divisional Wing to relieve 2/Lieut. DAKIN for duty as Town Major, HYTHE TUNNELS. Transport Lines shelled by 5.9's - four Other Ranks wounded and three Mules killed.	
- do -	18/5/18		Enemy artillery fairly active. Increased activity of Enemy Aircraft. On right of our Sector the 34th Infantry Brigade carried out a successful Raid. One Bosche and one Machine Gun captured.	
- do -	19/5/18		During day enemy very quiet. One enemy Aeroplane seen to come down out of control behind the Bosche Lines. Enemy Artillery fairly active during the night on our back areas.	
- do -	20/5/18		Everything quiet most of the day. Slight enemy artillery activity on our Back areas about 10.30 p.m.	
- do -	21/5/18		Our 6" Trench Mortars active during the day cutting enemy wire in front of enemy front line. Otherwise very quiet.	
- do -	22/5/18		Enemy artillery fairly active firing on vacinity of Left Company Front.	

Army Form C. 2118.

WAR DIARY
or
INTELLIGENCE SUMMARY.
(Erase heading not required.)

Instructions regarding War Diaries and Intelligence Summaries are contained in F. S. Regs., Part II. and the Staff Manual respectively. Title pages will be prepared in manuscript.

Place	Date	Hour	Summary of Events and Information	Remarks and references to Appendices
HILL 70 SECTOR.	23/5/18		About 10.30 a.m. Enemy made a silent raid on advanced Observation Post of our Left Company ("B" Company) and succeeded in capturing the post (6 O.R.s.) Two men of Battalion Headquarters slightly wounded. The Gas was discharged A Gas "Beam" Attack was made from the Divisional Front on our Right. at 12 mid-night.	
- do -	24/5/18		Battalion was relieved by the 9th Bn: Royal Sussex Regiment. Relief was completed by 11.45 pm. Billets were allotted to Battalion in LES BREBIS with Battalion Headquarters at the Chateau.	
- do -	25/5/18		All ranks engaged in cleaning up.	
- do -	26/5/18		Battalion Headquarters moved to the Mine Buildings LES BREBIS. Parades under Company arrangements. Working Party of One Company found for FOSSE 7 Defences.	
- do -	27/5/18		Working Parties as usual. One Company engaged in making Barbed Wire Concertinas. Yellow Cross Gas Shells dropped in LES BREBIS - no casualties.	
- do -	28/5/18		Parades and Working Parties as usual. Battalion occupied Reserve Battle Positions.	
- do -	29/5/18		Parades and Working Parties as usual. Battalion Concert given in the Church Army Hut - LES BREBIS.	
- do -	30/5/18		Battalion relieved the 13th Bn: Middlesex Regiment. Relief good. Completed at 12.50 am. "A" and "D" Companies ... Front Line. "C" Company ... Support - Loos Trench. "B" Company ... Reserve - Village Line. Battalion Headquarters ... TOSH ALLEY.	
- do -	31/5/18		Night quiet. Enemy Gas Projectors and shells (phosgine) (phosgine) sent over on our front starting about 11-30 p.m. Our total Casualties were 12 other Ranks - 1 O.R. dead - 11 O.R's evacuated. Enemy Artillery (Whizz-Bangs) on TOSH DUMP and FORT GLATZ 10.30 p.m.	

---oOo---

7th SERVICE BATTALION NORTHAMPTONSHIRE REGIMENT.

WAR DIARY for JUNE, 1918.

Army Form C. 2118.

WAR DIARY
or
INTELLIGENCE SUMMARY.
(Erase heading not required.)

Instructions regarding War Diaries and Intelligence Summaries are contained in F.S. Regs., Part II. and the Staff Manual respectively. Title pages will be prepared in manuscript.

Place	Date	Hour	Summary of Events and Information	Remarks and references to Appendices
Hill 70.	1st June 1918.		Enemy artillery slightly active during day. 3 O.Rs. reported suffering from gas.	
Hill 70.	2nd June 1918		Two more O.Rs. reported died from gas. Enemy quiet.	
Hill 70	3rd. June 1918		1 O.R. wounded (died from wounds later) 1 O.R. died from gas. Enemy artillery slightly active during the day. 7.7.cm. and 4.2 shells dropped in vicinity of Front line Company H.Q. and LOOS TRENCH, RAILWAY ALLEY, HUMBUG ALLEY. Several yellow cross gas shells on RAILWAY ALLEY and TOSH ALLEY - no casualties.	
Hill 70	4th June 1918.		2 O.Rs. reported died from Gas. This making total of deaths from gas sent over on the night of the 31st May - 1st June - 6 O.Rs. The 9th Royal Sussex Regiment made a raid from our Right Company front at 11-15 p.m by HUMBUG SAP. Two prisoners were captured. Casualties - 4 O.Rs. wounded and 2 O.Rs. missing.	
Hill 70	5th June 1918		Inter-Company Relief - disposition as follows - C Coy. Right Front Company - B Company, Left Front Coy - A Coy., Support Coy. in LOOS Trench - D COY., Reserve Coy in VILLAGE LINE. Relief carried out by daylight. 1 O.R. of C Coy. Wounded. Enemy Gas shells on Left Coy. Front, also on Brigade on our left. Our casualties were Nil.	
Hill 70	6th June 1918		Orders to extend our Battalion Front to the extent of Right Coy area of Battalion on our left. Our Support Coy. took this over. Two platoons of the Royal Fusiliers were attached to our Support Company. Enemy quiet during the day but very active at night with 7.7. cm. and "Minnies" on our Front Company areas.	
Hill 70..	7th June 1918		Front quiet during the day. A Gas Beam attack ordered for 1 a.m. (8th June) but cancelled.	

Army Form C. 2118.

WAR DIARY
or
INTELLIGENCE SUMMARY.
(Erase heading not required.)

Instructions regarding War Diaries and Intelligence Summaries are contained in F. S. Regs., Part II. and the Staff Manual respectively. Title pages will be prepared in manuscript.

Place	Date	Hour	Summary of Events and Information	Remarks and references to Appendices
Hill 70.	8th June 1918	"	During the morning enemy shelled vicinity of HUMBUG ALLEY - HORSE ALLEY - O.G.1. very heavily. A direct hit on Coy. H.Q. dug-out (B Coy) in O.G.1 Killed 3 and wounded 2 O.Rs. Our artillery very active during the day and night. Orders for our Right Coy. to take over Coy Front already taken over on the 6th inst by our Support Coy. The 13th Middlesex Regt. took over our right Front Coy's area. By this re-adjustment our Battalion Front extended from HUMBUG ALLEY (inclusive) to CHALK PIT ALLEY (inclusive) Our Support Coy moved with dispositions as follows:- 1 platoon and Coy H.Q. LOOS - & 1 Platoon GUN TRENCH SWITCH - 1 Platoon ENGLISH ALLEY - 1 Platoon "D" KEEP. Much movement was observed behind enemy lines and large numbers of Bosche troops were reported eight miles behind. An enemy attack in the morning was considered probable.	
Hill 70.	9th June 1918	"	The morning was quiet. Orders were issued for a Gas Beam attack from our Brigade front to take place at 1 a.m. 10th June. Enemy gas shells in vicinity of CRUCIFIX, LOOS.	
Hill 70	10th June 1918	"	As ordered gas was successfully discharged at 1 a.m. Owing to the little amount of wind our trenches were difficult to clear and our Right Coy which had been withdrawn was not able to occupy normal positions until about 4-30 a.m. During the day enemy was very quiet.	
Hill 70	11th June 1918	"	Battalion releived by the 9th Royal Sussex Regt. Relief was good - complete at 1-20 a.m. Billets allotted in LES BREBIS, Battn. H.Q. at Mine Buildings.	
LES BREBIS	12th June 1918	"	Lt.Col.S.S.Hayne left the Battalion to take over command of the 2nd. Bn. Northamptonshire Regiment. Battalion Engaged in Cleaning up - men paid.	
LES BREBIS	13th June 1918	"	Lt. Col. Grune took over command of the Battalion. Working parties were found as follows :- One Company at FOSSE 7 defences - Working Party for Div. H.Q. 100 men on Buried Cable - ST. PATRICKS. Training under Coy. arrangements was carried out during the day	

Army Form C. 2118.

WAR DIARY
or
INTELLIGENCE SUMMARY.
(Erase heading not required.)

Instructions regarding War Diaries and Intelligence Summaries are contained in F. S. Regs., Part II. and the Staff Manual respectively. Title pages will be prepared in manuscript.

Place	Date	Hour	Summary of Events and Information	Remarks and references to Appendices
Les BREBIS.	14th June 1918.		Training under Coy arrangements. Working parties as usual except Buried Cable which was finished on 13th.	
LES BREBIS	15th June 1918		All Officers reconnoitre Reserve Battle positions. Parades under Coy arrangements. Working parties as usual.	
LES BREBIS.	16th June 1918		Parades and working parties as usual. One officer and one N.C.O. per Coy reconnoitre Company areas to be taken over from 13th Middlesex Regt tomorrow (17th June).	
LES BREBIS	17th June 1918		Inspection parades by Companies. Outbreak of PYREXIA in the Battalion. (this disease resembles influenza of a very virulent type and developes very quickly) 30 cases between noon and 7 p.m. Battalion relieved the 13th Middlesex Regt The relief which was quite successful was completed at 1 a.m. (18/6/18). B Coy. Front Line - C Coy. Front Line TUNNEL - D Coy. Support, LOOS - A Coy. reserve VILLAGE LINE.	
Hill 70.	18th June 1918		Division on left carried out strong raid at 7 a.m. Retaliation on our Front inconsiderable. Very quiet day. Night also quiet.	
Hill 70.	19th June 1918		Total cases of Pyrexia now 59. Morning quiet. Enemy shelled HURDLE, HUMBUG, and HELL vicinity heavily from 10 p.m. to 2-45 a.m. (20/6/18) One O.R. Killed one slightly wounded. Our artillery active on front and back areas. LOOS Roads shelled about midnight.	
Hill 70.	20th June 1918		Gas bombs dropped by enemy planes in our front area, 12-10 ; 8-30 - 9-45 Heavy shelling in HURDLE, HELL, HYTHE and O.G.1. Afternoon quiet. In the evening regular salvoes of 7-7 on Hurdle and Hell. Several further cases of Pyrexia.	
Hill 70	21st June 1918		Pyrexia still increasing (3 Officers affected) Total 80. A few salvoes of 7-7-cm at irregular intervals during the morning in forward areas. One casualty - 1 O.R. Killed. Hostile artillery in Gun-fire all night especially on HURDLE AND HUMBUG Trenches.	

Army Form C. 2118.

WAR DIARY
or
INTELLIGENCE SUMMARY.
(Erase heading not required.)

Instructions regarding War Diaries and Intelligence Summaries are contained in F. S. Regs., Part II. and the Staff Manual respectively. Title pages will be prepared in manuscript.

Place	Date	Hour	Summary of Events and Information	Remarks and references to Appendices
Hill 70	22nd June 1918.	w.e.e.	Hostile shelling heavy in early morning 1-30 - 8 a.m. in forward areas. Casualties 10.R. filled 10.R. wounded. Quiet then until 6 p.m. Gases of Pyrexia over 150. Salvoes of 7-7-cm - 10 p.m. - 1 a.m.(23/6/18) on front line.	
Hill 70	23rd June 1918	w.e.e.	Cases of Pyrexia over 200. Our artillery very active on enemy back areas in early morning. Salvoes on HURDLE, HELL also on HUMBUG and HEAVEN 7 - 7.15, 11 - 40 - 1-25 during night.	
Hill 70	24th June 1918	w.e.e.	Morning quiet - cases of Pyrexia on the decrease. Repulse of the Austrians in the Austro-Italian battle for VENICE etc. 8 gas shells on HURDLE at 10 p.m. Usual hostile salvoes at irregular intervals on our front areas and on LOOS at ration time.	
Hill 70	25th June 1918.	w.e.e.	Further good news from Italian Front, Austrians driven across the PIAVE River with great loss. 900,000 Americans reported in France. Morning quiet. Irregular salvoes on front area. Considerable shelling of LOOS at night.25-26. Successful discharges of gas on enemy's lines at 12.40 and 2 a.m. No enemy response. Considerably less cases of Pyrexia.	
Hill 70	26th June 1918	w.e.e.	Enemy shelling of HYTHE ALLEY and HURDLE TRENCH in forenoon. 8- 10 p.m. shelling of HELL & HUMBUG TRENCHES, several direct hits. Pyrexia cases less.	
Hill 70	27th June 1918	w.e.e.	Successful small raid by 1st Bn. Royal Fusiliers at 8 a.m. 2 prisoners no casualties. Prisoners state that opposite our sector from N. S are 3rd Bar.R.I.R., 61st. R.I.R., 54th I.R.,5th R.I.R. Sentries in front line, remainder in dug-outs in second line. No retaliation for raid . Heavy bombardment of HURDLE, HUMBUG,HYTHE etc. - one casualty - 10.R. wounded. 40 - 7.7 on LOOS - 8 a.m. Further shelling of HURRAH - HELL - HUMBUG 1 - 2.30 p.m. Our own artillery very active all day . During night salvoes of Gas shells on O.G.1. at intervals from 10 p.m. to 4 a.m. (28/6/18). Total cases of Pyrexia 290. 'Morning Post '27/6/18 "The health of the British and American troops is un	

Army Form C. 2118.

WAR DIARY
or
INTELLIGENCE SUMMARY.
(Erase heading not required.)

Instructions regarding War Diaries and Intelligence Summaries are contained in F. S. Regs., Part II. and the Staff Manual respectively. Title pages will be prepared in manuscript.

Place	Date	Hour	Summary of Events and Information	Remarks and references to Appendices
Hill 70	27th June 1918		British and American troops is uniformly good and the influenza scourge has not made its appearance in our camps or trenches.	
Hill 70	28th June 1918		100 aerial darts on HEAVEN – HURDLE – HUMBUG 8 – 10 a.m. Casualties, 1 O.R. wounded slightly. Shells on HYTHE and HURDLE 11.20 – 12 noon. Afternoon quiet. Artillery during night normal.	
Hill 70	29th June 1918		3 a.m. Salvo in vicinity of ST.PATRICKS – quiet morning. 20 7.7 cm. in O.G.1. at 4.45 p.m. Battalion relieved by 9th Royal Sussex Regt., relief completed 2 a.m. 30/6/18. Battalion in reserve at LES BREBIS.	
LES BREBIS	30th June 1918		REST.	

Vol 34

7th (SERVICE) BATTALION NORTHAMPTONSHIRE REGIMENT.

WAR DIARY.

FOR THE MONTH OF JULY, 1918.

Army Form C. 2118.

WAR DIARY
or
INTELLIGENCE SUMMARY
(Erase heading not required.)

Instructions regarding War Diaries and Intelligence Summaries are contained in F. S. Regs., Part II. and the Staff Manual respectively. Title pages will be prepared in manuscript.

Place	Date	Hour	Summary of Events and Information	Remarks and references to Appendices
LES BREBIS.	1st July 1918.	A.A.	Brigade Armourer inspects Lewis Guns. A & B Companies put into shorts. Medical Officer inspects all Companies.	
LES BREBIS.	2nd July 1918.	A.A.	Brigade Armourer inspects arms of C & D Companies - C & D Companies put into shorts. Baths allotted to the Battalion.	
LES BREBIS.	3rd July 1918.	A.A.	Brigade Armourer inspects arms of C & D Companies.- Training etc.- Battn. Cricket Team play 12th Sherwoods during afternoon - Working party found by B Coy.	
LES BREBIS.	4th July 1918.	A.A.	Working party found by D Coy.- Training etc for other Companies, carried out under Company arrangements.	
LES BREBIS.	5th July 1918.	A.A.	All Box Respirators inspected by the Bde Gas N.C.O. C.O. lectures all Officers and N.C.O's. Battn relieve 13th Middlesex Regt. in Left Sector on night of 5th/6th. Battn. disposed as follows :- A Coy. Left Front - B Coy. Right Front - D Coy. Support - C Coy. Reserve (VILLAGE LINE). Relief complete by 12.55 a.m. 6th. Our artillery active on back areas 6 - 9 p.m. 5 planes patrolling over our lines 7.30 p.m.	
HILL 70. SECTOR.	6th July 1918.	A.A.	Salvoes of 5.9's around PUITS 14, 2.15 a.m. Very little shelling during morning and afternoon. A few 7.7's North of LOOS Our artillery quite marked.	
HILL 70 SECTOR.	7th July 1918.	A.A.	11.55 a.m. 40 5.9's around PUITS 14 BIS, - 2.20 p.m. 40 7.7's around HYTHE and O.G.1. - 3.p.m. 50 7.7's around HURRAH and HUP. Our artillery active on back areas. Low flying patrol of our planes over enemy lines at 5.15 p.m. 30 4.2's and 5.9's on LOOS CRATER 11.45 p.m. Considerable artillery activity North of our Sector 8 p.m to 12 midnight. Occasional 7.7. salvoes on LOOS during night.	

Army Form C. 2118.

WAR DIARY
or
INTELLIGENCE/SUMMARY.
(Erase heading not required.)

Instructions regarding War Diaries and Intelligence Summaries are contained in F. S. Regs., Part II. and the Staff Manual respectively. Title pages will be prepared in manuscript.

Place	Date	Hour	Summary of Events and Information	Remarks and references to Appendices
HILL 70 SECTOR.	8th July 1918.		2 a.m. 20 5.9's over HORSE. Low flying planes over our lines at 3.30 a.m. and 5 a.m. - 40 7.7's around HUGO & HUMBUG, several salvoes on PRATT DUMP & O.G.1. 7 p.m. to 8 p.m. 5.9 barrage on out-post line - 11 p.m. - 3 a.m. usual salvoes on dumps. Occasional 4.2's in HUMBUG & HORSE.	A.a.
HILL 70 SECTOR.	9th July 1918.		Our air patrols very active from dawn until 10 a.m. Our artillery fairly active. No enemy artillery activity in morning or afternoon. Usual salvoes of small shells on dumps and roads in LOOS during the night. Slight hostile T.M. activity at 6.40 p.m. and 10 p.m. C Company relieves A Company in front line. D Company relieves B Company in 1st. Support. B Company now become reserve Company, A Company 2nd Support.	A.a.
HILL 70 SECTOR.	10th July 1918.		Low flying E.A. over our lines from at 5.40 a.m. Our planes active patrolling enemy lines from 7.45 a.m. to 9.15 a.m. Hostile shelling 13 5.9's in vicinity of HOP TRENCH AT 8.40 a.m. and 14 on NEW CUT at 1.45 p.m. 6 on NEW CUT at 1.45 p.m. mostly direct hits. Salvoes of 7.7's on PRATT DUMP & LOOS during the night. Our aircraft active during evening.	A.a.
HILL 70 SECTOR.	11th July 1918.		Hostile artillery fairly active. 9 5.9's on CRUCIFIX, LOOS at 8 a.m. 40 5.9's on HELL and HUMBUG 2.15 p.m. - 3.15 p.m. 25 5.9's on HUMBUG ALLEY at 2 p.m. Our aeroplanes active during the fine periods of the day. Gas attack by the Division on our Left ordered for tonight but cancelled at 6.34 p.m. Enemy shelled PUITS 14 BIS area with 7.7's from 11 p.m. to 12 midnight.	A.a.
HILL 70 SECTOR.	12th July 1918.		Enemy shelled PUITS 14 BIS area heavily with 7.7's and 5.9's from 3.15 a.m. to 4.15 a.m.- 2 other ranks wounded. 8 M.T.M.s on HORSE ALLEY at 7.35 a.m. Aircraft inactive. Hostile artillery less active at night on the Battalion area. Gas was discharged on our left at 12.30 a.m.	A.a.

Army Form C. 2118.

WAR DIARY
or
INTELLIGENCE/SUMMARY.
(Erase heading not required.)

Instructions regarding War Diaries and Intelligence
Summaries are contained in F. S. Regs., Part II.
and the Staff Manual respectively. Title pages
will be prepared in manuscript.

Place	Date	Hour	Summary of Events and Information	Remarks and references to Appendices
HILL 70 SECTOR.	13th July 1918.		Our artillery and T.M"s Active during morning.Hostile artillery fairly active throughout the day, chiefly from 10 a.m. to 11 a.m. when he put 37 5.9's on LOOS CRASSIER. Hostile aircraft active towards evening. Our artillery very active on our left in connection with the shoot on 11th Division Front. D Coy relieve C Company in front line position.	
HILL 70 SECTOR.	14th July 1918.		Hostile artillery fairly active during day. Salvoes of 4.2's on LOOS TRENCH at intervals from 6.15 am to 7.20 am, and salvoes of 7.7's on HURDLE TRENCH, HYTHE ALLEY, HELL AND HUMBUG TRENCHES during morning. 35 9.7's on LOOS CRASSIER 5 - 5.45 p.m. 1 O.R. slightly wounded.	
HILL 70 SECTOR.	15th July 1918.		Hostile artillery not so active. 12 4.2's on HORSE ALLEY at 7.30 a.m. 5 salvoes of 4.2's on HELL AND HULL ALLEYS at 9.45 a.m. 12 gas shells on CHALK PIT LOCALITY at 10.45 a.m.,also occasional shelling with small calibres on front areas. News received of German offensive from CHATEAU THIERRY Southwards. Brig.Gen. Coilins C.M.G, D.S.O. assumes command of 73rd. Infantry Brigade as from today, vice Brig. Gen.W. Dugan. C.M.G., D.S.O.	
HILL 70 SECTOR.	16th July 1918.		Readjustment of the dispositions of front and 1st. Support Coy ordered. This was completed by 10.50. a.m. Usual desultory shelling of our forward areas. Enemy aircraft fairly active. The Corps Commander Lieut. General Sir Aylmer Hunter-Weston K.C.B.,D.S.O.visited the Battalion Area today, and inspected the defensive localities,etc.	
HILL 70 SECTOR.	17th July 1918.		Our artillery very active throughout the day. Hostile artillery quiet. The Battalion was relieved in the line by the 9th Royal Sussex Regt. relief complete by 1am. Battalion proceeded to LES BREBIS and became Bn. in Reserve. 50 Officers and Other ranks of B Company isolated at MAISNIL BOUCHE owing to having been in contact with a case of infectious disease.	

Army Form C. 2118.

WAR DIARY
or
INTELLIGENCE SUMMARY.
(Erase heading not required.)

Instructions regarding War Diaries and Intelligence Summaries are contained in F. S. Regs., Part II. and the Staff Manual respectively. Title pages will be prepared in manuscript.

Place	Date	Hour	Summary of Events and Information	Remarks and references to Appendices
LES BREBIS.	18th July 1918.	A.A.	Day spent in cleaning up, etc. B Company inspected by M.O. Baths allotted to Companies.	
LES BREBIS.	19th July 1918.	A.A.	Bde Armourer inspects all Lewis Guns. Kit inspections and parades under Company arrangements.	
LES BREBIS.	20th July 1918.	A.A.	A & D Coys. allotted range. Parades, training etc., as usual. Bde Armourer inspects small arms of B & C Coys.	
LES BREBIS.	21st July 1918.	A.A.	Divine Services. Armourer Sgt inspects all small arms of A & D Coys. Lecture in evening by Capt. Wamand, M.C.	
LES BREBIS.	22nd July 1918.	A.A.	Training under Company arrangements. Baths allotted to the Battalion. 3 Officers and 50 O.Rs. of B Company carried out a raid on the enemy lines about HUNT SAP in front of CITE ST. AUGUSTE at 2 p.m.	
LES BREBIS.	23rd. July 1918.	A.A.	Battalion relieved the 13th Middlesex Regt. on Right Bn. Sector. The relief was good - dispositions were as follows :- A Coy. HYTHE TUNNEL B Coy. 1st Support - C Coy. 2nd Support - D Coy. Reserve Coy.	
HILL 70 SECTOR.	24th July 1918.	A.A.	Enemy quiet. Slight hostile artillery activity.	
HILL 70 SECTOR.	25th July 1918.	A.A.	During the day enemy very quiet - one of our aeroplanes brought down a little behind the enemy lines by three enemy machines. One of our Observation Balloons brought down by an Enemy Aeroplane.	
HILL 70 SECTOR.	26th July 1918.	A.A.	Slight hostile artillery activity during the early morning and after dusk. Our artillery fairly active most of the day.	
HILL 70 SECTOR.	27th July 1918.	A.A.	Very quiet all day, with the exception of a few salvoes, of 4.2's and Whizz-bangs in our Battalion area.	

Army Form C. 2118.

WAR DIARY
or
INTELLIGENCE/SUMMARY
(Erase heading not required.)

Place	Date	Hour	Summary of Events and Information	Remarks and references to Appendices
HILL 70 Sector.	28th July 1918.	AC	Inter-company relief took place, new dispositions as follows- C Coy. HYTHE TUNNEL - D Coy. 1st. Support - B Coy. 2nd Support - A Coy. RESERVE COY.	
HILL 70 SECTOR.	29th July 1918.	AC	In the morning enemy shelled Battalion area on our right with 5.9's. During the day he shelled our frontCompany's positions. During the night enemy artillery was fairly active. Our artillery was active most of the day.	
HILL 70 SECTOR.	30th July 1918.	AC	Enemy very quiet. Aircraft very active during the day.	
HILL 70 SECTOR.	31st July 1918.	AC	Enemy fairly quiet during the day. 9th East Surreys made a raid on our right at 11 p.m., results not at present known.	

CONFIDENTIAL.

7th SERVICE BATTALION NORTHAMPTONSHIRE REGIMENT.

W A R   D I A R Y, for month of AUGUST 1918.

Army Form C. 2118.

WAR DIARY

INTELLIGENCE SUMMARY.

(Erase heading not required.)

Instructions regarding War Diaries and Intelligence Summaries are contained in F. S. Regs., Part II. and the Staff Manual respectively. Title pages will be prepared in manuscript.

Place	Date	Hour	Summary of Events and Information	Remarks and references to Appendices
HILL 70 SECTOR.	Aug 1st 1918.		Enemy fairly quiet - our aircraft very active.	
HILL 70 SECTOR.	Aug 2nd 1918.		Slight hostile shelling in the morning, and at intervals after dusk.	
HILL 70 SECTOR.	Aug.3rd. 1918.		Quiet day - Slight hostile shelling at intervals after dusk.	
HILL 70 Sector.	Aug. 4th 1918.		Quiet day - Battalion relieved by 9th Bn Royal Sussex Regt., during night. Good relief.	
LES BREBIS.	Aug.5th 1918		Day spent in cleaning up generally. Companies allotted Baths.	
LES BREBIS.	Aug. 6th 1918.		Parades etc. under Company arrangements. N.C.O's classes under R.S.M. During an organised "Nail Hunt" Coys etc picked up 130½ lbs of nails in half an hour. Working party of 36 O.R's found.	
LES BREBIS.	Aug. 7th 1918.		Training - The Battalion carries out a scheme in the vicinity of MARQUEFFLES FARM. Companies afterwards carried out firing practice on the range. Working party of 36 O.R's found.	
LES BREBIS.	Aug. 8th 1918.		Battalion again carry out firing practice on the MARQUEFFLES RANGE. Usual Working party found.	
LES BREBIS.	Aug. 9th 1918.		430 O.R's of the Battalion conveyed to the Divisional Show in lorries. Battalion succeeded in winning first prize in H.D. horse class, and first in O.R. "V.C." race. Usual working party found.	

Army Form C. 2118.

WAR DIARY
INTELLIGENCE SUMMARY.
(Erase heading not required.)

Instructions regarding War Diaries and Intelligence Summaries are contained in F. S. Regs., Part II. and the Staff Manual respectively. Title pages will be prepared in manuscript.

Place	Date	Hour	Summary of Events and Information	Remarks and references to Appendices
LES BREBIS. Aug.10th 1918.			Inspection of Box Respirators by Brigade Gas Officer. Baths allotted to Coys etc. During the night enemy aircraft dropped a very large bomb (probably an aerial torpedo) on a billet occupied by 3rd R.B's. causing several casualties, and wrecking several of our billets in the vicinity. Usual working party found. See Appendix (?)	
LES BREBIS. Aug.11th 1918.			Battalion relieved the 13th Middlesex Regt. on Left (PUITS 14 BIS SECTOR). Relief was complete by 11.45 p.m. Dispositions as follows:- D Coy. - PUITS 14 BIS. - C Coy. 1st Support - A Coy. 2nd Support - B Coy. Reserve Coy.	
HILL70 Sector. Aug.12th 1918.			Enemy fairly quiet. A fair amount of movement observed during the day mostly in H.26 and 27.	
HILL 70 SECTOR. Aug.13th 1918.			Hostile artillery - PRATTS DUMP, NEW CUT, and LOOS received attention at intervals during the night. 30 aerial darts on HUMBUG. 5 aerial darts on HULL, 5 aerial darts on PUITS 14. Our planes active over enemy lines. Usual amount of movement seen during day, mostly in H.2?,22 and 26.	
HILL 70 SECTOR. Aug.14th 1918.			Usual amount of "Mad Minutes" straffs at intervals on LOOS,NEW CUT, and O.G.W 1. during the night. Quiet day.	
HILL 70 SECTOR. Aug.15th 1918.			Usual shelling at intervals on O.G.1, HULL and HORSE ALLEY, and LOOS during the night. One E.A. crossed our front during the day at about 3,000 ft.	
HILL 70 SECTOR. Aug.16th 1918.			Quiet day. More E.A. activity.	
HILL 70 SECTOR. Aug.17th 1918.			Normal day. Usual shelling at night on LOOS, HULL, HUMBUG,NEW CUT, PUITS 14 BIS.	

Army Form C. 2118.

WAR DIARY
INTELLIGENCE SUMMARY.
(Erase heading not required.)

Place	Date	Hour	Summary of Events and Information	Remarks and references to Appendices
HILL 70 SECTOR.	Aug. 18th 1918.		Enemy movement above normal during the day. Hostile shelling on RAILWAY ALLEY, HURDLE and HOP TRENCHES.	
HILL 70 SECTOR.	Aug. 19th 1918.		No activity on the part of the enemy during the day. Quiet night.	
HILL 70 SECTOR.	Aug. 20th 1918.		More movement during the day. LOOS shelled at intervals during the night with H.E. and Gas mixed, also TOSH ALLEY.	
HILL 70 SECTOR.	Aug. 21st 1918.		Quiet during the day. LOOS TRENCH, TOSH ALLEY, and LOOS shelled with Blue Cross Gas and H.E. mixed at intervals during the night. E.A. active during the evening.	
HILL 70 SECTOR.	Aug. 22nd 1918.		Hostile artillery active on back areas in the morning. Right Batt. reported gas shelling on LOOS early part of the night.	
HILL 70 SECTOR.	Aug. 23rd 1918.		Quiet morning. Heavy shelling of enemy trenches near HULLUCH in the afternoon. Retaliation for five minutes only. Two of our planes crashed during the day, one near FOSSE 3 by Bosch "Archies", and the other stopped one of our own shells.	
HILL 70 SECTOR.	Aug. 24th 1918.		Dummy raid carried out by Left Division in the early morning; slight retaliation later. Battalion relieved by 9th Royal Sussex Regt at 12.30 a.m. 25th inst. See Appendix (2).	
LES BREBIS.	Aug. 25th 1918.		Day spent in cleaning up and bathing, kit inspections, and the like.	

Army Form C. 2118.

WAR DIARY
INTELLIGENCE SUMMARY.
(Erase heading not required.)

Instructions regarding War Diaries and Intelligence Summaries are contained in F. S. Regs., Part II. and the Staff Manual respectively. Title pages will be prepared in manuscript.

Place	Date	Hour	Summary of Events and Information	Remarks and references to Appendices
LES BREBIS.	Aug.26th 1918.		Battalion fired on the MARQUEFFLES RANGE (less A Coy), but owing to the weather the shooting was prematurely finished. Orders received in the middle of the night that the Battalion would probably have to take over the front then held by the Left Bde of the Division on our Right, (20th Division).	
ditto.			Orders received that the Battalion would take over the line held by the 7th D.C.L.I. in LENS Sector today, and orders issued for the Battalion to parade at 6.30 p.m. to march to the line. Orders were however received that lorries would be available to take the troops to the line, and would be at the Square, LES BREBIS at 8.30 p.m. The Battalion was therefore formed up in readiness at 8.15 p.m. No lorries turned up however, and it was not until 12.5 a.m.; after considerable trouble, that they did arrive. The Battalion then embussed and proceeded to the line, eventually completing the relief by 5 a.m.	
LENS SECTOR.	Aug.27th 1918.		A considerable amount of movement observed behind LENS in the neighbourhood of LOISON in the early morning, but no movement actually seen in LENS. Counter-battery work was carried out by our artillery in the evening.	
LENS SECTOR.	Aug.28th 1918.		Parties consisting of from 5 to 10 Bosch were frequently seen near LOISON; they were engaged by our artillery and dispersed. No movement seen in LENS. Enemy very active against our aircraft during day with A.A. and Machine guns.	
LENS SECTOR.	Aug.29th 1918.		Usual movement seen in the morning but only in very small numbers. Slight hostile shelling from 8.30 to 10 p.m. E.A. activity, Nil. Our aircraft very active.	

Army Form C. 2118.

WAR DIARY
or
INTELLIGENCE SUMMARY.

(Erase heading not required.)

Place	Date	Hour	Summary of Events and Information	Remarks and references to Appendices
LENS SECTOR.	Aug 30th 1918.		Quiet morning. Slight hostile shelling during the afternoon on forward area and communications. An Officer and 6 O.R's left our line to reconnoitre PUITS 4 and found it unoccupied and reported no enemy movement.	
LENS SECTOR.	Aug 31st 1918.		Movement normal during the day. No movement seen in LENS. An officer and 6 O.R's again reconnoitred PUITS 4 and occupied it without opposition. At about 10.30 p.m. 2 officers and about 36 O.R's left our lines with the intention of ascertaining if the enemy was holding the GREEN CRASSIER. They were however held up by thick wire so returned to our line and reported no movement, except one patrol consisting of two men on the part of the enemy. Two German privates Pioneer Battalion, walked into our lines in the morning and gave us some very useful information; they had been employed on demolishing work, and stated that they were "fed up".	

Army Form C. 2118.

WAR DIARY
or
INTELLIGENCE SUMMARY.
(Erase heading not required.)

Instructions regarding War Diaries and Intelligence Summaries are contained in F. S. Regs., Part II. and the Staff Manual respectively. Title pages will be prepared in manuscript.

Place	Date	Hour	Summary of Events and Information	Remarks and references to Appendices
			A P P E N D I X.	
LES BREBIS.	Aug. 10th 1918.		Capt E. Wright, M.C., O.C. B Coy, and Lieut Hobbs succeeded in finding three men who were buried after three and a half hours search. One was dead, one badly wounded, and the other badly shaken.	
HILL 70 SECTOR	Aug. 24th 1918.		The Battalion represented the Division in three events in the VIII Corps Horse Show and succeeded in winning two out of the three events, namely - "V.C." race (mounted) and best stripped heavy draught.	

CONFIDENTIAL.

7th Bn Northamptonshire Regt

W A R   D I A R Y.

SEPTEMBER, 1918.

WAR DIARY
INTELLIGENCE/SUMMARY

Army Form C. 2118.

Place	Date	Hour	Summary of Events and Information	Remarks and references to Appendices
LENS SECTOR.	1/9/18		Movement normal. A party was sent out in the evening to cut wire to enable a platoon and 2 sections of B Coy to occupy the GREEN CRASSIER; this was successfully accomplished and the Crassier was taken without opposition about 3 a.m. The Battalion was relieved by the 9th Royal Sussex Regt in the evening, except one platoon and the two sections holding the GREEN CRASSIER, and became Support Battalion. All bridges and roads in LENS reported to be destroyed except one or two wooden bridges over the Canal.	
LENS SECTOR	2/9/18		Small enemy parties observed near LOISON East of LENS in the early morning; they were successfully dealt with by our artillery. Our aircraft very active over enemy territory during the day. The 9th Royal Sussex Regt relieved the platoon and two sections on the GREEN CRASSIER in the evening.	
LENS SECTOR	3/9/18		Enemy aircraft more active during the day, patrolling his own line, were engaged by our A.A. Enemy movement normal behind LENS.	
LENS SECTOR	4/9/18		Enemy aircraft very active during the morning.	
LENS SECTOR	5/9/18		Enemy aircraft unusually active. Intermittent shelling all day. 4.2's, 5.9's and occasional gas shells from 11.45 a.m. to 5.30 p.m., all localities.	
LENS SECTOR	6/9/18		Fierce shelling round M.29.b and d. 4.2's, 5.9's, and many gas shells from 11.30 p.m. to 2.30 a.m. A few slight gas casualties. Probably over 2,000 shells fell in vicinity.	
LENS SECTOR	7/9/18		Battalion relieved by the 9th Royal Sussex Regt. and proceeded to new quarters xxx at MARQUEFFLES FARM. Accomodation, Nissen Bow Huts. Condition of Camp - good.	
MARQUEFFLES FARM.	8/9/18		Day spent in cleaning and bathing, etc.	

Army Form C. 2118.

WAR DIARY
or
INTELLIGENCE SUMMARY.
(Erase heading not required.)

Instructions regarding War Diaries and Intelligence Summaries are contained in F. S. Regs., Part II. and the Staff Manual respectively. Title pages will be prepared in manuscript.

Place	Date	Hour	Summary of Events and Information	Remarks and references to Appendices
MARQUEFFLES	9/9/18		Training (with a view to semi-open warfare) under company arrangements, followed by opening stages of the competitions in general work, to be decided this week. First stages field firing.	
MARQUEFFLES	10/9/18		The day devoted to all round training (with lectures on varied subjects), and shooting competition.	
MARQUEFFLES	11/9/18		Training in wiring, bayonet fighting, close order drill, open order drill, and fire and movement.	
MARQUEFFLES	12/9/18		Route march via BOUVIGNY, GOUY SERVINS, VERDREL, etc., and back to MARQUEFFLES. Weather bad. Night operations.	
MARQUEFFLES	13/9/18		Training in all subjects under company arrangements.	
MARQUEFFLES	14/9/18		The Battalion proceeded up the line to relieve the 13th Middlesex Regt. (Daylight relief). D Coy.- GREEN CRASSIER and PUITS 4. B Coy.- 1st SUPPORT. C Coy.- 2nd Support. A Coy Reserve.	
LENS SECTOR	15/9/18		Dispositions of Companies altered :- D Coy. Right front Coy. C Coy. Left front Coy. B Coy. Right Support Coy. A Coy. Left support Coy. A platoon of B Coy reconnoitred and established posts in FOSSE 5. No opposition encountered. Enemy attitude, quiet. H.A., nil. A platoon of A Coy. reconnoitred with a view to establishing posts CHATEAU SPRIET; this was found to be strongly held by an alert enemy.	
LENS SECTOR	16/9/18		Orders received to withdraw platoon from FOSSE 5. A platoon of A Coy endeavoured to push forward a post, but owing to extreme darkness were unable to find a position to occupy. E.A., nil. Hostile artillery, quiet.	
LENS SECTOR	17/9/18		E.A., more active all day - 1 at 300 ft M.G. over GREEN CRASSIER. Our aircraft fairly active.	

Army Form C. 2118.

WAR DIARY
or
INTELLIGENCE/SUMMARY.
(Erase heading not required.)

Place	Date	Hour	Summary of Events and Information	Remarks and references to Appendices
LENS SECTOR	18/9/18		Our aircraft very active during day. E.A. fairly active. B Coy relieved C Coy. Enemy movement above normal.	
LENS SECTOR	19/9/18		A Coy relieved D Coy. D Coy. relieved C Coy. C Coy. relieved A Coy. Enemy shelled battalion Headquarters for one hour with 4.2's. A party of 6 Germans led by an officer advanced towards our post on BOULEVARD des ECOLE. Warning was sent by our roving patrol and enemy patrol was caught between our post and roving patrol, both of whom opened fire killing the officer and two other ranks. The Sgt. and Cpl. (wounded) were taken prisoner, the sixth man was wounded but got away.	
LENS SECTOR	20/9/18		E.A. nil. Enemy very quiet all day. A Coy patrolled ground up to Railway, and established posts along Railway in N.20.a. and N.20.b.00.20. PUITS 4 evacuated. A patrol of C Coy reconnoitred route into LENS by way of GREEN CRASSIER and CANAL BANK. It is found to be possible to enter LENS by this route except for one or two small enemy posts which could easily be dealt with.	
LENS SECTOR	21/9/18		An attempt was made by day to blow up house at N.14.d.50.00. - a party of one officer and 7 O.R's, and one N.C.O. and 4 O.R's (Australian Tunnellers) made the attempt. The party got to within 80 yards of the house when enemy opened rifle and machine gun fire. Three men of covering party were wounded - remainder returned to our lines at dusk. Generally, enemy very quiet.	
LENS SECTOR	22/9/18		E.A. fairly active. Battalion relieved by 9th Royal Sussex Regt and went into Support. A and B Coys at CITE de CAUMONT, C Coy LIEVIN, D Coy. BOIS de RIAUMONT. Batt. H.Q. ROLENCOURT. Our artillery active in the afternoon. More Boche in LENS than previously. Note:-	

Said a Sub, to one of his friends,
As she shewed him her latest from VENUS,
"Though they look most inviting
They're not so exciting
As the outskirts and undies of LENS"

(It is thought there may be tunnels in LENS).

Army Form C. 2118.

WAR DIARY
or
INTELLIGENCE SUMMARY.
(Erase heading not required.)

Instructions regarding War Diaries and Intelligence Summaries are contained in F. S. Regs., Part II. and the Staff Manual respectively. Title pages will be prepared in manuscript.

Place	Date	Hour	Summary of Events and Information	Remarks and references to Appendices
LENS SECTOR	23/9/18		Battalion in Support - Apart from working parties, Companies at disposal of Company Commanders - Drums up from Transport.	
LENS SECTOR	24/9/18		Training under Company arrangements in accordance with programme issued by C.O.	
LENS SECTOR	25/9/18		Training by Companies in accordance with programme. Battalion football team played a team from 13th Middlesex Regt at MARQUEVILLES - result 2-1 in favour of the Middlesex.	
LENS SECTOR	26/9/18		Training carried out as per programme under Company arrangements - N.C.O's instruction in map reading - very quiet.	
LENS SECTOR	27/9/18		Training carried on as for 26th. Our guns carried out a shoot in early morning in conjunction with dummy figures - no retalliation.	
LENS SECTOR	28/9/18		Training carried on under Company arrangements.	
LENS SECTOR	29/9/18		Inspection of "Fighting Order and equipment by C.O. Equipment arranged, 2 Companies leather, and 2 webbing. Representatives of the Battalions of the 58th Division came up to reconnoitre.	
LENS SECTOR	30/9/18		Battalion relieved by Battalions of the 58th Div. as follows:- Bn H.Q. and C Coy. by 10th London Regt. A.B. and D Coys by 12th London Regt. After relief Battalion marched to COUPIGNY Huts.	

7th Northampton
Vol 37

CONFIDENTIAL

War Diary   for month of October 1918.

Army Form C. 2118.

WAR DIARY
or
INTELLIGENCE/SUMMARY.
(Erase heading not required.)

Instructions regarding War Diaries and Intelligence Summaries are contained in F. S. Regs., Part II. and the Staff Manual respectively. Title pages will be prepared in manuscript.

Place	Date	Hour	Summary of Events and Information	Remarks and references to Appendices
Hersin-Coupigny.	1-10-18.		Battalion entrained at Hersin-Coupigny at 1 p.m. and detrained at Mondicourt at 9.20 p.m. and marched to billets at Grouches.	
Grouches.	2-10-18.		Training under Company arrangements.	
Grouches.	3-10-18.		Training under Company arrangements.	
Grouches.	4-10-18.		Training under Company arrangements.	
Grouches.	5-10-18.		Transport moved by march route to Moeuvres, halting for the night 5/6th at Boisleux au Mont.	
Grouches.	6-10-18.		Battalion proceeded by train to Hermies, where they detrained. Battalion marched to camp just East of Moeuvres, where they bivouaced for the night 6/7th (very cold night with frost in morning). 24th Division was now in support to 63rd Division and were told to be in readiness to pass through and follow up the enemy if he withdrew.	
Moeuvres.	7-10-18.		Battalion struck camp about 14.00 hrs and marched to area S.W. of Caintaing, where they relieved the 190 Bde (63rd Div.) Battalion was settled in bivouages by 19.00 hrs.	
Caintaing.	8-10-18.		63rd Division, having attacked and captured Niergnies, 72nd I.B. moved forward to Roumilly; the 73rd Bde being concentrated just East of Canal de St.Quentin. Battalion bivouaced for the night, with orders to be ready to move at 2 hours notice. Camp had settled down by 17.00 hrs. A few 5.9 shells fell in close proximity to camp. 1 O.R. wounded. Orders received about midnight that 72nd Bde were attacking in the morning (having relieved Battalion of the 63rd Div.) and that 73rd Bde were to keep in close touch.	
Awoingt.	9.10.18		Camp was struck about 05.00 hrs. Battalion moved off at 06.15 hrs. Order of march, 9th Royal Sussex Regiment, 7th Northamptonshire Regt., 13th Middlesex Regt. Information received that 72nd I.B. attack had met with no opposition, and that they had pushed on to Railway East of Awoingt. 73rd Bde followed 72nd Bde, keeping close touch. At 13.00 hrs the Battalion had reached a point just N.W. of Awoingt. At 14.00 hrs the Battalion were ordered to reconnoitre ground towards the Sugar Factory, and to concentrate just beyond ready to attack village of Cagnoncles. A troop of the 6th Dragoon Guards went forward to reconnoitre high ground between Cagnoncles and the "Canadians" who were on our left. By 17.00 hrs., after overcoming intence M.G.opposition the Battalion had captured all the high ground overlooking the village.	

WAR DIARY

INTELLIGENCE SUMMARY

Army Form C. 2118.

Place	Date	Hour	Summary of Events and Information	Remarks and references to Appendices
Awoingt.	9-10-18.		Order of attack :- D Coy. (Capt Pearson M.C.) Left Front - B Coy. (Capt B.Wright M.C.) Right Front - C Coy. (2/Lieut W.W.Boal) Left Support - A Coy. (Capt Williamson M.C.) Right Support. Having taken the high ground on his sector, Capt Pearson went personally with a strong patrol to reconnoitre the village, and failed to return. 2/Lieut Boal, whilst moving forward with Support Company was mortally wounded by a shell. 2/Lieut Cutting and 2/Lieut Clements were both killed whilst leading their men forward. 2/Lieut Cooke and 2/Lieut Osborn were wounded. The village being too strongly held chiefly with machine guns, which were continually sweeping the ridge and slope leading to village, it was decided to dig in and wait for artillery to give the necessary support. Battalion scouts who had been operating in front during the day, were sent forward to get in touch with Canadians on the left. This was done. Information received that 2/Lieut. Boal had died of wounds. Casualties - 4 Officers Killed, 2 Officers Wounded. 85 O.Rs. Killed and wounded.	
Cagnoncles.	10-10-18.		At 05.30 hrs after artillery barrage, Battalion advanced on Cagnoncles, capturing 11 prisoners, 13 machine guns and several L. and L.T.Ms. Opposition weak. The Battalion continued to advance meeting with no opposition. At 08.30 hrs. Battalion scouts reported village of Rieux to be apparently evacuated. 2/Lieut Harrison went forward with patrol, arriving on far side of village about 09.00 hrs. Cavalry and cyclist patrols passed through shortly afterwards. At 10.00 13th Middlesex Regt passed through Battalion, which now became Support.	
Rieux.	11-10-18.		At 03.00 hrs orders were received for the Battalion to remain in its present position, in deep cutting W. of Rieux. Lt.Col.Hingley M.C. commanding 13th Middlesex Regt. seriously wounded. Battalion moved into billets in Rieux.	
Rieux.	12-10-18.		Day spent in sleep, cleaning up and reorganisation.	
Rieux.	13-10-18.		Re-organisation.	
Rieux.	14-10-18.		Battalion moved forward to billets in Avesnes-lez-Aubert. Attack on Haussy, which had been arranged to be carried out by 24th Division, cancelled.	
Avesnes-Lez-Aubert.	15-10-18.		B.G.C. inspected Battalion.	

Army Form C. 2118.

WAR DIARY
or
INTELLIGENCE/SUMMARY.
(Erase heading not required.)

Instructions regarding War Diaries and Intelligence Summaries are contained in F. S. Regs., Part II. and the Staff Manual respectively. Title pages will be prepared in manuscript.

Place	Date	Hour	Summary of Events and Information	Remarks and references to Appendices
St.Aubert.	16-10-18.	07.30	At 07.30 hrs. Battalion received sudden and unexpected orders to move in two hours time to St. Aubert in close support to 72nd I.B. Dispositions:- Headquarters and 2 Coys. St.Aubert - 2 Coys. High ground West of La Selle River. At 13.00 hrs the R.Essex(7thxxxx) Right Battalion of the 72nd I.B. was heavily counter-attacked and forced back to West bank of River Haussy. At 16.00 hrs Battalion was ordered to relieve remaining elements of 9th East Surrey Regt and 8th R.W.Kent Regt. with 2 Coys. This was successfully carried out, with few casualties. At 01.00 (17th) information was received that A Coy. had been surrounded by the enemy who had taken possession of the bridge heads. A wounded man who returned shortly afterwards stated that Capt Williamson, on realising the seriousness of his position gave orders to rush the bridge heads, every man for himself. This prompt decision undoubtedly unabled a considerable number of men to get across before the enemy could exploit his success. All officers and 48 O.Rs. returned. This number could have been increased if the men had seen the river by day, as they were undoubtedly under the impression that it was much wider and deeper.	
Haussy.	17-10-18.		At 05.30 hrs D Coy was ordered to withdraw from village of Haussy and take up position on high ground overlooking village. This was done. After a very busy day the Battalion was relieved by Bn Worcester Regt., 56th Div., and marched back to billets in Avesnes.	
Avesnes lez Aubert.	18-10-18.		Battalion fell in at 14.00 hrs and marched to Caurior, arriving at 16.30 hrs.	
Caurior.	19-10-18.		Baths and cleaning.	
Caurior.	20-10-18.		Brigade Church Parade. Remainder of the day left to the men.	
Caurior.	21-10-18.		Companies trained under their own arrangements. A and B Coys, tactical training - C and D Coys on the range, at B.15.a. (Sheet 51c.)	
Caurior.	22-10-18.		Box respirators tested by the Brigade Gas Officer. Baths allotted from 8.00 hrs to 13.00 hrs.	
Caurior.	23-10-18.		Training in open warfare and battle patrols. Inspection of all arms by the Brigade Armourer Sgt.	
Caurior.	24-10-18.		C and D Coys carry out a tactical scheme at 09.00 hrs. Inoculation carried out by the M.O. Transport inspected by the O.C. 24th Divisional Train.	

Army Form C. 2118.

WAR DIARY
or
INTELLIGENCE/SUMMARY.
(Erase heading not required.)

Instructions regarding War Diaries and Intelligence Summaries are contained in F. S. Regs., Part II. and the Staff Manual respectively. Title pages will be prepared in manuscript.

Place	Date	Hour	Summary of Events and Information	Remarks and references to Appendices
Caurior.	25-10-18		Baths allotted to C and D Coys from 8 - 12.00 hrs. A and B Coys practice Field Firing. All Companies carry out one hours patrol after dark. A nail hunt held today resulted in 102 lbs of nails being collected.	
Caurior.	26-10-18		The Battalion moved to Haussy via Avesnes les Aubert - St. Vaast. at 8.00 hrs and arrived at 12 noon.	
Haussy.	27-10-18		Brigade Church Parade. The B.G.C. afterwards took the march past.	
Haussy.	28-10-18		Companies at Company Commanders disposal. 1½ hours night training carried out. Brigade Sports held in which the Battalion won 7 of the events.	
Haussy.	29-10-18		All officers and N.C.Os.of B C and D Coys parade under the C.O. at 09.15 hrs. Remainder carry on with arm drill. Recreational training and gas drill.	
Haussy.	30-10-18		Company tactical training in the morning. Cross country run in the afternoon.	
Haussy.	31-10-18		Tactical scheme - all companies take part.	

C O N F I D E N T I A L.

W A R   D I A R Y

O F

7th SERVICE BATTALION NORTHAMPTONSHIRE REGIMENT

FROM :- NOVEMBER 1st. 1918

TO :- NOVEMBER 30th. 1918

--*-*-*-*-*-*-*-*-*-

IN THE FIELD

DECEMBER 1st. 1918.

Army Form C. 2118.

WAR DIARY
INTELLIGENCE SUMMARY.
(Erase heading not required.)

Instructions regarding War Diaries and Intelligence Summaries are contained in F. S. Regs., Part II. and the Staff Manual respectively. Title pages will be prepared in manuscript.

Place	Date	Hour	Summary of Events and Information	Remarks and references to Appendices
HAUSSY	2/11/18		Battalion moved from the village of HAUSSY into billets at BERMERAIN arriving there at 5.30 p.m.	
BERMERAIN	3/11/18		Company Commanders left early in the morning to reconnoitre forward area. Stores were issued and Companies moved off at 4 p.m. to a position of assembly west of SEPMERIES and then bivouaced for the night. A few shells fell into village and along the road.	
	4/11/18		"B" and "D" Companies were detailed as support to the 9th Bn. Royal Sussex Regiment who were to attack along the whole Brigade front from a line which had been established West of the ENLAIN - VILLERS POL Road. Capt. A.Elliman was in command of "D" Company and supported right flank, and Capt B.Wright the left flank. These two Companies moved off at 3 a.m., crossed the river RONELLE by bridges which had been put into position by "A" Company the night previous, and took up their position by early morning. "A" and "C" Companies remained in the positions occupied the previous night until 6 a.m. and then moved in rear of the general line of advance. The barrage commenced at 6 a.m. and the Companies moved forward. "D" Company was caught in the un counter-barrage and a number of casualties were caused. The remainder were lead onward and in time formed part of the front line. By 8 a.m. they were on the high ground in front of WARGNIES-LE-PETIT. Capt. A.Elliman and 2nd.Lt.W.Metley had both become casualties (wounded). "B" Company successfully eluded the counter-barrage on the left (N) flank and succeeded in establishing themselves in a position which dominated the small bridge over the river AUNELLE. This bridge carried the main ENLAIN - BAVAY Road which separated WARGNIES-LE-GRAND and WARGNIES-LE-PETIT and by concentrated Lewis Gun and rifle fire and by forward patrols they managed to keep it whole. The enemy was shelling the sunken roads and were sweeping the ridge with machine gun fire. The position having become stationary, it was decided to relieve the pressure by outflanking both villages from the North. The 13th Bn.Middlesex Regiment was allotted WARGNIES-LE-GRAND and the 7th Bn.Northamptonshire Regiment, WARGNIES-LE-PETIT.	
		14.30 hours.	"A" and "C" Companies were detailed for this duty. They were to cross by the bridge keeping their left on the main road and push through the village and then onward to the high ground East of it. "C" Company formed the front line under 2nd.Lt.W.C.Pike and "A" Company under Capt.G. A.Williamson M.C. were in support. Machine gun fire was met with but overcome by grenades and rifle fire and both Companies established themselves well forward of the village.	

/continued.

Army Form C. 2118.

WAR DIARY

INTELLIGENCE SUMMARY.

(Erase heading not required.)

Instructions regarding War Diaries and Intelligence Summaries are contained in F. S. Regs., Part II. and the Staff Manual respectively. Title pages will be prepared in manuscript.

Place	Date	Hour	Summary of Events and Information	Remarks and references to Appendices
	4/11/18 (cont)		"B" Company now became Support and "D" Company went into reserve. The enemy began to shell the outskirts and roads leading to the villages which were inhabited by a fair number of French civilians. 50 prisoners were taken during the operations.	
	5/11/18		This morning the 17th Infantry Brigade passed through out positions and continued the advance and the Battalion moved into billets in WARGNIES-LE-PETIT.	
	6/11/18		Companies reorganised and rested.	
	7/11/18		Battalion received orders to be ready to move forward and march through LA BOIS GRETTE, ST.WAAST-la-VALLEE and on to billets in BAVAY arriving there at 6 p.m. Transport overcame difficulty of bad roads and brought rations up same night.	
BAVAY	8/11/18		Battalion now became Support Battalion to 9th East Surrey Regt (72nd Infantry Brigade) and moved to LA LOUVION - then onward to MXXX Le LONGUEVILLE. At 4 p.m. "D" Company armed with bill-hooks etc. went off to clear a track through the BOIS LE LONGUEVILLE in a N.E. direction from the west side to the East side leading on to the road to LA BERLIERE. Orders were received that the advance would be continued in the morning, the 73rd Infantry brigade taking over a 3000 yards front, the Battalion being allotted 1000 yards North of left flank of 72nd Infantry B Brigade. the 17th I.B. being in Support - the Division taking over the Corps front.	
	9/11/18		"A" Company was detailed as advance guard with "C" Company in Support. Battalion moved off at 5.45 a.m. Scouts went forward and found LES GUELARDS clear of the enemy and joined hands with the Royal West Kents who came into the village from the Southern end. "A" Company went forward, meeting with no opposition, passing through LE FLORICAMP and to the high ground beyond MAIRIEUX. The Battalion Scouts were well to the front the whole time and, in conjunction with the Cyclists and Cavalry, did some good work. An outpost line was established by picqueting the roads leading into MAIRIEUX, the forward company held the roads withdrawn to the west of it. A Platoon held the RUE D'en BAS - "A" Company held the FORT DES SART and "B" Company in LE FLORICAMP. "D" Company in Reserve at ROTELEUX Farm where Battalion Headquarters was established. The enemy shelled the roads just west of MAIRIEUX during the night and "C" Company had one man killed.	

(38753) Wt. W4355/2369 600,000 12/17 D. D. & L.   Sch. 52a.   Forms/C2118/15.

Army Form C. 2118.

WAR DIARY

~~INTELLIGENCE SUMMARY~~

(Erase heading not required.)

Instructions regarding War Diaries and Intelligence Summaries are contained in F.S. Regs., Part II. and the Staff Manual respectively. Title pages will be prepared in manuscript.

Place	Date	Hour	Summary of Events and Information	Remarks and references to Appendices
	10/11/18.		The Battalion was relieved by a Battalion of the Rifle Brigade, 20th Division about mid-day and went into billets at LE RAGUELLE near FEIGNIES.	
	11/11/18.		Battalion moved off at 6.50 a.m. and marched to billets in LOUVIGNIES-BAVAY area arriving at 10 a.m. News of the signing of an Armistice was received on the way.	
	12/11/18.		Reorganisation of Companies. Kit inspections and shoemakers inspection etc..	
	13/11/18.		Cleaning up etc. Inspection of Lewis Guns.	
	14/11/18.		Inspection of "A" and "D" Companies by Commanding Officer.	
	15/11/18.		Battalion inspected by Brigadier General Commanding 73rd Infantry Brigade.	
	16/11/18.		Inspection of "B" and "C" Companies by Commanding Officer.. Training etc under Company arrangements.	
	17/11/18.		Battalion moved by march route to WARGNIES-LE-GRAND.	
	18/11/18.		Battalion moved by march route to the DENAIN area and was accommodated in billets for the night.	
	19/11/18.		Battalion moved by march route to AUBERCHICOURT.	
	20/11/18.		Cleaning up etc..	
	21/11/18.		Parades, inspections, etc. under Company arrangements.	
	22/11/18.		Commanding Officer and Medical Officer inspect billets. Parades under Coy. arrangements.	
	23/11/18.		Parades, training, under Company arrangements.	

Army Form C. 2118.

WAR DIARY
INTELLIGENCE SUMMARY.
(Erase heading not required.)

Place	Date	Hour	Summary of Events and Information	Remarks and references to Appendices
	24/11/18.		Divine Service, etc..	
	25/11/18.		Battalion moved by march route to RUMEGIES Area and was accommodated in billets for the night.	
	26/11/18.		Battalion moved by march route to MOUuIN Area - the whole Battalion being billetted in an old brewery.	
	27/11/18.		Parades under company arrangements.	
	28/11/18.		Battalion paraded for drill under the Commanding Officer.	
	29/11/18.		Parades etc under company arrangements.	
	30/11/18.		Parades etc under company arrangements.	

7TH. SERVICE BATTALION NORTHAMPTONSHIRE REGIMENT.

WAR DIARY.

DECEMBER, 1918.

Army Form C. 2118.

WAR DIARY
INTELLIGENCE/SUMMARY
(Erase heading not required.)

Instructions regarding War Diaries and Intelligence Summaries are contained in F. S. Regs., Part II. and the Staff Manual respectively. Title pages will be prepared in manuscript.

Place	Date	Hour	Summary of Events and Information	Remarks and references to Appendices
Mouchin.	1-12-1918.		Training etc under Company arrangements.	
Mouchin.	2-12-1918.		Training etc. The Commanding Officer addressed all regular soldiers on parade.	
Mouchin.	3-12-1918.		Usual parades under Company arrangements. Improvements of billets, etc.	
Mouchin.	4-12-1918.		Training. Battalion drill parade under the Commanding Officer.	
Mouchin.	5-12-1918.		Battalion moved by march route to billets at Bachy.	
Bachy.	6-12-1918.		Day spent in cleaning up and generally improving billets, etc.	
Bachy.	7-12-1918.		Inspection of all billets by the Commanding Officer. Instruction in ploughing. Road repairs by all Companies.	
Bachy.	8-12-1918.		Divine Services.	
Bachy.	9-12-1918.		The Battalion proceeded to Lamain to play football against the 2nd Batt. Northamptonshire Regt. The 7th Battalion won by 1 goal to Nil. The Battalion returned to billets by 17.00 hours.	
Bachy.	10-12-1918.		Training etc under Company Arrangements. - Educational classes.	
Bachy.	11-12-1918.		Training etc. Road cleaning and assistance to farmers. The Corps Flat Race Meeting was held on the Aerodrome, Mouchin.	
Bachy.	12-12-1918.		Training etc. Assistance in ploughing lent to farmers.	
Bachy.	13-12-1918.		Training etc. Assistance in ploughing lent to farmers - road repairs.	
Bachy.	14-12-1918.		The Battalion formed up on the Aerodrome, Bachy, for one hours Company and Ceremonial Drill. Companies inspected by the Commanding Officer. - Educational training.	
Bachy.	15-12-1918		Divine Services.	

Army Form C. 2118.

WAR DIARY
or
INTELLIGENCE/SUMMARY.
(Erase heading not required.)

Instructions regarding War Diaries and Intelligence
Summaries are contained in F. S. Regs., Part II.
and the Staff Manual respectively. Title pages
will be prepared in manuscript.

Place	Date	Hour	Summary of Events and Information	Remarks and references to Appendices
Bachy.	16-12-1918.		The Battalion formed up in mass on the Aerodrome Bachy, in full marching order, for inspection by the Commanding Officer. Orders were received that the Battalion was to take over billets in Esplechin. Advance parties were despatched to take over.	
Bachy.	17-12-1918.		The move to Esplechin cancelled.	
Bachy.	18-12-1918.		Training and Educational classes. Assistance lent to farmers.	
Bachy.	19-12-1918.		Training - Specialists and Educational classes.	
Bachy.	20-12-1918.		Training - Assistance in ploughing lent to farmers.	
Bachy. and Tournai.	21-12-1918.		The Battalion moved to billets in Tournai. Other ranks were billetted in the ASYLUM. Officers in private billets in the town. At 18.00 hrs a fire broke out in the west wing of the Asylum, and it was only prevented from spreading by the prompt action of a party of the Battalion in destroying a passage which connected the wing with the main building. There were no casualties, but the occupants of the building had to beat a hurried retreat. The French Fire Engines arrived, and after considerable delay succeeded in getting one stream of water on the few flames. The cause of the fire is still an unsolved mystery.	
Tournai	22-12-1918.		Cleaning and improvements of billets.	
Tournai.	~~22-12-1918~~		~~Parades etc. under Company arrangements.~~	
Tournai	23-12-1918.		Training and Education. Baths allotted to the Battalion.	
Tournai	24-12-1918.		Training and Educational classes.	
Tournai	25-12-1918.		No parades, except Divine Service. The troops were provided with Xmas Dinner out of the Canteen Funds.	
Tournai	26-12-1918.		No parades.	
Tournai	27-12-1918.		Two Company march. Order Company arrangements.	

Army Form C. 2118.

WAR DIARY
or
INTELLIGENCE SUMMARY.
(Erase heading not required.)

Instructions regarding War Diaries and Intelligence Summaries are contained in F. S. Regs., Part II. and the Staff Manual respectively. Title pages will be prepared in manuscript.

Place	Date	Hour	Summary of Events and Information	Remarks and references to Appendices
Tournai	28-12-1918		Training and Educational classes.	
Tournai	29-12-1918		Divine Services.	
Tournai	30-12-1918		Company and Platoon Drill - Educational classes.	
Tournai	31-12-1918		Training - Educational classes - Baths allotted to the Battalion.	

7TH SERVICE BATTALION NORTHAMPTONSHIRE REGIMENT

War diary for the month of January 1919.   Original.

Sidney Browne
................Lieut Col Commanding,
7th Bn Northamptonshire Regiment.

Army Form C. 2118.

WAR DIARY
or
INTELLIGENCE SUMMARY.
(Erase heading not required.)

Instructions regarding War Diaries and Intelligence Summaries are contained in F.S. Regs., Part II. and the Staff Manual respectively. Title pages will be prepared in manuscript.

Place	Date	Hour	Summary of Events and Information	Remarks and references to Appendices
TOURNAI	1/1/19.		PARADES Parades under Company arrangements - educational classes etc.	
"	2/1/19.		Parades etc. Educational training. Football in afternoon.	
"	3/1/19.		Usual military and educational training. Battalion run in afternoon.	
"	4/1/19.		Kit inspection under Company arrangements. Educational classes.	
"	5/1/19.		Divine services. Football match in afternoon.	
"	6/1/19.		Parades, fatigues and educational classes. Rugby match in afternoon.	
"	7/1/19.		Physical and educational training. Baths allotted to Transport Section.	
"	8/1/19.		Cleaning of equipment and Lewis guns. Educational classes.	
"	9/1/19.		Educational classes. Baths allotted to A & B Coys. Riding class for officers. Captain A.T. Webb and No.8629 Cpl. Kisby Mentioned in Despatches.	
"	10/1/19.		Educational classes. Court of enquiry on recent fire held. Bathing for C & D Coys.	
"	11/1/19.		Educational classes. Fatigues etc. Boxing classes commenced. 6 O.R. despatched for demobilization.	
"	12/1/19.		Divine services. 3 O.R. despatched for demobilization.	
"	13/1/19.		Parades - educational classes fatigues etc. Baths allotted to Coys.	
"	14/1/19.		Usual military and educational training. Fatigues etc. 3 O.R. despatched for demobilization.	
"	15/1/19.		Kit inspection. Educational training. Kit/inspection etc. 1 O.R. demobilized.	
"	16/1/19.		Parades under Company arrangements. Educational classes etc.	

Army Form C. 2118.

WAR DIARY
or
INTELLIGENCE SUMMARY.
(Erase heading not required.)

Place	Date	Hour	Summary of Events and Information	Remarks and references to Appendices
TOURNAI	17/1/19.		Usual military and educational training - fatigues etc.	
"	18/1/19.		Lecture by Medical officer to C & D Coys. Educational classes. 5 O.R. demobilized.	
"	19/1/19.		Divine services. 4 O.R. demobilized.	
"	20/1/19.		Parades under Coy arrangements. Educational classes. Disinfection of blankets. 8 O.R. despatched for demobilization.	
"	21/1/19.		Educational training - fatigues. 4 O.R. demobilized.	
"	22/1/19.		Company parades - educational classes - fatigues. 13 O.R. demobilized.	
"	23/1/19.		Usual parades - educational classes and fatigues. Football match in afternoon.	
"	24/1/19.		Fatigues - educational and other training. 10 O.R. demobilized.	
"	25/1/19.		Fatigues - educational classes. 12 O.R. demobilized.	
"	26/1/19.		Divine services. Lecture by the C.O. 14 O.R. demobilized.	
"	27/1/19.		Parades under Coy arrangements. Educational classes. Fatigues. 2/Lt Harrison and 6 O.R. demobilized.	
"	28/1/19.		Usual parades and educational classes. 2/Lt Ireland and 14 O.R. demobilized.	
"	29/1/19.		Fatigues - educational classes. 10 O.R. demobilized.	
"	30/1/19.		Ceremonial drill under Captain Wright. Educational training.	
"	31/1/19.		Battalion ceremonial drill under the commanding officer. Educational classes.	

Confidential.

WAR DIARY

7th (S) Bn Northamptonshire Regiment, for the month of February 1919.

In the Field.
1/3/1919.

Army Form C. 2118.

WAR DIARY
or
INTELLIGENCE SUMMARY.
(Erase heading not required.)

Instructions regarding War Diaries and Intelligence Summaries are contained in F. S. Regs., Part II. and the Staff Manual respectively. Title pages will be prepared in manuscript.

Place	Date	Hour	Summary of Events and Information	Remarks and references to Appendices
Tournai.	1/2/1919.		2/Lt. J. D. Clarke and 9 O.R.s despatched to England for demobilization. Ceremonial parade under the Commanding Officer.	
	2/2/1919		Divine service at the Concert Hall, Grand Place, Tournai. 13 Other ranks demobilized.	
	3/2/1919		Lieut. W.L.Mayne, and 11 Other ranks demobilized.	
	4/2/1919		Educational classes.	
	5/2/1919		Educational classes.	
	6/2/1919		7 O.R.s demobilized, and 3 Reenlisted soldiers sent to England for their leave.	
	7/2/1919		10 O.R. demobilized.	
	8/2/1919		Captain. C.A.Williamson and 8 O.R.s demobilized.	
	9/2/1919		9 O.R.s demobilized. Baths allotted to B and C Coys.	
	10/2/1919		2/Lieut. A.M.Hoare and 2 O.R.s demobilized. Church parade.	
	11/2/1919		Education classes as usual.	
	12/2/1919		4 Companies were amalgamated and formed into two Companies owing to the strength, under the command of Captain A.H Webb and Captain. A.C.Marshall respectively. Baths allotted to Bn. Headquarters and Transport section.	
	13/2/1919		19 O.R.s demobilized.	
	14/2/1919		8 O.R.s demobilized.	
	15/2/1919		21 O.R.s on the 15th demobilized. Ceremonial parade under the Commanding Officer.	

Army Form C. 2118.

WAR DIARY
or
INTELLIGENCE SUMMARY.
(Erase heading not required.)

Instructions regarding War Diaries and Intelligence Summaries are contained in F.S. Regs., Part II. and the Staff Manual respectively. Title pages will be prepared in manuscript.

Place	Date	Hour	Summary of Events and Information	Remarks and references to Appendices
Tournai.	16/2/19		34 O.R.s demobilized.	
	17/2/19		19 O.R.s demobilized.	
	18/2/19		Education classes. Practice ceremonial parade.	
	19/2/19		Ceremonial parade. Colours were presented to the Battalion (and remainder of 73rd Brigade) on the CHAMPS DE MANOEUVRES, TOURNAI today by the General Officer commanding the First Army. The parade was commented upon by the G.O.C. as being very well carried out.	
	20/2/19		19 O.R.s demobilized.	
	21/2/19		30 O.R.s demobilized.	
	22/2/19		2/Lt. R.W.Waterfield and 15 O.R.s demobilized.	
	23/2/19		9 O.R.s demobilized, and 3 reenlisted soldiers sent to England for leave.	
	24/2/19		Church Parade. Owing to strength of Bn. only 6 were available for parade. Education classes as usual.	
	25/2/19.		Ditto.	
	26/2/19		Ditto.	
	27/2/19.		7 O.R.s demobilized.	
	28/2/19.		9 O.R.s demobilized.	

Confidential
NRG. 1541/1

Headquarters,
73rd Bde.

****

Herewith War Diary for the month of March 1919.

(signed)

Captain, commdg.
7th (S) Bn. Northamptonshire Regiment.

2/4/19.

Instructions regarding War Diaries and Intelligence Summaries are contained in F. S. Regs., Part II. and the Staff Manual respectively. Title pages will be prepared in manuscript.

WAR

INTELLIGEN

(*Erase headi*

Place	Date	Hour		Summ

D. D. & L., London, E.C.
(A8004) Wt W1771/M2031 750,000 5/17 **Sch. 32** Forms/C2118/14

WAR DIARY
INTELLIGENCE SUMMARY

Confidential.

Original.

War Diary

of

the 7th (Service) Battalion Northamptonshire Regt.

for

the month of March 1919.

Army Form C. 2118.

WAR DIARY
or
INTELLIGENCE SUMMARY.

(Erase heading not required.)

Instructions regarding War Diaries and Intelligence Summaries are contained in F. S. Regs., Part II. and the Staff Manual respectively. Title pages will be prepared in manuscript.

Place	Date	Hour	Summary of Events and Information	Remarks and references to Appendices

(A8004) Wt W1771/M2031 750,000 3/17 **Sch. 52** Forms/C2118/14
D. D. & L. London, E.C.

Army Form C. 2118.

WAR DIARY
or
INTELLIGENCE SUMMARY.
(Erase heading not required.)

Instructions regarding War Diaries and Intelligence Summaries are contained in F. S. Regs., Part II. and the Staff Manual respectively. Title pages will be prepared in manuscript.

Place	Date	Hour	Summary of Events and Information	Remarks and references to Appendices
Tournai	1/3/9		1 O.R. Demobilized. Usual fatigues, clearing up etc.	
"	2nd		Church Parade at the Cinema, Rue de l'Hôpital. Tournai. at 11 am.	
"	3rd		2 O.R. demobilized. Usual fatigueparties.	
"	4th		Fatigue party found for No. 51 C.C.S. Remainder of Bn. paraded for recreational training.	
"	5th		Recreational Training.	
"	6th		Court of Inquiry held to investigate loss of bicycle on 27th Febry 1919.	
"	7th		Fatigue parties engaged in clearing out Asylum, and closing portions of same not now in use.	
"	8th		12 men demobilized.	
"	9th		Church Parade at the Cinema, Rue de l'Hôpital. Tournai at 11 am.	
"	10th		Baths at 51 C.C.S. allotted to the Bn. from 9/30 to 12 noon.	
"	11th		Inspection by Commanding Officer of all men who are being retained for the Army of Occupation. Fatigue party of 70 O.R. engaged in road mending under Lt. C... Halcrow.	
"	12th		Recreational training.	
"	13th		17 O.R.s demobilized. Fatigue parties clearing up roads adjacent to Asylum	
"	14th		Draft consisting of Lieut. H. D. Williams, Lieut. C... Halcrow, Lieut. E.A.Dakin, Lieut. F. North, 2/Lieut. R.W. Parnell. and 151 other ranks proceeded to join the 4th Battalion Suffolk Regiment, on the Rhine.	
"	15th		Fatigue party engaged on clearing out part of the Asylum not now in use, which is being closed down. The Battalion is now reduced to 1 Company, under the command of Capt. B. Wright M.C.	

Army Form C. 2118.

WAR DIARY
or
INTELLIGENCE SUMMARY.

(Erase heading not required.)

Place	Date	Hour	Summary of Events and Information	Remarks and references to Appendices
Tournai	16th		Accounts of all Companies closed down, and all books and records etc handed in to the Orderly Room. Party of 6 men engaged on cleaning up.	
"	17th		Fatigues as usual.	
"	18th		Ditto. Pay parade at 2/30 pm. All spare vehicles, loaded with mob. Equipment etc are parked at BAISEUX, as the scarcity of horses requires little transport to be used.	
"	19th		Parade for all available on the Tennis Court, Asylum, for lecture by Capt. Passmore.	
"	20th		Fatigue parties as usual. Baths at 51st C.C.S. allotted to the Battalion 9/30 to 10/30 am.	
"	21st		Ditto.	
"	22nd		Fatigue parties, and clearing up party under 2/Lieut. W. Battershell.	
"	23rd		Church Parade at Y.M.C.A. Tournai at 11 am.	
"	24th		Guard of 4 men (cadre) sent to Baiseux to guard transport. Usual fatigue parties	
"	25th		2/Lieut. J. J. Judge and 2/Lieut. J. W. Harred, and 7 O.R.s demobilized.	
"	26th		Headquarters, 73rd Brigade (Cadre) are affiliated to the Battalion from today. Recreational training under Captain Marshall.	
"	27th		Orders received that the Battalion would move to CREPLAINE were cancelled at the last moment and instructions that the Cadre would remain in Tournai and the remainder move to Creplaine were received. The move was carried out at a few hours notice, and Bn. Headquarters opened at the RUE DES MEULES, TOURNAI at 4pm. 2/Lieut. T.V. Norman demobilized.	
"	28th		Guard of 1 NCO and 18 O. R. provided for duty at the Station, Tournai, also 5 O.R.s for the R.T.O. Tournai.	

Army Form C. 2118.

WAR DIARY
of
INTELLIGENCE SUMMARY.
(Erase heading not required.)

Instructions regarding War Diaries and Intelligence Summaries are contained in F. S. Regs., Part II. and the Staff Manual respectively. Title pages will be prepared in manuscript.

Place	Date	Hour	Summary of Events and Information	Remarks and references to Appendices
Tournai	29th		Usual guard for Station, Tournai, and Fatigue party for R.T.O.	
"	30th		Ditto.	
"	31st		Ditto.	

Confidential

M.R.G.1633.

TO:- No.
24th Div.Group

Herewith War Diary (Duplicate) for the
month of April 1919.

Sidney ------- Lt.Colonel.
commanding 7th Northamptonshire Rgt.

1/5/1919.

Confidential

NW 43

7TH NORTHAMPTONSHIRE REGT.

War Diary
for
the month of April 1919

Army Form C. 2118.

WAR DIARY
or
INTELLIGENCE SUMMARY.
(Erase heading not required.)

Instructions regarding War Diaries and Intelligence Summaries are contained in F. S. Regs., Part II. and the Staff Manual respectively. Title pages will be prepared in manuscript.

Place	Date	Hour	Summary of Events and Information	Remarks and references to Appendices
	1/4/19	-	Usual Guard found for the Station. Tournai and fatigue party for R.T.O.	
	2/4/19	-	Same guards and fatigues as on 1/4/19	
	3/4/19	-	Usual guards and fatigues. Draft of 25 O.R.s with Lieut Lunford (conducting Officer) despatched to 4th Bn Suffolk Regt. (A.g.O) Today	
	4.4.19		Draft of 25 O.R.s with Capt. J. Chitis despatched to 4th Suffolk Regt	
	5.4.19		Draft of 25 O.R.s with W.O.O. Hobbs dispatched to 4th Suffolk Rgt	
	6.4.19		Orders received to despatch draft of 30 O.R.s to 4th Suffolk Regt. Rain & now practically arrived to cease	
	7.4.19		Draft of 14 O.R.s proceeded to 4th Suffolk Regt.	
	8.4.19		Usual guard and fatigues	
	9.4.19		1 Officer & 2 O.R.s to England for demobilization	
	10.4.19		Usual guard &c.	
	11.4.19		Guards and fatigues as usual	
	12.4.19		Usual Guards &c	
	13.4.19		2/Lt O.G. Ashley despatched to England to join Regular Bn.	
	14.4.19		Guards and fatigues as usual. Baths allotted to Coie	
	15.4.19		Lieut Bennett to England to join Regular Bn	

Army Form C. 2118.

WAR DIARY
or
INTELLIGENCE SUMMARY.
(Erase heading not required.)

Instructions regarding War Diaries and Intelligence Summaries are contained in F. S. Regs., Part II. and the Staff Manual respectively. Title pages will be prepared in manuscript.

Place	Date	Hour	Summary of Events and Information	Remarks and references to Appendices
Tournai	16.1.19		2Lt Rothwell L. and Grier F.I. despatched for demobilization	
	17.1.19		Usual Guards and fatigues	
	18.1.19			
	19.1.19		A/Cpt Campbell demobilized (scheduled men)	
	20.1.19		2Lt B.C. Clow trans. from 5th Labour Group	
	21.1.19		Usual guards and fatigues	
	22.1.19			
	23.1.19		Guard of 1 S.N.C.O. & 8 O.R. mounted as usual. Parties & working parties to Tournai	
	24.1.19		Guard for R.E.D. Depot as usual	
	25.1.19			
	26.1.19		Capt Ashton Proceeded to 21 dispatch to Dept. (Valenciennes)	
	27.1.19		Usual guards to R.E.D. Tournai	
	28.1.19		d.do	
	29.1.19		d.do	
	30.1.19		d.do. All work now being dealt with by 5th 2nd Div Employment Coy Staff now	
	31.1.19		have taken the Administration	

A5945. Wt. W14277/M1160 350,000 12/16 D.D.&L. Forms/C./2118/14.

908 44
Ceased

7TH NORTHAMPTONSHIRE REGT.

WAR DIARY FOR
MAY 1919

WAR DIARY or INTELLIGENCE SUMMARY

Army Form C. 2118.

(Erase heading not required.)

Place	Date	Hour	Summary of Events and Information	Remarks and references to Appendices
	1/5/19		Guard furnished for R.S.O. (?)	
	2/5/19		Ditto. 1 OR (Reinhold) despatched to England for furlough	
	3/5/19		Nothing unusual happened	
	4/5/19		Normal guard provided	
	5/5/19		Three OR's despatched on leave	
	6/5/19		Orders received that Establishment of Cadre is to be reduced to 16 OR and 36 OR all	
	7/5/19		Above 1 Off and 10 OR for Headquarters. Remainder personnel and vehicles is even	
			for guard duties.	
	8/5/19		Normal guards and fatigues	
	9/5/19		ditto	
	10/5/19		Capt. & O Maistre proceeds to England (anticipating) for demobilisation	
	11/5/19		2 OR's despatched to No 3 Concentration Camp for demob.	
	12/5/19		Normal guards. News received that Abnormal Cadre would proceed to England in 16 (?)	
	13/5/19		Orders issued that the Cadre would proceed to England on 11th instant via Ostende. Later, news cancelled in view of further action to be taken in question	

Army Form C. 2118.

WAR DIARY
or
INTELLIGENCE SUMMARY.
(Erase heading not required.)

Instructions regarding War Diaries and Intelligence Summaries are contained in F. S. Regs., Part II. and the Staff Manual respectively. Title pages will be prepared in manuscript.

Place	Date	Hour	Summary of Events and Information	Remarks and references to Appendices
	14/5/19		Nothing to record	
	15/5/19		4 ORs demobilized	
	16/5/19		2 OR's despatched to 4" B" Support hut (China)	
	17.5.19		Nothing to report	
	18.5.19		— do —	
	19.5.19		— do —	
	20.5.19		— do —	
	21.5.19		No news yet to hand regarding issue of clothes	
	22.5.19		Nothing to record	
	23.5.19			
	24.5.19		1 OR from France joined today	
	25.5.19		Football match between Castro Union and Ionian team resulted in 3-2	
	26.5.19		Proposed redivision of Cadre L.I.Q and B. ORs - no definite steps taken under public notice	
	27.5.19		Nothing to record	
	28.5.19			
	29.5.19		Football match between Cadre team and Ionian team resulted in another victory 3-2	
	30.5.19		Orders received this f.s. wanted proceed (Kephers) via Antwerp on 3" June	
	31.5.19			

A6943 Wt. W14422/M1160 350,000 12/16 D.D. & L. Form=C./2118/14.

Vol 45
Cencel

7th Northamptonshire Regiment.

W A R   D I A R Y.

for

the month of June 1919.

Army Form C. 2118.

WAR DIARY
or
INTELLIGENCE SUMMARY.
(Erase heading not required.)

Instructions regarding War Diaries and Intelligence Summaries are contained in F. S. Regs., Part II. and the Staff Manual respectively. Title pages will be prepared in manuscript.

Place	Date	Hour	Summary of Events and Information	Remarks and references to Appendices
Cairo	1.6.19		Orders received that the whole Brigade was to be on Service Leave.	
Cairo	2.6.19		The order was presented and the return was made. Entrain of troops on 3rd and 5th. Entraining commenced at 3pm and finished at 11pm.	
Cairo	3.6.19		Arrived at Antwerp at 9am. The remainder of 5th Battalion arrived at further transport arranged. On the way to Cairo proceeded to the front.	
Cairo	4.6.19		Day spent in clearing up and loading Vehicles onto store.	
Cairo	5.6.19		Orders received to embark a civilian team. Cars, Lorries were packed with clean clothing. Embarkation commenced at 11am and was completed by 4.15pm. Stores and vehicles were loaded on the "KALIS" and Stewed afterwards hay stored on the rail.	
	9.6.19		Arrived at TILBURY Docks at 9.30am and disembarked	

— FINIS —

Stray /wo/95/L

www.ingramcontent.com/pod-product-compliance
Lightning Source LLC
Chambersburg PA
CBHW081428300426
44108CB00016BA/2327